# GREAT CONCERT MUSIC

PHILIP HALE'S BOSTON SYMPHONY

PROGRAMME NOTES

# GREAT CONCERT MUSIC

**PHILIP HALE'S BOSTON SYMPHONY PROGRAMME NOTES**

*Historical, Critical, and Descriptive Comment on Music and Composers*

Edited by
JOHN N. BURK

With an Introduction by
LAWRENCE GILMAN

GREENWOOD PRESS, PUBLISHERS
WESTPORT, CONNECTICUT

Originally published in 1939
by Garden City Publishing Company, Inc., New York

First Greenwood Reprinting 1971

Library of Congress Catalogue Card Number 75-109742

SBN 8371-4232-6

Printed in the United States of America

# EDITOR'S NOTE

THIS BOOK, assembling the musical writings of Philip Hale, draws principally upon the programme books for which he wrote descriptive notes for thirty-two years of concerts by the Boston Symphony Orchestra. Since the notes were addressed to audiences approaching the music with, presumably, open minds, the writer judiciously withheld his individual opinion. This opinion he freely expressed in his newspaper reviews of the same concerts, extending over an even longer period, and it has seemed advisable, by combining the two, to bring together the critic and the historian. The editor has found, in the newspaper files, pertinent critical paragraphs which are here used to introduce the programme notes about each particular work. The transition from criticism to descriptive note is indicated by a typographical ornament.

In going through the scrapbooks in the Allen A. Brown Room of the Boston Public Library, wherein the newspaper criticisms of Philip Hale's forty active years are carefully preserved, the editor came across this observation by him, in the Boston *Herald* of March 13, 1912: "In 1945 some student in the Brown Room of the Public Library will doubtless be amused by opinions expressed by us all, of works first heard in 1912. Some of us will not then be disturbed by his laughter or by quotations ornamented with exclamation marks of contempt or wonder."

There is cause for wonder, to a student at a time ten years short of the year Mr. Hale mentioned; wonder, however, at his quick perception of essential values upon first hearing what time has since proved a masterpiece, or considerably less than a masterpiece, as the case may be. Few indeed are the professional judges of music who are not glad to leave undisturbed in the dust of the newspaper files some skeletons of their past—appalling errors of denunciation or proclamation. Again and again, when his fellow critics of another day wrote laughably of a then new tone poem of Richard Strauss or pastel of Claude Debussy, Philip Hale delivered a sane and still quotable judgment.

No attempt has been made to modify by omissions Mr. Hale's frank expressions of personal preferences among the composers. This writer never spoke as a major prophet, but as one who might be discussing a favorite subject over a demi-tasse. Anyone is privileged to disagree, and those insisting upon their eternal verities are referred to any one of a hundred books where the musical monuments are enshrined in ringing platitudes of praise. When this critic wrote, with the very opposite of solemnity, about Bach, or Brahms, or Wagner, his ridicule was always directed against a certain snobbish element in his public—a genus which sat at the feet of these composers. "There is, it is true, a gospel of Johannes Brahms," he wrote as long ago as 1896, "but Brahms, to use an old New England phrase, is often a painful preacher of the word.—Brahms is a safe play in Boston. Let me not be unthankful; let me be duly appreciative of my educational opportunities in this town."

It is a joyful privilege to be the agent of bringing the treasure of Philip Hale's musical knowledge and commentary within the permanence and general accessibility of two covers. It was at first hoped that the author could assist in the compilation, but, failing in health, he was unable to give more than his whole-hearted assent to the project. His death, November 30, 1934, came before the book was far under way.

The material drawn upon is of vast proportions. From the autumn of 1901 through the spring of 1933, Philip Hale contributed programme notes for everything played by the Boston Symphony

Orchestra in its regular concerts—upward of a thousand works. As music critic, Mr. Hale commented upon these and many more. He wrote for the Boston *Home Journal* from 1889 to 1891; the Boston *Journal* (like the other publication, long since extinct), from 1891 to 1903; and from then until his retirement in 1933 for the Boston *Herald*. There were also the editorials on various musical topics which he contributed anonymously to the *New Music Review* for many years. Acknowledgment is due for the quotations made from all of these publications; in particular the Boston Symphony Orchestra Concert Bulletins, which have provided the bulk of this book, and the Boston *Herald*, from which by far the larger number of critical paragraphs are drawn. To these should be added the innumerable writers to whom Mr. Hale himself has referred in the course of his programme notes. The helpful advice of Mrs. Philip Hale in the choice of the frontispiece is gratefully acknowledged.

The problem of selecting from the vast accumulation of Philip Hale's writings became somewhat less formidable when a large number of works now forgotten, and others still current but of lesser importance, were eliminated. One hundred and twenty-five works have been chosen, with the aim of including those most often encountered upon symphony programmes. The works of recent composers were necessarily limited to those which had been played by the Boston Symphony Orchestra, and therefore described in its programmes, up to April, 1933. They are still further limited by the exigencies of space. The quoted reviews have been kept clear, for the sake of continuity, of dates and sources; documentation in the programme notes has been minimized. These notes are given in the form in which they most recently appeared. Their partial curtailment is justified by the readiness of their author to adjust them to the space of the programme in hand. To have used each note in its fullest form would have reduced the number of works which the book could contain. As regards the newspaper quotations, they are largely of recent years, and in any case represent the writer's reconsidered opinion. A disproportion in the space given to a certain composer or certain work may be set down to the fact that in a few instances Mr. Hale did not happen at any time to write one of his inimitable essays in miniature which could be detached from the discussion of the occasion and the performance.

## Note On Second Edition

For purposes of accuracy, notation has been made in this edition of the dates of the death of several composers who have died since Philip Hale himself. No attempt, however, has been made to modify his comment where it refers to the artist in the present tense.

# CONTENTS

# INTRODUCTION

SOME DAY an inquisitive musicologist will consider the part played in the history of musical education and musical taste by that seemingly indispensable adjunct of the symphonic concert room, the Programme Note. When that time comes, the contributions made by Philip Hale to the musical civilization of his time will appear in their true proportions. For more than a generation, from the beginning of the twentieth century to the fifth year of the Great Depression, Hale provided programme notes for everything played by the Boston Symphony Orchestra in its regular concerts—"upward of a thousand works", as Mr. Burk informs us in his valuable note to the present collection. The annual issue by the Boston Symphony Orchestra of the bound volumes containing Philip Hale's annotations was an event in the musical world of America that exceeded in importance and interest the appearance of the average new symphonic work upon the Orchestra's programmes. A decade ago, in commenting upon the issue of one of those momentous and liberal tomes (sometimes they included more than two thousand pages), I remarked that it provided a musical education in one volume. Those famous annotations—modestly indicated on the title-page, in small and light-faced type, as "historical and descriptive notes by Philip Hale"—constitute a library of musical information the like of which is not to be found elsewhere on this sufficiently book-congested sphere.

Though Hale was a New Englander by birth, he had not the normal New England suspicion of entertainment as an educational ingredient; and he did not scruple to amuse. He was almost indecently readable. He never hesitated to lighten musical instruction with diversion and with wit. He knew much besides music; and he was able to peptonize for the reader his vast and curious erudition. He could tell you about the maceration of Oriental women, and what action is described by the word "tutupomponeyer", and who invented the first chess-playing automaton, and how locomotive engines are classified, and what Pliny said concerning the bird called penelope. He knew all about the various editions of the singular *Commentaires sur les epistres d'Ovide* by Claude Gaspar Bachet, Sieur de Meziriac, in which the parentage of Ulysses is discussed. He could tell you why the river Ebro bears that name; and what Louis XIV ate for supper—which, you may like to be reminded, often consisted of four plates of different soups, the whole of a pheasant, a partridge, a heaped-up plate of salad, two huge slices of ham, mutton stewed with garlic, and a plate of pastries topped off with fruit and hard-boiled eggs. As for all the other things that Hale knew, you must turn to his writings if you would appreciate their range and number.

And all this fantastically varied learning—which not only seemed boundless in extent, but which was also incredibly exact and circumstantial—adorned a general culture that was nourishing and humane, and a specifically musical culture which conceived no relevant fact as inconsiderable, no anecdote unimportant, no human aspect unrevealing. The average programme note is a deadly and a stifling thing; but these amazing annotations, traversing all history and the ceaseless tragi-comedy of life, assure us that a programme note may sometimes, if an artist has contrived it, be more rewarding than the music that occasioned it.

Philip Hale transformed the writing of programme notes from an arid and depressing form of musical pedagogy into an exhilarating variety of literary art. The formidable weight of learning which he bore was employed with an ease and finesse, a lightness of touch, a charm of manner, a wit and conciseness and flexibility, which belong among the achievements of distinguished letters. His predecessor as annotator of the Boston Symphony Orchestra's programmes, the accomplished William Foster Apthorp, had prepared the way for Hale's achievement. Apthorp's notes, written between 1892 and 1901, surpassed in brilliance and acumen anything that had come out of Europe or America. But Philip Hale, by reason of his exceptional width of intellectual range, and the well of knowledge which he drew upon, and his insatiable, devouring, delighted curiosity, established himself almost at once as the master of an enlivened order of creative musical scholarship which was a new thing under the tonal sun.

One might justly say of him, as critic, commentator, analyst, what Sir George Grove said of Schubert—a saying that Hale himself was fond of quoting: "There never has been one like him, and there never will be another."

LAWRENCE GILMAN.

GREAT CONCERT MUSIC

PHILIP HALE'S BOSTON SYMPHONY

PROGRAMME NOTES

# JOHANN SEBASTIAN
# BACH

(Born at Eisenach on March 21, 1685;
died at Leipsic on July 28, 1750)

---

No matter how well old music may be performed by chorus, orchestra, virtuoso, many audiences are bored by it today. There is one exception: the music of Bach. "He is the forerunner, the prophet that foresaw our epoch and our tastes." This speech is often heard, as is the remark: "There is not one ultra-modern harmonic thought that is not to be found somewhere in Bach's music." Bach is one of the great fetishes in music. The late John S. Dwight really believed in the plenary inspiration of the indefatigable weaver of counterpoint. No matter how formal, how dull a page of music looked or sounded, Mr. Dwight was in ecstasy the moment he was told the page was signed with Bach's name.

Mme Wanda Landowska (in *Musique ancienne*) says entertainingly: "The idea that the Cantor of Eisenach, though dedicating his music to Frederick the Great and princes of his period, composed it solely with a view to a Châtelet audience is so consecrated a commonplace that I hardly dare to dream of combating it." Von Bülow and others have declared that Bach's *Chromatic Fantasy* is an anticipation of modern romanticism; but the composers hinted at in this piece are more modern than Beethoven, Chopin, Schumann. Frescobaldi, Buxtehude, Couperin, and the writers for the lute are more modern because they are less known. And Bach not only knew their works but followed them rather than the advanced ideas of his own epoch; for Bach was a conservative rather than a radical.

## THE BRANDENBURG CONCERTOS

*No. 1 in F, for two horns, three oboes and bassoon, with strings*
*No. 2 in F, for violin, flute, oboe, trumpet, with strings*
*No. 3 in G, for three string orchestras*
*No. 4 in G, for violin and two flutes, with strings*
*No. 5 in D, for pianoforte, flute, and violin, with strings*
*No. 6 in B, for two viole da braccia, two viole da gamba, violoncello, and bass*

THE SIX Brandenburg Concertos, completed on March 24, 1721, were written in answer to the wish of a Prussian prince, Christian Ludwig, Margraf of Brandenburg, the youngest son of the Great Elector by a second wife. This prince was provost of the Cathedral at Halberstadt. He was a bachelor, living now at Berlin and now on his estate at Malchow. Fond of music, and not in an idle way, he was extravagant in his tastes and mode of life, and often went beyond his income of nearly fifty thousand thalers. In May, 1718, Prince Leopold of Anhalt-Cöthen, at whose court Bach was *Kapellmeister,* journeyed to Carlsbad to drink the waters. He took with him Bach and a quintet from his orchestra; also his clavicembalo with three "servants to care for it"; he was also thus attended when he visited Carlsbad in 1720. The Margraf may have been at Carlsbad, and as he was very fond of music and had his own orchestra, he undoubtedly attended Leopold's musical parties. At any rate, he gave Bach a commission. It was on March 24, 1721, that Bach—possibly someone at the Court—wrote a dedication in French:

*"A son altesse royale, Monseigneur Crétien Louis, Margraf de Brandenbourg, etc., etc., etc.*

*"Monseigneur,*

"Two years ago, when I had the honor of playing before your Royal Highness, I experienced your condescending interest in the insignificant musical talents with which heaven has gifted me, and understood your

Royal Highness's gracious willingness to accept some pieces of my composition. In accordance with that condescending command, I take the liberty to present my most humble duty to your Royal Highness in these Concerti for various instruments, begging your Highness not to judge them by the standards of your own refined and delicate taste, but to seek in them rather the expression of my profound respect and obedience. In conclusion, Monseigneur, I most respectfully beg your Royal Highness to continue your gracious favor toward me, and to be assured that there is nothing I so much desire as to employ myself more worthily in your service.

"With the utmost fervor, Monseigneur, I subscribe myself,

"Your Royal Highness's most humble and most obedient servant,

"JEAN SEBASTIAN BACH.

"Coethen, 24 March, 1721."[1]

These concertos—*"Concerts avec plusieurs instruments"*—were intended as a gift for the Margraf's birthday in March. Nothing is known about the reception in Berlin, nor is it positively known whether they were ever played at the palace of the Margraf. "The condition of the autograph suggests that, like the parts of the 'Kyrie' and 'Gloria' of the B minor Mass at Dresden, it was never performed by the recipient." It was the Margraf's habit to catalogue his library. The name of Bach was not found in the list, although the names of Vivaldi, Venturini, Valentiri, Brescianello, and other writers of concertos were recorded. After the death of the Margraf in 1734, Bach's score was put for sale with other manuscripts in a "job lot." The Brandenburg Concertos came into the possession of J. P. Kirnberger. They were later owned by the Princess Amalie, sister of Frederick the Great and a pupil of Kirnberger. Their next and final home was the Royal Library, Berlin, No. 78 in the Amalienbibliothek. They were edited by S. W. Dehn and published by Peters, Leipsic, in 1850.

[1]Translation into English by Charles Sanford Terry: *Bach: A Biography,* London, 1928.

## THE CONCERTOS FOR PIANOFORTE

*D minor (with strings)*
*E major (with strings)*
*D major (with strings)*
*A major (with strings)*
*F minor (with strings)*
*G minor (with strings)*
*F major (with two flutes and strings)*
*A minor (with flute, violin and strings)*
*D major (with flute, violin and strings)*

LITTLE is known about these concertos. It is supposed that the seven were formed by putting together various separate movements, or were arrangements or transcriptions for the clavier. "In all the concertos for clavier, whether for one instrument or many, there are passages for the solo instrument unaccompanied which anticipate the procedure of modern concertos, with considerable use of *arpeggios,* and even occasional *cadenza* passages. Bach follows the Italian types in the general scheme and easy style of the quick movements, and they are rather homophonic in feeling, with the exception of the last movement of the double concerto in C major, which is a fugue of the most vivacious description. . . . Bach clearly enjoyed writing in the concerto form and found it congenial. It would be even natural to infer that he found opportunities for performing the works, as in many cases the same concertos appear in versions both for violin and clavier."[2]

Parry also says: "When Bach writes slow movements for the clavier, he makes them serve as phases of contrast to the quick movements, in which some rather abstract melody is discussed with a certain aloofness of manner, or treated with elaborate ornamentation, such as was more suited to the instrument than passages of sustained melody pure and simple. The alternative presented in the admirable concerto for the clavier in D minor is to give a *Siciliano* in place of the central slow

[2]C. H. H. Parry: *Johann Sebastian Bach,* 1909.

movement, a course which provides a type of melody well adapted to the limited sustaining power of the harpsichord. . . . The finest of them [the concertos] is that in D minor, above mentioned, which from its style would appear to have been written at Cöthen."

It is supposed that there was use of the general bass in these concertos. A second clavier was usually employed; but there is reason to believe that a portable organ, or lutes, theorbos, and the like were also used in accompaniment. Dr. Albert Schweitzer wrote in his *J. S. Bach* (Leipsic, 1905): "The seven concertos for clavier are in effect, and with one exception only, transcriptions made at Leipsic after 1730 at a time when Bach saw himself obliged to write concertos for the performances of the Telemann Society, which he began to conduct in 1729, and for the little family concerts at his own home. These transcriptions are of unequal worth. Some were made carefully and with art, while others betray impatience in the accomplishment of an uninteresting task. Only one of the pianoforte concertos is not derived from a violin concerto."

## THE ORCHESTRAL SUITES

*No. 1. Suite in C (for two oboes, and bassoon, with strings)*

*No. 2. Suite in B minor (for flute with strings)*

*No. 3. Suite in D (for two oboes, three trumpets, and drums, with strings)*

*No. 4. Suite in D (for three oboes, bassoon, three trumpets, and drums, with strings)*

The term "suite" was not given by Bach to the four compositions that now are so named—the suites in C major, B minor, and two in D major. He used the word *"ouverture."* The original parts of these overtures were handed over in 1854 by the Singakademie of Berlin to the Royal (now Stadt) Library of that city.

Bach probably composed the four suites during his stay at Cöthen (1717–23), as *Kapellmeister* to Prince Leopold of Anhalt-Cöthen. The prince was then nearly twenty-four years old, an amiable, well-educated young man, who had traveled and was fond of books and pictures. He played the violin, the viol da gamba, and the harpischord. Furthermore, he had an agreeable bass voice and was more than an ordinary singer. Bach said of him, "He loved music, he was well acquainted with it, he understood it." The music at the Court was chiefly chamber music, and here Bach passed happy years.

Under the reign of Leopold's puritanical father there was no Court orchestra, but in 1707 Gisela, Leopold's wife, set up to please her husband an establishment of three musicians. When Leopold returned from his grand tour he expanded the orchestra. In 1714 he appointed Augustinus Reinhard Stricker *Kapellmeister,* and Stricker's wife Catherine soprano and lutanist. In 1716 the orchestra numbered eighteen players who, "with some omissions and additions," constituted its membership under Bach. Stricker and his wife retired in August, 1717. Leopold offered the post of *Kapellmeister* to Bach, "who was known to him since his sister's wedding at Nienburg in the previous year." This orchestra, reinforced by visiting players, probably played the Brandenburg music before it was performed elsewhere.

## LUDWIG VAN
# BEETHOVEN

(Born at Bonn, December 16 (?), 1770;
died at Vienna, March 26, 1827)

---

## SYMPHONY NO. 1, IN C MAJOR, OP. 21

*I. Adagio molto; allegro con brio*
*II. Andante cantabile con moto*
*III. Menuetto: allegro molto e vivace; trio*
*IV. Finale: adagio; allegro molto e vivace*

WHY DEBATE whether the music of this First symphony is wholly Mozartian; whether there are traces of the "greater" Beethoven? Let the music be taken for what it is, music of the end of the eighteenth century. At the same time let us recall the fact that when this symphony was played in Paris a hundred years ago, two or three critics protested against the "astonishing success" of Beethoven's works as "a danger to musical art." "It is believed," said one, "that a prodigal use of the most barbaric dissonances and a noisy use of all the orchestral instruments will make an effect. Alas, the ear is only stabbed; there is no appeal to the heart."

In spite of pages of mere routine, the music still has a certain freshness and a quaint beauty. The symphony will always remain a charming work with trivial passages, not to be compared as a whole with the three great symphonies of Mozart or the latter symphonies of Haydn.

The symphony in C major, No. 1, probably originated in 1800, was sketched at an earlier period, and elaborated in 1799.

The first performance was at a concert given by Beethoven at the National Court Theater, "next the Burg," Vienna, April 2, 1800.

The concert began at 6:30 P.M. The prices of admission were not raised. It was the first concert given in Vienna by Beethoven for his own benefit. A correspondent of the *Allgemeine Musikalische Zeitung* (October 15, 1800) gave curious information concerning the performance. "At the end a symphony composed by him was performed. It contains much art, and the ideas are abundant and original, but the wind instruments are used far too much, so that the music is more for a band of wind instruments than an orchestra." The performance suffered on account of the conductor, Paul Wranitzky. The orchestra men disliked him and took no pains under his direction. Furthermore, they thought Beethoven's music too difficult. "In the second movement of the symphony they took the matter so easily that there was no spirit, in spite of the conductor, especially in the performance of the wind instruments. . . . What marked effect, then, can even the most excellent compositions make?" The parts were published in 1801 and dedicated to Baron von Swieten.

Berlioz[1] wrote concerning it as follows: "This work is wholly different in form, melodic style, harmonic sobriety, and instrumentation from the compositions of Beethoven that follow it. When the composer wrote it, he was evidently under the sway of Mozartian ideas. These he sometimes enlarged, but he has imitated them ingeniously everywhere. Especially in the first two movements do we find springing up occasionally certain rhythms used by the composer of *Don Giovanni,* but these occasions are rare and far less striking. The first *allegro* has for a theme a phrase of six measures, which is not distinguished in itself but becomes interesting through the artistic treatment. An episodic melody follows, but it has little distinction of style. By means of a half cadence, repeated three or four times, we come to a figure in imitation for wind instruments; and we are the more surprised to find it here, because it had been so often employed in several overtures to French operas. The *andante* contains an accompaniment of drums, *piano,* which appears today rather ordinary, yet we recognize in it a hint at striking effects produced later by Beethoven with the aid of this instrument, which is seldom or badly employed as a rule by his predecessors. This movement is full of charm; the theme is graceful and lends itself easily to fugued development, by means of which the

[1]Hector Berlioz: *À travers champs,* 1862.

composer has succeeded in being ingenious and piquant. The *scherzo* is the first-born of the family of charming *badinages* or *scherzi,* of which Beethoven invented the form and determined the pace; which he substituted in nearly all of his instrumental works for the minuet of Mozart and Haydn with a pace doubly less rapid and with a wholly different character. This *scherzo* is of exquisite freshness, lightness and grace. It is the one truly original thing in this symphony in which the poetic idea, so great and rich in the majority of his succeeding works, is wholly wanting. It is music admirably made, clear, alert, but slightly accentuated, cold, and sometimes mean and shabby, as in the final *rondo,* which is musically childish. In a word, this is not Beethoven."

This judgment of Berlioz has been vigorously combated by all fetishists that believe in the plenary inspiration of a great composer. Thus Michel Brenet[2] (1882), usually discriminative, found that the introduction begins in a highly original manner. Marx took the trouble to refute the statement of Ulibichev,[3] that the first movement was an imitation of the beginning of Mozart's *"Jupiter"* symphony—a futile task. We find Dr. Prof. H. Reimann[4] in 1899 stoutly maintaining the originality of many pages of this symphony. Thus in the introduction the first chord with its resolution is a "genuine innovation by Beethoven." He admits that the chief theme of the *allegro con brio* with its subsidiary theme and jubilant sequel recalls irresistibly Mozart's *"Jupiter";* "but the passage *pianissimo* by the close in G major, in which the basses use the subsidiary theme, and in which the oboe introduces a song, is new and surprising, and the manner in which by a crescendo the closing section of the first chapter is developed is wholly Beethovenish"! He is also lost in admiration at the thought of the development itself. He finds the true Beethoven in more than one page of the *andante.* The trio of the *scherzo* is an example of Beethoven's "tone-painting." The introduction of the *finale* is "wholly original, although one may often find echoes of Haydn and Mozart in what follows."

Colombani combated the idea that the symphony is a weak imitation of symphonies by Haydn and Mozart. Ulibichev wrote that Beethoven, in order to reveal himself, waited for the minuet. "The rhythmic movement is changed into that of a *scherzo,* after the manner instituted by the composer in his first sonatas." When the symphony was first per-

[2]Michel Brenet (Marie Bobillier): *Histoire de la Symphonie à l'orchestre.*

[3]Alexander von Ulibichev: *Beethoven, ses critiques, et ses glossateurs,* 1857.

[4]Heinrich Reimann: *Musikalische Ruckblicke.*

formed at Leipsic, a critic described it as a "confused explosion of the outrageous effrontery of a young man." At Vienna in 1810, the work was described as "more amiable" than the second symphony.

## SYMPHONY NO. 2, IN D MAJOR, OP. 36

*I. Adagio molto; allegro con brio*
*II. Larghetto*
*III. Scherzo*
*IV. Allegro molto*

THE SYMPHONY is an answer to those who insist that the inner emotions of a composer must find a vent in the music composed at the time. Never was Beethoven more wretched physically and mentally than when he wrote this symphony, music that breathes forth serenity, beauty, gayety, and courage.

In 1801 Beethoven's deafness, which had begun with a roaring in his ears, grew on him. He suffered also from frightful colic. He consulted physician after physician; tried oil of almonds, cold baths and hot baths, pills and herbs and blisters; he was curious about galvanic remedies, and in his distress he wrote: "I shall as far as possible defy my fate, although there must be moments when I shall be the most miserable of God's creatures. . . . I will grapple with fate; it shall never pull me down."

Dr. Schmidt sent him in 1802 to the little village of Heiligenstadt, where, as the story goes, the Emperor Protus planted the first vines of Noricum. There was a spring of mineral water—a spring of marvelous virtues—which had been blessed by St. Severinus, who died in the village and gave the name by which it is known today. Beethoven's house was on a hill outside the village, isolated, with a view of the Danube valley. Here he lived for several months like a hermit. He saw only his physician and Ferdinand Ries, his pupil, who visited him occasionally.

Nature and loneliness did not console Beethoven. He had been in dismal mood since the performance of the First symphony (April,

1800). The powers of darkness, *"finstere Mächte,"* to quote Wasielewski's phrase, had begun to torment him. He had already felt the first attacks of deafness. It is possible that the first symptoms were in 1796, when, as a story goes, returning overheated from a walk, he plunged his head into cold water. "It would not be safe to say that the smallpox, which in his childhood left marks on his face, was a remote cause of his deafness." In 1800–01 Beethoven wrote about his deafness and intestinal troubles to Dr. Wegeler, and to the clergyman, Carl Amenda, in Kurland. It was at the beginning of October, 1802, that Beethoven, at Heiligenstadt, almost ready to put an end to his life, wrote a letter to his brothers, the document known as "Beethoven's will," which drips yew-like melancholy.

Furthermore, Beethoven was still passionately in love with Giulietta Guicciardi, of whom he wrote to Wegeler, November 16, 1801: "You can hardly believe what a sad and lonely life I have passed for two years. My poor hearing haunted me as a specter, and I shunned men. It was necessary for me to appear misanthropic, and I am not this at all. This change is the work of a charming child who loves me and is loved by me. After two years I have again had some moments of pleasure, and for the first time I feel that marriage could make me happy. Unfortunately, she is not of my rank in life, and now I certainly cannot marry." Beethoven, however, asked for her hand. One of her parents looked favorably on the match. The other, probably the father, the Count Guicciardi, refused to give his daughter to a man without rank, without fortune, and without a position of any kind. Giulietta became the Countess Gallenberg. Beethoven told Schindler that after her marriage she sought him out in Vienna, and she wept, but that he despised her.

Yet during the sad period of the winter of 1802–03, Beethoven composed the Second symphony, a joyous, "a heroic lie," to borrow the descriptive phrase of Camille Bellaigue.

The first performance of the Second symphony was at the Theater an der Wien, April 5, 1803. The symphony was performed at Leipsic, April 29, 1804, and Spazier characterized it as "a gross monster, a pierced dragon which will not die, and even in losing its blood (in the *finale*), wild with rage, still deals vain but furious blows with his tail, stiffened by the last agony." Spazier, who died early in 1805, was described by his contemporaries as a learned and well-grounded musician and a man of sound judgment.

A Leipsic critic found that the symphony would gain if certain passages were abbreviated and certain modulations were sacrificed. Another declared that it was too long; that there was an exaggerated use of the wind instruments; that the *finale* was bizarre, harsh, savage. Yet he added that there was such fire, such richness of new ideas, such an absolutely original disposition of these ideas, that the work would live; "and it will always be heard with renewed pleasure when a thousand things that are today in fashion will have been long buried."

The sketch of Berlioz may here serve as an analysis: "In this symphony everything is noble, energetic, proud. The introduction (*largo*) is a masterpiece. The most beautiful effects follow one another without confusion and always in an unexpected manner. The song is of a touching solemnity, and it at once commands respect and puts the hearer in an emotional mood. The rhythm is already bolder, the instrumentation is richer, more sonorous, more varied. An *allegro con brio* of enchanting dash is joined to this admirable *adagio*. The *gruppetto* which is found in the first measure of the theme, given at first to the violas and violoncellos in unison, is taken up again in an isolated form, to establish either progressions in a *crescendo* or imitative passages between wind instruments and the strings. All these forms have a new and animated physiognomy. A melody enters, the first section of which is played by clarinets, horns, and bassoons. It is completed *en tutti* by the rest of the orchestra, and the manly energy is enhanced by the happy choice of accompanying chords.

"The *andante* [*larghetto*] is not treated after the manner of that of the First symphony: it is not composed of a theme worked out in canonic imitations, but it is a pure and frank song, which at first is sung simply by the strings, and then embroidered with a rare elegance by means of light and fluent figures whose character is never far removed from the sentiment of tenderness which forms the distinctive character of the principal idea. It is a ravishing picture of innocent pleasure which is scarcely shadowed by a few melancholy accents.

"The *scherzo* is as frankly gay in its fantastic capriciousness as the *andante* has been wholly and serenely happy; for this symphony is smiling throughout; the warlike bursts of the first *allegro* are wholly free from violence; there is only the youthful ardor of a noble heart in which the most beautiful illusions of life are preserved untainted. The composer still believes in immortal glory, in love, in devotion. What abandon in his gayety! What wit! What sallies! Hearing these various instruments disputing over fragments of a theme which no one of them plays in its complete form, hearing each fragment thus colored with a thousand nuances as it passes from one to the other, it is as though you were watching the fairy sports of Oberon's graceful spirits.

"The *finale* is of like nature. It is a second *scherzo* in two time, and its playfulness has perhaps something still more delicate, more piquant."

## SYMPHONY NO. 3, IN E FLAT MAJOR "EROICA," OP. 55

*I. Allegro con brio*
*II. Marcia funebre: Adagio assai*
*III. Scherzo: Allegro vivace; Trio*
*IV. Finale: Allegro molto*

IT IS INTERESTING to note the difference in the expression of heroism between this symphony and Strauss's *Heldenleben.* To be sure, Beethoven had Bonaparte at first in mind, while in *Heldenleben* the hero is—Richard Strauss, defying his enemies, rejoicing vaingloriously in his immortality as a composer. It is not necessary to accept the theories of Beethoven's commentators. The excellent Nietzel finds that, in the second theme of the first movement, "the hero, having for the first time exerted his force, turns about to look at the path he has trod." Wagner sees Man, not merely a triumphant soldier, the hero. Schindler believes the symphony to be the celebration of the French Revolution. And so on and so on. It is enough that the structure and the spirit of the symphony are heroic, that there is the grand gesture, that even in the Funeral March there is no whine of pessimism, no luxury of woe. It is a heroic lamentation over heroes slain in defence of freedom, a lamentation in which there is exultation, even in grief.

At Nussdorf in the summer of 1817, Beethoven, who had then composed eight symphonies, and the poet Christian Kuffner were having a fish dinner at the Tavern Zur Rose. Kuffner asked him which of his symphonies was his favorite.

"Eh! Eh!" said Beethoven. "The *Eroica.*"

"I should have guessed the C minor," said Kuffner.

"No, the *Eroica.*"

---

Anton Schindler wrote in his life of Beethoven:

"First in the fall of 1802 was his [Beethoven's] mental condition so much bettered that he could take hold afresh of his long-formulated plan and make some progress: to pay homage with a great instrumental work to the hero of the time, Napoleon. Yet not until 1803 did he set himself seriously to this gigantic work, which we now know under the title of *Sinfonia Eroica:* on account of many interruptions it was not finished until the following year. . . . The first idea of this symphony is said to have come from General Bernadotte, who was then French Ambassador at Vienna and highly treasured Beethoven. I heard this from many friends of Beethoven. Count Moritz Lichnowsky, who was often with Beethoven in the company of Bernadotte, . . . told me the same story."[5] Schindler also wrote, with reference to the year 1823: "The correspondence of the King of Sweden led Beethoven's memory back to the time when the King, then General Bernadotte, Ambassador of the French Republic, was at Vienna, and Beethoven had a lively recollection of the fact that Bernadotte indeed first awakened in him the idea of the *Sinfonia Eroica.*"

These statements are direct. Unfortunately, Schindler, in the third edition of his book, mentioned Beethoven as a visitor at the house of Bernadotte in 1798, repeated the statement that Bernadotte inspired the idea of the symphony, and added: "Not long afterward the idea blossomed into a deed"; he also laid stress on the fact that Beethoven was a stanch republican and cited, in support of his admiration of Napoleon, passages from Beethoven's own copy of Schleiermacher's translation of Plato.

Thayer admits that the thought of Napoleon may have influenced the form and the contents of the symphony; that the composer may have based a system of politics on Plato; "but," he adds, "Bernadotte had been long absent from Vienna before the Consular form of government was adopted at Paris, and before Schleiermacher's Plato was published in Berlin."

[5]English translation by Ignatz Moscheles, 1841.

The symphony was composed in 1803–04. The story is that the title page of the manuscript bore the word "Buonaparte," and at the bottom of the page "Luigi van Beethoven"; and "not a word more," said Ries, who saw the manuscript. "I was the first," also said Ries, "to bring him the news that Bonaparte had had himself declared emperor, whereat he broke out angrily: 'Then he's nothing but an ordinary man. Now he'll trample on all the rights of men to serve his own ambition; he will put himself higher than all others and turn out a tyrant!' " There is also the story that when the death of Napoleon was announced, Beethoven exclaimed: "Did I not foresee the catastrophe when I wrote the Funeral March in the *Eroica?"* Vincent d'Indy argues against Schindler's theory that Beethoven wished to celebrate the French Revolution *en bloc. "C'était l'homme de Brumaire"* that Beethoven honored by his dedication. The autograph score, sold at auction in Vienna in 1827 for three florins, ten kreutzers, shows the erasure of two words under *"Sinfonia grande"* on the title page: one is plainly "Bonaparte"; under his own name, Beethoven wrote, in large characters, "Written on Bonaparte." Paul Bekker, arguing that the *Eroica* is not the portrait of any one hero, but that the symphony represents his concept of human heroism, believes that the first movement is the only one of direct connection with Napoleon: "The hero's deeds have resulted in victory, the restless will has achieved fulfilment."[6]

There can be nothing in the statements that have come down from Czerny, Dr. Bartolini, and others: the first *Allegro* describes a sea fight; the Funeral March is in memory of Nelson or General Abercrombie, etc. There can be no doubt that Napoleon, the young conqueror, the Consul, the enemy of kings, worked a spell over Beethoven, as over Berlioz, Hazlitt, Victor Hugo; for, according to W. E. Henley's paradox, although, as despot, Napoleon had "no love for new ideas and no tolerance for intellectual independence," yet he was "the great First Cause of Romanticism."

The first performance of the symphony was at a private concert at Prince Lobkowitz's in December, 1804. The composer conducted, and in the second half of the first *Allegro* he brought the orchestra to grief, so that a fresh start was made. The first performance in public was at a concert given by Clement at the Theater an der Wien, April 7, 1805. The symphony was announced as "A new grand Symphony in D sharp

[6]Paul Bekker: *Beethoven,* translated by M. M. Bozman, 1925.

by Herr Ludwig van Beethoven, dedicated to his Excellence Prince von Lobkowitz." Beethoven conducted. Czerny remembered that someone shouted from the gallery: "I'd give another kreutzer if they would stop." Beethoven's friends declared the work a masterpiece. Some said it would gain if it were shortened, if there were more "light, clearness, and unity." Others found it a mixture of the good, the grotesque, the tiresome.

The symphony was published in October, 1806. The title in Italian stated that it was to celebrate the memory of a great man. And there was this note: "Since this symphony is longer than an ordinary symphony, it should be performed at the beginning rather than at the end of a concert, either after an overture or an aria, or after a concerto. If it be performed too late, there is the danger that it will not produce on the audience, whose attention will be already wearied by preceding pieces, the effect which the composer purposed in his own mind to attain."

The theme of the first movement is note for note the same as that of the first measures of the Intrade written by Mozart in 1768, at Vienna, for his one-act operetta, *Bastien et Bastienne,* performed that year in a Viennese garden house. Beethoven's theme is finished by the violins and developed at length. There is a subsidiary theme, which begins with a series of detached phrases distributed among wood-wind instruments and then the violins. The second theme, of a plaintive character, is given out alternately by wood-wind and strings. The development is most elaborate, full of striking contrasts, rich in new ideas. The passage in which the horn enters with the first two measures of the first theme in the tonic chord of the key, while the violins keep up a tremolo on A flat and B flat, has given rise to many anecdotes and provoked fierce discussion. The *coda* is of unusual length.

The Funeral March, *Adagio assai,* C minor, 2-4, begins, *pianissimo e sotto voce,* with the theme in the first violins, accompanied by simple chords in the other strings. The theme is repeated by the oboe, accompanied by wood-wind instruments and strings; the strings give the second portion of the theme. A development by full orchestra follows. The second theme is in C major. Phrases are given out by various wood-wind instruments in alternation, accompanied by triplet *arpeggios* in the strings. This theme, too, is developed; and there is a return to the first theme in C minor in the strings. There is fugal development at length of a figure that is not closely connected with either of the two themes. The first theme reappears for a moment, but strings and brass enter *fortissimo* in A flat major. This episode is followed by another; and at last the first theme returns in fragmentary form in the first violins, accompanied by a *pizzicato* bass and chords in oboes and horns.

M. d'Indy,[7] discussing the patriotism of Beethoven as shown in his music, calls attention to the *militarisme,* the adaptation of a warlike rhythm to melody, that characterizes this march.

*Scherzo: allegro vivace,* E flat major, 3–4. Strings are *pianissimo* and *staccato,* and oboe and first violins play a gay theme which Marx says is taken from an old Austrian folk song. This melody is the basic material of the *scherzo.* The trio in E flat major includes hunting calls by the horns, which are interrupted by passages in wood-wind instruments or strings.

*Finale: allegro molto,* E flat major, 2–4. A theme, or, rather, a double theme, with variations. Beethoven was fond of this theme, for he had used it in the *finale* of his ballet, *Die Geschöpfe des Prometheus,* in the Variations for pianoforte, Op. 35, and in a country dance. After a few measures of introduction, the bass to the melody which is to come is given out, as though it were an independent theme. The first two variations in the strings are contrapuntal. In the third the tuneful second theme is in the wood-wind against runs in the first violins. The fourth is a long fugal development of the first theme against a counter subject found in the first variation. Variations in G minor follow, and the second theme is heard in C major. There is a new fugal development of the inverted first theme. The tempo changes to *poco andante,* wood-wind instruments play an expressive version of the second theme, which is developed to a *coda* for full orchestra, and the symphony ends with a joyful glorification of the theme.

First performances: London, 1814. Paris (at a rehearsal in 1815 everybody laughed after the first and second movement; this happened at another attempt some years later), Conservatory Orchestra, 1828. St. Petersburg, 1834. Rome, 1860. Madrid, 1878.

[7]Vincent d'Indy: *Beethoven, a Critical Biography,* 1911; translated by Dr. Theodore Baker, 1913.

## SYMPHONY NO. 4, IN B FLAT MAJOR, OP. 60

*I. Adagio; Allegro vivace*
*II. Adagio*
*III. Allegro vivace. Trio. Un poco meno allegro*
*IV. Finale: Allegro, ma non troppo*

Of the nine symphonies of Beethoven the Fourth and Sixth are the least impressive. The First is historically interesting, and its *finale* is delightfully gay. The Second is also interesting as showing the development of Beethoven's musical mind. After the *Eroica,* the Fourth seems a droop in the flight of imagination. Yet there are noble and strange things in this symphony, things that only Beethoven could have written: the introduction, the mysterious measures with the *crescendo* that majestically reëstablishes the chief tonality in the first movement; the superb *adagio.*

The old theory that the Fourth was inspired by Beethoven's love for Therese Brunswick; that he was betrothed to her, which made happiness the keynote to the music, has been disproved, if ever it was accepted by students of Beethoven's life. As a matter of fact, nothing is known about the "origin" of the music. A German commentator has recently spoken of "indecisiveness of mood" as "part of the imaginative scheme of the whole work"; he even sees in the *adagio* "the stimulus of some tense emotion" such as inspired the love letter, whether aroused by the "Immortal" or some other beloved. Is it not enough to hear the serene, nobly emotional *adagio* without vain speculation as to why Beethoven was so deeply moved? Nor is it necessary to see Berlioz's Archangel Michael, who, by the way, was the warlike leader of the angelic hosts, sighing and overcome by melancholy, as "he contemplated the worlds from the threshold of the empyrean." One might ask why should

Michael grow melancholy at the glorious sight? Nor can Beethoven's *adagio* be justly characterized as melancholy.

The composition of Beethoven's Symphony No. 5 in C minor was interrupted by work on the Symphony in B flat major, No. 4, a symphony of a very different character. The symphony was probably planned and composed in the summer of 1806. "Having been played in March, 1807, at one of the two subscription concerts at Lobkowitz's," Thayer is justified in adding solemnly that "it must have been finished at that time."

After the performance of the *Eroica,* Beethoven also worked on his opera, *Fidelio*. The French army entered Vienna November 13, 1805; on the 15th, Napoleon sent to the Viennese a proclamation dated at Schönbrunn, and on November 20, 1805, *Fidelio* was performed for the first time, before an audience largely composed of French officers. There were three performances, and the opera was withdrawn until March 29, 1806, when it was reduced from three acts to two. The opera was again coldly received; there were two performances; and there was no revival in Vienna until 1814.

Beethoven, disturbed by the disaster which attended the first performances of his *Fidelio* in Vienna, during the French invasion, went in 1806 to Hungary to visit his friend, Count Brunswick. He visited the Prince Lichnowsky at Castle Grätz, which was near Troppau in Silesia. It has been said that at Martonvásár, visiting the Brunswicks, he found that he loved Therese and that his love was returned. Some, therefore, account for the postponement of the Fifth symphony, begun before the Fourth, "by the fact that in May, 1806, Beethoven became engaged to the Countess Therese. . . . The B flat symphony has been mentioned as 'the most tenderly classical' of all works of its kind; its keynote is 'happiness'—a contentment which could have come to the master only through such an incident as the one above set forth—his betrothal." We do not see the force of this reasoning.

It is better to say with Thayer that nothing is known about the origin of the Fourth beyond the inscription put by the composer on the manuscript which belongs to the Mendelssohn family: *"Sinfonia 4ta 1806. L. v. Bthvn."*

This we do know: that, while Beethoven was visiting Prince Lichnowsky at the latter's Castle Grätz, the two called on Franz, Count Oppersdorff, who had a castle near Grossglogau. This count, born in 1778, rich and high-born, was fond of music; he had at this castle a well-drilled orchestra, which then played Beethoven's Symphony in D major in the presence of the composer. In June, 1807, he commissioned Beethoven to compose a symphony, paid him two hundred florins in advance and one hundred and fifty florins more in 1808. Beethoven accepted the offer, and purposed to give the Symphony in C minor to the Count; but he changed his mind, and in November, 1808, the Count received, not the symphony, but a letter of apology, in which Beethoven said that he had been obliged to sell the symphony which he had composed for him, and also another—these were probably the Fifth and the Sixth—but that the Count would receive soon the one intended for him. The Fifth and Sixth were dedicated to Prince Lobkowitz and Count Rasoumowsky. Oppersdorff at last received the Fourth symphony, dedicated to him, a symphony that was begun before he gave the commission; he received it after it had been performed. He was naturally offended, especially as the Fourth symphony at first met with little favor. He did not give Beethoven another commission, nor did he meet him again, although Beethoven visited again the Castle Grätz in 1811. The Count died January 21, 1818.

The Fourth symphony was performed for the first time at one of two concerts given in Vienna about the 15th of March, 1807, at Prince Lobkowitz's. The concert was for the benefit of the composer. The *Journal des Luxus und der Moden* published this review early in April of that year:

"Beethoven gave in the dwelling house of Prince L. two concerts in which only his own compositions were performed: the first four symphonies, an overture to the tragedy *Coriolanus,* a pianoforte concerto, and some arias from *Fidelio.* Wealth of ideas, bold originality, and fullness of strength, the peculiar characteristics of Beethoven's Muse, were here plainly in evidence. Yet many took exception to the neglect of noble simplicity, to the excessive amassing thoughts, which on account of their number are not always sufficiently blended and elaborated, and therefore often produce the effect of uncut diamonds."

Was this "Prince L." Lobkowitz or Lichnowsky? Thayer decided in favor of the former.

Berlioz writes of this symphony:

"Here Beethoven abandons wholly the ode and the elegy—a reference to the *Eroica* symphony—to return to the less lofty and somber but perhaps no less difficult style of the Second symphony. The character of this score is generally lively, nimble, joyous, or of a heavenly sweetness. If we except the meditative *adagio,* which serves as an introduction, the first movement is almost entirely given up to joyfulness. The motive in detached notes, with which the *allegro* begins, is only a canvas, on which the composer spreads other and more substantial melodies, which thus render the apparently chief idea of the beginning an accessory. This artifice, although it is fertile in curious and interesting results, has already been employed by Mozart and Haydn with equal success. But we find in the second section of this same *allegro* an idea that is truly new, the first measures of which captivate the attention; this idea, after leading the hearer's mind through mysterious developments, astonishes it by its unexpected ending. . . . This astonishing *crescendo* is one of the most skillfully contrived things we know of in music: you will hardly find its equal except in that which ends the famous *scherzo* of the Symphony in C minor. And this latter, in spite of its immense effectiveness, is conceived on a less vast scale, for it sets out from *piano* to arrive at the final explosion without departing from the principal key, while the one whose march we have just described starts from *mezzo-forte,* is lost for a moment in a *pianissimo* beneath which are harmonies with vague and undecided coloring, then reappears with chords of a more determined tonality, and bursts out only at the moment when the cloud that veiled this modulation is completely dissipated. You might compare it to a river whose calm waters suddenly disappear and only leave the subterranean bed to plunge with a roar in a foaming waterfall.

"As for the *adagio*—it escapes analysis. It is so pure in form, the melodic expression is so angelic and of such irresistible tenderness, that the prodigious art of the workmanship disappears completely. You are seized, from the first measure, by an emotion which at the end becomes overwhelming in its intensity; and it is only in the works of one of these giants of poetry that we can find a point of comparison with this sublime page of the giant of music. Nothing, indeed, more resembles the impression produced by this *adagio* than that which we experience when we read the touching episode of Francesca da Rimini in the *Divina Commedia,* the recital of which Virgil cannot hear 'without weeping in sobs,' and which, at the last verse, makes Dante 'fall, as falls a dead body.' This movement seems to have been sighed by the archangel Michael, one day when, overcome by melancholy, he contemplated the worlds from the threshold of the empyrean.

"The *scherzo* consists almost wholly of phrases in binary rhythm forced to enter into combinations of 3–4 time. . . . The melody of the trio, given to wind instruments, is of a delicious freshness; the pace is a little slower than that of the rest of the *scherzo,* and its simplicity stands out in still greater elegance from the opposition of the little phrases which the violins throw across the wind instruments, like so many teasing but charming allurements.

"The *finale,* gay and lively, returns to ordinary rhythmic forms; it consists of a jingling of sparkling notes, interrupted, however, by some hoarse and savage chords, in which are shown the angry outbursts which we have already had occasion to notice in the composer."

## SYMPHONY NO. 5, IN C MINOR, OP. 67

*I. Allegro con brio*
*II. Andante con moto*
*III. Allegro; trio—*
*IV. Allegro*

As for the Fifth symphony, what words can be said of its composer more fitting than those of De Quincey's apostrophe to Shakespeare: "O mighty poet! Thy works are not those of other men, simply and merely great works of art, but are also like the phenomena of nature, like the sun and the sea, the stars and the flowers, the frost and the dew, hailstorm and thunder, which are to be studied with entire submission of our own faculties, and in the perfect faith that in them there can be no too much or too little, nothing useless or inert, but that the farther we press in our discoveries, the more we shall see proofs of design and self-supporting arrangement where the careless eye had nothing but accident!"

In all modern music there is no page more thrilling than that of the mysterious, unearthly transition from the *scherzo* to the *finale,* and the preceding pages are the triumph of absolute music over that which needs a programme or is the translation of something into music. Here is music that was not suggested, but it suggests that which can only be imagined, not spoken, not painted, not written in lofty rhyme or passionate prose.

Beethoven sketched motives of the *Allegro, Andante,* and *scherzo* of this symphony as early as 1800 and 1801. We know from sketches that while he was at work on *Fidelio* and the pianoforte concerto in G major—1804–06—he was also busied with this symphony, which he put aside to compose the Fourth symphony, in B flat.

The Symphony in C minor was finished in the neighborhood of Heiligenstadt in 1807. Dedicated to the Prince von Lobkowitz and the Count Rasoumowsky, it was published in April, 1809. It was first performed at the Theater an der Wien, Vienna, December 22, 1808.

Instead of inquiring curiously into the legend invented by Schindler —"and for this reason a statement to be doubted," as Bülow said— that Beethoven remarked of the first theme, "So knocks Fate on the door!" (it is said that Ferdinand Ries was the author of this explanation and that Beethoven was grimly sarcastic when Ries, his pupil, made it known to him), instead of investigating the statement that the rhythm of this theme was suggested by the note of a bird—oriole or goldfinch—heard during a walk; instead of a long analysis, which is vexation and confusion without the themes and their variants in notation, let us read and ponder the words of the great Hector Berlioz:

"The most celebrated of them all, beyond doubt and peradventure, is also the first, I think, in which Beethoven gave the reins to his vast imagination, without taking for guide or aid a foreign thought. In the First, Second, and Fourth, he more or less enlarged forms already known, and poetized them with all the brilliant and passionate inspirations of his vigorous youth. In the Third, the *Eroica,* there is a tendency, it is true, to enlarge the form, and the thought is raised to a mighty height; but it is impossible to ignore the influence of one of the divine poets to whom for a long time the great artist had raised a temple in his heart. Beethoven, faithful to the Horatian precept, '*Nocturna versate manu, versate diurna,*' read Homer constantly, and in his magnificent musical epopee, which, they say, I know not whether it be true or false, was inspired by a modern hero, the recollections of the ancient Iliad play a part that is as evident as admirably beautiful.

"The Symphony in C minor, on the other hand, seems to us to come directly and solely from the genius of Beethoven; he develops in it his own intimate thought; his secret sorrows, his concentrated rage, his reveries charged with a dejection, oh, so sad, his visions at night, his bursts of enthusiasm—these furnish him the subject; and the forms of melody, harmony, rhythm, and orchestration are displayed as essentially individual and new as they are powerful and noble.

"The first movement is devoted to the painting of disordered sentiments which overthrow a great soul, a prey to despair; not the concentrated, calm despair that borrows the shape of resignation; not the dark and voiceless sorrow of Romeo who learns of the death of Juliet; but the terrible rage of Othello when he receives from Iago's mouth the poisonous slanders which persuade him of Desdemona's guilt. Now it is a frenetic delirium which explodes in frightful cries; and now it is the prostration that has only accents of regret and profound self-pity. Hear these hiccups of the orchestra, these dialogues in chords between wind instruments and strings, which come and go, always weaker and fainter, like unto the painful breathing of a dying man, and then give way to a phrase full of violence, in which the orchestra seems to rise to its feet, revived by a flash of fury; see this shuddering mass hesitate a moment and then rush headlong, divided in two burning unisons as two streams of lava; . . . and then say if this passionate style is not beyond and above everything that had been produced hitherto in instrumental music. . . .

"The *adagio*" [*andante con moto*] "has characteristics in common with the *allegretto* in A minor of the Seventh symphony and the slow movement of the Fourth. It partakes alike of the melancholy soberness of the former and the touching grace of the latter. The theme, at first announced by the united violoncellos and violas, with a simple accompaniment of the double-basses *pizzicato,* is followed by a phrase for wind instruments, which returns constantly, and in the same tonality throughout the movement, whatever be the successive changes of the first theme. This persistence of the same phrase, represented always in a profoundly sad simplicity, produces little by little on the hearer's soul an indescribable impression. . . .

"The *scherzo* is a strange composition. Its first measures, which are not terrible themselves, provoke that inexplicable emotion which you feel when the magnetic gaze of certain persons is fastened on you. Here everything is somber, mysterious; the orchestration, more or less sinister, springs apparently from the state of mind that created the famous scene of the Blocksberg in Goethe's *Faust*. Nuances of *piano* and *mezzoforte* dominate. The trio is a double-bass figure, executed with the full force of the bow; its savage roughness shakes the orchestral stands and reminds one of the gambols of a frolicsome elephant. But the monster retires, and little by little the noise of his mad course dies away. The theme of the *scherzo* reappears in *pizzicato*. Silence is almost established, for you hear only some violin tones lightly plucked and strange little cluckings of bassoons. . . . At last the strings give gently with the bow the chord of A flat and doze on it. Only the drums preserve the rhythm; light blows struck by sponge-headed drumsticks mark the dull rhythm amid the general stagnation of the orchestra. These drum notes are C's; the tonality of the movement is C minor; but the chord of A flat sustained for a long time by the other instruments seems to introduce a different tonality, while the isolated hammering of the C on the drums tends to preserve the feeling of the foundation tonality. The ear hesitates—but will this mystery of harmony end?—and the dull pulsations of the drums, growing louder and louder, reach the violins, which now take part in the movement and with a change of harmony, to the chord of the dominant seventh, G, B, D, F, while the drums roll obstinately their tonic C; the whole orchestra, assisted by the trombones, which have not yet been heard, bursts in the major into the theme of a triumphal march, and the *finale* begins. . . .

"Criticism has tried, however, to diminish the composer's glory by stating that he employed ordinary means, the brilliance of the major mode pompously following the darkness of a *pianissimo* in minor; that the triumphal march is without originality, and that the interest wanes even to the end, whereas it should increase. I reply to this: Did it require less genius to create a work like this because the passage from *piano* to *forte* and that from minor to major were the means already understood? Many composers have wished to take advantage of the same means; and what result did they obtain comparable to this gigantic chant of victory in which the soul of the poet-musician, henceforth free from earthly shackles, terrestrial sufferings, seems to mount radiantly towards heaven? The first four measures of the theme, it is true, are not highly original, but the forms of a fanfare are inherently restricted, and I do not think it possible to find new forms without departing utterly from the simple, grand, pompous character which is becoming. Beethoven wished only an entrance of the fanfare for the beginning of his *finale,* and he quickly found in the rest of the movement and even in the conclusion of the chief theme that loftiness and originality of style which never forsook him. And this may be said in answer to the reproach of his not having increased the interest to the very end; music, in the state known at least to us, would not know how to produce a more violent effect than that of this transition from *scherzo* to triumphal march; it was then impossible to enlarge the effect afterwards.

"To sustain one's self at such a height is of itself a prodigious effort; yet in spite of the breadth of the developments to which he committed himself, Beethoven was able to do it. But this equality from the beginning to end is enough to make the charge of diminished interest plausible, on account of the terrible shock which the ears receive at the beginning; a shock that, by exciting nervous emotion to its most violent paroxysm, makes the succeeding instant the more difficult. In a long row of columns of equal height, an optical illusion makes the most remote appear the smallest. Perhaps our weak organization would accommodate itself to a more laconic peroration, as that of Gluck's '*Notre général vous rappelle.*' Then the audience would not have to grow cold, and the symphony would end before weariness had made impossible further following in the steps of the composer. This remark bears only on the *mise en scène* of the work; it does not do away with the fact that this *finale* in itself is rich and magnificent; very few movements can draw near without being crushed by it."

## SYMPHONY NO. 6, IN F MAJOR, "PASTORALE," OP. 68

*I. Awakening of serene impressions on arriving in the country: allegro, ma non troppo*
*II. Scene by the brookside: andante molto moto*
*III. Jolly gathering of country folk: allegro; in tempo d'allegro*
*Thunderstorm; tempest: allegro*
*IV. Shepherd's song; gladsome and thankful feelings after the storm: allegretto*

WHEN JUSTLY READ, this symphony is indeed pastoral, light-hearted, something more than a fearsome length relieved only by the little ornithological passage in which nightingale, quail, and cuckoo are neatly imitated; at least, it is fair to suppose this; we have never heard the nightingale sing. Jean Cocteau, in his amusing little book full of aphorisms designed to make the bourgeois sit up, says that the nightingale sings badly. So we must not be unduly prejudiced by praise of the bird coming from Milton, Matthew Arnold, and other poetical enthusiasts. Then there is the thunderstorm—the tempest, to use the good country term that has come down from Shakespeare and before him. And how charming the first two movements! To borrow the Host's characterization of Master Fenton, the symphony smells April and May.

This symphony—*Sinfonia pastorale*—was composed in the country round about Heiligenstadt in the summer of 1808. It was first performed at the Theater an der Wien, Vienna, December 22, 1808. The descriptive headings were probably an afterthought. In the sketchbook, which contains sketches for the first movement, is a note: *"Characteristic Symphony. The recollections of life in the country."* There is also a note: *"The hearer is left to find out the situations for himself."*

M. Vincent d'Indy in his *Beethoven* (Paris, 1911) devotes several pages to Beethoven's love of nature. "Nature was to Beethoven not only a consoler for his sorrows and disenchantments; she was also a friend with whom he took pleasure in familiar talk, the only intercourse to which his deafness presented no obstacle." Nor did Beethoven understand Nature in the dryly theoretical manner of Jean Jacques Rousseau, whose writings then were in fashion, for there could be no point of contact between the doctrines of this Calvinist of Geneva and the effusions of Beethoven, a Catholic by birth and by education. Nor did Beethoven share the views of many Romantics about Nature. He would never have called her "immense, impenetrable, and haughty," as Berlioz addressed her through the mouth of his Faust. A little nook, a meadow, a tree—these sufficed for Beethoven. He had so penetrated the beauty of nature that for more than a dozen years all his music was impregnated by it.

His bedside book for many, many years soon after his passion for

Giulietta Guicciardi was the *Lehr und Erbauungs Buch* of Sturm. Passages underscored show the truth of the assertions just made, and he copied these lines that they might always be in his sight: "Nature can be justly called the school of the heart; it shows us beyond all doubt our duty towards God and our Neighbor. I wish therefore to become a disciple of this school, and offer my heart to it. Desirous of self-instruction, I wish to search after the wisdom that no disillusion can reject; I wish to arrive at the knowledge of God, and in this knowledge I shall find a foretaste of celestial joys."

Nature to Beethoven was the country near by, which he could visit in his daily walks. If he was an indefatigable pedestrian, he was never an excursionist.

M. d'Indy draws a picture of the little *Wirthschaften* in the suburbs of the large towns, humble inns "not yet ticketed with the pompous barbarism of 'restaurant.'" They were frequented by the bourgeoisie, who breathed the fresh air and on tables of wood ate the habitual sausage and drank the traditional beer. There was a dance hall with a small orchestra; there was a discreet garden with odorous alleys in which lovers could walk between the dances. Beyond was the forest where the peasant danced and sang and drank, but the songs and dances were here of a ruder nature.

Beethoven, renting a cottage at Döbling, Grinzing, or Heiligenstadt, which then were not official faubourgs, could in a few minutes be in the forest or open country. He did not attempt to reproduce the material, realistic impression of country sounds and noises, but only the spirit of the landscape.

Thus in the *Pastoral* symphony, to suggest the rustic calm and the tranquillity of the soul in contact with Nature, he did not seek curious harmonic conglomerations, but a simple, restrained melody which embraces only the interval of a sixth (from *fa* to *re*). This is enough to create in us the sentiment of repose—as much by its quasi-immobility as by the duration of this immobility. The exposition of this melody based on the interval of a sixth is repeated with different timbres, but musically the same, for fifty-two measures without interruption. In an analogous manner Wagner portrayed the majestic monotony of the river in the introduction to *Rheingold*. Thus far the landscape is uninhabited. The second musical idea introduces two human beings, man and woman, force and tenderness. The second musical thought is the thematic base of the whole work. In the *scherzo* the effect of sudden immobility produced by the bagpipe tune of the strolling musician (the oboe solo, followed by the horn), imposing itself on the noisy joy of the peasants, is due to the cause named above; here, with the exception of one note, the melody moves within the interval of a fifth.

The storm does not pretend to frighten the hearer. The insufficient kettledrums are enough to suggest the thunder, but in four movements of the five there is not a fragment of development in the minor mode. The key of F minor, reserved for the darkening of the landscape hitherto sunny and gay, produces a sinking of the heart and the distressing restlessness that accompany the approach of the tempest. Calm returns with the *ambitus* of the sixth, and then the shepherd's song leads to a burst of joyfulness. The two themes are the masculine and feminine elements exposed in the first movement.

According to M. d'Indy the *andante* is the most admirable expression of true nature in musical literature. Only some passages of *Siegfried* and *Parsifal* are comparable. Conductors usually take this *andante* at too slow a pace and thus destroy the alert poetry of the section. The brook furnishes the basic movement, expressive melodies arise, and the feminine theme of the first *allegro* reappears, alone, disquieted by the absence of its mate. Each section is completed by a pure and prayer-like melody. It is the artist who prays, who loves, who crowns the diverse divisions of his work by a species of Alleluia.

It has been said that several of the themes in this symphony were taken from Styrian and Carinthian folk songs. It is dedicated to Prince von Lobkowitz and Count Rasoumowsky. The work was published in 1809.

## SYMPHONY NO. 7, IN A MAJOR, OP. 92

*I. Poco sostenuto; vivace*
*II. Allegretto*
*III. Presto; assai meno presto; tempo primo*
*IV. Allegro con brio*

THE RHAPSODISTS have had their say; the commentators have pried and conjectured; the later symphonies are still sublime in their grandeur. They well-nigh express the inexpressible.

Nor have the legends, fondly believed for years, done injury to the music. It matters not whether the Seventh symphony be a description of Germany exulting in its deliverance from the French yoke, or the apotheosis of the dance; whether the allegretto picture a procession in the catacombs or be the love dream of an odalisque. Whenever the music is played, whenever it comes into the mind, it awakens new thoughts and each one dreams his own dreams.

Each writer in turn publishes in print or by word of mouth his little explanation, but Beethoven broods, mysterious, gigantic, above commentators, above even conductors when they misunderstand him, or plume themselves upon a new and striking interpretation, or in their endeavor to grasp and convey to others the essential greatness of the composer put their trust in din and speed.

The first sketches of this symphony were probably made before 1811 or even 1810. The score of the symphony was dedicated to the Count Moritz von Fries and published in 1816. The edition for the pianoforte was dedicated to the Tsarina Elizabeth Alexievna of All the Russias.

The Seventh and Eighth symphonies were probably played over for the first time at the Archduke Rudolph's in Vienna on April 20, 1813. Beethoven in the same month vainly endeavored to produce them at a concert. The first performance of the Seventh was at Vienna in the large hall of the university, on December 8, 1813.

Mälzel, the famous maker of automata, exhibited in Vienna during the winter of 1812–13 his automatic trumpeter and panharmonicon. The former played a French cavalry march with calls and tunes; the latter was composed of the instruments used in the ordinary military band of the period—trumpets, drums, flutes, clarinets, oboes, cymbals, triangle, etc. The keys were moved by a cylinder. Overtures by Handel and Cherubini and Haydn's Military symphony were played with ease and precision. Beethoven planned his *Wellington's Victory,* or *Battle of Vittoria,* for this machine. Mälzel made arrangements for a concert—a concert "for the benefit of Austrian and Bavarian soldiers disabled at the battle of Hanau."

This Johann Nepomuk Mälzel (Mälzl) was born at Regensburg, August 15, 1772. He was the son of an organ builder. In 1792 he settled at Vienna as a teacher of music, but he soon made a name for himself by inventing mechanical music works. In 1816 he constructed a metronome, though Winkel, of Amsterdam, claimed the idea as his. Mälzel also made ear trumpets, and Beethoven tried them, as he did others. His life was a singular one, and the accounts of it are contradictory. Two leading French biographical dictionaries insist that Mälzel's "brother Leonhard" invented the mechanical toys attributed to Johann, but they are wholly wrong. Fétis and one or two others state that he took the panharmonicon with him to the United States in 1826 and sold it at Boston to a society for four hundred thousand dollars—an incredible statement. No wonder that the Count de Pontécoulant, in his *Organographie,* repeating the statement, adds, "I think there is an extra cipher." But Mälzel did visit America, and he spent several years here. He landed at New York, February 3, 1826, and the *Ship News* announced the arrival of "Mr. Maelzel, Professor of Music and Mechanics, inventor of the Panharmonicon and the Musical Time Keeper." He brought with him the famous automata—the Chess Player, the Austrian Trumpeter, and the Rope Dancers—and opened an exhibition of them at the National Hotel, 112 Broadway, April 13, 1826. The Chess Player was invented by Wolfgang von Kempelen. Mälzel bought it at the sale of von Kempelen's effects after the death of the latter, at Vienna, and made unimportant improvements. The Chess Player had strange adventures. It was owned for a time by Eugène Beauharnais, when he was viceroy of the kingdom of Italy, and Mälzel had much trouble in getting it away from him. Mälzel gave an exhibition in Boston at Julien Hall, on a corner of Milk and Congress streets. The exhibition opened September 13, 1826, and closed October 28 of that year. He visited Boston again in 1828 and 1833. On his second visit he added *The Conflagration of Moscow,* a panorama, which he sold to three Bostonians for six thousand dollars. Hence, probably, the origin of the panharmonicon legend. He also exhibited an automatic violoncellist. Mälzel died on the brig *Otis* on his way from Havana to Philadelphia on July 21, 1838, and was buried at sea, off Charleston. The *United States Gazette* published his eulogy and said, with due caution: "He has gone, we hope, where the music of his harmonicons will be exceeded." The Chess Player was destroyed by fire in the burning of the Chinese Museum at Philadelphia, July 5,

1854. An interesting and minute account of Mälzel's life in America, written by George Allen, is published in the *Book of the First American Chess Congress,* pp. 420–84 (New York, 1859) see also *Métronome de Maelzel* (Paris, 1833); the *History of the Automatic Chess Player,* published by George S. Hilliard, Boston, 1826; Mendel's *Musikalisches Conversations-Lexicon;* and an article, *Beethoven and Chess,* by Charles Willing, published in *The Good Companion Chess Problem Club* of May 11, 1917 (Philadelphia), which contains facsimiles of Mälzel's programmes in Philadelphia (1845) and Montreal (1847). In Poe's fantastical "Von Kempelen and His Discovery" the description of his Kempelen, of Utica, N. Y., is said by some to fit Mälzel, but Poe's story was probably not written before 1848. His article, "Maelzel's Chess Player," a remarkable analysis, was first published in the *Southern Literary Messenger* of April, 1836. Portions of this article other than those pertaining to the analysis were taken by Poe from Sir David Brewster's *Lectures on Natural Magic.*

The programme of the Vienna concert was announced: "A brand-new symphony," the Seventh, in A major, by Beethoven; and also *Wellington's Sieg, oder die Schlacht bei Vittoria. Wellington's Sieg* was completed in October, 1813, to celebrate the victory of Wellington over the French troops in Spain on June 21 of that year. Mälzel had persuaded Beethoven to compose the piece for his panharmonicon. He furnished material for it and gave him the idea of using "God Save the King" as the subject of a lively fugue. He purposed to produce the work at concerts, so as to raise money enough for him and Beethoven to visit London. A shrewd fellow, he said that if the *"Battle"* symphony were scored for orchestra and played in Vienna with success, an arrangement for his panharmonicon would then be of more value to him. Beethoven dedicated the work to the Prince Regent, afterwards George IV, and forwarded a copy to him, but the "First Gentleman in Europe" never acknowledged the compliment. *Wellington's Sieg* was not performed in London until February 10, 1815, when it had a great run. The news of this success pleased Beethoven very much. He made a memorandum of it in the notebook which he carried with him to taverns.

The benefit concert was brilliantly successful, and there was a repetition of it December 12 with the same prices of admission, ten and five florins. The net profit of the two performances was four thousand six gulden. Spohr tells us that the new pieces gave "extraordinary pleasure, especially the symphony; the wondrous second movement was repeated at each concert; it made a deep, enduring impression on me. The performance was a masterly one, in spite of the uncertain and often ridiculous conducting by Beethoven." Glöggl was present at a rehearsal when violinists refused to play a passage in the symphony and declared that it could not be played. "Beethoven told them to take their parts home and practise them; then the passage would surely go." It was at these rehearsals that Spohr saw the deaf composer crouch lower and lower to indicate a long *diminuendo,* and rise again and spring into the air when he demanded a climax. And he tells of a pathetic yet ludicrous blunder of Beethoven, who could not hear the soft passages.

Beethoven was delighted with his success, so much so that he wrote a public letter of thanks to all that took part in the two performances. "It is Mälzel especially who merits all our thanks. He was the first to conceive the idea of the concert, and it was he who busied himself actively with the organization and the ensemble in all the details. I owe him special thanks for having given me the opportunity of offering my compositions to the public use and thus fulfilling the ardent vow made by me long ago of putting the fruits of my labor on the altar of the country."

The first movement opens with an introduction, *poco sostenuto,* A major, 4–4. The main body is *vivace,* 6–8. The *allegretto* is in A minor, 2–4; the third movement, *presto,* F major, 3–4. The *finale, allegro con brio,* A major, 2–4, is a wild rondo on two themes. Here, according to Mr. Prod'homme and others, as Beethoven achieved in the *scherzo* the highest and fullest expression of exuberant joy—"unbuttoned joy," as the composer himself would have said—so in the *finale* the joy becomes orgiastic. The furious bacchantic first theme is repeated after the exposition, and there is a sort of coda to it, "as a chorus might follow upon the stanzas of a song."[8]

[8]J. G. Prod'homme: *Les Symphonies de Beethoven,* 1906.

## SYMPHONY NO. 8, IN F MAJOR, OP. 93

*I. Allegro vivace e con brio*
*II. Allegretto scherzando*
*III. Tempo di menuetto*
*IV. Allegro vivace*

BEETHOVEN characterized his Eighth symphony as "a little symphony" and in the same letter spoke of the Seventh as a great one; yet if Czerny is to be believed the composer was vexed because the audience was cool when the Eighth was first performed. He said, "because it is much better" than the Seventh, which was played at the same concert. Authors often pronounce strange judgments on their works, as parents often favor a stupid or unpleasant child; but this composer had a right to be proud of the little Benjamin—the colossal Ninth was not then born—for the Eighth symphony is charged with the spirit of the greater Beethoven.

Some commentators have endeavored to read a programme into the symphony, thinking perhaps thus to give it greater importance. One speaks of the symphony as a "military trilogy"; another thinks the *allegretto* is a parody of Rossini's manner, but the movement was written in 1812, and Vienna did not go mad over the Olympian Rossini until after that year. We even find Vincent d'Indy citing the Eighth as revealing impressions of Nature made on the composer's soul; the trio of the pompous minuet is to M. d'Indy a representation in grotesque fashion of a peasant band, and the Hungarian theme in the *finale,* the hymn of Hunyadi, denotes the arrival of gypsy musicians in the midst of a festival.

The symphony needs not such support to excite extraneous interest. In the music we find Beethoven in reckless mood, whimsical, delighting in abrupt contrasts, shouting his joy, ready to play a practical joke. There is, no doubt, the absence of the "fine taste" which Debussy misses in the case of Beethoven and finds ruling the musical life of Bach and Mozart. No, Beethoven was not Paterian in a struggle after taste. He was an elemental person, coarse in his life, with an enormous capacity for hard work. There are others who have been condemned for a lack of taste: Euripides, Rabelais, Shakespeare, Verdi, Walt Whitman. De Quincey, a stylist, found Goethe lacking in taste when he wrote *Wilhelm Meister*.

And in this symphony, characterized by mad jollity, and a playfulness that at times approaches buffoonery, there are exquisite musical thoughts; there are passages that for a moment sound the depths and reach the heights.

The Eighth symphony was composed at Linz in the summer of 1812. Beethoven was in poor physical condition in that year, and as Staudenheim, his physician, advised him to try Bohemian baths, he went to Töplitz by way of Prague; to Carlsbad, where a note of the postillion's horn found its way among the sketches for the Eighth symphony; to Franzensbrunn, and again to Töplitz; and lastly to his brother Johann's home at Linz, where he remained until into November.

At the beginning of 1812 Beethoven contemplated writing three symphonies at the same time; the key of the third, D minor, was already determined, but he postponed work on this; and as the autograph score of the first of the remaining two, the Symphony in A, No. 7, is dated May 13, it is probable that he contemplated the Seventh before he left Vienna on his summer journey. His sojourn in Linz was not a pleasant one. Johann, a bachelor, lived in a house too large for his needs, and so he rented a part of it to a physician, who had a sister-in-law, Therese Obermeyer, a cheerful and well-proportioned woman of an agreeable if not handsome face. Johann looked on her kindly, made her his housekeeper, and according to the gossips of Linz, there was a closer relationship. Beethoven meddled with his brother's affairs, and, finding him obdurate, visited the bishop and the police authorities and persuaded them to banish her from the town, to send her to Vienna if she should still be in Linz on a fixed day. Naturally, there was a wild scene between the brothers. Johann played the winning card: he married Therese on November 8. Ludwig, furious, went back to Vienna and took pleasure afterwards in referring to his sister-in-law in both his conversation and his letters as the "Queen of Night."

This same Johann said that the Eighth symphony was completed from sketches made during walks to and from the Pöstlingberge, but Thayer considered him to be an untrustworthy witness.

The two symphonies were probably played over the first time at the Archduke Rudolph's in Vienna, April 20, 1813. Beethoven in the same month endeavored to produce them at a concert, but without success. The Seventh was not played until December 8, 1813, at a concert organized by Mälzel. The first performance of the Eighth symphony was at a concert given by Beethoven at Vienna in the Redoutensaal on Sunday, February 27, 1814.

The *Allgemeine Musik-Zeitung,* in a review of this concert, stated that the Seventh symphony was again heartily applauded, and the *allegro* was repeated. "All were in anxious expectation to hear the new symphony (F major, 3-4), the latest product of Beethoven's muse; but this expectation *after one hearing* was not fully satisfied, and the applause which the work received was not of that enthusiastic nature by which a work that pleases universally is distinguished. In short, the symphony did not make, as the Italians say, a *furore.* I am of the opinion that the cause of this was not in weaker or less artistic workmanship (for in this, as in all of Beethoven's works of this species, breathes the peculiar genius which always proves his originality), but partly in the mistake of allowing this symphony to follow the one in A major, and partly in the satiety that followed the enjoyment of so much that was beautiful and excellent, whereby natural apathy was the result. If this symphony in future should be given alone, I have no doubt concerning its favorable reception."

There were in the orchestra at this concert eighteen first violins, eighteen second violins, fourteen violas, twelve violoncellos, seven double basses. The audience numbered about three thousand, although Schindler spoke of five thousand.

We know from his talk noted down that Beethoven originally planned an elaborate introduction to this symphony.

It is often said that the second movement, the celebrated *allegretto scherzando,* is based on the theme of a "three-voice circular canon, or round, *Ta, ta, ta, lieber Mälzel,* sung in honor of the inventor of the metronome at a farewell dinner given to Beethoven in July, 1812, before his leaving Vienna for his summer trip into the country."

This story was first told by Schindler, who, however, did not say that the dinner was given to Beethoven alone, and did say that the dinner was in the spring of 1812. Beethoven was about to visit his brother Johann in Linz; Mälzel was going to England to produce there his automaton trumpeter but was obliged to defer this journey. Beethoven, who among intimate friends was customarily "gay, witty, satiric, 'unbuttoned,' as he called it," improvised at this parting meal a canon, which was sung immediately by those present. The *allegretto* was founded on this canon, suggested by the metronome, according to Schindler. Thayer[9] examined this story with incredible patience, and he drew these conclusions: the machine that we now know as Mälzel's metronome was at first called a musical chronometer, and not until 1817 could the canon include the word "Metronom." Schindler, who was seventeen years old in 1812, heard the story from Count Brunswick, who was present at the meal, but was not in Vienna from March, 1810, till the end of February, 1813, four months after the completion of the symphony. Furthermore, Beethoven is reported as having said: "I, too, am in the second movement of the Eighth symphony—ta, ta, ta, ta—the canon on Mälzel. It was a right jolly evening when we sang this canon. Mälzel was the bass. At that time I sang the soprano. I think it was toward the end of December, 1817." Thayer says: "That Mälzel's 'ta, ta, ta' suggested the *allegretto* to Beethoven, and that at a parting meal the canon on this theme was sung, are doubtless true; but it is by no means sure that the canon preceded the symphony. . . . If the canon was written before the symphony, it was not improvised at this meal; if it was then improvised, it was only a repetition of the *allegretto* theme in canon form." However this may be, the persistent ticking of a wind instrument in sixteenth notes is heard almost throughout the movement, of which Berlioz said: "It is one of those productions for which neither model nor pendant can be found. This sort of thing falls entire from heaven into the composer's brain. He writes it at a single dash, and we are amazed at hearing it."

[9]A. W. Thayer: *"Ludwig van Beethoven's Leben,"* 1866–79; revision in English by H. E. Krehbiel.

## SYMPHONY NO. 9, IN D MINOR, WITH FINAL CHORUS ON SCHILLER'S "ODE TO JOY," OP. 125

*I. Allegro, ma non troppo, un poco maestoso*
*II. Molto vivace; presto*
*III. Adagio molto e cantabile*
*IV. Presto*
*Allegro assai*
*Presto*
*Baritone recitative*
*Quartet and chorus: allegro assai*
*Tenor solo and chorus: allegro assai vivace, alla marcia*
*Chorus: allegro assai*
*Chorus: andante maestoso*
*Adagio, ma non troppo, ma divoto*
*Allegro energico, sempre ben marcato*
*Quartet and chorus: allegro ma non tanto; prestissimo*

MUCH HAS BEEN written about the Ninth symphony, a symphony that has been and is a stumbling block to certain conductors and hearers. It is easy to smile at such books as *Le Livre de la Genèse de la IX Symphonie de Beethoven,* by Ricciotto Canudo, with its fantastical theories and titles given to the leading themes, but the comments of more ordinary mortals have led conductors into singular experiments. Some have rewritten passages. Some, fearing the inherent difficulties in the *finale,* have transposed this *finale* a tone lower. There are hearers who, knowing the theory of Wagner —that the Ninth symphony was the logical end of purely instrumental music, and Beethoven introduced singers in the finale to show his impatience with the orchestra as a medium of full expression—look on the symphony as a polemical work and in turn deny all absolute music written after Beethoven's death.

The music remains, in spite of the commentators and the too anxious conductors. The instrumental movements are among the proudest achievements of man. Mr. Canudo may begin his "explanation" of the opening *allegro* by saying: "In the beginning was space; and all possibilities were in space; and life was space"; he may find in a certain page the "religious affirmation of Creation"; he may entitle the first theme of the *adagio* "The rhythm of the blessed cosmic night" and thus take his pleasure.

The music of the first three movements is not the less sublime or beautiful because it has no programme, because it has no text for singers. With the exception of a few stupendous passages in the *finale,* where Beethoven is among the stars, the *finale* falls below the movements that precede it. There is more frenzied joy in the *scherzo;* there is greater, world-embracing humanity, a loftier, nobler spirit in the *adagio*. The theme of Joy is not in itself one of Beethoven's most fortunate inventions, and there are pages both for singers and for orchestra that disconcert even if they do not seem to the hearer abnormal and impotent. The answer made by some is that if an ideal performance could be attained the grandeur of the thought would then be overwhelming. Unfortunately, human voices have their limitations.

Yet if the first three movements are performed alone, there is a sense of incompleteness. If the *finale* is transposed, the effect is diminished. And so the Ninth symphony as a whole is still a stumbling block to many.

Beethoven made sketches for his Ninth symphony as early as 1815. The symphony was completed about February, 1824. The idea of adding a chorus to the last movement probably came to him only in the course of his work, for there are sketches of a purely instrumental *finale* which Nottebohm says were made in June or July, 1823; but Schiller's *Hymn to Joy* had long tempted Beethoven. At Bonn, in 1792, he thought of setting music to it. His *Fantaisie* for piano, orchestra, and chorus (1800) contains the melodic germ that he afterwards used for Schiller's words. Perhaps the "mother melody" may be found in a folk song, "Freu' dich sehr, O meine Selle, und vergiss' all' Noth und Qual." Wasielewski thinks the origin is in a song of Beethoven's, "Kleine Blümen, kleine Blätter," with text by Goethe, while the music was composed in 1810.

According to Beethoven's sketchbooks, he was planning two symphonies; one, for England, was to be purely instrumental; the other was the *Sinfonie allemand,* either with variations after the chorus when it entered, or without variations; the *finale* with "Turkish music"—that is, bass drum, cymbals, and triangle—"and choral song."

In 1817, there was correspondence between the Philharmonic Society of London and Beethoven with reference to the latter's visiting England. He was offered 300 guineas if he would come to London and superintend the production of two symphonies to be composed for the Society. Beethoven asked for 400 guineas; 150 to be paid in advance (one hundred were for traveling expenses). The previous offer was repeated, but Beethoven abandoned his intention of going to London.

At the first performance of the Ninth symphony in England (March 21, 1825), the programme read: "New Grand Characteristic Sinfonia, MS. with vocal *finale,* the principal parts to be sung by Madame Caradori, Miss Goodall, Mr. Vaughan, and Mr. Phillips; *composed expressly for this Society.*" There was also a note in which it was said that in 1822 the directors of the Philharmonic had offered Beethoven £50 for a symphony to be delivered at the stipulated time; and as it had been performed and published at Vienna before the Society could use it, the remuneration was ample. It should be remembered that the Philharmonic Society, learning of Beethoven's sickness in 1827, sent him £100. Beethoven acknowledged in most grateful terms, eight days before his death, the receipt of the sum given him by these "generous" Englishmen, and spoke of a tenth symphony wholly sketched, also a new overture, that he might send to them. He had written to Ries in 1823 that only his poverty compelled him to write the Ninth symphony for the Philharmonic; he had sent to it the overture *The Dedication of the House,* and he asked Ries to drive as good a bargain as he could for it. He had been vexed because the Philharmonic Society had characterized three overtures delivered for 75 guineas in 1815: *Ruins of Athens, King Stephen,* and *Zur Namensfeier,* as "unworthy" of the composer.

After Beethoven's death, the Philharmonic Society reclaimed the gift of £100, but was persuaded to withdraw the claim. A portion of the money was applied to the payment of the funeral expenses.

The first performance of the Ninth symphony was at the Kärthnerthor Theater, Vienna, on May 7, 1824. Musicians and wealthy amateurs organized the concert, for the Gesellschaft der Musikfreunde had refused the undertaking on account of the expense. Beethoven then proposed to give the first performance of the symphony and the great Mass in Berlin, where Count Brühl, the Intendant of the Royal theaters there, was favorably inclined. This led the Viennese patrons and musicians to sign a petition, begging Beethoven to spare Vienna the shame. He reflected, and consented. The programme, approved by the police, was as follows: Grand Overture, Op. 124; Three Grand Hymns for solo voices and chorus; Grand Symphony with a *finale* in which solo voices and chorus enter, on the text of Schiller's "Ode to Joy." The three "Hymns" were the *Kyrie, Credo, Agnus Dei*, of the Mass in D. Sedlinsky, the chief of police, acting on the advice of the Archbishop, had forbidden the printing of "Sacred words" on a playbill, and the church authorities were opposed to the performance of missal music in a theater.

The solo singers were Henriette Sontag, Karolina Unger, Anton Haitzinger, and J. Seipelt. The chorus was composed of amateurs from the Gesellschaft der Musikfreunde. Ignaz Schuppanzigh was the concertmaster; Michael Umlauf conducted. Beethoven asked for twenty-four violins, ten violas, twelve violoncellos and double basses, and a doubling of wind instruments. The rehearsals were laborious. The solo singers had great difficulty in learning their parts. Mmes Sontag and Unger begged Beethoven to make changes in their music. He was obdurate. Mme Unger called him to his face "tyrant over all the vocal organs." When he refused to change the music, she said to Mme Sontag: "Well, then we must go on torturing ourselves in the name of God." The success of the symphony was great, though the performance was imperfect. "There was lack of homogeneous power, a paucity of nuance, a poor distribution of lights and shades." When the drum alone beat the *scherzo* motive, the audience applauded so that a repetition seemed inevitable. (It was of the *scherzo* that Rossini, hearing the symphony in Paris, exclaimed, "I could not have written that.") Mme Unger led Beethoven to the edge of the stage that he might see the crowd waving hats and handkerchiefs. He bowed and was calm.

Mme Grebner, who had sung in the chorus, told Felix Weingartner that Beethoven sat in the middle of the orchestra and followed the score. Thalberg, the pianist, who was in the audience, told A. W. Thayer that Beethoven was dressed in a black dress-coat, white neckerchief and waistcoat, black satin small-clothes, black silk stockings, shoes with buckles; but Thalberg was mistaken if Schindler's story is true, for he called on Beethoven just before the concert and said, "O great master, you do not own a black frock-coat! The green one will have to do. The theater will be dark, and no one will notice it. In a few days the black one will be ready."

The success was unprecedented; the net pecuniary result was a sum equivalent to sixty dollars. Beethoven was angry. Some days after the concert, dining in a restaurant with Schindler and Duport, he accused them of having swindled him; nor would he be persuaded by Schuppanzigh that the charge was absurd, for Beethoven's brother Johann and nephew Karl had watched the cashiers.

There was a second performance in Vienna on May 23, 1824, in the large Hall of the Redoutes. Duport assumed all the expenses, and guaranteed Beethoven 500 florins. The programme was not the same, but it included the symphony, the *Kyrie,* and the overture. The hour, noon, was unfavorable. Duport lost some hundreds of florins. These were the only performances at which Beethoven could be present.

Beethoven had purposed to dedicate the symphony to the Tsar Alexander; he finally dedicated it to Friedrich Wilhelm III, the King of Prussia. The King answered, expressing appreciation, and saying that he had sent to him a diamond ring. The gem turned out to be not a diamond, but a reddish stone valued by the court jeweler at 300 florins in paper money. The indignant Beethoven was inclined to return the ring; but he sold it to the jeweler who had appraised it. Some thought that the "reddish stone" had been substituted for the diamond ring on the way to Vienna.

Though Beethoven had long been fond of Schiller's "Ode to Joy," the Ninth symphony was not conceived at first as a celebration of joy. In 1818, he had the plan of introducing voices into a symphony "in the ancient modes," but the text was to be relating to some Greek myth, or a pious song.

The symphony begins *Allegro ma non troppo,* D minor, 2–4; but the chief theme, though hinted at, does not appear until after sixteen measures. There is a continuous melodic development which may be divided into several distinct periods, but there is no marked contrast in character between what might be called eight separate themes.

The second movement, *molto vivace,* D minor, 3–4, is a *scherzo,* though it is not so called in the score. It is built on three leading themes. The peculiar rhythm of the dotted triplet is maintained either in the melody or in the accompaniment.

The third movement, *adagio molto e cantabile,* B flat major, 4–4, has been described as a double theme with variations.

The *finale* begins with several orchestral sections, the first *presto,* D minor, 3–4. There are recitatives for the lower strings. Finally, the baritone enters with this recitative:

*O brothers, these sad tones no longer!*
*Rather raise we now together our voices,*
*And joyful be our song!*

*Allegro assai,* D major, 4–5. The baritone "with the encouragement of the basses of the choruses at the beginning," sings the first theme. Then follow passages for chorus, quartet, until the tempo changes to *allegro assai vivace alla marcia,* B flat major, 6–8. There are later changes in tempo until the final *prestissimo,* "in which the chorus goes stark mad with joy."

The following translation of Schiller's ode is by the late Henry G. Chapman:

## *TO JOY*

*Joy, thou spark from flame immortal*
*Daughter of Elysium!*
*Drunk with fire, O heav'n-born Goddess,*
*We invade thy halidom!*
*Let thy magic bring together*
*All whom earth-born laws divide;*
*All mankind shall be as brothers*
*'Neath thy tender wings and wide.*

*He that's had that best good fortune,*
*To his friend a friend to be,*
*He that's won a noble woman,*
*Let him join our Jubilee!*

*Ay, and who a single other*
*Soul on earth can call his own;*
*But let him who ne'er achieved it*
*Steal away in tears alone.*

*Joy doth every living creature*
*Draw from Nature's ample breast;*
*All the good and all the evil*
*Follow on her roseate quest.*
*Kisses doth she give, and vintage,*
*Friends who firm in death have stood;*
*Joy of life the worm receiveth,*
*And the Angels dwell with God!*

*Glad as burning suns that glorious*
*Through the heavenly spaces sway,*
*Haste ye brothers, on your way,*
*Joyous as a knight victorious.*

*Love toward countless millions swelling,*
*Wafts one kiss to all the world!*
*Surely, o'er yon stars unfurl'd,*
*Some kind Father has his dwelling!*

*Fall ye prostrate, O ye millions!*
*Dost thy Maker feel, O world?*
*Seek Him o'er yon stars unfurl'd,*
*O'er the stars rise His pavilions!*

## OVERTURE TO "LEONORE NO. 3," OP. 72

THE OVERTURE is in itself a condensation of what is dramatic in an opera that has commonplace, yes, bourgeois pages. Hearing the overture, one is spared the sight of a bulbous and shrieking prima donna; of a tenor whose throat had been seriously affected by a long confinement in a "dem'd moist" dungeon; of the operetta young man and woman chatting with a flatiron among the stage properties; of four persons, each with an individual sentiment, singing the same tune in an approved scholastic form.

It might be well to play in the same concert the three Leonore overtures in the order in which they were probably written: Nos. 2, 3, 1. A programme composed exclusively of piano sonatas by Beethoven is an invention of the Adversary, and it deserves the attention of the police as a deliberate act against public morals. Nor is an orchestral programme devoted exclusively to the works of any composer to be encouraged, except possibly when the Ninth symphony is given. But with these overtures the case is different, for here is a revelation of Beethoven's processes of musical and dramatic thought when he was mightily interested in the same subject. . . . How many composers, after the achievement of a *Leonore No. 2,* would have the courage or the ability to shape from it a *Leonore No. 3?* After the three were attentively heard and thoughtfully considered, then *No. 3* might be reasonably reserved for concert use and the other two put away neatly but surely on the shelf.

In the year that saw the production of *Fidelio* (November 20, 1805), Napoleon's army was hastening toward Vienna. There was an exodus from the town of the nobility, merchants, and other residents. The vanguard of the French army entered on November 13. Those of the Viennese who would have appreciated the opera had fled the town. The theater was not well filled. Many in the audience were or had been officers in Napoleon's army. The success of the opera was small. Only two performances followed the first. At the first and at the second the overture *Leonore No. 2* was performed. Anna Pauline Milder, afterwards Mme Hauptmann, was the heroine. "The opera was hastily put upon the stage, and the inadequacy of the singers thus increased by the lack of sufficient rehearsals." Beethoven had received the text in 1804. He worked on the music the following summer at Hetzendorf. On his return to Vienna, rehearsals were begun. In later years *Fidelio* was one of Anna Milder's great parts: "Judging from the contemporary criticism, it was now [1805] somewhat defective, simply from lack of stage experience."

*Leonore No. 2* was the overture played at the first performance in Vienna. The opera was withdrawn, revised, and produced again on March 29, 1806, when *Leonore No. 3,* a remodeled form of *No. 2,* was the overture. There was talk of a performance at Prague in 1807. Beethoven wrote for it a new overture, retaining the theme derived from Florestan's air, "In des Lebens Frülingstagen." The other material in *Nos. 2* and *3* was not used. The opera was not performed; the autograph of the overture disappeared. *Fidelio* was revived at Vienna in 1814. For this performance Beethoven wrote the *Fidelio* overture. We know from his diary that he "rewrote and bettered" the opera by working on it from March to May 15 of that year.

The dress rehearsal was on May 22, but the promised overture was not ready. On the 20th or 21st, Beethoven was dining at a tavern with his friend Bartolini. After the meal was over, Beethoven took a bill of fare, drew lines on the back of it, and began to write. "Come, let us go," said Bartolini. "No, wait a while: I have the scheme of my overture," answered Beethoven, and he sat until he had finished his sketches. Nor was he at the dress rehearsal. They waited for him a long time, then went to his lodgings. He was fast asleep in bed. A cup of wine and biscuits were near him, and sheets of the overture were on the bed and the floor. The candle was burnt out. It was impossible to use the new overture, which was not even finished. Schindler said a *Leonore* overture was played. According to Seyfried, the overture used was that to *The Ruins of Athens.*

The order, then, of these overtures, according to the time of composition, is now supposed to be *Leonore No. 2, Leonore No. 3, Leonore No. 1, Fidelio.* It was said that *Leonore No. 2* was rewritten because certain passages given to the wood-wind troubled the players. Others say it was too difficult for the strings and too long. In *No. 2,* as well as in *No. 3,* the chief dramatic stroke is the trumpet signal, which announces the arrival of the Minister of Justice, confounds Pizarro, and saves Florestan and Leonore.

The *Fidelio* overture is the one generally played before performances of the opera in Germany, although Weingartner has tried earnestly to restore *Leonore No. 2* to that position. *Leonore No. 3* is sometimes played between the acts of the opera. The objection to this is that the trumpet episode of the prison will then discount the dramatic ending of the overture when it comes in the following act, nor does the joyous ending of the overture prepare the hearer for the lugubrious scene with the Florestan soliloquy. Bülow therefore performed the overture at the end of the opera. Zumpe did likewise in Munich. They argued with Wagner that this overture is the quintessence of the opera, "the complete and definite synthesis of the drama that Beethoven had dreamed of writing." There has been a tradition that the overture should be played between the scenes of the second act.

The key of the *Leonore Overture No. 3* is C major. A short *fortissimo* is struck. It is diminished by wood-wind and horns, then taken up, *piano,* by the strings. From this G there is a descent down the scale of C major to a mysterious F sharp. The key of B minor is reached, finally A flat major, when the opening measures of Florenstan's air, "In des Lebens Frülingstagen" (Act II of the opera), is played. The theme of the *allegro,* C major, begins *pianissimo,* first violins and violoncellos, and waxes impetuously. The second theme has been described as "woven out of sobs and pitying sighs." The working out consists in alternating a pathetic figure, taken from the second theme and played by the wood-wind over a nervous string accompaniment, with furious outbursts from the whole orchestra. Then comes the trumpet call off stage. The twice-repeated call is answered in each instance by the short song of thanksgiving from the same scene. Leonore's words are: *"Ach! du bist gerettet! Grosser Gott!"* A gradual transition leads from this to the return of the first theme at the beginning of the third part (flute solo). The third part is developed in general as the first part and leads to a wildly jubilant *coda.*

## OVERTURE TO "EGMONT," OP. 84

Strange things have been done by conductors to Beethoven's overture. We remember Franz Wüllner in Berlin slackening the pace in the *allegro* section when he came to the heavy chords that are supposed by some commentators, finders of sunbeams in cucumbers, to represent Alva, and then playing the chords with brutal emphasis and a long pause between them. Another conductor, no less a person than Arthur Nikisch, made a long hold on the short, incisive violin stroke just before the *coda,* and then brought the figure slowly down *portamento.* We doubt if he did this in later years.

This overture was composed in 1810; it was published in 1811. The music to Goethe's play—overture, four entr'actes, two songs sung by Clärchen, "Clärchen's Death," "Melodrama," and "Triumph Symphony" (identical with the coda of the overture), for the end of the play, nine numbers in all—was performed for the first time with the tragedy at the Hofburg Theater, Vienna, May 24, 1810. Antonie Adamberger was the Clärchen.

When Hartl took the management of the two Vienna Court theaters, January 1, 1808, he produced plays by Schiller. He finally determined to produce plays by Goethe and Schiller with music, and he chose Schiller's *Tell* and Goethe's *Egmont.* Beethoven and Gyrowetz were asked to write the music. The former was anxious to compose the music for *Tell;* but, as Czerny tells the story, there were intrigues, and, as *Egmont* was thought to be less suggestive to a composer, the music for that play was assigned to Beethoven. Gyrowetz's music to *Tell* was performed June 14, 1810. It was described by a correspondent of a Leipsic journal of music as "characteristic and written with intelligence." No allusion was made at the time anywhere to Beethoven's *Egmont.*

The overture has a short, slow introduction, *sostenuto ma non troppo,* F minor, 3–2. The main body of the overture is an *allegro,* F minor, 3–4. The first theme is in the strings; each phrase is a descending *arpeggio* in the violoncellos, closing with a sigh in the first violins; the antithesis begins with a "sort of sigh" in the wood-wind, then in the strings; then there is a development into passage work. The second theme has for its thesis a version of the first two measures of the sarabande theme of the introduction, *fortissimo* (strings), in A flat major, and the antithesis is a triplet in the wood-wind. The coda, *allegro con brio,* F major, 4–4, begins *pianissimo.* The full orchestra at last has a brilliant fanfare figure, which ends in a shouting climax, with a famous shrillness of the piccolo against fanfares of bassoons and brass and between crashes of the full orchestra.

Long and curious commentaries have been written in explanation of this overture. As though the masterpiece needed an explanation! We remember one in which a subtle meaning was given to at least every half-dozen measures: The Netherlanders are under the crushing weight of Spanish oppression; Egmont is melancholy, his blood is stagnant, but at last he shakes off his melancholy (violins), answers the cries of his country-people, rouses himself for action; his death is portrayed by a descent of the violins from C to G; but his countrymen triumph. Spain is typified by the sarabande movement; the heavy, recurring chords portray the lean-bodied, lean-visaged Duke of Alva; "the violin theme in D flat, to which the clarinet brings the under-third, is a picture of Clärchen," etc. One might as well illustrate word for word the solemn ending of Thomas Fuller's life of Alva in *The Profane State:* "But as his life was a mirror of cruelty, so was his death of God's patience. It was admirable that his tragical acts should have a comical end; that he that sent so many to the grave should go to his own, and die in peace. But God's justice on offenders goes not always in the same path, nor the same pace; and he is not pardoned for the fault who is for a while reprieved from the punishment; yea, sometimes the guest in the inn goes quietly to bed before the reckoning for his supper is brought to him to discharge." The overture is at first a mighty lamentation. There are voices of an aroused and angry people, and there is at the last tumultuous rejoicing. The "Triumph Symphony" at the end of the play forms the end of the overture.

## OVERTURE TO "CORIOLANUS," OP. 62

Someone said—was it A. W. Thayer?—of this overture that he could not understand it—until he read Collin's tragedy; that he could not reconcile the music with Shakespeare's text. Pray, what would the gentleman have had? It is immaterial whether Beethoven had Collin or Shakespeare in mind. The name Coriolanus was enough, even if he knew it only from some schoolboy history of Rome; for in this music we hear the proud voice, we hear the haughty, inexorable bearing of the soldier-patrician. Nor does it matter whether the lyrical theme is the entreating voice of wife or mother. Possibly if one should read Collin's play he would wonder that Beethoven should have written an overture for it. There it is—one of Beethoven's greatest works. From his own disdain of the mob, from his own contempt of what the public thought of his music, he recognizes in Coriolanus a kindred spirit.

The original manuscript of the overture bears this inscription: *Overtura (zum Trauerspiel Coriolan) composta da L. v. Beethoven, 1807.* The words in parentheses are crossed out. The overture was published in 1808. The tragedy by Heinrich Joseph von Collin, in which the hero kills himself, was produced in Vienna on November 24, 1802. Collin (1771–1811) was jurist and poet. In 1803 he was ennobled. In 1809 he became court councillor. Other tragedies by him were *Regulus* and *Polyxena.* In 1807 Beethoven was expecting a libretto from him. Collin tried *Macbeth,* Tasso's *Jerusalem Delivered,* and a *Bradamante* to which J. F. Reichardt set music. But Beethoven wrote to Collin:

"Great irate poet, give up Reichardt. Take my *music* for your *poetry;* I promise that you will not thereby suffer. As soon as my concert is over . . . I will come to you, and then we will at once take in hand the opera—and it shall soon sound. For the rest you can ring out your just complaints about me by word of mouth." The libretto before this had seemed to Beethoven "too venturesome" in respect of its use of the supernatural. Collin's biographer, Laban, says that the *Macbeth* libretto was left unfinished in the middle of the second act "because it threatened to become too gloomy." At various times Beethoven thought of Grillparzer's *Melusine,* Körner's *Return of Ulysses,* Treitschke's *Romulus and Remus,* Berger's *Bacchus,* Shakespeare's *Romeo and Juliet,* Schiller's *Fiesco,* Grillparzer's *Dragomira,* Voltaire's tragedies, and Goethe's *Faust,* as operatic subjects. He told Rellstab that the material must be attractive to him; that it must be something he could take up with sincerity and love. "I could not compose operas like *Don Juan* and *Figaro.* They are repugnant to me. I could not have chosen such subjects; they are too frivolous for me!"

It is in one movement, *allegro con brio,* in C minor, 4–4, as written, *alla breve* as played. It begins with a succession of three long-held *fortissimo* C's in the strings, each one of which is followed by a resounding chord in the full orchestra. The agitated first theme in C minor soon gives place to the second lyrically passionate theme in E flat major.

The development of this theme is also short. The free fantasia is practically passage-work on the conclusion theme. The tendency to shorten the academic sonata form is seen also in the third part, or recapitulation. The first theme returns in F minor with curtailed development. The second theme is now in C major. The *coda* begins with this theme; passage-work follows; there is a repetition of the C's and the chords of the beginning; and the purely dramatic close in C minor may be suggestive of the hero's death.

## CONCERTO FOR PIANOFORTE, NO. 4, IN G MAJOR, OP. 58

*I. Allegro moderato*
*II. Andante con moto*
*III. Rondo: vivace*

THIS CONCERTO was probably composed for the most part, and it was surely completed, in 1806, although Schindler, on advice from Ries, named 1804 as the year, and an edition of the concerto published by Breitkopf & Härtel states that the year 1805 saw the completion.

The concerto was performed by Beethoven in one of two private subscription concerts of his works given in the dwelling house of Prince Lobkowitz, Vienna, in March, 1807. The first public performance was in the Theater an der Wien, Vienna, December 22, 1808.

The score was dedicated "humbly" by Beethoven to "his Imperial Highness, the Archduke Rudolph of Austria."

I. *Allegro moderato,* G major, 4–4. The first movement, contrary to the tradition that prevailed at the time, begins with the pianoforte alone. The pianoforte announces the first four measures of the first theme, five measures if an introductory chord be counted. (These measures are to be found in a sketchbook of Beethoven which is dated 1803, but in this book they end in the tonic, and not in the dominant.) The orchestra then enters in B major, but soon returns to G major, and develops the theme, until after a short climax with a modulation a second theme appears, which is given to the first violins. There is a third theme *fortissimo* in G major, with a supplement for the wood-wind instruments, and still another new theme, an expressive melody in B flat major.

II. *Andante con moto,* E minor, 2-4. This movement is free in form. Beethoven put a footnote in the full score to this effect: "During the whole *andante,* the pianist must use the soft pedal *(una corda)* unintermittently; the sign 'Ped' refers to the occasional use of the ordinary pedal." This footnote is contradicted at one point in the score by the marking *"tre corde"* for five measures near the end of the movement. A stern and powerful recitative for strings alternates with gentle and melodic passages for the pianoforte. "The strings of the orchestra keep repeating a forbidding figure of strongly marked rhythm in *staccato* octaves; this figure continues at intervals in stern, unchanging *forte* through about half the movement and then gradually dies away. In the intervals of this harsh theme the pianoforte as it were improvises little scraps of the tenderest, sweetest harmony and melody, rising for a moment into the wildest frenzied exultation after its enemy, the orchestra, has been silenced by its soft pleading, then falling back into hushed sadness as the orchestra comes in once more with a whispered recollection of its once so cruel phrase; saying as plainly as an orchestra can say it, 'The rest is silence!' "[10]

III. *Rondo: vivace.* The first theme, of a sunny and gay character, is announced immediately by the strings. The pianoforte follows with a variation. A short but more melodic phrase for the strings is also taken up by the pianoforte. A third theme, of a bolder character, is announced by the orchestra. The fourth theme is given to the pianoforte. The *rondo,* "of a reckless, devil-may-care spirit in its jollity," is based on this thematic material. At the end the tempo becomes *presto.*

## CONCERTO FOR PIANOFORTE, NO. 5, IN E FLAT MAJOR, OP. 73

*I. Allegro*
*II. Adagio un poco mosso*
*III. Rondo: allegro ma non tanto*

THERE ARE noble pages, also moments of tenderness, in the first movement; there is a majestic, compelling sweep. In the second movement there is simplicity, serenity of contemplation, Buddhistic

[10]William Foster Apthorp.

music of singular detachment, found only in certain measures of Beethoven and Handel; but the *finale* with the endless repetitions of a Kangaroo theme leads one to long for the end.

Beethoven, having made some sketches in 1808, wrote this concerto in 1809 at Vienna. The town was occupied by the French from May 12 to October 14.

It is said that the first public performance of which there is any record was at Leipsic on November 28, 1811. It is also stated that this performance was late in 1810. The pianist was Friedrich Schneider. The *Allgemeine Musik Zeitung* described the concerto as "without doubt one of the most original, imaginative, effective, but most difficult of all existing concertos." Schneider, it seems, played "with soul" as well as force, and the orchestra accompanied remarkably, for "it respected and admired composer, composition, and pianist."

The first performance with which Beethoven was concerned was at Vienna on February 12, 1812, when Karl Czerny (1791–1857) was the pianist. The occasion was a singular sort of entertainment. Theodor Körner, who had been a looker-on in Vienna only for a short time, wrote home on February 15: "Wednesday there took place for the benefit of the Charitable Society of Noble Ladies a concert and a representation of three pictures after Raphael, Poussin, and Troyes, as Goethe describes them in his *Elective Affinities*. A new concerto by Beethoven for the pianoforte did not succeed"; but Castelli's *Thalia* gave as the reason of this failure the unwillingness of Beethoven, "full of proud self-confidence," to write for the crowd. "He can be understood and appreciated only by the connoisseurs, and one cannot reckon on their being in a majority at such an affair." Thayer moralizes on this statement. "The trills of Miss Sessi and Mr. Siboni and Mayseder's Variations on the March from *Aline* were appropriate to the occasion and the audience."

The Vienna correspondent of the *Allgemeine Musik Zeitung* wrote that the extravagant length of the concerto diminished the total effect which the "noble production of the mind" would otherwise have made. As for Czerny, "he played with much accuracy and fluency, and showed that he has it in his power to conquer the greatest difficulties."

But the correspondent wished that there had been greater purity in his performance, a finer contour.

The tableaux pleased mightily, and each one was repeated.

The first movement, *allegro,* in E flat, 4–4, opens with a strong chord for full orchestra, which is followed by a *cadenza* for the solo instrument.

The first theme is given out by the strings and afterward taken up by the clarinets. The second theme soon follows, first in E flat minor, softly and staccato by the strings, then *legato* and in E flat major by the horns. It was usual at that time for the pianist to extemporize his *cadenza,* but Beethoven inserted his own with the remark, *"non si fa, una cadenza ma s'attacca subito il seguente"* (that is to say, "Do not insert a *cadenza,* but attack the following immediately"); and he then went so far as to accompany with the orchestra the latter portion of his *cadenza.*

The second movement, *adagio un poco moto,* in B major, 2–2, is in the form of "quasi-variations," developed chiefly from the theme given at the beginning by muted strings. This movement goes, with a suggestion hinted by the pianoforte of the coming first theme of the *rondo,* into the *rondo,* the *finale, allegro,* in E flat, 6–8. Both the themes are announced by the pianoforte and developed elaborately. The end of the *coda* is distinguished by a descending long series of pianoforte chords which steadily diminish in force, while the kettledrums keep marking the rhythm of the opening theme.

## CONCERTO FOR VIOLIN, IN D MAJOR, OP. 61

*I. Allegro ma non troppo*
*II. Larghetto*
*III. Rondo*

Beethoven composed this concerto in 1806 for the violinist, Franz Clement, who played it for the first time at the latter's concert in the Theater an der Wien, December 23 of that year.

Beethoven, often behindhand in finishing compositions for solo players—according to the testimony of Dr. Bartolini and others—did not have the concerto ready for rehearsal. Clement played it at the concert *a vista.*

The first movement, *allegro ma non troppo,* in D major, 4-4, begins with a long orchestral *ritornello.* The first theme is announced by oboes, clarinets, and bassoons. It is introduced by four taps of the kettledrums on D. (There is a story that these tones were suggested to the composer by his hearing a neighbor knocking at the door of his house for admission late at night.) The wind instruments go on with the second phrase. Then come the famous and problematical four D sharps in the first violins. The short second theme is given out by wood-wind and horns in D major, repeated in D minor, and developed at length. The solo violin enters after a half cadence on the dominant. The first part of the movement is repeated. The solo violin plays the themes or embroiders them. The working out is long and elaborate. A *cadenza* is introduced at the climax of the conclusion theme. There is a short *coda.*

The second movement, *Larghetto,* in G major, 4-4, is a romance in free form. The accompaniment is lightly scored. The theme is almost wholly confined to the orchestra, while the solo violin embroiders with elaborate figuration until the end, when it brings in the theme, but soon abandons it to continue the embroidery. A *cadenza* leads to the *finale.*

The third movement, *rondo,* in D major, 6-8, is based on a theme that has the character of a folk dance. The second theme is a sort of hunting call for the horns. There is place for the insertion of a free *cadenza* near the end.

Beethoven's great development of the symphony was in his use of the instruments—not in their number. For the most part, he called for virtually the same orchestra which his predecessors, Mozart and Haydn, evolved: two flutes, two oboes, two clarinets, two bassoons, two horns, two trumpets, kettledrums and strings. This applies to Beethoven's First, Second, Third, Fourth, Seventh, and Eighth symphonies (exceptions: the addition of a third horn in the *Eroica* symphony, and use of a single flute in the Fourth).

In the Fifth symphony, he gave greater sonority to his *finale* with three trombones, double bassoon, and piccolo.

In the Sixth, he added a piccolo for the storm, two trombones for the storm and *finale.*

In the Ninth, he increased his horns to four, added three trombones, and the following instruments in the *alla marcia* of the *finale:* piccolo, double bassoon, cymbals, triangle, and bass drum.

In the overtures here listed, Beethoven added to the above essential orchestration as follows: *Egmont*—two additional horns, piccolo; *Leonore*—two additional horns and three trombones. The concertos call for the minimum orchestration, "in twos."—EDITOR.

# HECTOR
# BERLIOZ

(Born at La Côte Saint-André, December 11, 1803; died at Paris, March 9, 1869)

---

THE MORE Berlioz is studied, the more the wonder grows at his colossal originality. Yet there are some who still insist that he had little melodic invention. They have ears, and they do not hear. They should read the essay of Romain Rolland, and the essay of Felix Weingartner in his *Akkorde,* for there are many, unfortunately, who do not trust their own judgment and are eager to accept the sayings of others who are considered men of authority.

Berlioz wrote his *Fantastic* symphony in a high-strung, hotly romantic period. Romanticism was in the air. Much that seems fantastic to us, living in a commercial and material period, was natural then. It was as natural to be extravagant in belief, theories, speech, manner of life, dress, as it was to breathe. And Berlioz was a revolutionary of revolutionaries. His "antediluvian hair" that rose from his forehead was as much of a symbol as was the flaming waistcoat worn by Théophile on the memorable first night of *Hernani.* We smile now at the eccentricities and the extravagancies of the period, but we owe the perpetrators a heavy debt of gratitude. They made the art of today possible.

It is easy to call Berlioz a *poseur,* but the young man was terribly in earnest. He put his own love tragedy into his *Fantastic* symphony; he was a man; he suffered; he was there; and so the music did not pass away with the outward badges of romanticism, with much of Byron's poetry, with plays and novels of the time. The emotions he expressed are still universal and elemental.

## SYMPHONIE FANTASTIQUE, IN C MAJOR, OP. 14 a

*I. Dreams, Passions: Largo: Allegro agitato e appassionato assai*
*II. A Ball: Waltz: allegro non troppo*
*III. Scene in the Meadows: Adagio*
*IV. March to the Scaffold: Allegretto non troppo*
*V. A Witches' Sabbath: Larghetto: allegro*

When one remembers that Beethoven had died only a few years before Berlioz wrote his symphony; that Schubert also had died; that Schumann and Wagner were not known as composers, one must regard this audacious work of Berlioz as nothing less than marvelous. No predecessor had given him hints for orchestration: he invented his own system; he thought and wrote orchestrally. Liszt, Meyerbeer, Wagner, Strauss, the Russian School, in fact, the musical world of the last century is indebted deeply to Hector Berlioz. Without him all would have been sadly at a loss.

One may smile in this matter-of-fact age at the frantic love of Berlioz for the Irish actress; at the programme of the *Fantastic* symphony, written when he was not twenty-seven years old. But there's no denying the genius in this work, the genius that has kept this music alive in spite of a few cheap or arid pages; for there is the imagination, the poetic sensitiveness that we rightly associate with genius. If one would gladly shorten the "Scene in the Fields," what is to be said against that masterpiece "The March to the Scaffold," with its haunting, nightmarish rhythm, its ghostly chatter of the bassoons, its mocking shouts of brass? Or who does not find beauty in the first movement, brilliance in the second, and a demoniacal spirit in the *finale?*

Ernest Newman has wisely said that the harmonies of Berlioz

suited exactly his aims; that however strange they may seem on paper, they are justified when they are heard. As for the charge of failure as a melodist, there are the songs; there is the pathetic air of Marguerite in *The Damnation of Faust,* the "Farewell of the Shepherds" in *The Childhood of Christ,* the grand arias in *Les Troyens.*

This symphony forms the first part of a work entitled *Épisode de la vie d'un artiste* (Episode in the Life of an Artist), the second part of which is a lyric monodrama, *Lélio, ou le retour à la vie* (Lelio; or, The Return to Life). Berlioz published the following preface to the full score of the symphony:

"PROGRAMME OF THE SYMPHONY

"A young musician of morbid sensibility and ardent imagination poisons himself with opium in a fit of amorous despair. The narcotic dose, too weak to result in death, plunges him into a heavy sleep accompanied by the strangest visions, during which his sensations, sentiments, and recollections are translated in his sick brain into musical thoughts and images. The beloved woman herself has become for him a melody, like a fixed idea which he finds and hears everywhere.

"PART I

"DREAMS, PASSIONS

"He first recalls that uneasiness of soul, that *vague des passions,* those moments of causeless melancholy and joy, which he experienced before seeing her whom he loves; then the volcanic love with which she suddenly inspired him, his moments of delirious anguish, of jealous fury, his returns to loving tenderness, and his religious consolations.

"PART II

"A BALL

"He sees his beloved at a ball, in the midst of the tumult of a brilliant fête.

"PART III

"SCENE IN THE FIELDS

"One summer evening in the country he hears two shepherds playing a *Ranz-des-vaches* in alternate dialogue; this pastoral duet, the scene around him, the light rustling of the trees gently swayed by the breeze, some hopes he has recently conceived, all combine to restore an unwonted calm to his heart and to impart a more cheerful coloring to his thoughts; but *she* appears once more, his heart stops beating, he is agitated with painful presentiments; if she were to betray him! . . . One of the shepherds resumes his artless melody, the other no longer answers him. The sun sets . . . the sound of distant thunder . . . solitude . . . silence.

"PART IV

"MARCH TO THE SCAFFOLD

"He dreams that he has killed his beloved, that he is condemned to death and led to execution. The procession advances to the tones of a march which is now sombre and wild, now brilliant and solemn, in which the dull sound of the tread of heavy feet follows without transition upon the most resounding outburst. At the end, the *fixed idea* reappears for an instant, like a last love-thought interrupted by the fatal stroke.

"PART V

"WALPURGISNIGHT'S DREAM

"He sees himself at the witches' Sabbath, in the midst of a frightful group of ghosts, magicians, and monsters of all sorts, who have come together for his obsequies. He hears strange noises, groans, ringing laughter, shrieks to which other shrieks seem to reply. The *beloved melody* again reappears; but it has lost its noble and timid character; it has become an ignoble, trivial, and grotesque dance tune; it is *she* who comes to the witches' Sabbath. . . . Howlings of joy at her arrival . . . she takes part in the diabolic orgy. . . . Funeral knells, burlesque parody on the *Dies Iræ*. Witches' dance. The Witches' dance and the *Dies Iræ* together."

In a preamble to this programme, relating mostly to some details of stage-setting when the *Épisode de la vie d'un artiste* is given entire,

Berlioz also writes: "If the symphony is played separately at a concert . . . the programme does not absolutely need to be distributed among the audience, and only the titles of the five movements need be printed, as the symphony can offer by itself (the composer hopes) a musical interest independent of all dramatic intention."

The score is dedicated to Nicholas I of Russia.

The symphony begins with a slow introduction, *Largo,* C minor, 4-4. Two measures of soft preluding lead to a plaintive theme played by the strings, *pianissimo.* This theme is a melody of romance composed by Berlioz in his youth and recurs in modified form in each movement. "Strange to say," wrote Berlioz of the imagined artist, "the image of the loved one never comes into his mind without the accompaniment of a musical thought in which he finds the characteristic grace and nobility attributed by him to his beloved. This double *idée fixe*—obsessing idea—constantly pursues him; hence the constant apparition in all the movements of the chief melody of the first *allegro.*"

The symphony is scored for two flutes (and piccolo), two oboes (and English horn), two clarinets and E flat clarinet, four bassoons, four horns, two cornets-à-pistons, two trumpets, three trombones, two tubas, two pairs of kettledrums (three players) bells, snaredrum, bass drum, cymbals, two harps, and strings.

What was the origin of this symphony? Who was the woman that inspired the music and was so bitterly assailed in the argument sent to his friend Ferrand? Boschot describes her as she looked in 1827: "Tall, lithe, with shoulders rather fat and with full bust, a supple figure, a face of an astonishing whiteness, with bulging eyes like those of the glowing Mme de Staël, but eyes gentle, dreamy, and sometimes sparkling with passion. And this Harriet Smithson had the most beautiful arms—bulbous flesh, sinuous line. They had the effect on a man of a caress of a flower. And the voice of Harriet Smithson was music."[1]

Harriet Constance Smithson, known in Paris as Henrietta Smithson, born at Ennis, Ireland, March 18, 1800, was seen as Ophelia by Berlioz at the Odéon, Paris, September 11, 1827, after engagements in Ireland and England. She appeared there first on September 6 with Kemble, Powers, and Liston. Her success was immediate and overwhelming. She appeared as Juliet, September 15 of the same year. Berlioz saw these first performances. He did not then know a word of English:

[1]Adolf Boschot: *La jeunesse d'un romantique,* 1906.

Shakespeare was revealed to him only through the mist of Letourneur's translation. After the third act of *Romeo and Juliet* he could scarcely breathe; he suffered as though "an iron hand was clutching" his heart, and he exclaimed, "I am lost." And the story still survives, in spite of Berlioz's denial, that he then exclaimed: "That woman shall be my wife! And on that drama I shall write my greatest symphony." He married her, and he was thereafter miserable. He wrote the *Romeo and Juliet* symphony. To the end he preferred the "Love Scene" to all his other music.

Berlioz has told in his Memoirs the story of his wooing. He was madly in love. After a tour in Holland, Miss Smithson went back to London, but Berlioz saw her always by his side; she was his obsessing idea, the inspiring muse. When he learned through the journals of her triumps in London in June, 1829, he dreamed of composing a great work, the *Episode in the Life of an Artist,* to triumph by her side and through her. He wrote Ferrand, February 6, 1830: "I am again plunged in the anguish of an interminable and inextinguishable passion, without motive, without cause. She is always at London, and yet I think I feel her near me: all my remembrances awake and unite to wound me; I hear my heart beating, and its pulsations shake me as the piston strokes of a steam engine. Each muscle of my body shudders with pain. In vain! 'Tis terrible! O unhappy one! if she could for one moment conceive all the poetry, all the infinity of a like love, she would fly to my arms, were she to die through my embrace. I was on the point of beginning my great symphony (*Episode in the Life of an Artist*), in which the development of my infernal passion is to be portrayed; I have it all in my head, but I cannot write anything. Let us wait."

He wrote Ferrand on April 16, 1830: "Since my last I have experienced terrible hurricanes, and my vessel has cracked and groaned horribly, but at last it has righted itself; it now sails tolerably well. Frightful truths, discovered and indisputable, have started my cure; and I think that it will be as complete as my tenacious nature will permit. I am about to confirm my resolution by a work which satisfies me completely." He then inserted a description of the work. "Behold, my dear friend, the scheme of this immense symphony. I am just writing the last note of it. If I can be ready on Whitsunday, May 30, I shall give a concert at the Nouveautés, with an orchestra of two hundred and twenty players. I am afraid I shall not have the copied parts ready. Just now I am stupid; the frightful effort of thought necessary to the production of my work has tired my imagination, and I should like to sleep and rest continually. But if the brain sleeps, the heart keeps awake."

He wrote to Ferrand on May 13, 1830: "I think that you will be satisfied with the scheme of my *Fantastic* symphony which I sent you in my letter. The vengeance is not too great; besides, I did not write the *Dream of a Sabbat Night* in this spirit. I do not wish to avenge myself. I pity her and I despise her. She's an ordinary woman, endowed with an instinctive genius for expressing the lacerations of the human soul, but she has never felt them, and she is incapable of conceiving an immense and noble sentiment, as that with which I honored her. I make today my last arrangements with the managers of the Nouveautés for my concert the 30th of this month. They are very honest fellows and very accommodating. We shall begin to rehearse the *Fantastic* symphony in three days; all the parts have been copied with the greatest care; there are 2,300 pages of music; nearly 400 francs for the copying. We hope to have decent receipts on Whitsunday, for all the theaters will be closed. . . . I hope that the wretched woman will be there that day; at any rate, there are many conspiring at the Feydeau to make her go. I do not believe it, however; she will surely recognize herself in reading the programme of my instrumental drama, and then she will take good care not to appear. Well, God knows all that will be said, there are so many who know my story!" He hoped to have the assistance of the "incredible tenor," Haizinger, and of Schröder-Devrient, who were then singing in opera at the Salle Favart.

The "frightful truths" about Miss Smithson were sheer calumnies. Berlioz made her tardy reparation in the extraordinary letter written to Ferrand, October 11, 1833, shortly after his marriage. He too had been slandered: her friends had told her that he was an epileptic, that he was mad. As soon as he heard the slanders, he raged, he disappeared for two days, and wandered over lonely plains outside Paris, and at last slept, worn out with hunger and fatigue, in a field near Sceaux. His friends had searched Paris for him, even the morgue. After his return he was obstinately silent for several days.

At last Berlioz determined to give a grand concert at which his cantata *Sardanapale,* which took the prix de Rome, and the *Fantastic* symphony would be performed. Furthermore, Miss Smithson was then in Paris. The concert was announced for November 14, 1830, but it was postponed till December 5 of that year. But Miss Smithson was not present;

she was at the Opéra at a performance for her benefit, and she mimed there for the first and last time the part of Fenella in Auber's *Muette de Portici.* The symphony made a sensation; it was attacked and defended violently, and Cherubini answered, when he was asked if he heard it: *"Ze n'ai pas besoin d'aller savoir comment il né faut pas faire."*

After Berlioz returned from Italy, he purposed to give a concert. He learned accidentally that Miss Smithson was still in Paris; but she had no thought of her old adorer; after professional disappointments in London, due perhaps to her Irish accent, she returned to Paris in the hope of establishing an English theater. The public in Paris knew her no more; she was poor and at her wit's end. Invited to go to a concert, she took a carriage, and then, looking over the programme, she read the argument of the *Fantastic* symphony which with *Lélio,* its supplement, was performed on December 9, 1832. Fortunately, Berlioz had revised the programme and omitted the coarse insult ("She is now only a courtesan worthy to figure in such an orgy") in the programme of the *Sabbat;* but, as soon as she was seen in the hall of the Conservatory, some who knew Berlioz's original purpose chuckled, and spread malicious information. Miss Smithson, moved by the thought that her adorer, as the hero of the symphony, tried to poison himself for her, accepted the symphony as a flattering tribute.

Tiersot[2] describes the scene at this second performance in 1832. The pit was crowded, as on the great days of romantic festival occasions—Dumas's *Antony* was then jamming the Porte Saint-Martin—with pale, long-haired youths, who believed firmly that "to make art" was the only worthy occupation on the earth; they had strange, fierce countenances, curled mustaches, Merovingian hair or hair cut brushlike, extravagant doublets, velvet-faced coats thrown back on the shoulders. The women were dressed in the height of the prevailing fashion, with coiffures *à la girafe,* high shell combs, shoulder-of-mutton sleeves, and short petticoats that revealed buskins. Berlioz was seated behind the drums, and his "monstrous antediluvian hair rose from his forehead as a primeval forest on a steep cliff." Heine was in the hall. He was especially impressed by the *Sabbat,* "where the Devil sings the mass, where the music of the Catholic church is parodied with the most horrible, the most outrageous buffoonery. It is a farce in which all the serpents that we carry hidden in the heart raise their heads, hissing with pleasure and biting their tails in the transport of their joy. . . . Mme Smithson

[2]Julien Tiersot: *Hector Berlioz et la société de son temps,* 1904.

was there, whom the French actresses have imitated so closely. M. Berlioz was madly in love with this woman for three years, and it is to this passion that we owe the savage symphony which we hear today." It is said that, each time Berlioz met her eyes, he beat the drums with redoubled fury. Heine added: "Since then Miss Smithson has become Mme Berlioz, and her husband has cut his hair. When I heard the symphony again last winter, I saw him still at the back of the orchestra, in his place near the drums. The beautiful Englishwoman was in a stage box, and their eyes again met: but he no longer beat with such rage on his drums."

Musician and play actress met, and after mutual distrust and recrimination there was mutual love. She was poor and in debt; on March 16, 1833, she broke her leg, and her stage career was over. Berlioz pressed her to marry him; both families objected; there were violent scenes; Berlioz tried to poison himself before her eyes; Miss Smithson at last gave way, and the marriage was celebrated on October 3, 1833. It was an unhappy one.

"A separation became inevitable," says Legouvé.[3] "She who had been Mlle Smithson, grown old and ungainly before her time, and ill besides, retired to a humble lodging at Montmartre, where Berlioz, notwithstanding his poverty, faithfully and decently provided for her. He went to see her as a friend, for he had never ceased to love her, he loved her as much as ever; but he loved her differently, and that difference had produced a chasm between them."

After some years of acute physical as well as mental suffering, the once famous play actress died, March 3, 1854. Berlioz put two wreaths on her grave, one for him and one for their absent son, the sailor. And Jules Janin sang her requiem in a memorable *feuilleton*.

## OVERTURE, "THE ROMAN CARNIVAL," OP. 9

Berlioz's overture, *Le Carnaval Romain,* originally intended as an introduction to the second act of *Benvenuto Cellini,* is dedicated to Prince de Hohenzollern-Hechingen. It was performed for the first time, and under the direction of the composer, at the Salle Herz, Paris, on February 3, 1844. The overture was composed in Paris in 1843, shortly after a journey in Germany. The score and parts were published in June, 1844.

[3]Ernest Legouvé: *Soixante Ans de Souvenirs,* 1886.

The chief thematic material of the overture was taken by Berlioz from his opera *Benvenuto Cellini,* originally in two acts, libretto by Léon de Wailly and Augusta Barbier. It was produced at the Opéra, Paris, on September 10, 1838.

The success of *The Roman Carnival* overture was immediate. The applause was so long-continued that the work was repeated then and there. Berlioz gives an account of the performance in the forty-eighth chapter of his Memoirs. He first says that Habeneck, the conductor at the Opéra, would not take the time of the *saltarello* fast enough.

"Some years afterwards, when I had written the overture *The Roman Carnival,* in which the theme of the *allegro* is the same *saltarello* which he never could make go, Habeneck was in the foyer of the Salle Herz the evening that this overture was to be played for the first time. He had heard that we had rehearsed it without wind instruments, for some of my players, in the service of the National Guard, had been called away. 'Good!' said he. 'There will surely be some catastrophe at this concert, and I must be there to see it!' When I arrived, all the wind players surrounded me; they were frightened at the idea of playing in public an overture wholly unknown to them.

" 'Don't be afraid,' I said; 'the parts are all right, you are all talented players; watch my stick as much as possible, count your rests, and it will go.'

"There was not a mistake. I started the *allegro* in the whirlwind time of the Transteverine dancers; the audience shouted, *'Bis!'* We played the overture again, and it went even better the second time. I went to the foyer and found Habeneck. He was rather disappointed. As I passed him, I flung at him these few words: 'Now you see what it really is!' He carefully refrained from answering me.

"Never have I felt more keenly than on this occasion the pleasure of conducting my own music, and my pleasure was doubled by thinking on what Habeneck had made me suffer.

"Poor composers, learn to conduct, and conduct yourselves well! (Take the pun, if you please.) For the most dangerous of your interpreters is the conductor. Don't forget this."

The overture is scored for two flutes (and piccolo), two oboes, English horn, two clarinets, two bassoons, four horns, two trumpets, two cornets, three trombones, kettledrums, two side drums, cymbals, triangle, and strings.

# ERNEST
# BLOCH

(Born at Geneva, Switzerland, July 24, 1880)

---

## "SCHELOMO" (SOLOMON), HEBREW RHAPSODY FOR VIOLONCELLO AND ORCHESTRA

Mr. Bloch is most inspired when he stands firmly and proudly on Jewish ground. The well equipped composer is seen in all that he writes, but his three Jewish Poems for orchestra, his Psalms, for voice and orchestra, his *Schelomo,* are far above his what might be called Gentile work, even above his concerto, not to mention the cycloramic *America.* As he has written in an account of himself and his artistic beliefs, it is the Jewish soul that interests him: "the complex, glowing, agitated soul" that he feels vibrating through the Bible. No wonder that the despair of the Preacher in Jerusalem and the splendor of Solomon alike appealed to him; the monarch in all his glory; the Preacher, who when he looked on all his works that his hands had wrought and on the labor that he had labored to do, could only explain: "And behold, all was vanity, and vexation of spirit, and there was no profit under the Sun." And so Mr. Bloch might have taken as a motto for this Hebrew rhapsody the lines of Rueckert:

*Solomon! Where is thy throne? It is gone in the wind*

. . . . . . . . . . . . . . .

*Say what is pleasure? A phantom, a mask undefined.*
*Science? An almond, whereof we can pierce but the rind.*
*Honor and affluence? Firmans that Fortune hath signed*
*Only to glitter and pass on the wings of the wind.*

Other composers have taken Solomon for their hero; as Handel in his oratorio; Goldmark, representing him as mighty and jealous in *The Queen of Sheba;* Gounod in the opera similarly entitled, based on the wildly fantastic tale of Gerard de Nerval; there are older operas, but all, or nearly all, are concerned with *Grand Turke,* the Sultan of the Ottomans. It was left for Mr. Bloch to express in music the magnificence and the pessimistic, despairing philosophy of the ruler to whom is falsely attributed the book, Ecclesiastes. Here is music that does not brook conventional analysis; music that is now purely lyrical, now dramatic, now pictorial; music that rises to gorgeous heights and sinks to the depths; with a conclusion that is not of the Preacher, the pious admonition after summing up the whole matter, but a conclusion voiced by the violoncello: "There is no work, nor device, nor knowledge, nor wisdom in the grave, whither thou goest." Here is no Solomon, lord of all creatures at whose name Afrites and evil genii trembled, the Solomon of the "Thousand Nights and a Night," here is the monarch that having known power and all the pleasures, enumerating them—even to "the delights of the sons of men, as musical instruments, and that of all sorts"—reasoned that everything was futile; that all was vanity.

One might therefore infer that this rhapsody is distressingly somber, for nothing is more wearisome than a long-drawn-out complaint. The inference would be wrong, for Mr. Bloch has imagined in tones, in superbly exultant measures, the pomp and sumptuousness of the King enthroned. There are orchestral bursts of glorification; between them are recitatives and lyric reflections for the jaded voluptuary, the embittered philosopher. The ingenuity displayed is as remarkable as the individuality, the originality shown by the composer stirred in his soul not only by the story of Solomon; moved mightily by the thought of ancient days, the succeeding trials and persecution of his race. More than once in the rhapsody, if there is a suggestion of Solomon's court and temple, there is also the suggestion of the Wailing Wall.

*Schelomo* was composed at Geneva, Switzerland, in the first two months of 1916. With the *Trois poèmes juifs* (composed in 1916) and the symphony *Israel* (1913–18), it is that portion of Mr. Bloch's work that is peculiarly Hebraic in character. In a letter to the writer of these notes in 1917, Mr. Bloch wrote that the Psalms, *Schelomo,* and *Israel* were more representative than the *Jewish Poems* because they came from the passion and the violence that he believed to be characteristics of his nature. "It is not my purpose, not my desire, to attempt a 'reconstitution' of Jewish music, or to base my works on melodies more or less authentic. I am not an archæologist. I hold it of first importance to write good, genuine music, my music. It is the Jewish soul that interests me, the complex, glowing, agitated soul, that I feel vibrating throughout the Bible; the freshness and naïveté of the Patriarchs; the violence that is evident in the prophetic books; the Jew's savage love of justice; the despair of the Preacher in Jerusalem; the sorrow and the immensity of the Book of Job; the sensuality of the Song of Songs. All this is in us; all this is in me, and it is the better part of me. It is all this that I endeavor to hear in myself and to transcribe in my music: the venerable emotion of the race that slumbers way down in our soul."

The *Musical Quarterly* of January, 1921, published a translation by Theodore Baker of Guido M. Gatti's estimate of *Schelomo* contributed to *La Critica musicale* of April–May, 1920:

"The Hebrew rhapsody for solo violoncello with orchestra bears the name of the great king Solomon. In this, without taking thought for development and formal consistency, without the fetters of a text requiring interpretation, he has given free course to his fancy; the multiplex figure of the founder of the Great Temple lent itself, after setting it upon a lofty throne, and chiseling its lineaments, to the creation of a phantasmagorical entourage of persons and scenes in rapid and kaleidoscopic succession. The violoncello, with its ample breadth of phrasing, now melodic and with moments of superb lyricism, now declamatory and with robustly dramatic lights and shades, lends itself to a reincarnation of Solomon in all his glory, surrounded by his thousand wives and concubines, with his multitude of slaves and warriors behind him. His voice resounds in the devotional silence, and the sentences of his wisdom sink into the heart as the seed into a fertile soil: 'Vanity of vanities, saith the Preacher, . . . all is vanity. What profit hath a man of all his labor which he taketh under the sun? One generation passeth away, and another generation cometh: but the earth abideth for ever. . . . He that increaseth knowledge increaseth sorrow.' . . . At times the sonorous voice of the violoncello is heard predominant amid a breathless and fateful obscurity throbbing with persistent rhythms, again, it blends in a phantasmagorical paroxysm of polychromatic tones, shot through with silvery clangors and frenzies of exultation. And anon one finds oneself in the heart of a dream-world, in an Orient of fancy, where men and women of every race and tongue are holding argument or hurling maledictions; and now and again we hear the mournful accents of the prophetic seer, under the influence of which all bow down and listen reverently. The entire discourse of the soloist, vocal rather than instrumental, seems like musical expression intimately conjoined with the Talmudic prose. The pauses, the repetitions of entire passages, the leaps of a double octave, the chromatic progressions, all find their analogues in the Book of Ecclesiastes—in the versicles, in the fairly epigraphic reiteration of the admonitions ('and all is vanity and vexation of spirit'), in the unexpected shifts from one thought to another, in certain *crescendi* of emotion that end in explosions of anger or grief uncontrolled."

*Schelomo* is scored for three flutes (and piccolo), two oboes (and English horn), two clarinets, bass clarinet, two bassoons, contra-bassoon, four horns, four trumpets, three trombones and tuba, kettledrums, tambourine, side drum, bass drum, cymbals, tam-tam, celesta, two harps, and strings.

# ALEXANDER PORPHIRIEVITCH BORODIN

(Born at St. Petersburg, November 12, 1833;[1] died there February 28, 1887)

---

## SYMPHONY NO. 2, IN B MINOR, OP. 5

I. *Allegro moderato*
II. *Molto vivo*
III. *Andante*
IV. *Allegro*

ONLY A RUSSIAN can do justice to this music, which is wildly Russian; that is to say, the Russia of the Orient. One is tempted, hearing the repetitions of the first leading theme, a motto phrase it may be called, to say with Hamlet: "Leave thy damnable faces and begin," but the monotony of repetition becomes irrepressive. A Russian critic was reminded more than once in the course of the first and last movements of the ancient Russian knights in their awkwardness, also in their greatness. We are told that Borodin intended to portray them in tones. He himself said that in the slow movement he wished to recall the songs of Slav troubadours; to picture in the first movement the gatherings of

[1]The year 1834 has been generally accepted as the year of Borodin's birth. M. D. Calvocoressi (in the *London Musical Times,* June, 1934) reported that Serge Dianin had examined the church registers in Leningrad, and other documents which proved the date to have been October 31 (November 12), 1833, not 1834. "Borodin himself knew this quite well until October 31, 1873, when he wrote to his wife: 'Today is my fortieth birthday.' But on that very day an old servant of his mother, Catherine Beltzman by name, assured him that he was thirty-nine years old, not forty. Borodin was delighted, and never troubled to verify the information."—EDITOR.

princes, and in the *finale* the banquets of heroes where the Russian Guzla and bamboo flute were heard while the mighty men caroused. It is easy in the lyrical passages to be reminded of corresponding phrases in *Prince Igor,* nor is this surprising, for he was working on the symphony and the opera at the same time. He was then obsessed by the life of feudal Russia.

No composer can be called great simply because he is a nationalist in his music. The folk tunes of a nation have often worked damage to the composer relying on them for his themes, and content with the mere exposition of them. Rimsky-Korsakov and Moussorgsky were nationalists, but their music passed the frontier; it gives pleasure in every country. Is Borodin to be ranked with them?

Eric Blom, speaking of Borodin as a pioneer, remembers how he was once condemned as an "incompetent amateur who wrote hideous discords because he did not know the rules of harmony"—an unwarranted and foolish condemnation, as unjust as Tchaikovsky's characterization in the bitter letter he wrote to Mme von Meck in 1878 the year after this symphony was first heard. Admitting that Borodin had talent, "a very great talent," he said that it had come to nothing for the want of teaching, "because blind fate has led him into the science laboratories instead of a vital musical existence." The reference was to Borodin's fame as a chemist at the Academy of Medicine. This was written when Tchaikovsky was accused of that atrocious crime, cosmopolitanism, by his fellow laborers in the Russian vineyard.

There are pages of splendid savagery in this symphony; there are a few wild, haunting melodies. No, the composer of the two symphonies, one at least of the string quartets, and a handful of exquisite songs is not to be flippantly dismissed.

Borodin's Symphony in B minor was written during the years 1871–77. The first performance was at St. Petersburg in the Hall of the

Nobility, February 14, 1877, and Eduard Napravnik was the conductor.

Borodin's First symphony, in E flat major, was begun in 1862 and completed in 1867. Stassov furnished him with the scenario of a libretto founded on an epic and national poem, the story of Prince Igor. This poem told of the expedition of Russian princes against the Polovtsi, a nomadic people of the same origin as the Turks, who had invaded the Russian Empire in the twelfth century. The conflict of Russian and Asiatic nationalities delighted Borodin, and he began to write his own libretto. He tried to live in the atmosphere of the bygone century. He read the poems and the songs that had come down from the people of that period; he collected folk songs even from Central Asia; he introduced in the libretto comic characters to give contrast to romantic situations; and he began to compose the music, when at the end of a year he was seized with profound discouragement. His friends said to him: "The time has gone by to write operas on historic or legendary subjects; today it is necessary to treat the modern drama." When anyone deplored in his presence the loss of so much material, he replied that this material would go into a second symphony. He began work on this symphony, and the first movement was completed in the autumn of 1871. But the director of the Russian opera wished to produce an operatic ballet, *Mlada*. The subject was of an epoch before Christianity. The fourth act was intrusted to Borodin: it included religious scenes, apparitions of the ghosts of old Slavonic princes, an inundation, and the destruction of a temple; and human interest was supplied by a love scene. Faithful to his theories, Borodin began to study the manners and the religion of this people. He composed feverishly and did not leave his room for days at a time. Although the work was prepared by the composers—Minkus was to write the ballet music, and Borodon, Cui, Moussorgsky, and Rimsky-Korsakov the vocal music—the scenery demanded such an expense that the production was postponed, and Borodin began work again on his Second symphony and *Prince Igor*. He worked under disadvantages: his wife, Catherine Sergeïevna Protopopova (she died August 9, 1887), an excellent pianist, was an invalid, and his own health was wretched. In 1877 he wrote: "We old sinners, as always, are in the whirlwind of life—professional duty, science, art. We hurry on and do not reach the goal. Time flies like an express train. The beard grows gray, wrinkles make deeper hollows. We begin a hundred different things. Shall we ever finish any of them? I am always a poet in my soul, and I nourish the hope of leading my opera to the last measure, and yet I often mock at myself. I advance slowly, and there are great gaps in my work."

Borodin in a letter (January 31, 1877) to his friend, Mme Ludmilla Ivanovna Karmalina, to whom he told his hopes, disappointments, enthusiasms, wrote: "The Musical Society had determined to perform my Second symphony at one of its concerts. I was in the country and did not know this fact. When I came back to St. Petersburg, I could not find the first movement and the *finale*. The score of these movements was lost; I had without doubt mislaid it. I hunted everywhere, but could not find it; yet the Society insisted, and there was hardly time to have the parts copied. What should I do? To crown all, I fell sick. I could not shuffle the thing off, and I was obliged to reorchestrate my symphony. Nailed to my bed by fever, I wrote the score in pencil. My copy was not ready in time, and my symphony will not be performed till the next concert. My two symphonies then will be performed in the same week. Never has a professor of the Academy of Medicine and Surgery been found in such a box!"

The Second symphony was at first unsuccessful. Ivanov wrote in the *Nouveau Temps:* "Hearing this music, you are reminded of the ancient Russian knights in all their awkwardness and also in all their greatness. There is heaviness even in the lyric and tender passages. These massive forms are at times tiresome; they crush the hearer." But Stassov tells us that Borodin endeavored by this music to portray the knights. "Like Glinka, Borodin is an epic poet. He is not less national than Glinka, but the Oriental element plays with him the part it plays for Glinka, Dargomijsky, Balakirev, Moussorgsky, Rimsky-Korsakov. He belongs to the composers of programme music. He can say with Glinka: 'For my limitless imagination I must have a precise and given text.' Of Borodin's two symphonies the second is the greater work, and it owes its force to the maturity of the composer's talent, but especially to the national character with which it is impregnated by the programme. The old heroic Russian form dominates it as it does *Prince Igor.*

The symphony is scored for three flutes (and piccolo), two oboes, English horn, two clarinets, two bassoons, four horns, two trumpets, three trombones, bass tuba, three kettledrums, bass drum, cymbals, triangle, tambourine, harp, and the usual strings.

It appears from the score that this symphony was edited by Rimsky-Korsakov and Glazounov.

I. *Allegro,* B minor, 2–2. The first movement opens with a vigorous theme given out by the strings in unison, while bassoons and horns reinforce each alternate measure. This theme may be taken for the motto of the movement, and it is heard in every section of it. Another motive, *animato assai,* is given to the wood-wind. After the alternation of these two musical thoughts, the expressive second theme, *poco meno mosso,* 3–2 time, is introduced by the violoncellos, and afterward by the wood-wind. The vigorous first theme is soon heard again from the full orchestra. There is development. The time changes from 2–2 to 3–2, but the motto dominates with a development of the first measure of the second subject. This material is worked at length. A pedal point, with persistent rhythm for the drum, leads to the recapitulation section, in which the theme undergoes certain modifications. The *coda, animato assai,* is built on the motto.

II. *Scherzo, prestissimo,* F major, 1–1 time. There are a few introductory measures with repeated notes for first and second horn. The chief theme is followed by a new thought (syncopated unison of all the strings). This alternates with the first theme.

*Trio: Allegretto,* 6–4. A melody for the oboe is repeated by the clarinet, and triangle and harp come in on each alternate half of every measure. This material is developed. The first part of the movement is repeated, and the *coda* ends *pianissimo.*

III. *Andante,* D flat major, 4–4. There are introductory measures in which a clarinet is accompanied by the harp. A horn sings the song of the old troubadours. *Poco animato.* There is a tremolo for strings, and the opening melody, changed somewhat, is heard from wood-wind instruments and horns. *Poco più animato,* 3–4. A new thought is given to the strings with a chromatic progression in the bass. After the climax the opening theme returns (strings), and the movement ends with the little clarinet solo. Then comes, without a pause, the

IV. *Finale. Allegro,* B major, 3–4. The movement is in sonata form. There is an introduction. The chief theme, *forte,* is given to the full orchestra. It is in 5–4. The second subject, less tumultuous, is given to clarinet, followed by flute and oboe. The chief theme is developed, *lento,* in the trombones and tuba, and in a more lively manner by strings and wood-wind. The second subject is developed, first by strings, then by full orchestra. The recapitulation section is preceded by the introductory material for the opening of the movement.

# JOHANNES
# BRAHMS

(Born at Hamburg, May 7, 1833;
died at Vienna, April 3, 1897)

---

THOSE WHO LIKE to know about composers as human beings rejoice in the knowledge that Beethoven was irascible, the despair of his landladies, given to rough joking; that Haydn was nagged by his shrew of a wife and fell in love in London with a widow; that Mozart was fond of punch and billiards; that César Franck's trousers were too short. There are many anecdotes about the great, some of them no doubt apocryphal.

In the excellent biography of Brahms by Walter Niemann[1] there is an entertaining chapter entitled "Brahms as a Man."

He was not fussy in his dress. At home he went about in a flannel shirt, trousers, a detachable white collar, no cravat, slippers. In the country he was happy in a flannel shirt and alpaca jacket, carrying a soft felt hat in his hand, and in bad weather wearing on his shoulders an old-fashioned bluish-green shawl, fastened in front by a huge pin. (In the 'sixties many New Englanders on their perilous journeys to Boston or New York wore a shawl.) He preferred a modest restaurant to a hotel table d'hôte. In his music room were pictures of a few composers, engravings—the Sistine Madonna among them—the portrait of Cherubini, by Ingres, with a veiled Muse crowning the composer—"I cannot stand that female," Brahms said to his landlady—a bronze relief of Bismarck,

[1]Walter Niemann: *Brahms,* 1920; translated by C. A. Phillips, 1929.

always crowned with laurel. There was a square piano on which a volume of Bach was usually standing open. On the cover lay notebooks, writing tablets, calendars, cigar cases, spectacles, purses, watches, keys, portfolios, recently published books and music, also souvenirs of his travels. He was passionately patriotic, interested in politics, a firm believer in German unity. He deeply regretted that he had not done military service as a young man. Prussia should be the North German predominant power.

A Viennese musician once said that whenever he heard one of Brahms' symphonies he was inclined to prefer it to the other three; but he was a passionate Brahmsite. The second has a freshness and a spontaneity that are perhaps not found in the others, though the third presses it hard in these respects; but there is a rugged grandeur in the first that puts it above the others.

Professor Schweizerhoffsteinlein, the celebrated Wagnerite, once said: "To me, however many movements there are in an orchestral work of Johannes Brahms, to me—hear me once—there are only two: he makes the first, and I make the second." But the eminent professor was no doubt unjust toward Brahms, in his clumsy ponderous way.

The sensuousness of Brahms is cerebral; it might be called Platonic. There are various kinds of sensuousness in music, as in human life. Some years ago Joséphin Péladan, the fantastical Sar of dark corners, likened the music of Brahms to a gypsy woman dancing in tight-fitting corsets. He detected "latent heat beneath the formal exterior."

## JOHANNES BRAHMS

# SYMPHONY NO. 1, IN C MINOR, OP. 68

*I. Un poco sostenuto; allegro*
*II. Andante sostenuto*
*III. Un poco allegretto e grazioso*
*IV. Adagio; allegro non troppo, ma con brio*

BRAHMS' First symphony contains remarkable pages, as those of the first movement, passages in the second, and the marvelously poetic introduction to the final *allegro*. Mr. Apthorp's belief that this introductory episode may have been suggested to Brahms by the tones of the Alpine horn is not too fanciful, and this impression is made on all that have heard the horn whether in the Oberland or high up in the Canton Vaud. Brahms' fondness for Switzerland is well known, and he had visited that country before the *finale* was performed. In this introductory *adagio* there is a lyric flight and at the same time an imaginative force in superb decoration that are seldom found in the purely orchestral compositions of Brahms.

Brahms was not in a hurry to write a symphony. He heeded not the wishes or demands of his friends, he was not disturbed by their impatience. As far back as 1854 Schumann wrote to Joachim: "But where is Johannes? Is he flying high or only under the flowers? Is he not yet ready to let drums and trumpets sound? He should always keep in mind the beginning of the Beethoven symphonies; he should try to make something like them. The beginning is the main thing; if only one makes a beginning, then the end comes of itself."

Max Kalbeck, of Vienna, the author of a life of Brahms in 2,138 pages, is of the opinion that the beginning, or rather the germ, of the Symphony in C minor is to be dated 1855. In 1854 Brahms heard in Cologne for the first time Beethoven's Ninth symphony. It impressed him greatly, so that he resolved to write a symphony in the same tonality. This symphony he never completed. The first two movements were later used for the Pianoforte concerto in D minor, and the third for "Behold all flesh" in *A German Requiem.*

A performance of Schumann's *Manfred* also excited him when he was twenty-two. Kalbeck has much to say about the influence of these works and the tragedy in the Schumann family over Brahms, as the composer of the C minor symphony. The contents of the symphony, according to Kalbeck, portray the relationship between Brahms and Robert and Clara Schumann. The biographer finds significance in the first measures, *poco sostenuto,* that serve as introduction to the first *allegro.* It was Richard Grant White who said of the German commentator on Shakespeare that the deeper he dived the muddier he came up.

Just when Brahms began to make the first sketches of this symphony is not exactly known. He was in the habit, as a young man, of jotting down his musical thoughts when they occurred to him. Later he worked on several compositions at the same time and let them grow under his hand. There are instances where this growth was of very long duration. He destroyed the great majority of his sketches. The few that he did not destroy are, or were recently, in the library of the Gesellschaft der Musikfreunde at Vienna.

In 1862 Brahms showed his friend Albert Dietrich an early version of the first movement of the symphony. It was then without the introduction. The first movement was afterwards greatly changed. Walter Niemann quotes Brahms as saying that it was no laughing matter to write a symphony after Beethoven; "and again, after finishing the first movement of the First symphony, he admitted to his friend Levi: 'I shall never compose a symphony! You have no conception of how the likes of us feel when we hear the tramp of a giant like him [Beethoven] behind us.'"

The first movement opens with a short introduction, *un poco sostenuto,* C minor, 6–8, which leads without a pause into the first movement proper, *allegro,* C minor. Second movement, *andante sostenuto,* E major, 3–4. The place of the traditional *scherzo* is supplied by a movement, *un poco allegretto e grazioso,* A flat major, 2–4. The *finale* begins with an *adagio,* C minor, 4–4, in which there are hints of the themes of the *allegro* which follows. Here William Foster Apthorp should be quoted:

"With the thirtieth measure the tempo changes to *più andante,* and we come upon one of the most poetic episodes in all Brahms. Amid hushed, tremulous harmonies in the strings, the horn and afterward the flute pour forth an utterly original melody, the character of which ranges from passionate pleading to a sort of wild exultation, according to the instrument that plays it. The coloring is enriched by the solemn tones of the trombones, which appear for the first time in this movement. It is ticklish work trying to dive down into a composer's brain, and surmise what special outside source his inspiration may have had; but one cannot help feeling that this whole wonderful episode may have been suggested to Brahms by the tones of the Alpine horn, as it awakens the echoes from mountain after mountain on some of the high passes in the Bernese Oberland. This is certainly what the episode recalls to anyone who has ever heard those poetic tones and their echoes. A short, solemn, even ecclesiastical interruption by the trombones and bassoons is of more thematic importance. As the horn tones gradually die away, and the cloudlike harmonies in the strings sink lower and lower—like mist veiling the landscape—an impressive pause ushers in the *allegro non troppo, ma con brio* (in C major, 4–4 time). The introductory *adagio* has already given us mysterious hints at what is to come; and now there bursts forth in the strings the most joyous, exuberant *Volkslied* melody, a very Hymn to Joy, which in some of its phrases, as it were unconsciously and by sheer affinity of nature, flows into strains from the similar melody in the *finale* of Beethoven's Ninth symphony. One cannot call it plagiarism: it is two men saying the same thing."

The symphony was produced at Carlsruhe by the Grand Duke's orchestra on November 4, 1876. Dessoff conducted from manuscript. Brahms was present. There was a performance a few days later at Mannheim, where Brahms conducted.

Richard Specht,[2] stating that the First symphony made its way slowly—even Hanslick was far from being enthusiastic—attributes the fact largely to unsatisfactory interpretations.

After the first performance in Boston (by the Harvard Musical Association, January 3, 1878), John S. Dwight wrote in his *Journal of Music* that the total impression made on him was "as something depressing and unedifying, a work coldly elaborated, artificial; earnest to

[2]Richard Specht: *Johannes Brahms,* translated by Eric Blom, 1930.

be sure, in some sense great, and far more satisfactory than any symphony by Raff, or any others of the day, which we have heard; but not to be mentioned in the same day with any symphony by Schumann, Mendelssohn, or the great one by Schubert, not to speak of Beethoven's. . . . Our interest in it will increase, but we foresee the limit; and certainly it cannot be popular; it will not be loved like the dear masterpieces of genius."

## SYMPHONY NO. 2, IN D MAJOR, OP. 73

*I. Allegro non troppo*
*II. Adagio non troppo*
*III. Allegretto grazioso, quasi andantino*
*IV. Allegro con spirito*

THE LATEST biographers of Johannes Brahms differ curiously concerning the character of the Second symphony. The excellent Walter Niemann finds a tragic undercurrent; "ghostly elements glimmering in a supernatural, uncanny way"; even "mysterious Wagnerian visions." The equally excellent Richard Specht finds sunshine, fair days, warm winds, clarity, and tenderness. Brahms can on occasion be gloomy and crabbed enough. Why cannot Mr. Niemann, a devoted admirer of Johannes, allow him to be cheerful once in a while, as in this Second symphony?

The Symphony in D is the most genial of the four, the most easily accepted by an audience, for, if there are pages of supreme beauty in it, as toward the end of the first movement, so there are pages that are Mendelssohnian in form and in the rhythm of the easily retained melodic thought. Mendelssohn, a shrewd composer, seldom, if ever, committed the blunder of surprising an audience. As in the theater, so in the concert hall, an audience does not wish to be left in doubt, and in this symphony, which is in reality a storehouse of truly beautiful things, there is every now and then a passage that is accepted by the hearer as an agreeable commonplace.

Chamber music, choral works, pianoforte pieces, and songs had made Brahms famous before he allowed his First symphony to be played. The Symphony in C minor was performed for the first time in 1876. Kirchner wrote in a letter to Marie Lipsius that he had talked about this symphony in 1863 or 1864 with Mme Clara Schumann, who then showed him fragments of it. No one knew, it is said, of the existence of a second symphony before it was completed.

The Second symphony, in D major, was composed, probably at Pörtschach-am-See, in the summer of 1877, the year that saw the publication of the first. Brahms wrote Dr. Billroth in September of that year: "I do not know whether I have a pretty symphony; I must inquire of skilled persons." He referred to Clara Schumann, Dessoff, and Ernst Frank. On September 19, Mme Schumann wrote that he had written out the first movement. Early in October he played it to her, also a portion of the *finale*. The symphony was played by Brahms and Ignaz Brüll as a pianoforte duet (arranged by the composer) to invited guests at the pianoforte house of his friend Ehrbar in Vienna a few days before the announced date of the orchestral performance, December 11, 1877. Through force of circumstances the symphony was played for the first time in public at the succeeding Philharmonic concert of December 30. Hans Richter conducted. The second performance, conducted by Brahms, was at the Gewandhaus, Leipsic, on January 10, 1878.

Certain German critics in their estimate of Brahms have exhausted themselves in comparison and metaphor. One claims that, as Beethoven's Fourth symphony is to his *Eroica,* so is Brahms' Second to his First; the one in C minor is epic, the one in D major is a fairy tale. When Bülow wrote that Brahms was an heir of Cherubini, he referred to the delicate filigree work shown in the *finale* of the second. Felix Weingartner, whose *Die Symphonie nach Beethoven* (Berlin, 1898) is a pamphlet of singularly acute and discriminative criticism, coolly says that the Second is far superior to the First: "The stream of invention has never flowed so fresh and spontaneous in other works by Brahms, and nowhere else has he colored his orchestration so successfully."

And after a eulogy of the movements he puts the symphony among the very best of the new classic school since the death of Beethoven—"far above all the symphonies of Schumann."

Richard Specht, in his Life of Brahms, writes: "The work is suffused with the sunshine and the warm winds playing on the water, which recall the summer at Pörtschach that gave it life. The comfortably swinging first subject at once creates a sense of well-being with its sincere and sensuous gladness. . . . This movement is like a fair day in its creator's life and outshines the other three sections—the brooding *andante,* the rather unimportant *scherzo* . . . the broad, sweeping *finale* which, for all its lively, driving motion, strikes one as cheerless and artificial in its briskness. The impression of the unsymphonic nature of this work is probably due partly to a prejudice that expects to see cosmic images and not mere genre pictures in such a composition, and partly to the meter adopted for the first movement. It is remarkable that Brahms did not employ the common time almost invariably used by the symphonic masters from Mozart to Schubert in their opening movements until he came to his Fourth symphony. The round-dance nature of the 3–4 measure in the D major symphony is especially difficult to take seriously, and rightly so; for this is a light-hearted work, a declaration of love in symphonic form.

"Brahms was particularly fond of this clear and tender composition, as might be judged from the little mystifications with which he raised the expectations his friends had of the new work that followed its elder sister within the space of a year. He persisted in describing it as gloomy and awesome, never to be played by any musicians without a mourning band on their sleeve." (As a matter of fact Brahms wrote to Elisabet von Herzogenberg on December 29, 1877: "The orchestra here play my new symphony with crape bands on their sleeves, because of its dirge-like effect. It is to be printed with a black edge, too.") "He replied in a tone of waggish secrecy to Elisabet, who was impatiently waiting for the score and scolded him for not rewarding her discretion by sending her the work, which she knew to be ready ('May the deuce take such modesty!') and who, incidentally, took exception to his spelling so noble a word as 'symphony' with an 'f'. 'It really is no symphony,' he writes, 'but merely a *Sinfonie,* and I shall have no need to play it to you beforehand. You merely sit down at the piano, put your little feet on the two pedals in turn, and strike the chord of F minor several times in succession, first in the treble, then in the bass *ff* and *pp* and you will gradually gain a vivid impression of my "latest."' And he was as pleased as Punch with the glad surprise and delight of the adored woman and of all his friends when they saw this sunny work."

## SYMPHONY, NO. 3, IN F MAJOR, OP. 90

*I. Allegro con brio*
*II. Andante*
*III. Poco allegretto*
*IV. Allegro*

SOME JUSTLY PREFER the Symphony in F major to the other three. It has no pages equal in imagination to the wonderful introduction to the *finale* of the First; it has nothing in it like the architectural grandeur of the Fourth's *finale;* but, as a whole, it is the most poetic of the four. Brahms wrote nothing more commanding than the opening of the first movement. Page after page thereafter might be cited in praise. And in this symphony the natural austerity of the composer is mellowed, his melancholy, as in the third movement, is tender, wistful, not pessimistic.

Brahms worked on his Third symphony in 1882, and in the summer of 1883 he completed it.

The first performance of the Third symphony was at a Philharmonic concert in Vienna, December 2, 1883. Hans Richter conducted. Brahms feared for the performance, although Richter had conducted four rehearsals. He wrote to Bülow that at these rehearsals he missed the Forum Romanum (the theater scene which in Meiningen served as a concert hall for rehearsals), and would not be wholly comfortable until the public gave unqualified approval. Max Kalbeck states that at the first performance in Vienna a crowd of the Wagner-Bruckner *ecclesia militans* stood in the pit to make a hostile demonstration, and there was hissing after the applause following each movement had died away; but the general public was so appreciative that the hissing was drowned and enthusiasm was at its height. Arthur Faber came near fighting a duel with an inciter of the *Skandal* sitting behind him, but forgot the disagreeable incident at the supper given by him in honor of the production of the symphony, with Dr. Billroth, Simrock, Goldmark, Dvořák, Brüll, Hellmesberger, Richter, Hanslick, among the guests. At this concert Franz Ondricek played the new violin concerto of Dvořák.

It is said that various periodicals asserted that this symphony was by far the best of Brahms' compositions. This greatly annoyed the composer, especially as it raised expectations which he thought could not be fulfilled. Brahms sent the manuscript to Joachim in Berlin and asked him to conduct the second performance where or at what time he liked. For a year or more the friendship between the two had been clouded, for Brahms had sided with Mrs. Joachim in the domestic dispute, or at least he had preserved his accustomed intimacy with her, and Joachim had resented this. The second performance, led by Joachim, was at Berlin, January 4, 1884. Dr. Franz Wüllner was then the conductor of the Berlin Philharmonic Orchestra Subscription Concerts. Brahms had promised him in the summer before the honor of conducting this symphony in Berlin for the first time. Joachim insisted that he should be the conductor. Churlish in the matter, he persuaded Brahms to break his promise to Wüllner by saying that he would play Brahms' violin concerto under the composer's direction if Brahms would allow him to conduct the symphony. Brahms then begged Wüllner to make the sacrifice. Joachim therefore conducted it at an Academy Concert, but Brahms was not present; he came about a fortnight later to Wüllner's first subscription concert, and then conducted the symphony and played his pianoforte concerto in D minor. The writer of these notes was at this concert. The symphony was applauded enthusiastically, but Brahms was almost as incompetent a conductor as Joachim. (His pianoforte playing in 1884 on that occasion was muddy and noisy.) Brahms conducted the symphony at Wiesbaden on January 18, 1884. The copyright of the manuscript was sold to the publisher Simrock, of Berlin, for 36,000 marks ($9,000) and a percentage on sums realized by performances.

Hans Richter in a toast christened this symphony when it was still in manuscript, the *"Eroica."* Hanslick remarked concerning this: "Truly, if Brahms' First symphony in C minor is characterized as the *'Pathetic'* or the *'Appassionata'* and the second in D major as the *'Pastoral,'* the new symphony in F major may be appropriately called his *'Eroica'"*; yet Hanslick took care to add that the key word was not wholly to the point, for only the first movement and the *finale* are of heroic character. This Third symphony, he says, is indeed a new one. "It repeats neither the poignant song of Fate of the first, nor the joyful Idyl of the second; its fundamental note is proud strength that rejoices in deeds. The heroic element is without any warlike flavor; it leads to no tragic action, such as the Funeral March in Beethoven's *Eroica.* It recalls in its musical character the healthy and full vigor of Beethoven's second period, and nowhere the singularities of his last period; and every now and then in passages quivers the romantic twilight of Schumann and Mendelssohn."

Max Kalbeck thinks that the statue of Germania near Rüdesheim inspired Brahms to write this symphony.[8] Joachim found Hero and Leander in the *finale!* He associated the second motive in C major with the bold swimmer breasting the waves. Clara Schumann entitled the symphony a "Forest Idyl" and sketched a programme for it.

The first movement, *allegro con brio,* in F major, 6–4, opens with three introductory chords (horns, trumpets, wood-wind), the upper voice of which, F, A flat, F, presents a short theme that is an emblematic figure, or device, which recurs significantly throughout the movement. Although it is not one of the regular themes, it plays a dominating part. Some find in a following cross-relation—A flat of the bass against the preceding A natural of the first theme, the "Keynote to some occult dramatic signification." Enharmonic modulation leads to A major, the tonality of the second theme. There is first a slight reminiscence of the "Venusberg" scene in *Tannhäuser—"Naht euch dem Strande!"* Dr. Hugo Riemann goes so far as to say that Brahms may have thus paid a tribute to Wagner, who died in the period of the composition of this symphony. The second theme is of a graceful character, but of compressed form, in strong contrast with the broad and sweeping first theme. The second movement, *andante* in C major, 4–4, opens with a hymnlike passage, which in the first three chords reminds some persons of the "Prayer" in *Zampa.* The third movement is a *poco allegretto,* C minor, 3–8, a romantic substitute for the traditional *scherzo. Finale, allegro,* in F minor, 2–2. At the end the strings in tremolo bring the original first theme of the first movement, "the ghost" of this first theme, as Apthorp called it, over sustained harmonies in the wind instruments.

[8]See Kalbeck's *Brahms,* Vol. III, Part II, pp. 384–85, Berlin, 1912.

## SYMPHONY NO. 4, IN E MINOR, OP. 98

*I. Allegro non troppo*
*II. Andante moderato*
*III. Allegro giocoso*
*IV. Allegro energico e passionato*

Much of the Fourth symphony is melancholy and lamentful, but it is relieved by the consolatory beatitude of the *andante* and the elevating stateliness of the conclusion. . . . The austerity with which the composer has been reproached—in many instances unjustly—is here pronounced. The solidity of the structure may be admired, but the structure itself is granitic and unrelieved. The symphony has not the epic grandeur of the first, the geniality of the second, the wealth of varied beauty that distinguishes the third.

This symphony was first performed at Meiningen, October 25, 1885, under the direction of the composer.

It was composed in the summers of 1884 and 1885 at Mürzzuschlag in Styria: Miss Florence May in her Life of Brahms says that the manuscript was nearly destroyed in 1885: "Returning one afternoon from a walk, he [Brahms] found that the house in which he lodged had caught fire, and that his friends were busily engaged in bringing his papers, and amongst them the nearly finished manuscript of the new symphony, into the garden."

In a letter, Brahms described this symphony as "a couple of entr'actes," also as "a choral work without text." He was doubtful about its worth. He consulted his friends, and he and Ignaz Brüll played a pianoforte arrangement in the presence of several of them. He judged from their attitude that they did not like it and he was much depressed. There was a preliminary orchestral rehearsal at Meiningen in October, 1885, conducted by Hans von Bülow. Brahms arrived in time for the first performance. The symphony was most warmly applauded, and the audience endeavored, but in vain, to obtain a repetition of the third movement.

The symphony was performed at a Philharmonic concert in Vienna on March 7, 1897, the last Philharmonic concert heard by Brahms. We quote from Miss May's biography: "The Fourth symphony had never become a favorite work in Vienna. Received with reserve on its first performance, it had not since gained much more from the general public of the city than the respect sure to be accorded there to an important work by Brahms. Today [*sic*], however, a storm of applause broke out at the end of the first movement, not to be quieted until the composer, coming to the front of the artist's box in which he was seated, showed himself to the audience. The demonstration was renewed after the second and the third movements, and an extraordinary scene followed the conclusion of the work. The applauding, shouting house, its gaze riveted on the figure standing in the balcony, so familiar and yet in present aspect so strange, seemed unable to let him go. Tears ran down his cheeks as he stood there, shrunken in form, with lined countenance, strained expression, white hair hanging lank; and through the audience there was a feeling as of a stifled sob, for each knew that they were saying farewell. Another outburst of applause and yet another; one more acknowledgment from the master; and Brahms and his Vienna had parted forever."

Heinrich Reimann gives a short description of the symphony: "It begins as in ballad fashion. Blaring fanfares of horns and cries of pain interrupt the narration, which passes into an earnest and ardent melody (B major, violoncellos). The themes, especially those in fanfare fashion, change form and color. 'The formal appearance, now powerful, prayerful, now caressing, tender, mocking, homely, now far away, now near, now hurried, now quietly expanding, ever surprises us, is ever welcome: it brings joy and gives dramatic impetus to the movement.' A theme of the second movement constantly returns in varied form, from which the chief theme, the staccato figure given to the wind, and the melodious song of the violoncellos are derived. The third movement, *allegro giocoso,* sports with old-fashioned harmonies, which should not be taken too seriously. This is not the case with the *finale,* an artfully contrived *ciacona* of antique form, but of modern contents. The first eight measures give the 'title-page' of the *ciacona.* The measures that follow are variations of the leading theme; wind instruments prevail in the first three, then the strings enter; the movement grows livelier, clarinets and oboes lead to E major; and now comes the solemn climax of this movement, the trombone passage. The old theme enters again after the *fermata,* and rises to full force, which finds expression in a *più allegro* for the close."[4]

## VARIATIONS ON A THEME BY JOSEF HAYDN, IN B FLAT MAJOR, OP. 56a

At Bonn, in August, 1873, Brahms with Clara Schumann played to a few friends the *Variations on a Theme by Haydn* in the version (Op. 56b) for two pianofortes.

It is not definitely known whether the orchestral version or the one for two pianofortes was the earlier. The orchestral stands first in thematic catalogues of Brahms' compositions, but the pianoforte version was published first—in November, 1873. The probability is that the orchestral version was the first. The autograph manuscript of Op. 56b is dated at the end "Tutzing July 1873." It was in November, 1870, that C. F. Pohl showed Brahms the compositions of Haydn, an *andante* from a symphony and the *chorale* that gave Brahms his theme. Kalbeck believed that the score of Haydn's *chorale* put Brahms in mind of the excellent wind choir of the Detmold Court Orchestra, and the thought of the Vienna Philharmonic Orchestra gave him greater desire to write an orchestral work.

The theme is taken from a collection of *divertimenti* for wind instruments by Haydn. In the original score it is entitled *Chorale St. Antoni.* The *divertimento* in which this theme occurs is in B flat major; it is composed for two oboes, two horns, three bassoons, and a serpent. For the third bassoon and the serpent Brahms substituted a double bassoon. The *divertimento* was composed by Haydn probably about 1782–84 and for open-air performance. It was performed at a concert in London in March, 1908. As then played, it consisted of a lively introduction, the *Chorale Sancti Antonii,* a *minuetto* and a *rondo.* It was then questioned whether Haydn composed the *chorale,* and why the folk-song-like tune was so named.

The theme is announced by Brahms in plain harmony by wind instruments over a bass for violoncellos, double basses, and double bassoon.

[4]Heinrich Reimann: *Johannes Brahms,* 1930.

Variation I. *Poco più andante.* The violins enter, and their figure is accompanied by one in triplets in the violas and violoncellos. These figures alternately change places. Wind instruments are added.

II. B flat minor, *più vivace.* Clarinets and bassoons have a variation of the theme, and violins enter with an *arpeggio* figure.

III. There is a return to the major, *con moto,* 2–4. The theme is given to the oboes, doubled by the bassoons an octave below. There is an independent accompaniment for the lower strings. In the repetition the violins and violas take the part which the wind instruments had, and the flutes, doubled by the bassoons, have *arpeggio* figures.

IV. In minor, 3–8. The melody is sung by oboe with horn; then it is strengthened by the flute with the bassoon. The violas and shortly after the violoncellos accompany in scale passage. The parts change place in repetition.

V. This variation is a *vivace* in major, 6–8. The upper melody is given to flutes, oboes, and bassoons, doubled through two octaves. In the repetition the moving parts are taken by the strings.

VI. *Vivace,* major, 2–4. A new figure is introduced. During the first four measures the strings accompany with the original theme in harmony, afterwards in *arpeggio* and scale passages.

VII. *Grazioso,* major, 6–8. The violins an octave above the clarinets descend through the scale, while the piccolo doubled by violas has a fresh melody.

VIII. B flat minor, *presto non troppo,* 3–4. The strings are muted. The mood is *pianissimo* throughout. The piccolo enters with an inversion of the phrase.

The *finale* is in the major, 4–4. It is based throughout on a phrase, an obvious modification of the original theme, which is used at first as a ground bass—"a bass passage constantly repeated and accompanied each successive time with a varied melody and harmony." This obstinate phrase is afterwards used in combination with other figures in other passages of the *finale.* The original theme returns in the strings at the climax; the wood-wind instruments accompany in scale passages, and the brass fills up the harmony. The triangle is now used to the end. Later the melody is played by wood and brass instruments, and the strings have a running accompaniment.

The late Max Kalbeck in his long-winded and ponderous Life of Brahms has much to say about these Variations. Which St. Anthony was in Hadyn's mind is immaterial. Kalbeck decided that Brahms' hero is the St. Anthony of Thebes. Brahms was a friend and admirer of Anselm Feuerbach, the artist, who had painted a life-size Temptation of St. Anthony, the monk kneeling with a book, a scourge, and a skull near him, while a woman begs him to leave his religious meditation and enter into life. This picture was so ridiculed that the sensitive Feuerbach destroyed it, but it had been engraved and photographed.

Kalbeck finds a *crescendo* of musical psychology in the Variations, which, as they are developed, remind him of musical dissolving views. The seventh Variation pictures the severest test undergone by the saint: "The most atrocious because it is the sweetest." In this Siciliano he sees the apparition of the tempting woman. The music is "the quintessence of human voluptuousness, which according to Master Eckhart is 'mixed with bitterness.' After it comes death. Blessed is the man that has withstood the temptation! The *finale,* which includes seventeen and more variations, celebrates him."

Did Brahms have all this in mind when he wrote these Variations? Was not Kalbeck like the man "of meager aspect with sooty hands and face" seen by Captain Lemuel Gulliver at the Academy of Lagado engaged for eight years upon a project for extracting sunbeams from cucumbers?

## "TRAGIC" OVERTURE, OP. 81

THE *Tragic* overture is among the greatest works of Brahms; by its structure, and by its depths of feeling. There is no hysterical outburst; no shrieking in despair; no peevish or sullen woe; no obtruding suggestion of personal suffering. The German commentators have cudgeled their brains to find a hero in the music: Hamlet, Faust, this one, that one. They have labored in vain. The soul of Tragedy speaks in the music.

Although the *Tragic* overture is Op. 81 and the *Academic* is Op. 80, the *Tragic* was composed and performed before the *Academic:* it was performed for the first time at the Fourth Philharmonic Concert at Vienna in 1880.

The *Tragic* overture may be said to be a musical characterization of the principles of tragedy as laid down by Aristotle or Lessing; it mirrors, as Reimann puts it, the grandeur, the loftiness, the deep earnestness, of tragic character; "calamities, which an inexorable fate has imposed on him, leave the hero guilty; the tragic downfall atones for the guilt; this downfall, which by purifying the passions and awakening fear and pity works on the race at large, brings expiation and redemption to the hero himself." Or as Dr. Dieters says: "In this work we see a strong hero battling with an iron and relentless fate; passing hopes of victory cannot alter an impending destiny. We do not care to inquire whether the composer had a special tragedy in his mind, or if so, which one; those who remain musically unconvinced by the unsurpassably powerful theme, would not be assisted by a particular suggestion."[5]

The overture was composed in 1880 and published in 1881.

## ACADEMIC FESTIVAL OVERTURE, OP. 80

JOHANNES BRAHMS desired to give thanks publicly to the University of Breslau because he had received from the illustrious dignitaries of that university the degree of Doctor of Philosophy. How best could he express his thanks in music? By something stately, pompous? Or by something profound and cryptic? Brahms acted with shrewdness in the matter; he took for his thematic material well-known students' songs. These songs are familiar throughout Germany, and it is not as though a composer called upon, for instance, to write an appropriate overture for an approaching jubilee at Yale should take songs peculiar to that college; nor is it as though a composer should take "Eli Yale" and "Fair Harvard" and a Dartmouth or Williams song for his themes. Wherever Brahms' overture is heard by a German student, whether of Heidelberg, Bonn, Berlin, or Breslau, the themes are old friends and common property.

But where is the reckless gayety of student life in this overture? Much of it is dry, on account of the orchestration. For even

[5]Dr. Hermann Dieters: *Johannes Brahms,* a biographical sketch, translated by Rosa Newmarch, 1888.

when you admit that Brahms was a master builder of musical structures, you are not thereby estopped from saying in clear, bell-like tones that he was also color deaf.

The Brahmsite turns triumphantly to the *Fuchslied*—"Was kommt dort von der Höh"—which is introduced by two bassoons, accompanied by 'cellos and violas *pizzicati*. "There! there!" he exclaims, "that is excruciatingly funny. Only a master, only St. Johannes could make so easily a master stroke!" If you cross-examine him you will find that the humor consists in the choice of instruments.

Somebody once said that the bassoon is the clown of the orchestra. Therefore the double bassoon should be twice as funny—perhaps even a Shakespearean clown. And simply because somebody gave the poor bassoon this name, it must be regarded as funny *per se*. "Funny"? The bassoon is lugubrious, ghostly, spectral, weird, unearthly, demoniacal. It smells of mortality. It suggests the glow-worm and the grave. The wicked nuns in *Robert le Diable* heard it and obeyed the spell, for corruption called to corruption. It lends a flavor of the charnal house to Tchaikovsky's *Pathétique*. It pictures the mood of Leonora without Di Luna's tower. It chatters and gibbers as the murderous artist in the *Symphonie fantastique* goes his wretched way to the scaffold. It is the instrument dear to all that inhabit the night air, the cemetery, the diseased mind.

But these bassoons appear in Brahms' overture *"etwas plötzlich"* —a phrase I once heard used in a Berlin beer hall by a dapper and corseted and monocled officer, who was extremely thirsty and thus addressed the waiter. And I defy any sober-minded person who has not the fear of Brahms before his eyes to find the introduction or the treatment of the song spontaneously gay or humorous. The song itself is a good freshman hazing song.

Some of the books—and books of authority—say that the *Academic* was written for performance at Breslau on the occasion of Brahms' receiving the degree of Doctor of Philosophy. He did receive the degree, but it was on March 11, 1879, and if anyone doubts this I shall be happy to quote to him the degree in the original Latin—which I cannot construe, except as regards the date. I like to think of Brahms as a doctor of philosophy. The degree goes so well with the man. It also explains some—not all—of his music. Let the overture be considered and weighed as the night work of a Doctor of Philosophy.

Brahms wrote two overtures in the summer of 1880 at Ischl—the *Academic* and the *Tragic.* They come between the Symphony in D major and that in F major in the list of his orchestral works. It is said by Heuberger that Brahms wrote two "Academic Festival overtures"; so he must have destroyed one of them. When the *Academic* was first played at Breslau, the rector and Senate and members of the Philosophical faculty sat in the front seats at the performance, and the composer conducted his work. Brahms was not a university man, but he had known with Joachim the joyous life of students at Göttingen—at the university made famous by Canning's poem:

*Whene'er with haggard eyes I view*
*This dungeon that I'm rotting in,*
*I think of those companions true*
*who studied with me at the U-*
*niversity of Göttingen—*
*niversity of Göttingen;*

—the university satirized so bitterly by Heine.

Brahms wrote to Bernard Scholz that the title *Academic* did not please him. Scholz suggested that it was "cursedly academic and boresome," and suggested *Viadrina,* for that was the poetical name of the Breslau University. Brahms spoke flippantly of this overture in the fall of 1880 to Max Kalbeck. He described it as a "very jolly potpourri on students' songs à la Suppé"; and, when Kalbeck asked him ironically if he had used the "Foxsong," he answered contentedly, "Yes, indeed." Kalbeck was startled, and said he could not think of such academic homage to the "leathery Herr Rektor," whereupon Brahms duly replied, "That is also wholly unnecessary."

The first of the student songs to be introduced is Binzer's "Wir hatten gebauet ein stattliches Haus" (We had built a stately house, and trusted in God therein through bad weather, storm, and horror). The first measures are given out by the trumpets with a peculiarly stately effect. The melody of "Der Landesvater" is given to the second violins. And then for the first time is there any deliberate attempt to portray the jollity of university life. The "Fuchslied" (Freshman Song) is introduced suddenly by two bassoons. There are hearers undoubtedly who remember the singing of this song in Longfellow's "Hyperion"; how the freshman entered the *Kneipe,* and was asked with ironical courtesy concerning the health of the leathery *Herr Papa* who reads in Cicero. Similar impertinent questions were asked concerning the *Frau Mama* and the *Mamsell Sœur;* and then the struggle of the freshman with the first pipe of tobacco was described in song. "Gaudeamus igitur," the melody that is familiar to students of all lands, serves as the *finale.*

## CONCERTO FOR PIANOFORTE, NO. 1, IN D MINOR, OP. 15

*I. Maestoso*
*II. Adagio*
*III. Rondo: allegro non troppo*

THIS CONCERTO was played for the first time at Hanover, on January 22, 1859. Brahms was the pianist; Joachim conducted.

Brahms, living in Hanover in 1854, worked in the spring and summer on a symphony. The madness of Schumann and his attempt to commit suicide by throwing himself into the Rhine had deeply affected him. He wrote to Joachim in January, 1855, from Düsseldorf, "I have been trying my hand at a symphony during the past summer, have even orchestrated the first movement and composed the second and third."

This symphony was never completed. The work as it stood was turned into a sonata for two pianofortes. The first two movements became later the first and the second of the Pianoforte concerto in D minor; the third is the movement "Behold all flesh" in *A German*

*Requiem.* The sonata for two pianofortes was frequently played in private in the middle 'fifties by Brahms with Clara Schumann, or his friend Julius Otto Grimm, who had assisted him in the orchestration of the symphony. Grimm (1827–1903), philologist, conductor, lecturer, doctor of philosophy, composer of a symphony, suites and other works, declared that the musical contents of this sonata deserved a more dignified form, and persuaded Brahms to put them into a concerto. The task busied Brahms for two years or more. The movements were repeatedly sent to Joachim, whose advice was of much assistance. In 1858 the *Signale* reported that Brahms had arrived in Detmold, and it was hoped that some of his compositions might be performed there. "He has completed, among other things, a pianoforte concerto, the great beauties of which have been reported to us." The musicians at Detmold were not inclined to appreciate Brahms; it is said that the *Kapellmeister,* Kiel, was prejudiced against him; but the concerto was rehearsed at Hanover, and Joachim, in spite of a certain amount of official opposition, put it on the programme of the Hanover Subscription Court Concerts, the third of the series for 1858–59.

The concerto was then coldly received. The Hanover correspondent of the *Signale* wrote, "The work had no great success with the public, but it aroused the decided respect and sympathy of the best musicians for the gifted artist." Brahms played the concerto at a Gewandhaus concert in Leipsic on January 27, 1859. The public and the critics were unfriendly. The composer wrote to Joachim: "A brilliant and decided failure. . . . In spite of all this, the concerto will please some day when I have improved its construction." Breitkopf & Härtel refused to publish it; but Rieter-Biedermann gave it to the world in 1861.

## CONCERTO NO. 2, IN B FLAT MAJOR, FOR PIANOFORTE AND ORCHESTRA, OP. 83

*I. Allegro non troppo*
*II. Allegro appassionato*
*III. Andante*
*IV. Allegretto grazioso*

THE CHOICE of this concerto shows the high purpose and the pure aim; for the Second concerto of Brahms is not one to tickle the ear, stun the judgment, and provoke cheap and boisterous applause. And as the Second symphony of Brahms is to the First, so is the Second concerto of Brahms to the First. In each case, while the passion is less stormy, the thoughts are less crabbed and gnarled. Only in the first movement of the B flat major concerto does Brahm "keep up a terrible thinking."

The second fascinates by its sturdiness and rhythmic capriciousness; the third movement is Brahms at his noblest, when his thought is as lofty and serenely beautiful as a summer sky at noon. And who can describe in words the enchanting, haunting delight of the *finale*—music like unto the perfect verse of a supreme poet whose imagination is kindled by wild or melancholy tales told him in youth by gypsy lips.

This concerto was performed for the first time at Budapest, from manuscript, November 9, 1881, when the composer was the pianist.

On April 8, 1878, Brahms, in company with Dr. Billroth and Carl Goldmark, made a journey to Italy. Goldmark, who went to Rome to be present at the last rehearsals of his opera *Die Königin von Saba*—production was postponed until the next year on account of the illness of the leading soprano—did not accompany his friends to Naples and Sicily. Returning to Pörtschach, Brahms sketched themes of the Concerto in B flat major on the evening before his birthday; but he left the sketches, in which "he mirrored the Italian spring turning to summer," undeveloped.

His violin concerto originally contained a *scherzo* movement. Conferring with Joachim, he omitted this movement. Max Kalbeck thinks that this *scherzo* found a home in the second pianoforte concerto.

In March, 1881, Brahms set out on a second journey in Italy. He visited Venice, Florence, Siena, Orvieto, Rome, Naples, and Sicily. He returned to Vienna on his birthday of that year with his mind full of Italian scenes in springtime and with thoughts of the pianoforte concerto inspired by his first visit. On May 22 he went to Pressbaum near Vienna and lived in the villa of Mme Heingartner. In 1907, Orestes Ritter von Connevay, then the possessor of the villa, erected a monument to Brahms in the garden. A bronze bust stands on a stone pedestal. An iron tablet bears this inscription: "Here in the summer of 1881 Johannes Brahms completed *Nänie,* Op. 82, and the pianoforte concerto, Op. 83." Brahms was moved by the death of Anselm Feuerbach, the painter, to set music for chorus and orchestra to Schiller's poem, "Nänie."

Miss May says in her life of Brahms that the manuscript of *Nänie,* and portions of the concerto, were soon lent by Brahms to Dr. Billroth, "the concerto movements being handed to him with the words, 'A few little pianoforte pieces.'" "It is always a delight to me," wrote Billroth, "when Brahms, after paying me a short visit, during which we have talked of indifferent things, takes a roll out of his greatcoat pocket and says casually, 'Look at that and write me what you think of it.'"

## CONCERTO FOR VIOLIN, IN D MAJOR, OP. 77

*I. Allegro non troppo*
*II. Adagio*
*III. Allegro giocoso, ma non troppo vivace*

THIS CONCERTO was written, during the summer and the fall of 1878, at Pörtschach on Lake Wörther in Carinthia for Joseph Joachim, dedicated to him, and first played by him under the direction of the composer at a Gewandhaus concert, Leipsic, on January 1, 1879.

Brahms, not confident of his ability to write with full intelligence for the solo violin, was aided by Joachim, who it appears from the correspondence between him and Brahms, gave advice inspired by his own opinions concerning the violinist's art. Richard Specht, in his *Johannes Brahms* (1928), says that Brahms agreed to scarcely anything but "bow marks and fingering; otherwise he adhered to his text, and not always to the advantage of his notation, which has often been misread by violinists." There was a dispute concerning the writing of "ties over staccato dots, which has not the same meaning for the violinist as for the pianist." Joachim tried to explain this difference, but Brahms obstinately refused to alter his notation, "which was afterwards duly misinterpreted."

The concerto was originally in four movements. It contained a *scherzo* which was thrown overboard. Max Kalbeck, the biographer of

Brahms, thinks it highly probable that it found its way into the Second pianoforte concerto. The *adagio* was so thoroughly revised that it was practically new. "The middle movements have gone," Brahms wrote, "and of course they were the best! But I have written a poor *adagio* for it." Specht suggests that Brahms may have intended to save the rejected two movements for a second violin concerto, "of which he made sketches immediately after the first."

Florence May in her life of Brahms quotes Dörffel with regard to the first performance at Leipsic: "Joachim played with a love and devotion which brought home to us in every bar the direct or indirect share he has had in the work. As to the reception, the first movement was too new to be distinctly appreciated by the audience, the second made considerable way, the last aroused great enthusiasm." Miss May adds that the critic Bernsdorf was less unsympathetic than usual.

Kalbeck, a still more enthusiastic worshiper of Brahms than Miss May, tells a different story. "The work was heard respectfully, but it did not awaken a bit of enthusiasm. It seemed that Joachim had not sufficiently studied the concerto or he was severely indisposed." Brahms conducted in a state of evident excitement. A comic incident came near being disastrous. The composer stepped on the stage in gray street trousers, for on account of a visit he had been hindered in making a complete change of dress. Furthermore he forgot to fasten again the unbuttoned suspenders, so that in consequence of his lively directing his shirt showed between his trousers and waistcoat. "These laughter-provoking trifles were not calculated for elevation of mood."

In spite of Leipsic, Brahms soon recovered his spirits. He wrote to Elisabet von Herzogenberg from Vienna in January: "My concert tour was a real downhill affair after Leipsic; no more pleasure in it. Perhaps that is a slight exaggeration, though, for friends and hospitality are not everything on a concert tour. In some trifling ways it was even more successful; the audiences were kinder and more alive. Joachim played my piece more beautifully with every rehearsal, too, and the *cadenza* went so magnificently at our concert here that the people clapped right on into my *coda*. But what is all that compared to the privilege of going home to Humboldtstrasse and being pulled to pieces by three womenkind—since you object to the word 'females'?"

The composition is fairly orthodox in form. The three movements are separate, and the traditional *tuttis, soli, cadenzas,* etc., are pretty much as in the old-fashioned pieces of this kind; but in the first movement the long solo *cadenza* precedes the taking up of the first theme by the violin. The modernity is in the prevailing spirit and in the details. Furthermore, it is not a work for objective virtuoso display.

The orchestra which Brahms requires in his symphonies is practically the same as that which Beethoven used in the first three movements of his Ninth: two flutes, two oboes, two clarinets, two bassoons and double bassoon, four horns, two trumpets, three trombones, kettledrums, and strings. This is the orchestration of Brahms' First symphony (the trombones being reserved for the final movement). The Second omits the double bassoon but adds a tuba. The Third lists the same orchestra as the First. The Fourth adds a piccolo, and in this symphony the trombones are not heard until the opening chords of the *finale*.

To the above basic orchestration Brahms added, in his *Tragic* overture, a piccolo and tuba, and in his *Academic* overture, a piccolo, a third trumpet, tuba, bass drum, cymbals, and triangle. The *Variations* add piccolo and triangle but omit trombones. The concertos follow the usual orchestration, with but two trombones in the piano concertos—none in the violin concerto.—EDITOR.

## ANTON
# BRUCKNER

(Born at Ansfelden, in Upper Austria, September 4, 1824; died at Vienna, October 11, 1896)

---

BOTH THE ADMIRERS of Bruckner and those that dislike his music lay stress on the fact that he was born a peasant and was essentially a peasant to the day of his death, although the Rector Magnificus of the University of Vienna bowed before him when he presented him with the honorary degree of doctor. The detractors find in Bruckner's peasanthood his salient faults. The former say that by reason of the simplicity and purity of his character Bruckner was as Paul caught up in the body or out of the body, they cannot tell, to the third heaven, caught up into paradise where he heard unspeakable words, which it was not lawful for him to utter, but it was allowed him to hint at them in music. The latter insist that his peasant naïveté is revealed in his interminable chatter, in his vague wanderings, in his lack of continuity and cohesion in the expression of thought.

The wretched game of politics is still played with Bruckner. Because he worshipped Wagner and because Brahms, or rather Hanslick—who was to Brahms both elephantier and thurifer—was opposed to Wagner, the Wagnerites therefore pitted Bruckner against Brahms and proclaimed the former the great successor to Beethoven in the field of absolute music. As a matter of fact, Brahms was neither bitterly hostile toward Wagner nor did he sneer at Bruckner. There was room for both Brahms and Bruckner

—except in Vienna and except in the shaggy breasts of Wagnerites. Hanslick is dead, "the executioner of Bruckner," as William Ritter characterizes him, "the man who derided all the true glories of the music of his time for Brahms' sole benefit"; but Hanslick in his lifetime did not kill Bruckner, who had friendly audiences in Vienna before his death, whose fame has steadily grown.

In order to appreciate fully and yet with discrimination the indisputable talent, the irregular, uncontrolled genius of Bruckner, it is not necessary to inquire curiously into Bruckner's humble origins, or into the character of his father and mother. It was the theory of Sainte-Beuve that the superior man is found, at least in part, in his parents, and especially in his mother; but I doubt in this instance whether an intimate acquaintance with Therese, the daughter of the innkeeper and administrator Ferdinand Helm, at Neuzeng, would explain the inconsistencies and contradictions in her son's music. She was no doubt a strong, lusty woman, and she bore her husband a dozen children. As for Bruckner being a peasant, poor, now rude in behavior and speech, and now almost cringing in his desire to be courteous, shabbily educated, very few of the greatest composers have been born in rooms of purple hangings, very few have been distinguished for the elegance of their manners or the depth and breadth of their general learning.

The wonder is that Bruckner, the long-ignored, poor, humble school teacher, grotesque in appearance, a peasant in speech and action, should have had apocalyptic visions and spoken musically with the tongues of angels.

## SYMPHONY NO. 7, IN E MAJOR

*I. Allegro moderato*
*II. Adagio: sehr feierlich und langsam*
*III. Scherzo: allegro. Trio: etwas langsamer*
*IV. Finale: bewegt, doch nicht schnell*

THIS CERTAINLY is a gigantic work, abounding in lofty and noble pages, abounding also in trivialities, tiresome repetitions, and fussy and insignificant details. As in the other symphonies of Bruckner that we have heard, there is a lack of continuity in each movement; there are impressive preparations that lead to nothing: "In the name of the Prophet—Figs!" The composer had little sense of structure. To use Disraeli's phrase, he was intoxicated with his own verbosity. His taste in ornamentation was more than doubtful. He could crown a noble façade with gingerbread work; he would plan an extension of cheap stucco to a pure temple of marble.

And yet in the Seventh symphony there are pages that come closer to Beethoven at his greatest than we find in the symphonies of other composers. There are grand thoughts expressed in a masterly manner in Franck's symphony and in the symphony in B flat by Vincent d'Indy; the introduction to the *finale* of Brahms' First symphony has elemental grandeur and spiritual intensity; but Bruckner's spirit in the *adagio* and in the main body of the *scherzo* of the Seventh symphony is nearer akin to that of Beethoven.

Bruckner's Symphony in E major was composed in the time between September, 1881, and September, 1883. The first movement was completed December 29, 1882; the third, October 16, 1882; the fourth, September 5, 1883. The symphony is dedicated "To His Majesty the King, Ludwig II of Bavaria, in deepest reverence," and was published in 1885.

The statement is often made that the *adagio* was composed as funeral music in memory of Richard Wagner. As a matter of fact, this *adagio* was completed in October, 1882. Wagner died February 13, 1883.

The singular statement has been made that a premonition of Wagner's death inspired Bruckner to compose a dirge—this *adagio*. Bruckner, who had what the Germans call "peasant cunning," may have agreed to this in the presence of those who were thus affected by the thought, but he himself knew, as will be seen by his letters to Felix Mottl in 1885 concerning the first performance at Carlsruhe, that the movement had not in all respects the character of a dirge. Indeed, he pointed out the measures of the funeral music: "At X in the *adagio* (Funeral music for tubas and horns)" etc.; also, "Please take a very slow and solemn tempo. At the close, in the Dirge (In memory of the death of the Master), think of our Ideal! . . . Kindly do not forget the *fff* at the end of the Dirge."

Bruckner wrote to Mottl in a letter published February 10, 1900: "At one time I came home and was very sad; I thought to myself, it is impossible that the Master can live for a long time, and then the *adagio* in C sharp minor came into my head."

The symphony is scored for two flutes, two oboes, two clarinets, two bassoons, four horns, three trumpets, three trombones, four Wagner tubas, bass tuba, kettledrums, triangle, cymbals, strings.

I. *Allegro moderato,* E major, 2-2. The first theme is announced by horn and violoncellos against the violins, tremolo, and clarinets, violas, and violoncellos add a subsidiary theme. The chief theme appears in a richer orchestral dress. There is a *crescendo* based on the subsidiary theme, and the whole orchestra enters, but there is quickly a *diminuendo,* and the mood becomes more nervous, more uncertain. The second theme, one of complaint, is given to oboe and clarinet, with horns and trumpet in the accompaniment. This theme with its peculiar instrumentation and its changing tonality is in marked opposition to the first. This second chief theme is developed at length. (The first assumes greater importance later.) In this development there are evidences in the manner of leading the voices of Bruckner's partiality for the organ. The mood becomes more restful, although the theme of complaint is not silent, but soon appears, inverted, in the violins. It may here be said that Bruckner delighted in this manner of varying a theme. A mighty *crescendo* is based on a phrase of this inverted theme over an organ-point, F sharp, but instead of the arrival of the expected climax a theme of somewhat mournful character is given to wood-wind instruments with counterpoint in the strings. The rhythm of this counterpoint is maintained in the final section of the exposition part. An episode for the brass follows. There is soon a calmer mood, and gentle horn and clarinet tones mingle with the voices of the strings.

The free fantasia begins with an inversion of the first theme (clarinet). The rhythm of the characteristic counterpoint just mentioned appears, but a solemn, religious mood is soon established (trombones, *pianissimo*). The second chief theme appears in its inverted form, also the "contrapuntal figure." The mood is now one of doubt and perplexity, but the decisive, inexorable first theme enters, inverted, C minor, in the full orchestra, *fortissimo,* and with canonic imitation.

The beginning of the third, or recapitulation, part of the movement is quietly worked. The first theme appears *piano* (violoncellos and horn); there is an inversion of the theme for violins and flute, and there is canonic imitation for oboe and trumpet. As in the first part, the subsidiary leads to the second chief theme, which is now in E minor and is given to the clarinet. There is an end to the delicate instrumentation. There is a great *crescendo,* which ends in an inversion of the second chief theme, *fortissimo,* for full orchestra. Other *crescendos* follow, one with the second theme to an episode of choral character, others based on the "contrapuntal figure." The great climax comes in the elaborate *coda,* which is built on a long organ-point on the bass E, with the first subsidiary theme and with the first chief theme, which now has its true and heroic character.

II. *Adagio, sehr feierlich und langsam* (in a very solemn and slow manner), C sharp minor, 4-4. This movement is thought by many to be Bruckner's masterpiece and monument. It undoubtedly established his fame when there were few to recognize his irregular genius. The *adagio* was played in cities of Germany in memory of the composer shortly after his death, as at the Philharmonic Concert, Berlin, led by Mr. Nikisch, October 26, 1896.

In this movement, as in the *finale,* Bruckner introduced the Bayreuth tubas, to gain effects of peculiar solemnity and also, no doubt, to pay homage to the master whom he loved and venerated.

The chief melody of the *adagio* is given to the lower strings and tubas and is answered by all the strings.

There is a passage of stormy lamentation, and then consolation comes in a melody for violins (*moderato,* F sharp major, 3-4). This theme is developed, chiefly by the strings. Then there is a return to the first and solemn theme, with wood-wind instruments and strings in alternation. There is a great *crescendo* with bold modulations until the entrance, C major, of the chief theme (second violins, supported by horn, oboes, and clarinets), which is soon followed by a variant of the answer to this theme. The answer soon appears in E flat major and in its original form and is maintained for a long time (G major). There is a modulation to A flat major, and the *cantilena* is repeated. After the entrance again of the chief melody and the restoration of the original tonality there is a *crescendo* of great and imposing force. This is over, and the tubas chant the answer to the chief theme and after an interlude for strings the chief theme itself, C sharp major. The horns take up the *cantilena,* and the last chord, C sharp major, dies away in brass instruments to a *pizzicato* of the strings.

III. *Scherzo: sehr schnell* (very fast), A minor, 3–4. This *scherzo* is based chiefly on two themes—the first for trumpet (*piano*), then clarinet, with a figure for strings; the second, a wild and raging one. The *scherzo* ends after a great *crescendo.* Drumbeats lead to the trio, F major, *etwas langsamer* (somewhat slower), with an expressive melody for strings. The theme of this trio is made at first out of an inversion of the *scherzo* theme, but the trio is in all respects in marked contrast to the *scherzo,* which after the trio is repeated.

*Finale: bewegt, doch nicht schnell* (with movement, but not fast), E major, 2–2. The first theme, given to the violins, has a certain resemblance, as far as intervals are concerned, to the chief theme of the first movement, but it is joyous rather than impressive. Flutes and clarinets enter at times, and horn tones also enter and lead to the second theme, which has the character of a choral, with an accompanying *pizzicato* bass. The tubas are then heard in solemn chords. A new theme of a dreamy nature follows (strings), and then at the beginning of the free fantasia an orchestral storm breaks loose. This dies away, and a theme appears which is derived from the first and main motive, which in turn enters, inverted, and with a *pizzicato* bass. The choral theme is also inverted, but it gives way to the chief motive, which is developed and leads to another tempestuous burst, ended suddenly with a pause for the whole orchestra. The repetition section brings back the themes in inverted order. The second chief theme is heard in C major. After a time there is a *crescendo* built on passages of this motive, which leads to a powerful episode in B major, with a theme in the bass derived from the chief motive. This motive is given to violins and clarinets, and there are contrapuntal imitations. The choral theme, appearing at the end of the free fantasia, is heard no more. The first chief theme dominates to the end. There is an imposing *coda.*

I am indebted in a measure to the analysis of this symphony by Mr. Johannes Reichert, prepared for the concerts of the Royal Orchestra of Dresden.

## SYMPHONY NO. 8, IN C MINOR

*I. Allegro moderato*
*II. Scherzo: allegro—andante—allegro moderato*
*III. Adagio*
*IV. Finale: Feierlich, nicht schnell*

BRUCKNER's Eighth is in all respects to be numbered with his greatest. The structure is nobler, the form more clearly recognized than in his other symphonies. There is less perplexing or boresome detail. The digressions do not cause the main line of musical argument to be forgotten. The interest is more steadily maintained. The instrumentation is richer in color and in contrasts. Above all, the invention shown, both in thematic lines and in wealth of development, is little less than marvelous, for Bruckner was sixty years old when he began work on this symphony.

Much has been said in European cities about the extraordinary length of the work. This length does not seem distressing. Bruckner had a great deal to say, and whereas in other symphonies he sometimes stammers and often falters, as though he were not able to express his thoughts, as though they were so great to him that he hesitated to put them into even musical speech, which comes nearest to the full expression of the inherently inexpressible, in this symphony he is master of his speech; he is convincing, authoritative, eloquent. Furthermore, he is more discriminative in his use of material. In other symphonies he is seen building indifferently with marble and clay. His Eighth symphony is as a stately temple, in which mortals forget the paltry cares and tribulations of earth, and gods appear calm and benignant.

There are pages that remind one of the visions seen by John on the isle of Patmos. "And I heard, as it were, the voice of a great multitude, and as the voice of many waters, and as the voice of mighty thunderings."

There are also pages of ravishing beauty, as those of the trio in the *scherzo,* as those devoted to the exposition of the first and second themes of the *adagio,* as those of the second theme in the *finale.* The *scherzo,* with rough humor and its episode of rare melodic beauty finely orchestrated, is of this earth, but the other movements leave the earth behind in a sustained and fearless flight. This is especially true of the first movement and the *adagio.*

In the *finale* there is here and there a drooping of the wings, but the opening measures of this *finale* and the close are towering and exultant.

This symphony, begun in 1885, was completed in 1890. It was performed for the first time in Vienna, December 18, 1892, at a Philharmonic concert led by Hans Richter. Even Hanslick admitted in his bitter review (*Neue Freie Presse,* December 23, 1892) of the symphony that the concert was a triumph for the composer. "How was the new symphony received? Boisterous rejoicing, waving of handkerchiefs from those standing, innumerable recalls, laurel wreaths," etc.

The symphony is dedicated to the composer's "imperial and royal apostolic Majesty Francis Joseph I, Emperor of Austria and apostolic King of Hungary." It is scored for three flutes, three oboes, three clarinets, three bassoons (and double bassoon), eight horns, three trumpets, three trombones, bass tuba, kettledrums, triangle, cymbals, three harps, and usual strings.

It appears that, when the symphony was first performed, there was an explanatory programme written by some devout disciple. This programme stated that the first theme of the first movement was "the form of the Æschylean Prometheus"; and a portion of this movement was entitled "the greatest loneliness and silence." The *scherzo* was supposed to typify "The German Michael." *"Der deutsche Michel"* may be translated "the plain, honest, much enduring (but slow) German," and "Michel" in a figurative sense means yokel, boor, clodhopper. Hanslick wrote: "If a critic had spoken this blasphemy, he would probably have been stoned to death by Bruckner's disciples; but the composer himself gave this name, the German Michael, to the *scherzo,* as may be read in black and white in the programme." The published score bears no motto. The programme-maker found in the *scherzo* "the deeds and sufferings of Prometheus reduced in the way of parody to the smallest proportions." And in the *adagio* was disclosed "the all-loving Father of mankind in his measureless wealth of mercy." The *finale* was characterized by him as "heroism in the service of the Divine," and the trumpet calls in the *finale* were explained as "the announcers of eternal salvation, heralds of the idea of divinity." On the other hand, it is said that the beginning of the *finale* was suggested to Bruckner by the meeting of the three emperors!

In the published score there is nothing to give the idea that the music has any programme, any argument. Yet Johannes Reichert in his analysis[1] of the symphony, referring to Josef Schalk's vision of "Prometheus Bound" in the first movement, found something of Prometheus or of Faust in the music.

I. *Allegro moderato,* C minor, 2–2. The first and chief motive is given to violas, violoncellos, and double basses. It is announced *pianissimo;* it is decisively rhythmed, and its rhythm and its upward leap of a sixth are important factors in the development. After a short *crescendo,* the strings are about to return to a *pianissimo* when the theme is proclaimed with the full force of the orchestra.

The first violins have the expressive and questioning second theme. Wood-wind instruments answer the question. The rhythm of the second theme, a rhythm that is characteristically Brucknerian, is used in counterpoint to a new *cantilena* sung by horns and first violins.

There is a modulation to the dominant of the chief tonality. The second theme now assumes an obstinate, arrogant character. Wood-wind instruments conduct over *pianissimo* and sustained chords of tubas, with the use of the first measures of the chief motive, to the second subsidiary section. In spite of the interrupting springs of the

[1]*Programme Book* of the Symphony Concert of the Royal Orchestra of Dresden, December 13, 1907.

seventh there is a return to a quiet mood. Then comes a chromatic and mighty *crescendo* for full orchestra, which reaches a climax with trumpet fanfares. The chief motive returns and is given out thrice *pianissimo.* The first horn has the chief motive in augmentation, and there is a double echo of it: from first oboe; from tenor tuba.

The "working-out" section begins with the indication "very quietly." Oboes and tubas introduce constituent parts of the chief motive in augmentation; then the motive itself appears in inversion and as in a *stretto.* This form of elaboration is long continued. And now the second theme appears inverted, and gives with its compelling rhythm the impetus to a great crescendo which reaches its climax with the encounter of the two themes *fortississimo.* This shock occurs three times without a decisive result. The orchestra seems to lose its force. There are wandering fragments of the two motives, while the trumpet keeps up monotonously the rhythm of the chief theme. A fragment of the first theme leads to the repetition section.

The repetition is at first free, whereas as a rule in Bruckner's symphonies it is literal. The first theme, now a lamentation, is given to the first oboe. The clarinet answers in another tonality. After bold modulations the second theme is repeated. The prevailing mood of unrest ends with a long held *fermata.* The second subsidiary section is repeated quietly, and, as in the first chief section of the movement, it is used in a *crescendo;* but here the climax is built on a *coda* motive of a bitterly complaining character, while horns and trumpets repeat incessantly the chief theme. Grief itself soon loses its voice. The violins sigh the chief motive thrice *pianissimo.* Only the last portion of the theme is then heard, and it dies away in the violas.

II. *Scherzo, Allegro moderato,* C minor, 3–4. The chief theme (violas and violoncellos) has a rough humor, while violins have a contrasting figure of a whispering and mysterious nature. This figure brings in a great *crescendo* in which the theme is blown by horns, later by trumpets, and at last by the bass tuba. At the end of the section a rhythm appears (E flat major, bassoons, drums, basses) that is slightly reminiscent of a rhythm in Beethoven's Symphony No. 8. The whispering figure is inverted. The first section is repeated.

The trio begins *langsam* ("slow"), 2–4, softly and delicately (first violins). The horn enters. There are pleasant harmonies in E major. "The whole episode breathes smiling happiness."

The harp is used here and in the *adagio,* the only instances of the use of this instrument in a symphony by Bruckner. A second subject brings the return to A flat major. The beginning of the trio is repeated with changes in tonality, and the whole first part of the *scherzo* is repeated with an ending in C major.

III. The *adagio* is said to be probably the longest symphonic *adagio* movement in existence, and there are some that put it at the head of all *adagios* by reason of its solemnity, nobility, and elevated thought. It begins, "solemn, slow, but not dragging," D flat major, 4–4. The first violins sing (on the G string) a long and intimate song to the accompaniment of the second violins and lower strings. "This theme contains three moments of mood. For the first four measures the violins complain softly; then sighing clarinets and bassoons enter in gasps; the four last measures are only an extension to strengthen the mood." A strange organ-point puts an end to the mood of doubt and brings in triumphant certainty. The violins, playing with greater breadth, lead to a calm close in F. There is a repetition of what has gone before, with the exception of a few measures of the chief theme.

The second theme is sung by the violoncellos, and they lead to the serenely quiet song of the tubas. Some measures based on fragments of the second theme bring in the "working-out" section. The chief theme appears. Portions of the long *cantilena* are combined, and there is fresh and melodic counterpoint. There is at the same time a *crescendo*. After the climax the second theme becomes prominent, with interruptions by the tubas.

The first theme appears with lively figuration at the beginning of the second section of development. A portion of this theme is used in augmentation. "Then appears suddenly and in a decided manner the rhythm for horns of the 'Siegfried' motive in *The Ring*." The accompaniment for strings grows livelier; the chief theme is more and more impressive in the brass. The second theme enters, and there are tranquillizing episodes, but there is no checking the course of the *crescendo* or the acceleration in pace. "*À tempo* (though in a lively movement)." The third section of the chief theme is now in powerful augmentation. There is a return to the prevailing tempo. The mood is milder. The violins "intimately and softly" remember once more the second theme. The *coda* brings in a peaceful close. In the third and fourth measures before the end the tubas indicate *pianissimo* the chief rhythm of the *finale* that follows.

IV. *Finale,* C minor, "solemnly, not fast," 2–2. The heavily rhythmed chief theme contains three important motives. It first appears in F sharp, as the enharmonically changed subdominant of the preceding tonality, D flat major (or as the dominant of the dominant of C minor). Joyful fanfares sound in D flat. The whole is repeated, and there is a modulation from A flat to E flat. Then appears sonorously the conclusion of the whole theme in the prevailing tonality, C minor. Out of the counterpoint arises a lamenting strain for oboes.

There is a pause. The melodious and religious second theme is sung in slower tempo. The accompanying voices for horn and violas might well be reckoned as thematic. The third theme, wood-wind and strings, is practically a double theme, and the lower voice has much importance, later. The concluding section of this theme is developed in choral fashion, and it is then combined with the lower voice. After a pause comes the working-out section. As the introduction indicated, it gives the impression of a mighty struggle. A blend of the two just preceding themes leads to a new melody for violins. There is a powerful *crescendo* for full orchestra. The rhythm of the chief theme of the first movement is heard. The first measures of the *finale* are now played softly by the horns, then by the flutes. Preceding themes are again combined. The repetition section opens powerfully. The decisive rhythm of the chief theme spurs the full orchestra. The *coda* begins quietly, but it soon becomes intense. In the triumphant ending in C major, chief themes of the four movements are heard exulting.

I am indebted in a measure for the preceding sketch of the contents of this symphony to the analysis by Werner Wolff, published in the programme book of the Philharmonic Orchestra, Berlin, October 29, 1906; and to the analysis of Johannes Reichert which has already been mentioned. They that wish to study the symphony may consult with profit the analysis by Willibald Kähler (*Musikführer* No. 262). These analysts are by no means unanimous in their designation of the chief themes. I have followed chiefly in the footsteps of Mr. Wolff.

It may help to a better understanding of the music of Bruckner if light be thrown on the personal nature and prejudices not only of the composer but of his contemporaneous partisans and foes. This simple man, who had known the cruelest poverty and distress, and in Vienna lived the life of an ascetic, made enemies by the very writing of music.

There appeared in Vienna in 1901 a little pamphlet entitled *Meine*

*Erinnerung an Anton Bruckner.* The writer was Carl Hruby, a pupil of Bruckner. The pamphlet is violent, malignant. In its rage there is at times the ridiculous fury of an excited child. There are pages that provoke laughter and then pity; yet there is much of interest about the composer himself, who now, away from strife and contention, is still unfortunate in his friends. We shall pass over Hruby's ideas on music and the universe, nor are we inclined to dispute his proposition (p. 7) that Shakespeare, Goethe, Beethoven, Wagner, were truer heroes and supporters of civilization than Alexander, Cæsar, Napoleon, who, nevertheless, were, like Hannibal, very pretty fellows in those days. When Hruby begins to talk about Bruckner and his ways, then it is time to prick up ears.

As a teacher, Bruckner was amiable, patient, kind, but easily vexed by frolicsome pupils who did not know his sensitive nature. He gave each pupil a nickname, and his favorite phrase of contentment and disapproval was *"Viechkerl!"*—"You stupid beast!" There was a young fellow whose name began "Sachsen"; but Bruckner could never remember the rest of it, so he would go through the list of German princes, "Sachsen"—"Sachsen"—"Sachsen-Coburg-Gotha, Sachsen"—and at last the name would come. Another pupil, afterwards a harp virtuoso, was known to his teacher only as "Old Harp." Bruckner had a rough, at the same time, sly, peasant humor. One of his pupils came into the class with bleached and jaded face. Bruckner asked what ailed him. The answer was: "I was at the Turnverein till two o'clock." "Yes," said Bruckner, "oh, yes, I know the Turnverein that lasts till 2 A.M." The pupil on whom he built fond hope was Franz Nott, who died young and in the madhouse. When Bruckner was disturbed in his work, he was incredibly and gloriously rude.

Bruckner was furious against all writers who discovered "programmes" in his music. He was warmly attached to the ill-fated Hugo Wolf, and was never weary of praising the declamation in his songs: "The fellow does nothing all day but compose, while I must tire myself out by giving lessons," for at sixty years Bruckner was teaching for three guldens a lesson. Beethoven was his idol, and after a performance of one of the greater symphonies he was as one insane. After a performance of the *Eroica,* he said to Hruby—would that it were possible to reproduce Bruckner's dialect—"I think that if Beethoven were alive, and I should go to him with my Seventh symphony and say, 'Here, Mr. Van Beethoven, this is not so bad, this Seventh, as certain gentlemen would make out' . . . I think he would take me by the hand and say, 'My dear Bruckner, never mind, I had no better luck; and the same men who hold me up against you even now do not understand my last quartets, although they act as if they understood them.' Then I'd say to him, 'Excuse me, Mr. Van Beethoven, that I have gone beyond you in freedom of form, but I think a true artist should make his own forms for his own works, and stick by them.'" He once said of Hanslick, "I guess Hanslick understands as little about Brahms as about Wagner, me, and others. And the Doctor Hanslick knows as much about counterpoint as a chimney sweep about astronomy."

Hanslick was to Bruckner as a pursuing demon. (We are giving Hruby's statement, and Hanslick surely showed a strange perseverance and an unaccountable ferocity in criticism that was abuse.) Hruby likens this critic to the *Phylloxera vastatrix* in the vineyard. He really believes that Hanslick sat up at night to plot Bruckner's destruction. He affirms that Hanslick tried to undermine him in the Conservatory and the Imperial Chapel, that he tried to influence conductors against the performance of his works. And he goes so far as to say that Hans Richter, thus influenced, had never performed a symphony by Bruckner in England. As a matter of fact, Richter produced Bruckner's Seventh in London, May 23, 1887. There is a story that when the Emperor Franz Josef asked Bruckner if he could honor him in any way, he asked if the Emperor would not stop Hanslick abusing him in print.

He was never mean or hostile toward Brahms, as some would have had him. He once said that Brahms was not an enemy of Wagner, as the Brahmsites insisted; that down in his heart he had a warm admiration for Wagner, as was shown by the praise he had bestowed on *Die Meistersinger*.

Just before his death Bruckner's thoughts were on his Ninth symphony: "I undertook a stiff task," he said. "I should not have done it at my age and in my weak condition. If I never finish it, then my *'Te Deum'* may be used as a *finale*. I have nearly finished three movements. This work belongs to my Lord God."

Although he had the religion of a child, he had read the famous book of David Strauss, and he could talk about it reasonably. Someone asked him about the future life and prayer. "I'll tell you," he replied. "If the story is true, so much the better for me. If it is not true, praying cannot hurt me."

# JOHN ALDEN CARPENTER

(Born at Park Ridge, Ill., February 28, 1876)

## SUITE, "ADVENTURES IN A PERAMBULATOR"

I. *En Voiture*
II. *The Policeman*
III. *The Hurdy-gurdy*
IV. *The Lake*
V. *Dogs*
VI. *Dreams*

MR. CARPENTER has told us in music the outing of a child. One of his first compositions was a collection of humorous *Improving Songs for Children.* This fondness for children as subjects for art he shares with Victor Hugo; with Swinburne, who abandoned the shrine of Venus to sing of children's beauty and innocence—after Watts-Dunton had docked him of his rum. In the *Perambulator* there is no sentimentalism, no Sunday-school address to "you, little girl with the blue sash"; but his music is as his child saw and thought, when wheeled about.

This suite is not only an ingenious work: it has true fancy, true humor, pages of truly poetic feeling. Mr. Carpenter displays imagination; witness his glorification of the lake that supplies Chicago with water. But even his imagination was dormant at the thought of the Chicago River. An unflinching realist would have introduced the child's visit to the stockyards and slaughter houses.

The composition of this suite was begun in July, 1914, and completed in December of that year. The suite was performed for the first time at the concerts of the Chicago Symphony Orchestra, Frederick Stock conductor, March 19–20, 1915.

The suite is scored for these instruments: three flutes (and piccolo), two oboes, English horn, two clarinets, bass clarinet, two bassoons, four horns, two trumpets, three trombones, bass tuba, kettledrums, bass drum, cymbals, triangle, tambourine, xylophone, glockenspiel, bells, harp, celesta, pianoforte, and the usual strings.

This programme is printed as preface to the score:

I. *En Voiture.* Every morning—after my second breakfast—if the wind and the sun are favorable, I go out. I should like to go alone, but my will is overborne. My nurse is appointed to take me. She is older than I, and very powerful. While I wait for her, resigned, I hear her cheerful steps, always the same. I am wrapped in a vacuum of wool, where there are no drafts. A door opens and shuts. I am placed in my perambulator, a strap is buckled over my stomach, my nurse stands firmly behind—and we are off!

II. *The Policeman.* Out is wonderful! It is always different, though one seems to have been there before. I cannot fathom it all. Some sounds seem like smells. Some sights have echoes. It is confusing, but it is Life! For instance, the Policeman—an Unprecedented Man! Round like a ball; taller than my Father. Blue—fearful—fascinating! I feel him before he comes. I see him after he goes. I try to analyze his appeal. It is not buttons alone, nor belt, nor baton. I suspect it is his eye and the way he walks. He walks like Doom. My nurse feels it, too. She becomes less firm, less powerful. My perambulator hurries, hesitates, and stops. They converse. They ask each other questions—some with answers, some without. I listen, with discretion. When I feel that they have gone far enough, I signal to my nurse, a private signal, and the Policeman resumes his enormous Blue March. He is gone, but I feel him after he goes.

III. *The Hurdy-gurdy.* Then suddenly there is something else. I think it is a sound. We approach it. My ear is tickled to excess. I find that the absorbing noise comes from a box—something like my music box, only much larger, and on wheels. A dark man is turning the music out of the box with a handle, just as I do with mine. A dark lady, richly dressed, turns when the man gets tired. They both smile. I smile too, with restraint, for music is the most insidious form of noise. And such music! So gay! I tug at the strap over my stomach. I have a wild thought of dancing with my nurse and my perambulator—all three of us together. Suddenly, at the climax of our excitement, I feel the approach of a phenomenon that I remember. It is the Policeman. He has stopped the music. He has frightened away the dark man and the lady with their music box. He seeks the admiration of my nurse for his act. He walks away, his buttons shine, but far off I hear again the forbidden music. Delightful forbidden music!

IV. *The Lake*. Sated with adventure, my nurse firmly pushes me on, and before I recover my balance I am face to face with new excitement. The land comes to an end, and there at my feet is the Lake. All other sensations are joined in one. I see, I hear, I feel the quiver of the little waves as they escape from the big ones and come rushing up over the sand. Their fear is pretended. They know the big waves are amiable, for they can see a thousand sunbeams dancing with impunity on their very backs. Waves and sunbeams! Waves and sunbeams! Blue water—white clouds—dancing, swinging! A white sea gull floating in the air. That is *My Lake!*

V. *Dogs*. We pass on. Probably there is nothing more in the World. If there is, it is superfluous. *There* IS. It is Dogs! We are coming upon them without warning. Not *one* of them—all of them. First, one by one; then in pairs; then in societies. Little dogs, with sisters; big dogs, with aged parents. Kind dogs, brigand dogs, sad dogs, and gay. They laugh, they fight, they run. And at last, in order to hold my interest, the very littlest brigand starts a game of "Follow the Leader," followed by all the others. It is tremendous!

VI. *Dreams*. Those dogs have gone! It is confusing, but it is Life! My mind grows numb. My cup is too full. I have a sudden conviction that it is well that I am not alone. That firm step behind reassures me. The wheels of my perambulator make a sound that quiets my nerves. I lie very still. I am quite content. In order to think more clearly, I close my eyes. My thoughts are absorbing. I deliberate upon my mother. Most of the time my mother and my nurse have but one identity in my mind, but at night or when I close my eyes, I can easily tell them apart, for my mother has the greater charm. I hear her voice quite plainly now, and feel the touch of her hand. It is pleasant to live over again the adventures of the day—the long blue waves curling in the sun, the Policeman who is bigger than my father, the music-box and my friends, the Dogs. It is pleasant to lie quite still and close my eyes, and listen to the wheels of my perambulator. How very large the world is! How many things there are!

# CLAUDE ACHILLE
# DEBUSSY

(Born at Germain [Seine and Oise], August 22, 1862;
died at Paris, March 25, 1918)

---

DEBUSSY SUFFERED at the hands of the ultra-orthodox and the snobs in music. The former could not find either melodic lines or the semblance of form in his orchestral and chamber works, his songs and pianoforte pieces. The snobs, secretly bored, thought it the thing to swoon at the mere mention of his name. In New York and Boston, as in Paris, there were *"Pelléastres,"* to use the contemptuous term coined by Jean Lorraine. There were some that spoke of Debussy as an ignorant fellow who, not being able to achieve greatness in the conventional manner, wrote in an eccentric way to attract attention, to make the bourgeois sit up. They forgot that Debussy had taken the chief prize at the Paris Conservatory, where harmony and counterpoint are taught rigorously. Debussy fashioned his own musical speech. It is easy to say that he learned much from Moussorgsky's *Boris Godounov*—but no one has yet pointed out exactly what he borrowed or imitated. That Debussy sojourned in Russia was enough to excite those who are unwilling to admit that any innovator has originality, for Debussy was an innovator, not a developer of what was handed down to him. It is more probable that he learned from the gypsies in Russia than from Moussorgsky.

The question arises whether in his compositions of the few last years Debussy did not merely imitate himself, whether he had anything more to say. The believer in plenary inspiration of course shouts with joy on hearing the three sonatas that have been played in this country. Admiring Debussy greatly as we do, we cannot in this instance shout with him. Debussy can surely rest his fame on the string quartet; *L'Après-midi d'un faune; Gigues, Ibéria, Pelléas et Mélisande,* and some of the songs and the pianoforte pieces.

As for *Pelléas and Mélisande,* we believe it to be the perfect example in opera of music wedded to words and situations, an opera more remarkable in this respect than even *Tristan and Isolde.*

## "PRÉLUDE À L'APRÈS-MIDI D'UN FAUNE" (ECLOGUE BY STÉPHANE MALLARMÉ)

Debussy's *Prelude to the Afternoon of a Faun* is a masterpiece of imaginative poetry in tones; it is a thing of flawless beauty. It matters not whether the symbolism of Mallarmé be cryptic or intelligible. It matters not whether the explanation of Gosse or of another be ingenious and plausible. The title is enough to give a clue to the hearer, if a clue be needed. Debussy himself has composed nothing more charming in strictly orchestral music.

There is the suggestion of sunlight and warmth, forest and meadow dear to fauns and nymphs. There is the gentle melancholy that is associated with a perfect afternoon. There is the exquisite melodic line, and there is harmonic suggestion with inimitable coloring that is still more exquisite.

*Prélude à l'après-midi d'un faune,* completed in 1892, was played for the first time at a concert of the National Society of Music, Paris, December 23, 1894. The conductor was Gustave Doret. According to Charles Koechlin, there had been insufficient rehearsal, so the performance left much to be desired, and the acoustics of the Salle d'Harcourt were unfavorable. When the second performance took place at a Colonne concert, a critic wrote: "This composer seems to dread banality." "And yet," says Koechlin, "the charm of this music is so simple, so melodic. But every *new* melody should be heard several times. Besides, even the construction—a supple melodic line that is expanded—could be disconcerting. For certain writers about music, Debussy was a dangerous artist with a diabolical fascination: the worst possible example. Diabolical or not, the work has lasted. It has the votes of the élite: that is enough."

The second performance was at a Colonne concert, Paris, October 20, 1895. In the *Annales du théâtre,* we find this singular note: "Written after a poem by Stéphane Mallarmé so sadistic that M. Colonne did not dare to print the text; young girls attend his concerts."

To Debussy is attributed a short "explanation of his *Prelude,* a very free illustration of Mallarmé's poem": The music evokes "the successive scenes in which the longings and the desire of the Faun pass in the heat of the afternoon."

Stéphane Mallarmé formulated his revolutionary ideas concerning style about 1875, when the *Parnasse contemporain* rejected his first poem of true importance, *L'Après-midi d'un faune.* The poem was published in 1876 as a quarto pamphlet, illustrated by Manet.

Gosse gave this explanation of the poem that suggested music to Debussy: "It appears in the *florilège* which he has just published, and I have now read it again, as I have often read it before. To say that I understand it bit by bit, phrase by phrase, would be excessive. But, if I am asked whether this famous miracle of unintelligibility gives me pleasure, I answer, cordially, Yes. I even fancy that I obtain from it as definite and as solid an impression as M. Mallarmé desires to produce.

"This is what I read in it: A faun—a simple, sensuous, passionate being—wakens in the forest at daybreak and tries to recall his experience of the previous afternoon. Was he the fortunate recipient of an actual visit from nymphs, white and golden goddesses, divinely tender and indulgent? Or is the memory he seems to retain nothing but the shadow of a vision, no more substantial than the 'arid rain' of notes from his own flute? He cannot tell. Yet surely there was, surely there is, an animal whiteness among the brown reeds of the lake that shines out yonder. Were they, are they, swans? No! But Naiads plunging? Perhaps! Vaguer and vaguer grows that impression of this delicious experience. He would resign his woodland godship to retain it. A garden of lilies, golden-headed, white-stalked, behind the trellis of red roses? Ah! the effort is too great for his poor brain. Perhaps if he selects one lily from the garth of lilies, one benign and beneficent yielder of her cup to thirsty lips, the memory, the ever receding memory, may be forced back. So when he has glutted upon a bunch of grapes, he is wont to toss the empty skins in the air and blow them out in a visionary greediness. But no, the delicious hour grows vaguer; experience or dream, he will never know which it was. The sun is warm, the grasses yielding; and he curls himself up again, after worshiping the efficacious star of wine, that he may pursue the dubious ecstasy into the more hopeful boskages of sleep.

"This, then, is what I read in the so excessively obscure and unintelligible. *L'Après-midi d'un faune;* and, accompanied as it is with a perfect suavity of language and melody of rhythm, I know not what more a poem of eight pages could be expected to give. It supplies a simple and direct impression of physical beauty, of harmony, of color; it is exceedingly mellifluous, when once the ear understands that the poet, instead of being the slave of the Alexandrine, weaves his variations round it, like a musical composer."

*The Afternoon of a Faun* is scored for three flutes, two oboes, English horn, two clarinets, two bassoons, four horns, two harps, small antique cymbals, strings. It is dedicated to Raymond Bonheur.

The chief theme is announced by the flute, *très modéré,* E major, 9–8. Louis Laloy gives the reins to his fancy: "One is immediately transported into a better world; all that is leering and savage in the snub-nosed face of the faun disappears; desire still speaks, but there is a veil of tenderness and melancholy. The chord of the wood-wind, the distant call of the horns, the limpid flood of harp tones, accentuate this impression. The call is louder, more urgent, but it almost immediately dies away, to let the flute sing again its song. And now the theme is developed: the oboe enters in, the clarinet has its say; a lively dialogue follows, and a clarinet phrase leads to a new theme which speaks of desire satisfied; or it expresses the rapture of mutual emotion rather than the ferocity of victory. The first theme returns, more languorous, and the croaking of muted horns darkens the horizon. The theme comes and goes, fresh chords unfold themselves; at last a solo violoncello joins itself to the flute; and then everything vanishes, as a mist that rises in the air and scatters itself in flakes."[1]

## NOCTURNES

*a. Nuages*
*b. Fêtes*
*c. Sirènes*

BAUDELAIRE's prose poem, "The Stranger," might serve as motto for the first nocturne, and for a hint to performance.

*"Enigmatical man, whom do you love best? Tell me—your mother, your sister, or your brother?"*

*"I have neither father, mother, sister, nor brother."*

*"Your friends?"*

*"You now use a word which to this day has been meaningless to me."*

*"Your country?"*

*"I do not know under what latitude it lies."*

*"Beauty?"*

*"I would love her gladly; goddess and immortal."*

*"Well, what do you love, extraordinary stranger?"*

*"I love the clouds, the clouds that pass, yonder, the marvellous clouds."*

*Festivals,* with its strange processional march, its whirring capriciousness, makes a more direct appeal. Does the third movement answer the old question put by Tiberius to the grammarians and repeated by Sir Thomas Browne, "What song did the sirens sing?" Here is music of waves and of sea—women: music that never was heard on a casino-lined coast, but sounds that might go with "The light that never was, on sea or land." Here is music that is subtly poetic, music of ineffable beauty. Suppose that Debussy had put

[1]Louis Laloy: *Claude Debussy,* 1909.

words to this song; how he would have cheapened the nocturne! To each hearer on the ship of Ulysses, or to each hearer of Debussy's music, the sirens sang of what might well lure him.

The first two nocturnes, *Nuages* and *Fêtes,* were produced at a Lamoureux concert, Camille Chevillard conductor, Paris, December 9, 1900, and they were played by the same orchestra January 6, 1901. The third, *Sirènes,* was first produced—in company with the other two—at a Lamoureux concert, October 27, 1901. The third is for orchestra with chorus of female voices. At this last concert the friends of Debussy were so exuberant in manifestations of delight that there was sharp hissing as a corrective. The *Nocturnes* were composed in 1898, and published in 1899.

Debussy furnished a programme for the suite; at least, this programme is attributed to him. Some who are not wholly in sympathy with what they loosely call "the modern movement" may think that the programme itself needs elucidation. Debussy's peculiar forms of expression in prose are not easily Englished, and it is well-nigh impossible to reproduce certain shades of meaning.

"The title *Nocturnes* is intended to have here a more general and, above all, a more decorative meaning. We, then, are not concerned with the form of the Nocturne, but with everything that this word includes in the way of diversified impression and special lights.

*"Clouds:* the unchangeable appearance of the sky, with the slow and solemn march of clouds dissolving in a gray agony tinted with white.

*"Festivals:* movement, rhythm dancing in the atmosphere, with bursts of brusque light. There is also the episode of a procession (a dazzling and wholly idealistic vision) passing through the festival and blended with it; but the main idea and substance obstinately remain—always the festival and its blended music—luminous dust participating in the universal rhythm of all things.

*"Sirens:* the sea and its innumerable rhythm; then amid the billows silvered by the moon the mysterious song of the Sirens is heard; it laughs and passes."

Alfred Bruneau with regard to the *Nocturnes:* "Here, with the aid of a magic orchestra, he has lent to clouds traversing the sombre sky the various forms created by his imagination; he has set to running and dancing the chimerical beings perceived by him in the silvery dust scintillating in the moonbeams; he has changed the white foam of the restless sea into tuneful sirens."

Questioning the precise nature of the form that shapes these *Nocturnes,* the reader may well ponder the saying of Plotinus in his "Essay on the Beautiful": "But the simple beauty of color arises, when light, which is something incorporeal, and reason and form, entering the obscure involutions of matter, irradiates and forms its dark and formless nature. It is on this account that fire surpasses other bodies in beauty, because, compared with the other elements, it obtains the order of form: for it is more eminent than the rest, and is the most subtle of all, bordering as it were on an incorporeal nature."

The *Nocturnes* are scored as follows:

I. Two flutes, two oboes, English horn, two clarinets, three bassoons, four horns, kettledrums, harp, strings. The movement begins *modéré,* 6–4.

II. Three flutes, two oboes, English horn, two clarinets, three bassoons, four horns, three trumpets, three trombones, bass tuba, two harps, kettledrums, cymbals, and snare drum, strings. *Animé et très rhythmé,* 4–4.

III. Three flutes, oboe, English horn, two clarinets, three bassoons, four horns, three trumpets, two harps, eight soprano voices, eight mezzo-soprano voices, strings, *modérément animé,* 12–8.

Debussy before his death made many changes in the instrumentation of these *Nocturnes.*

## "LA MER," TROIS ESQUISSES SYMPHONIQUES

*I. De l'aube à midi sur la mer*
*II. Jeux de vagues*
*III. Dialogue du vent et de la mer*

As THESE SKETCHES are frankly impressionistic, the enjoyment of the hearer depends largely on his own susceptibility and imagination. There are persons who do not like the ocean. Oscar Wilde was disappointed in the Atlantic; but there are more normal beings, far from being poseurs, who cannot exclaim with Jules Laforgue, "the sea, always new, always respectable!" We know a man who was doomed to spend a vacation in a summer hotel on a bluff looking down on Nantucket Sound. Whenever he sat on a bench he turned his back to the ocean and faced pine trees, giving as an excuse that "the sea got on his nerves."

Debussy's *Sea* is not for them, neither is it for those who find pleasure in Mendelssohn's overture, *Sea Calm and Prosperous Voyage,* for Debussy knows a wilder ocean, many-faced, now exulting in Æschylean laughter, now spasmodic, sinister, terrible, and never so terrible as when calm, or inviting mortals to sport with it, and smiling—as though it were forgetful of rotting ships and sunken treasure and the drowned far down that were for a time regarded curiously by monsters of the deep.

These orchestral pieces (I. *From Dawn till Noon on the Ocean;* II. *Play of the Waves;* III. *Dialogue of Wind and Sea*) were performed for the first time at a Lamoureux concert in Paris, October 15, 1905. Camille Chevillard conducted.

Debussy wrote in August, 1903, from Bichain to his publisher Jacques Durand[2] that he was at work on *La Mer.* "If God will be good to me the work will be in a very advanced state on my return [to Paris]." He wrote later that the sketches would have there titles: *Mer belle aux Îles Sanguinaires; Jeux de vagues; Le Vent fait danser la mer;* and in September he said the work was intended for Chevillard. In September, 1904, he wrote from Dieppe, "I wanted to finish *La Mer* here, but I must still work on the orchestration, which is as tumultuous and varied as the sea (with all my excuses to the latter)." In January, 1905, he was not sure that the title, *"De l'Aube à midi sur la mer"* would do: "So many contradictory things are dancing in my head, and this last attack of grippe has added its particular dance." He also wrote that he had remade the end of *Jeux de vagues.* He was disturbed because Chevillard spoke of the difficulties in the music, but if he gave the score to Colonne

[2] *Lettres de Claude Debussy à son éditeur;* published by Jacques Durand, 1927.

there might be a row. In July and September, 1905, he complained of "very curious corrections" made by someone in the proofs; and the idea of a performance at Chevillard's first concert seemed to him as bad as a performance at the last one of the season. At rehearsal it was found that the proofs had been badly read.

The Sketches, dedicated to Jacques Durand, were published at Paris in 1905. Debussy made an arrangement for two pianos; André Caplet made one in 1908 for three pianos.

*La Mer* is scored for piccolo, two flutes, two oboes, English horn, two clarinets, three bassoons and contra-bassoon, four horns, three trumpets, two *cornets-à-pistons,* three trombones, bass tuba, kettledrums, bass drum, cymbals, tam-tam, glockenspiel, two harps, and strings.

### Debussy and the Sea

Debussy loved and respected the ocean. In 1905 he wrote from Eastbourne: "The sea rolls with a wholly British correctness. There is a lawn combed and brushed on which little bits of important and imperialistic English frolic. But what a place to work! No noise, no pianos, except the delicious mechanical pianos, no musicians talking about painting, no painters discussing music. In short, a pretty place to cultivate egoism."

At Le Puy near Dieppe, August, 1906: "Here I am again with my old friend the sea, always innumerable and beautiful. It is truly the one thing in nature that puts you in your place; only one does not sufficiently respect the sea. To wet in it bodies deformed by the daily life should not be allowed; truly these arms and legs which move in ridiculous rhythms—it is enough to make the fish weep. There should be only Sirens in the sea, and could you wish that these estimable persons would be willing to return to waters so badly frequented?"

Houlgate, 1911: "Here life and the sea continue—the first to contradict our native savagery, the second to accomplish its sonorous going and coming, which cradles the melancholy of those who are deceived by the beach."

Pourville, August, 1915: "Trees are good friends, better than the ocean, which is in motion, wishing to trespass on the land, bite the rocks, with the anger of a little girl—singular for a person of its importance. One would understand it if it sent the vessels about their business as disturbing vermin."

## CLAUDE ACHILLE DEBUSSY

### "IBÉRIA": "IMAGES" FOR ORCHESTRA, NO. 2

*I. Par les rues et par les chemins (In the Streets and By-ways)*
*II. Les Parfums de la nuit (The Fragrance of the Night)*
*III. Le Matin d'un jour de fête (The Morning of a Festival Day)*

THE *Images,* of which *Ibéria* is the second movement, are remarkable in many ways and to be ranked among the first compositions of this genius. They are impressionistic, but there is a sense of form; there is also the finest proportion. This music is conspicuous for exquisite effects of color. There are combinations of timbres and also contrasts that were hitherto unknown. There are hints of Spanish melodies; melodies not too openly exposed; there are intoxicating rhythms, sharply defined, or elusive, and then they are the more madding.

This music is pleasingly remote from photographic realism. The title might be "Impressions of Spain." There is the suggestion of street life and wild strains heard on bleak plains or savage mountains; of the music of the people; of summer nights, warm and odorous; of the awakening of life with the break of day; of endless jotas, tangos, seguidillas, fandangoes; of gypsies with their spells brought from the East; of women with Moorish blood. *Ibéria* defies analysis and beggars description.

What phrase-mongering, however ingenious, would impart the beauty of *Odors of the Night* to him that did not hear the music? The music that haunts should not be lightly or openly talked about. The impression made by it should be guarded or confided only to the closest friend.

To speak of Debussy's use of instruments to gain effects, of his ability to reproduce what had not been heard by others, though they may have felt it feebly and had the wish to hear it clearly and put it in notation, would be a classroom task. To write of it for the general reader would be only to rhapsodize. Now Debussy is a rhapsodist of the rarest nature, and his musical speech is not to be translated by a rhapsody in words.

*Ibéria* is the second in a series of three orchestral compositions by Debussy entitled *Images.*

The first, *Gigues*—it was originally entitled *Gigue Triste*—was published in 1913 and performed for the first time at a Colonne concert, Paris, January 26, 1913. *Ibéria* was performed for the first time at a Colonne concert in Paris on February 20, 1910, Gabriel Pierné, conductor.

M. Boutarel wrote after the first performance that the hearers are supposed to be in Spain. The bells of horses and mules are heard, and the joyous sounds of wayfarers. The night falls; nature sleeps and is at rest until bells and *aubades* announce the dawn, and the world awakens to life. "Debussy appears in this work to have exaggerated his tendency to treat music with means of expression analogous to those of the impressionistic painters. Nevertheless, the rhythm remains well defined and frank in *Ibéria.* Do not look for any melodic design, nor any carefully woven harmonic web. The composer of *Images* attaches importance only to tonal color. He puts his timbres side by side, adopting a process like that of the *Tachistes* or the 'stipplers' in distributing coloring." The Debussyites and *"Pelléastres"* wished *Ibéria* repeated, but, while the majority of the audience was willing to applaud, it did not long for a repetition. Repeated the next Sunday, *Ibéria* aroused "frenetic applause and vehement protestations."

*Ibéria* is scored for these instruments: piccolo, three flutes (one interchangeable with a second piccolo), two oboes, English horn, three clarinets, three bassoons, double bassoon, four horns, three trumpets, three trombones, bass tuba, kettledrums, side drum, tambourine, castanets, xylophone, celesta, cymbals, three bells (F, G, A), two harps, and the usual strings.

Debussy wrote on May 16, 1905, to Jacques Durand, his publisher, that he was preparing these compositions for two pianofortes: "I. *Gigues tristes.* II. *Ibéria.* III. *Valse* (?)." In September of that year he hoped to finish them. 1906, August 8: "I have at present three different ways of finishing *Ibéria.* Shall I toss up a coin or search for a fourth?"

In September, 1907, the *Images* would be ready as soon as the *Rondes* were *"comme je le veux et comme il faut."* In 1908 Debussy was hard at work on his opera, *The Fall of the House of Usher,* an opera of which, it is said, no sketches have been found. (Durand received Debussy's libretto in 1917.) In 1909 he wrote that he had laid the *Images* aside "to the advantage of Edgar Allan Poe." He also worked on an opera, *The Devil in the Belfry.*

In 1910: "I have seen Pierné. I think he exaggerates the difficulties in a performance of *Ibéria.*"

Debussy wrote on December 4, 1910, from Budapest, where he gave a concert of his works, that *Ibéria* was especially successful. "They could not play *The Sea* no more the *Nocturnes,* from want of rehearsal. I was assured that the orchestra knew *The Sea,* for it had been played through three times. Ah! my friend, if you had heard it! . . . I assure you to put *Ibéria* right in two rehearsals was, indeed, an effort. . . . Don't forget that these players understood me only through an interpreter—a sort of Doctor of Law—who perhaps transmitted my thought only by deforming it. I tried every means. I sang, made the gestures of Italian pantomime, etc.—it was enough to touch the heart of a buffalo. Well, they at last understood me, and I had the last word. I was recalled like a ballet girl, and if the idolatrous crowd did not unharness the horses of my carriage, it was because I had a simple taxi. The moral of this journey is that I am not made to exercise the profession of composer of music in a foreign land. The heroism of a commercial traveler is needed. One must consent to a sort of compromise which decidedly repels me."

# ANTON DVOŘÁK

(Born at Mühlhausen [Nelahozeves] near Kralup, Bohemia, September 8, 1841; died at Prague, May 1, 1904)

---

THE WINNING and endearing qualities of childhood were in Dvořák's best music: artless simplicity, irresistible frankness, delight in nature and life. His music was best when it smacked of the soil, when he remembered his early days, the strains of vagabond musicians, the dances dear to his folk. One of a happily primitive people, he delighted in rhythm and color. He was not the man to translate pictures, statues, poems, a system of metaphysics, a gospel of pessimism into music. He was least successful when he would be heroic, mystical, profound. It was an evil day for him when England "discovered" him, patronized him, ordered oratorios from him for her festivals, made him a doctor of music (as though he were a cathedral organist), and tried to turn this *Naturmensch* into a drawing-room and church celebrity. When Dvořák is dull, he is very dull. His Slavonic Dances and such a song as "Als die alte Mutter" are worth a wilderness of "St. Ludmilas" and "Heldenlieds." And his work as a creative musician was no doubt at an end when he left this country to go back to his beloved Prague.

Some have been inclined to think lightly of Dvořák because his best and vital qualities were recognized by the people. This popularity irritated those who believe that pure art is only for the few—the purists; they forget Mozart, Beethoven, Schubert, Chopin,

Verdi, Wagner, Tchaikovsky. But this popularity was based on the quick recognition of essential qualities: melody, rhythm, color. Slavonic intensity has a purpose, an esoteric meaning. Dvořák might have replied to lecturers, essayists, and the genteel in Whitman's words:

> *Do you guess I have some intricate purpose? Well,*
> *I have—for the Fourth-month showers have, and the*
> *mica on the side of a rock has.*
> *Do you take it I would astonish? Does the daylight*
> *astonish? Does the early redstail, twittering through*
> *the woods?*

Dvořák had his faults, and they were tiresome and exasperating. His naïveté became a mannerism. Like a child, he delighted in vain repetitions; he was at times too much pleased with rhythms and colors, so that he mistook the exterior dress for the substance and forgot that after all there was little or no substance behind the brilliant trappings. We believe that he will ultimately be ranked among the minor poets of music. His complete works may gather dust in libraries; but no carefully chosen anthology will be without examples of his piquancy, strength, and beauty in thought and expression.

## SYMPHONY NO. 5, IN E MINOR, "FROM THE NEW WORLD," OP. 95

*I. Adagio; allegro molto*
*II. Largo*
*III. Scherzo*
*IV. Allegro con fuoco*

Dvořák was an Austrian of a sort, and lived his time in Vienna, like the others. But he had Czech blood in his veins, and had, moreover, pretty well formed his style before coming to Vienna; besides, he was a peasant and had not only been brought up in, but had a native affinity for, the peasant musical atmosphere; Vienna taught him no dancing-master tricks. It is at once curious and delightful to note how, in this symphony, Dvořák sticks to his peasant dialect. Once, in the *scherzo,* he rises to the Schubert pitch of civilization (and Schubert himself was an incorrigible man of the people), but for the rest remains peasant as he was born and bred. And as his dialect is really his native lingo, it has all the charm of reality and does not offend nor bore you—as so-called dialect novels do. Here in this symphony Dvořák has done, perhaps, the best work of his life; not the most genuine, for he is hardly ever anything but genuine, but the most thoroughly poetic and beautiful. There are parts of the *finale* that seem clearly intended as a picture of—or say, rather, clearly inspired by memories of—a peasant's Sunday afternoon *Keilerei,* or free fight (of the "where you see a head, hit" sort).

Dvořák in 1892–93 was living in New York as the director of the National Conservatory of Music. He made many sketches for this symphony. In the first of the three books used for this purpose, he noted "Morning, December 19, 1892." Fuller sketches began January 10, 1893. The slow movement was then entitled *"Legenda."* The *scherzo* was completed January 31; the *finale,* May 25, 1893. A large part of the instrumentation was done at Spillville, Ia., where many Bohemians dwelt.

This symphony was performed for the first time, in manuscript, by the Philharmonic Society of New York on Friday afternoon, December 15, 1893. Anton Seidl conducted. Dvořák was present.

When this symphony was played at Berlin in 1900, Dvořák wrote to Oskar Nedbal, who conducted it: "I send you Kretzschmar's analysis of the symphony, but omit that nonsense about my having made use of 'Indian' and 'American' themes—that is a lie. I tried to write only in the spirit of those national American melodies. Take the introduction to the symphony as slowly as possible."

The symphony aroused a controversy in which there was shedding of much ink. The controversy long ago died out, and is probably forgotten even by those who read the polemical articles at the time and expressed their own opinions. The symphony remains. It is now without associations that might prejudice. It is now enjoyed or appreciated, or possibly passed by, as music, and not as an exhibit in a case on trial.

Yet it may be good to recall the circumstances of the symphony's origin. In the feverish days of the discussion excited by the first performance of this symphony, it was stated that Mr. Krehbiel and others called the attention of Dvořák, who was then living in New York, to Negro melodies and rhythms; that the Bohemian composer then wept with joy and rushed after music paper; that he journeyed to a Western town inhabited chiefly by Bohemians, a town in Iowa, where he could find the stimulating atmosphere to write masterpieces of a truly American nature. Some may also remember that soon after the first performances of the symphony there was a distressing rumor that portions of it had been composed long before Dvořák came to New York; long before his eyes were dimmed and his knees turned to water by hearing Negro tunes.

The conclusion of the whole matter, according to several Czechs whom William Ritter (author of a life of Smetana) consulted, is as follows:

I. The *New World* symphony expresses the state of soul of an uncultured Czech in America, the state of a homesick soul remembering his native land and stupefied by the din and hustle of a new life.

II. The uncultured Czech is a born musician, a master of his trade. He is interested in the only traces of music that he finds in America. Negro airs, not copied, adapted, imitated, tint slightly two or three passages of the symphony without injury to its Czech character.

III. The symphony leaped, Minerva-like, from the head of this uncultured genius. As nearly all his other compositions, except the operas, it was not stimulated by any foreign assistance, by any consultation of authors, or by quotations, reading, etc., as was especially the case with Brahms.

IV. The national Czech feeling in this work, quickened by homesickness, is so marked that it is recognized throughout Bohemia, by the learned and by the humblest.

These are the conclusions of Mr. Ritter after a painstaking investigation. That Dvořák was most unhappy and pathetically homesick during his sojourn in New York is known to many, though Mr. Ritter does not enter into any long discussion of the composer's mental condition in this country.

Yet some will undoubtedly continue to insist that the symphony *From the New World* is based, for the most part, on Negro themes, and that the future of American music rests on the use of Congo, North American Indian, Creole, Greaser, and Cowboy ditties, whinings, yawps, and whoopings.

The symphony is scored for two flutes and piccolo, two oboes (one interchangeable with English horn), two clarinets, two bassoons, four horns, two trumpets, three trombones, bass tuba, kettledrums, cymbals, triangle, and strings.

# EDWARD WILLIAM
# ELGAR

(Born at Broadheath, near Worcester, England, June 2, 1857; died at Worcester, February 23, 1934)

---

NEARLY ONE HUNDRED years ago, William Hazlitt wrote a few words concerning a speech on Indian affairs by the Marquis Wellesley, the eldest brother of the Duke of Wellington. These words may be justly applied to Sir Edward Elgar, composer of *The Dream of Gerontius,* two symphonies, the popular march *Pomp and Circumstance,* and other works familiar to our concert audiences.

"Seeming to utter volumes in every word, and yet saying nothing; retaining the same unabated vehemence of voice and action without anything to excite it; still keeping alive the promise and the expectation of genius without once satisfying it—soaring into mediocrity with adventurous enthusiasm, harrowed up by some plain matter of fact, writhing with agony under a truism, and launching a commonplace with all the fury of a thunderbolt."

## VARIATIONS ON AN ORIGINAL THEME, "ENIGMA," OP. 36

*Theme: Andante.*

*Variations.*

*I. "C.A.E." L'istesso tempo*

*II. "H.D.S.-P." Allegro*

*III. "R.B.T." Allegretto*

*IV. "W.M.B." Allegro di molto*

*V. "R.P.A." Moderato*
*VI. "Ysobel" Andantino*
*VII. "Troyte" Presto*
*VIII. "W.N." Allegretto*
*IX. "Nimrod" Moderato*
*X. "Dorabella—Intermezzo." Allegro*
*XI. "G.R.S." Allegro di molto*
*XII. "B.G.N." Andante*
*XIII. "X.X.X.—Romanza." Moderato*
*XIV. "E.D.U.—Finale"*

ELGAR's Variations were once regarded as a brilliant show-piece for an orchestra. There was a time when Elgar was held to be a "great" composer. Time, the Old Man with a Scythe, has a disconcerting way of handling it. The music with a few exceptions seems at the best respectable in a middle-class manner; the sort of music that gives the composer the degree of Mus. Doc. from an English university. In Elgar's case, his music won him knighthood, and to this day there are "Elgar Festivals" in England. Was Cecil Gray too severe when he wrote of Elgar: "He never gets entirely away from the atmosphere of pale, cultured idealism and the unconsciously hypocritical, self-righteous, Pharisaical gentlemanliness which is so characteristic of British art in the last century"?

These Variations, composed at Malvern in 1899, were first performed at one of Hans Richter's concerts in London, June 19, 1899. Mr. Felix Borowski, the excellent editor of the Chicago Orchestra's Programme Books, says: "Richter had never met the English composer when, in Vienna, he received the score of the Variations from his agent in the British capital; but the conductor determined to exploit a work which appeared to him to possess qualities of strength and skill that had not been made evident in many English compositions. 'The *Enigma* Variations,' wrote Robert J. Buckley, 'toured by Richter's band, set the seal on Elgar's reputation. Richter did for Elgar what he had done for Wagner thirty years before. England was won for Wagner by Richter and the *Tannhäuser* overture. England was won for Elgar by Richter and the *Enigma* Variations.'[1] It should, however, be pointed out that the Variations, as produced by Richter in June, 1899, were not quite the same composition as that which has been made familiar to every concert-going audience in the world. After the first performance, Elgar, at the instigation of Hans Richter, added a *coda,* and he made various changes in the orchestration throughout the piece. In this revised form it was produced at the Worcester Festival, the composer conducting his work, September 13, 1899." The Variations were first played in Germany at a concert of the Städtische Musikverein, Düsseldorf, February 7, 1901; Julius Buths, conductor.

The score, which includes a theme and fourteen variations, is dedicated by the composer to his "friends pictured within." Elgar himself said: "It is true that I have sketched, for their amusement and mine, the idiosyncrasies of fourteen of my friends, not necessarily musicians; but this is a personal matter and need not have been mentioned publicly. The Variations should stand simply as a 'piece' of music. The Enigma I will not explain—its 'dark saying' must be left unguessed, and I warn you that the apparent connection between the Variations and the theme is often of the slightest texture; further, through and over the whole set another and larger theme 'goes' but is not played. . . . So the principal theme never appears, even as in some late dramas—e.g., Maeterlinck's *L'Intruse* and *Les Sept Princesses:* the chief character is never on the stage."

Elgar's work is scored for two flutes and piccolo, two oboes, two clarinets, two bassoons, double bassoon, four horns, three trumpets, three trombones, bass tuba, snare drum, bass drum, triangle, cymbals, organ (*ad lib.*), and strings.

## THEME

The theme, or the "Enigma," is an *andante,* G minor, 4–4, of a melancholy nature, with a halting and sighing melody. A few measures of musical notation would show more clearly the nature of the following variations than any verbal description, however graphic.

Elgar wrote to the late August Johannes Jaeger that he had composed

[1]Robert J. Buckley: *Sir Edward Elgar,* 1904.

thirteen variations, but, yielding to superstition, he had called the *finale* the fourteenth.

## VARIATIONS

I. "C.A.E." *L'istesso tempo,* G minor, 4–4. The initials are Lady Elgar's. The theme, changed in rhythm, is given to the second violins and violas tremolo; flute and clarinet in octaves. The close, *pianississimo,* is in G major.

II. "H.D.S.-P." *Allegro,* G minor, 3–8. The theme finally appears in the violoncellos and basses under a staccato figure for wood-wind, later violins.

III. "R.B.T." *Allegretto,* G major, 3–8. Fragments of the theme are played by oboe and violins (*pizzicato*) against a counter theme for wood-wind.

IV. "W.M.B." A spirited, vigorous variation. *Allegro di molto,* G minor-major 3–4. Strings, wood-wind, and horns proclaim the theme. The last measures call for the full strength of the orchestra.

V. "R.P.A." *Moderato,* C minor, 12–8 (4–4). A counter melody is developed against the theme (bassoons, violoncellos, and double basses), first above the theme and then below it.

VI. "Ysobel." *Andantino,* C major 3–2. A lyrical movement with a *cantilena* for solo viola, while gentle phrases are given to the wood-wind and horns.

VII. "Troyte." *Presto,* C major, 4–4. Wood-wind and violins have a bold figure over a *basso ostinato* for violoncellos, double basses, kettle-drums. This figure, changed, is afterwards given to the basses.

VIII. "W.N." *Allegretto,* G major, 6–8. Clarinets vary the theme.

IX. "Nimrod." *Moderato,* E flat major, 3–4. This and the next variations are in strong contrast to each other and to those that precede. "Nimrod" is a tribute to Elgar's friend Jaeger. Elgar's Variations were performed at a memorial concert to Jaeger in London on January 24, 1910. Hans Richter conducted. Elgar wrote this note for the programme: "The Variations are not all 'portraits.' . . . Something ardent and mercurial, in addition to the slow movement (No. IX), would have been needful to portray the character and temperament of A. J. Jaeger. The variation is a record of a long summer evening talk, when my friend grew nobly eloquent (as only he could) on the grandeur of Beethoven, and especially of his slow movements." The strings (2d violins, violas, and violoncellos divided) sing the theme, *pianissisimo*. Later the wood-wind and brass enlarge it.

X. "Dorabella-Intermezzo." *Allegretto,* G major, 3–4, a sparkling, joyous variation, scored lightly for muted strings and wood-wind; a horn is heard in one measure, and there are a few strokes on the kettledrums.

XI. "G.R.S." *Allegro di molto,* G minor, 2–2. An English reviewer says of this variation: "The furious pedaling in the basses seems to confirm our suspicion that this is the 'picture' of a well-known Cathedral organist." This organist is probably Dr. George Roberton Sinclair, a friend and neighbor of Elgar at Hereford. The basses play a staccato variation of the theme. Later the brass has it *fortissimo.*

XII. "B.G.N." *Andante,* G minor, 4–4. A song for violoncellos in which violas join later with first violins for the climax.

XIII. "X.X.X.—Romanza." *Moderato,* G major, 3–4. The story is that "X.X.X." was at sea when Elgar wrote this variation. We quote from Mr. Daniel Gregory Mason's essay on Elgar: "Violas in a quietly undulating rhythm suggests the ocean expanse; an almost inaudible tremor of the drum gives the throb of the engines; a quotation from Mendelssohn's *Calm Sea and Prosperous Voyage* (clarinet) completes the story. Yet 'story' it is not—and there is the subtlety of it. Dim sea and dreamlike steamer are only accessories, after all. The thought of the distant friend, the human soul there, is what quietly disengages itself as the essence of the music."[2] Ernest Newman speaks of the "curious drum roll, like the faint throb of the engines of a big liner."[3]

XIV. "E.D.U.—Finale." *Allegro,* G major, with an introduction. There are various modifications of tempo; the final section is a *presto.* The organ part was added after the first performance. "The *finale* is an elaborate movement, starting *pianissimo,* but soon developing strength and brilliancy in a richly scored marchlike strain, with which anon the *ritmo di tre* of Variation IX, 'Nimrod' (but in augmentation) is combined in a grandiose and triumphant passage, which virtually forms the climax of the work." There is also a reminiscence of the opening strain of Variation I, *pianississimo.*

[2]D. G. Mason: *Contemporary Composers,* 1918.
[3]Ernest Newman: *Elgar,* 1906.

MANUEL

# DE FALLA

(Born at Cadiz, November 23, 1876)

---

## BALLET-PANTOMIME: "EL AMOR BRUJO"

THE SUITE derived from de Falla's "choreographic fantasy," *Love, the Sorcerer,* does not suffer so much by its separation from the theatrical situations, action, and stage settings as other suites arranged from ballets. There are many pages that are enjoyable as pure music without thought of a plot and the evolutions of a ballet, without the question of whether this number or that is illustrative of an episode in the ballet. If de Falla expresses the wildness of Spanish gypsy music in a fascinating manner, he is equally fortunate in the expression of gentle emotions. There is little that is sensuous or voluptuous in the suite. The music for the scene of the appearance of a ghost which cools the amorous ardor of Candelas when her new lover would approach her—here one is reminded of the chief theme of Anatole France's amusing and satirical *Histoire comique*—is, perhaps, imbued with passionate fervor for performance on the stage.

This *Gitaneria* (Gypsy Life) in one act and two scenes, a choreographic fantasy with voice and small orchestra, book by Gregorio Martinez Sierra (known in this country by the plays *A Romantic Young Lady, Cradle Song, The Kingdom of God*), was produced at the Teatro de Lara, Madrid, April 15, 1915, with the Señora Pastora Imperio assisting. A concert version was performed at Madrid in 1916,

E. Fernandez Arbos conductor, at a concert of the Sociedad Nacional de Música. According to G. Jean-Aubry, "De Falla drew from the music certain symphonic excerpts, in which he suppressed the spoken or sung parts and enlarged the instrumentation. . . . But this did not alter the essential character of the work, which is to be found in its particular color, or the semi-Arabian style of its idioms."

This suite was performed for the first time in London on November 23, 1921.

Sierra based the libretto of de Falla's ballet pantomime on an Andalusian gypsy story. *Brujo* means a wizard, a male witch. Mr. Trent, in his *Manuel de Falla and Spanish Music,* writes: "*L'Amour sorcier* has misled both audiences and English translators. *Love the Wizard* gives an entirely wrong impression; *Wedded by Witchcraft,* proposed as an alternative, is a description, more or less, of what happens; and even that would be better as *Wedded in Spite of Witchcraft.*"

There was a small orchestra when the work was first produced. As finally revised, the score calls for piccolo, two flutes, oboe, two clarinets, bassoon, two horns, two trumpets, kettledrums, bells (A, D, C), piano, and strings. A mezzo-soprano sings "behind"; but in concerts the voice is replaced by a horn, or in one place an English horn.

When Mr. Arbos conducted this work in St. Louis, the Programme Book, edited by Harry R. Burke, contained this synopsis of the story published as a preface to the piano score:

"Candelas, a young, very beautiful and passionate woman has loved a wicked, jealous and dissolute, but fascinating and cajoling Gypsy. Although having led a very unhappy life with him, she has loved him intensely and mourned his loss, unable ever to forget him. Her memory of him is something like a hypnotic dream, a morbid, gruesome, and maddening spell. She is terrified by the thought that the dead may not be entirely gone, that he may return, that he continues to love her in that fierce, shadowy, faithless, and caressing way. She lets herself become a prey to the past as if under the influence of a specter; yet she is young, strong, vivacious. Spring returns, and with it love, in the shape of Carmelo.

"Carmelo, a handsome youth, enamored and gallant, makes love to her. Candelas, not unwilling to be won, almost unconsciously returns his love; but the obsession of her past weighs against her present inclination. When Carmelo approaches her and endeavors to make her share his passion, the Specter returns and terrifies Candelas, whom he separates from her lover. They cannot exchange the kiss of perfect love.

"Carmelo being gone, Candelas languishes and droops; she feels as if bewitched, and her past love seems to flutter heavily about her like malevolent and foreboding bats. But this evil spell has to be broken, and Carmelo believes he has found a remedy. He has once been the comrade of the Gypsy whose specter haunts Candelas. He knows that the dead lover was the typical faithless and jealous Andalusian gallant. Since he appears to retain, even after his death, his taste for beautiful women, he must be taken on his weak side and thus diverted from his posthumous jealousy in order that Carmelo may exchange with Candelas the perfect kiss against which the sorcery of love cannot prevail.

"Carmelo persuades Lucia, a young and enchantingly pretty Gypsy girl, the friend of Candelas, to simulate acceptance of the Specter's addresses. Lucia, out of love for Candelas and from feminine curiosity, agrees. The idea of a flirtation with a ghost seems to her attractive and novel. And then the dead man was so mirthful in life. Lucia takes up the sentinel's post. Carmelo returns to make love to Candelas, and the Specter intervenes . . . but he finds the charming little Gypsy, and neither can nor will resist the temptation, not being experienced in withstanding the allurements of a pretty face. He makes love to Lucia, coaxing and imploring her, and the coquettish young Gypsy almost brings him to despair. In the meantime Carmelo succeeds in convincing Candelas of his love, and life triumphs over death and the past. The lovers at last exchange the kiss that defeats the evil influence of the Specter, who perishes, definitely conquered by love."

## THREE DANCES TAKEN FROM THE BALLET "THE THREE-CORNERED HAT"

*I. The Neighbors*
*II. The Miller's Dance*
*III. Final Dance*

THE SCORE calls for piccolo, two flutes, two oboes, English horn, two clarinets, two bassoons, four horns, two trumpets, three trombones, bass tuba, kettledrums, side drum, bass drum, cymbals, triangle, xylophone, tam-tam, castanets, celesta, harp, piano, and the usual strings.

When the Russian Ballet visited Spain, Serge de Diaghilev was so much interested in the work of de Falla that he commissioned him to write a ballet on the subject of Alarcón's novel, *El Sombrero de Tres Picos.*

This ballet *The Three-cornered Hat* was performed for the first time on any stage by the Russian Ballet at the Alhambra, London. Joaquin Turina says (*The Chesterian,* May, 1920) that the first version of *The Three-cornered Hat* was produced at the Eslava Theater, Madrid, under the title of *El Corregidor y la Molinera.* Turina was then conducting this theater's orchestra. The "pantomime" of de Falla was accompanied by only seventeen players. "The composer was confronted with one great difficulty, and that was to follow musically the action of the play without spoiling the unity of his score. The music therefore continually reflected a certain anxiety on the composer's part, as if he were trying to disentangle himself, so to speak, from the external network. The transformation of the 'pantomime' into a ballet at once cleared away all these difficulties. This is quite natural, for in the new version the action became reduced to a strictly indispensable minimum, and the dances became predominant, those already existing being considerably amplified."

Turina finds the Miller's Dance the most interesting "because of its typically Andalusian character, its fascinating rhythm which is like an affirmation of Southern art, and its Moorish character." In the Final Dance the *jota* and the folk theme called *vito* are introduced.

The *Daily Telegraph* (London, July 24, 1919) said of the ballet:

"Over the whole brisk action is the spirit of frivolous comedy of a kind by no means common only to Spain of the eighteenth century. A young miller and his wife are the protagonists, and if their existence be idyllic in theory, it is extraordinarily strenuous in practice—choreographically. But that is only another way of saying that M. Massine and Mme Karsavina, who enact the couple, are hardly ever off the stage, and that both of them work with an energy and exuberance that almost leave one breathless at moments. The miller and his wife between them, however, would scarcely suffice even for a slender ballet plot. So we have as well an amorous *corregidor* (or governor), who orders the miller's arrest so that the way may be cleared for a pleasant little flirtation—if nothing more serious—with the captivating wife. Behold the latter fooling him with a seductive dance, and then evading her admirer with such agility that, in his pursuit of her, he tumbles over a bridge into the mill stream. But, as this is comedy, and not melodrama, the would-be lover experiences nothing worse than a wetting, and the laugh, which is turned against him, is renewed when, having taken off some of his clothes to dry them and gone to rest on the miller's bed, his presence is discovered by the miller himself, who, in revenge, goes off in the intruder's garments after scratching a message on the wall to the effect that 'Your wife is no less beautiful than mine!' Thereafter a 'gallimaufry of gambols' and—curtain!"

# CÉSAR FRANCK

(Born at Liège, Belgium, December 10, 1822; died at Paris, November 8, 1890)

---

WHAT A characteristic figure is this artist of the nineteenth century, whose profile stands out so boldly from the surroundings in which he lived! An artist of another age, whose work makes one think of that of the great Bach! Franck went through this life as a dreamer, seeing little or nothing of that which passed about him, thinking only of his art, and living only for it. True artists are subject to this kind of hypnotism—the inveterate workers, who find the recompense of their labor in the accomplished fact, and an incomparable joy in the pure and simple toil of each day. They have no need to search for the echo in the crowd.

When Ysaye and Lachaume introduced Franck's violin sonata (in Boston) in 1895; when these and others introduced the magnificent piano quintet in 1898, leading musicians of this city shook wise heads and said with an air of finality: "This will never do." The string quartet was only tolerated, endured because it was produced at a Kneisel concert, and at that time the Kneisels could do no wrong. *The Wild Huntsman,* produced here by Theodore Thomas in 1898, was looked on as the work of an eccentric and theatrical Frenchman.

When Mr. Gericke produced the symphony in 1899, the storm broke loose. There were letters of angry protest. A leading critic characterized the symphony as "dismal." Several subscribers to the concerts called it "immoral" and vowed they would not attend any concert at which music by Franck was to be played.

Nor did Franck fare better for a time in New York. Even the broad-minded James Huneker dismissed him as a sort of Abbé Liszt, now in the heavily scented boudoir, now with self-conscious devotion in the church. Franck in the boudoir! Poor *"Père"* Franck!

And so Franck had to make his way here, as in Paris, misunderstood, abused, regarded by some as an anarchist, by some as a bore. This, men and brethren, should make us all tolerant, even cautious in passing judgment on contemporary composers whose idiom is as yet strange to us. Cocksure opinions are valuable chiefly to the one who expresses them.

Let us hear what is going on in the musical world, even if it is going on noisily and queerly in our ears. It is not enough to say: "I don't like it. Why does —— put such pieces on the programme?" Inherently bad music will soon disappear of itself, unless it is so bad, with such obviously vulgar tunes, that it becomes popular. But music is not necessarily bad because it is of a strange and irregular nature. For audiences to have no curiosity about new works, no spur to hot discussion concerning them, is a sign of stagnation in art. Thus César Franck, a great teacher, teaches us all indirectly a lesson.

## SYMPHONY IN D MINOR

*I. Lento; allegro non troppo*
*II. Allegretto*
*III. Allegro non troppo*

As THE *"Pelléastres"* for a time did Debussy harm, so the "Franckists" injured the reputation of César Franck. They insisted on his aloofness from earthly strife, joy, sorrow, passion. They proclaimed him a mystic, dwelling in the seventh heaven and hearing, if not the celestial choir, at least the music of the spheres. His compositions were of plenary inspiration: not a note could be added; not a note could be taken away.

A reaction was inevitable. Younger composers, escaping his influence, were tired of his alleged perfection. Older composers, envious no doubt of his fame, were wearied by the recital of his private and musical virtues. Was he overestimated soon after his death? For some years it has been the fashion to underestimate him; to speak of "the false mysticism of the old Belgian angel." Too frequent repetitions of his music, even of that masterpiece the violin sonata and of his symphony, were not of benefit to him. (It was as with Tchaikovsky and his *Pathetic* symphony.)

Today it is only just to recognize Franck's eminence among composers. To say that his symphony is flawless is not so easy. We believe that in the first movement the return of the somber introduction, even with a changed tonality, before the full exposition, development and continuance of the main body of the movement, was a mistake. It might reasonably be said that there is in this movement overelaboration, a surplusage of detail, unnecessary repetitions of thematic fragments given in turn to various instruments or choirs of instruments, a favorite device of Tchaikovsky's. There might something be said with regard to diffuseness in the other movements.

This symphony was produced at the Conservatoire, Paris, February 17, 1889. It was composed in 1888 and completed August 22 of that year.

Vincent d'Indy[1] in his Life of Franck gives some particulars about the first performance of the Symphony in D minor. "The performance was quite against the wish of most members of the famous orchestra, and was only pushed through thanks to the benevolent obstinacy of the conductor, Jules Garcin. The subscribers could make neither head nor tail of it, and the musical authorities were much in the same position. I inquired of one of them—a professor at the Conservatoire, and

[1]Vincent d'Indy: *César Franck*, 1906; translated by Rosa Newmarch, 1929.

a kind of factotum on the committee—what he thought of the work. 'That a symphony?' he replied in contemptuous tones. 'But, my dear sir, who ever heard of writing for the English horn in a symphony? Just mention a single symphony by Haydn or Beethoven introducing the English horn. There, well, you see—your Franck's music may be whatever you please, but it will certainly never be a symphony!'" This was the attitude of the Conservatoire in the year of grace 1889.

"At another door of the concert hall, the composer of *Faust,* escorted by a train of adulators, male and female, fulminated a kind of papal decree to the effect that this symphony was the affirmation of incompetence pushed to dogmatic lengths. For sincerity and disinterestedness we must turn to the composer himself, when, on his return from the concert, his whole family surrounded him, asking eagerly for news. 'Well, were you satisfied with the effect on the public? Was there plenty of applause?' To which 'Father Franck,' thinking only of his work, replied with a beaming countenance: 'Oh, it sounded well; just as I thought it would!'"

D'Indy describes Gounod leaving the concert hall of the Conservatoire after the first performance of Franck's symphony, surrounded by incense burners of each sex, and saying particularly that this symphony was "the affirmation of impotence pushed to dogma." Perhaps Gounod made this speech; perhaps he didn't; some of Franck's disciples are too busy in adding to the legend of his martyrdom. D'Indy says little about the structure of this symphony, although he devotes a chapter to Franck's string quartet.

Speaking of Franck's sonata for violin and pianoforte, he calls attention to the fact that the first of its organic germs is used as the theme of the four movements of the work. "From this moment cyclical form, the basis of modern symphonic art, was created and consecrated." He then adds:

"The majestic, plastic, and perfectly beautiful Symphony in D minor is constructed on the same method. I purposely use the word *method* for this reason: After having long described Franck as an empiricist and an improviser—which is radically wrong—his enemies (of whom, in spite of his incomparable goodness, he made many) and his ignorant detractors suddenly changed their views and called him a musical mathematician, who subordinated inspiration and impulse to a conscientious manipulation of form. This, we may observe in passing, is a common reproach brought by the ignorant Philistine against the dreamer and the genius. Yet where can we point to a composer in the second half of the nineteenth century who could—and did—think as loftily as Franck, or who could have found in his fervent and enthusiastic heart such vast ideas as those which lie at the musical basis of the symphony, the quartet, and *The Beatitudes?*

"It frequently happens in the history of art that a breath passing through the creative spirits of the day incites them, without any previous mutual understanding, to create works which are identical in form, if not in significance. It is easy to find examples of this kind of artistic telepathy between painters and writers, but the most striking instances are furnished by the musical art.

"Without going back upon the period we are now considering, the years between 1884 and 1889 are remarkable for a curious return to pure symphonic form. Apart from the younger composers, and one or two unimportant representatives of the old school, three composers who had already made their mark—Lalo, Saint-Saëns, and Franck—produced true symphonies at this time, but widely different as regards external aspects and ideas.

"Lalo's Symphony in G minor, which is on very classical lines, is remarkable for the fascination of its themes, and still more for charm and elegance of rhythm and harmony, distinctive qualities of the imaginative composer of *Le Roi d'Ys*.

"The C minor symphony of Saint-Saëns, displaying undoubted talent, seems like a challenge to the traditional laws of tonal structure; and although the composer sustains the combat with cleverness and eloquence, and in spite of the indisputable interest of the work—founded, like many others by this composer, upon a prose theme, the *Dies Iræ*—yet the final impression is that of doubt and sadness.

"Franck's symphony, on the contrary, is a continual ascent towards pure gladness and life-giving light because its workmanship is solid, and its themes are manifestations of ideal beauty. What is there more joyous, more sanely vital, than the principal subject of the *finale,* around which all the other themes in the work cluster and crystallize? While in the higher registers all is dominated by that motive which M. Ropartz has justly called 'the theme of faith.'"

The symphony is scored for two flutes, two oboes, English horn, two clarinets, bass clarinet, two bassoons, four horns, two trumpets, two cornets, three trombones, bass tuba, tympani, harps, and strings. The score is dedicated to Henri Duparc.

# GEORG FRIDERIC
# HANDEL

(Born at Halle, February 23, 1685;
died at London, April 14, 1759)

---

MR. GEORG FRIDERIC HANDEL," Mr. Runciman once wrote, "is by far the most superb personage one meets, in the history of music. He alone, of all the musicians, lived his life straight through in the grand manner."[1] When Handel wrote *"pomposo"* on a page, he wrote not idly. What magnificent simplicity in outlines! . . . For melodic lines of such chaste and noble beauty, such Olympian authority, no one has approached Handel. "Within that circle none durst walk but he." His nearest rival is the Chevalier Gluck.

And this giant of a man could express a tenderness known only to him and Mozart, for Schubert, with all his melodic wealth and sensitiveness, could fall at times into sentimentalism, and Schumann's intimate confessions were sometimes whispered. Handel in his tenderness was always manly. No one has approached him in his sublimely solemn moments! Few composers, if there is anyone, have been able to produce such pathetic or sublime effects by simple means, by a few chords even. He was one of the greatest melodists. His fugal pages seldom seem labored; they are distingushed by amazing vitality and spontaneity. In his slow movements, his instrumental airs, there is a peculiar dignity, a peculiar serenity, and a direct appeal that we find in no other composer.

Would that we could hear more of Handel's music! At present he is known in this country as the composer of *The Messiah,* the

[1]John F. Runciman: *Old Scores and New Readings,* 1899.

variations entitled *The Harmonious Blacksmith,* and the monstrous perversion of a simple operatic air dignified, forsooth, by the title "*Handel's Largo.*"

## TWELVE CONCERTI GROSSI, FOR STRING ORCHESTRA

| | |
|---|---|
| *No. 1, in G major* | *No. 7, in B flat major* |
| *No. 2, in F major* | *No. 8, in C minor* |
| *No. 3, in E minor* | *No. 9, in F major* |
| *No. 4, in A minor* | *No. 10, in D minor* |
| *No. 5, in D major* | *No. 11, in A major* |
| *No. 6, in G minor* | *No. 12, in B minor* |

HANDEL apparently took a peculiar pride in his Concerti Grossi. He published them himself, and by subscription. They would probably be more popular today if all conductors realized the fact that music in Handel's time was performed with varied and free inflections; that his players undoubtedly employed many means of expression. As German organists of forty years ago insisted that Bach's preludes, fugues, toccatas, should be played with full organ and rigidity of tempo, although those who heard Bach play admired his skill in registration, many conductors find in all of the *allegros* of Handel's concertos only a thunderous speech and allow little change in tempo. In the performance of this old music, old but fresh, the two essential qualities demanded by Handel's music, suppleness of pace and fluidity of expression, named by Volbach, are usually disregarded. Unless there be elasticity in performance, hearers are not to be blamed if they find the music formal, monotonous, dull.

The twelve concertos were composed within three weeks. Kretzschmar has described them as impressionistic pictures, probably without strict reference to the modern use of the word "impressionistic." They are not of equal worth. Romain Rolland[1] finds

[1]Romain Rolland: *Handel,* 1910; translated by A. E. Hull, 1916.

the seventh and three last mediocre. In the tenth he discovers French influences and declares that the last *allegro* might be an air for a music box. Yet the music at its best is aristocratic and noble.

Handel's twelve grand concertos for strings were composed between September 29 and October 30, 1739. The London *Daily Post* of October 29, 1739, said: "This day are published proposals for printing by subscription, with His Majesty's royal license and protection, Twelve Grand Concertos, in Seven Parts, for four violins, a tenor, a violoncello, with a thorough-bass for the harpsichord. Composed by Mr. Handel. Price to subscribers, two guineas. Ready to be delivered by April next. Subscriptions are taken by the author, at his house in Brook Street, Hanover Square, and by Walsh." In an advertisement on November 22 the publisher added, "Two of the above concertos will be performed this evening at the Theatre Royal, Lincoln's Inn." The concertos were published on April 21, 1740. In an advertisement a few days afterwards Walsh said, "These concertos were performed at the Theatre Royal in Lincoln's Inn Fields, and now are played in most public places with the greatest applause." Victor Schoelcher made this comment in his *Life of Handel:* "This was the case with all the works of Handel. They were so frequently performed at contemporaneous concerts and benefits that they seem, during his lifetime, to have quite become public property. Moreover, he did nothing which the other theaters did not attempt to imitate. In the little theater of the Haymarket, evening entertainments were given in exact imitation of his 'several concertos for different instruments, with a variety of chosen airs of the best master, and the famous *Salve Regina* of Hasse.' The handbills issued by the nobles at the King's Theatre make mention also of 'several concertos for different instruments.' "[2]

The year 1739, in which these concertos were composed, was the year of the first performance of Handel's *Saul* (January 16) and *Israel in Egypt* (April 4)—both oratorios were composed in 1738—also of the music to Dryden's *Ode for St. Cecilia's Day* (November 22).

Romain Rolland, discussing the form *concerto grosso,* which consists essentially of a dialogue between a group of soloists, the *concertino*

[2]Victor Schoelcher: *The Life of Handel,* 1857.

(trio of two solo violins and solo bass with cembalo) and the chorus of instruments, *concerto grosso,* believes that Handel at Rome in 1708 was struck by Corelli's works in this field, for several of his concertos of Opus 3 are dated 1710, 1716, 1722. Geminiani introduced the concerto into England—three volumes appeared in 1732, 1735, 1748—and he was a friend of Handel.

It is stated that the word "concerto," as applied to a piece for a solo instrument with accompaniment, first appeared in a treatise by Scipio Bargaglia (Venice, 1587); that Giuseppe Torelli, who died in 1708, was the first to suggest a larger number of instruments in a concerto, and to give the name *concerto grosso* to this species of composition. But Michelletti, seventeen years before, had published his *Sinfonie e concerti a quatro,* and in 1698 his *Concerti musicali,* while the word "concerto" occurs frequently in the musical terminology of the seventeenth century. It was Torelli who, determining the form of the grand solo for violin, opened the way to Archangelo Corelli, the father of modern violinists, composers, or virtuosos.

Romain Rolland insisted that the instrumental music of Handel has the nature of a constant improvisation, music to be served piping hot to an audience, and should preserve this character in performance. "When you have studied with minute care each detail, obtained from your orchestra an irreproachable precision, tonal purity, and finish, you will have done nothing unless you have made the face of the improvising genius rise from the work."

## FRANZ JOSEF
# HAYDN

(Born at Rohrau, Lower Austria, March 31, 1732; died at Vienna, May 31, 1809)

---

HAYDN HAS BEEN sadly misunderstood by present followers of tradition who have spoken of him as a man of the old school, while Mozart was a forerunner of Beethoven. Thus they erred. Mozart summed up the school of his day and wrote imperishable music. There has been only one Mozart, and there is no probability of another being born for generations to come; but Haydn was often nearer in spirit to the young Beethoven. It is customary to speak lightly of Haydn as an honest Austrian who wrote light-hearted *allegros,* also minuets by which one is not reminded of a court with noble dames smiling graciously on gallant cavaliers, but sees peasants thumping the ground with heavy feet and uttering joyful cries.

It is said carelessly that Haydn was a simple fellow who wrote at ease many symphonies and quartets that, to quote Berlioz, recall "the innocent joys of the fireside and the *pot-au-feu.*" But Haydn was shrewd and observing—read his diary, kept in London—and if he was plagued with a shrewish wife he found favor with other women. Dear Mrs. Schroeter of London received letters from him breathing love, not manly complimentary affection. And it is said of Haydn that he was only sportive in his music, having a fondness for the bassoon. But Haydn could express tenderness, regret, sorrow in his music.

FRANZ JOSEF HAYDN

# LONDON SYMPHONIES

## SYMPHONY NO. 104, IN D MAJOR (B. & H. NO. 2)

*I. Adagio; allegro*
*II. Andante*
*III. Menuetto; trio*
*IV. Allegro spiritoso*

HAYDN'S SYMPHONY is ever fresh, spontaneous, yet contrapuntally worked in a masterly manner. What a skillful employment of little themes in themselves of slight significance save for their Blakelike innocence and gayety! Yet in the introduction there is a deeper note, for, contrary to current and easy belief, Haydn's music is not all beer, skittles, and dancing. There are even gloomy pages in some of his quartets; tragic pages in his *Seven Last Words,* and the prelude to *The Creation,* depicting chaos, is singularly contemporaneous.

Haydn composed twelve symphonies in England for Salomon. His name began to be mentioned in England in 1765. Symphonies by him were played in concerts given by J. C. Bach, Abel, and others in the 'seventies. Lord Abingdon tried in 1783 to persuade Haydn to take the direction of the Professional Concerts which had just been founded. Gallini asked him his terms for an opera. Salomon, violinist, conductor, manager, sent a music publisher, one Bland—an auspicious name—to coax him to London, but Haydn was loath to leave Prince Esterhazy. Prince Nicolaus died in 1790, and his successor, Prince Anton, who did not care for music, dismissed the orchestra at Esterház and kept only a brass band; but he added 400 gulden to the annual pension of 1,000 gulden bequeathed to Haydn by Prince Nicolaus. Haydn then made Vienna his home. And one day, when he was at work in his house, the "Hamberger" house in which Beethoven also once lived, a man appeared, and said: "I am Salomon from London, and come to fetch you with me. We will agree on the job tomorrow." Haydn was intensely amused by the use of the word "job." The contract for one season was as follows: Haydn should receive three hundred pounds for an opera written for the manager Gallini, £300 for six symphonies and £200 for the copyright, £200 for twenty new compositions to be produced in as many concerts under Haydn's direction, £200 as guarantee for a benefit concert, Salomon deposited 5,000 gulden with the bankers, Fries & Company, as a pledge of good faith. Haydn had 500 gulden ready for traveling expenses, and he borrowed 450 more from his prince. Haydn agreed to conduct the symphonies at the piano.

Salomon about 1786 began to give concerts as a manager, in addition to fiddling at concerts of others. He had established a series of subscription concerts at the Hanover Square Rooms, London. He thought of Hadyn as a great drawing card. The violinist W. Cramer, associated with the Professional Concerts, had also approached Haydn, who would not leave his prince. The news of Prince Esterhazy's death reached Salomon, who then happened to be at Bonn. He therefore hastened to Vienna.

The first of the Salomon-Haydn concerts was given March 11, 1791, at the Hanover Square Rooms. Haydn, as was the custom, "presided at the harpsichord"; Salomon stood as leader of the orchestra. The symphony was in D major, No. 2, of the London list of twelve. The *adagio* was repeated, an unusual occurrence, but the critics preferred the first movement.

The orchestra was thus composed: twelve to sixteen violins, four violas, three violoncellos, four double basses, flute, oboe, bassoon, horns, trumpets, drums—in all about forty players.

Haydn and Salomon left Vienna on December 15, 1790, and arrived at Calais by way of Munich and Bonn. They crossed the English Channel on New Year's Day, 1791. From Dover they traveled to London by stage. The journey from Vienna took them seventeen days. Haydn was received with great honor.

Haydn left London towards the end of June, 1792. Salomon invited him again to write six new symphonies. Haydn arrived in London, February 4, 1794, and did not leave England until August 15, 1795. The orchestra at the opera concerts in the grand new concert hall of the King's Theatre was made up of sixty players. Haydn's engagement was again a profitable one. He made by concerts, lessons, symphonies, etc.,

£1,200. He was honored in many ways by the King, the Queen, and the nobility. He was twenty-six times at Carlton House, where the Prince of Wales had a concert room; and, after he had waited long for his pay, he sent a bill from Vienna for 100 guineas, which Parliament promptly settled.

# LONDON SYMPHONIES

## SYMPHONY NO. 94, IN G MAJOR, "SURPRISE" (B. & H. NO. 6)

*I. Adagio cantabile e vivace assai*
*II. Andante*
*III. Menuetto*
*IV. Allegro di molto*

THIS SYMPHONY, known as the *"Surprise,"* and in Germany as the symphony "with the drumstroke," is the third of the twelve Salomon symphonies as arranged in the order of their appearance in the catalogue of the Philharmonic Society (London).

Composed in 1791, this symphony was performed for the first time on March 23, 1792, at the sixth Salomon concert in London. It pleased immediately and greatly. *The Oracle* characterized the second movement as one of Haydn's happiest inventions, and likened the "surprise" —which is occasioned by the sudden orchestral crash in the *andante*— to a shepherdess, lulled by the sound of a distant waterfall, awakened suddenly from sleep and frightened by the unexpected discharge of a musket.

Griesinger in his Life of Haydn (1810) contradicts the story that Haydn introduced these crashes to arouse the Englishwomen from sleep. Haydn also contradicted it; he said it was his intention only to surprise the audience by something new. "The first *allegro* of my symphony was received with countless 'Bravos,' but enthusiasm rose to its highest pitch after the *andante* with the drumstroke. *'Ancora! ancora!'* was cried out on all sides, and Pleyel himself complimented me on my idea." On the other hand, Gyrowetz, in his Autobiography, page 59 (1848), said that he visited Haydn just after he had composed the *andante,* and Haydn was so pleased with it that he played it to him on the piano, and sure of his success, said with a roguish laugh: "The women will cry out here!" C. F. Pohl[1] added a footnote, when he quoted this account of Gyrowetz, and called attention to Haydn's humorous borrowing of a musical thought of Martini to embellish his setting of music to the commandment, "Thou shalt not steal," when he had occasion to put music to the Ten Commandments. The *Surprise* symphony was long known in London as "the favorite grand overture."

# PARIS SYMPHONIES

## SYMPHONY NO. 88, IN G MAJOR (B. & H. NO. 13)

*I. Adagio; allegro*
*II. Largo*
*III. Menuetto; trio*
*IV. Finale: allegro con spirito*

THE PARISIAN ORCHESTRA, which Haydn undoubtedly had in mind, was a large one—forty violins, twelve violoncellos, eight double basses—so that the composer could be sure of strong contrasts in performance by the string section. Fortunate composer—whose symphonies one can, sitting back, enjoy without inquiring into psychological intention or noting attempts at realism in musical seascapes and landscapes—music not inspired by book or picture—just music; now pompous, now merry, and in more serious moments, never too sad, but with a constant feeling for tonal grace and beauty.

Haydn wrote a set of six symphonies for a society in Paris known as the *Concert de la loge olympique.* They were ordered in 1784, when Haydn was living at Esterház. Composed in the course of the years 1784–89, they are in C, G minor, E flat, B flat, D, A. No. 1, in C, has

[1] C. F. Pohl: *Josef Haydn,* 1875, 1882.

been entitled the "*Bear*"; No. 2, in G minor, has been entitled the "*Hen*"; and No. 4, in B flat, is known as the "*Queen of France*." This symphony is the first of a second set, of which five were composed in 1787, 1788, 1790. If the sixth was written, it cannot now be identified. This one in G major was written in 1787, and is numbered 88 in the full and chronological listing of Mandyczewski (given in Grove's Dictionary).

I. The first movement opens with a short, slow introduction, *adagio,* G major, 3–4 which consists for the most part of strong *staccato* chords which alternate with softer passages. The main body of the movement *allegro,* G major, begins with the first theme, a dainty one, announced *piano* by the strings without double basses and repeated *forte* by the full orchestra with a new counter figure in the bass. A subsidiary theme is but little more than a melodic variation of the first. So, too, the short conclusion theme—in oboes and bassoon, then in the strings—is only a variation of the first. The free fantasia is long for the period and is contrapuntally elaborate. There is a short *coda* on the first theme.

II. *Largo,* D major, 3–4. A serious melody is sung by oboe and violoncellos to an accompaniment of violas, double basses, bassoon, and horn. The theme is repeated with a richer accompaniment; while the first violins have a counter figure. After a transitional passage the theme is repeated by a fuller orchestra, with the melody in first violins and flute, then in the oboe and violoncello. The development is carried along on the same lines. There is a very short *coda.*

III. The *Menuetto, allegretto,* G major, 3–4, with trio, is in the regular minuet form in its simplest manner.

IV. The *finale, allegro con spirito,* G major, 2–4, is a *rondo* on the theme of a peasant country dance, and it is fully developed. Haydn in his earlier symphonies adopted for the *finale* the form of his first movement. Later he preferred the *rondo* form, with its couplets and refrains, or repetitions of a short and frank chief theme. "In some *finales* of his last symphonies," says Brenet,[2] "he gave freer reins to his fancy, and modified with greater independence the form of his first *allegros;* but his fancy, always prudent and moderate, is more like the clear, precise arguments of a great orator than the headlong inspiration of a poet. Moderation is one of the characteristics of Haydn's genius; moderation in the dimensions, in the sonority, in the melodic

[2]Michel Brenet (Marie Bobillier): *Haydn,* 1909; English translation, 1926.

shape; the liveliness of his melodic thought never seems extravagant, its melancholy never induces sadness."

The usual orchestration of Haydn's symphonies (including those listed above) consisted of one (or two) flutes, two oboes, two bassoons, two horns, two trumpets, kettledrums, and strings. In his last years (from 1791) he followed Mozart's lead in introducing two clarinets. The clarinets accordingly appear in the London symphony in D major, described in this chapter.—EDITOR.

# PAUL
# HINDEMITH

(Born at Hanau, on November 16, 1895)

---

## "KONZERTMUSIK" FOR STRING AND BRASS INSTRUMENTS

There was a time in Germany when Hindemith was regarded as the white-haired boy; the hope for the glorious future; greater even than Schönberg. In England, they look on Hindemith coolly—an able and fair-minded critic there has remarked: "The more one hears of the later Hindemith, the more exasperating his work becomes. From time to time some little theme is shown at first in sympathetic fashion, then submitted to the most mechanical processes known to music. Any pleasant jingle seems to mesmerize the composer, who repeats it much as Bruckner repeats his themes —Hindemith abuses the liberty shown to a modern."

But Hindemith is not always mesmerized by a pleasant jingle. Witness his oratorio, performed with great success. The title is forbidding, *The Unending,* but the performance takes only two hours. The *Concert Music,* composed for the fiftieth anniversary of the Boston Symphony Orchestra, is more than interesting. It cannot be called "noble," not even "grand," but it holds the attention by its strength in structure, its spirit, festal without blatancy. For once there is no too evident desire to stun the hearer. It is as if the composer had written for his own pleasure. It is virile music with relieving passages—few in number—that have genuine and simple beauty of thought and expression; exciting at times by the rushing rhythm.

Hindemith, at the age of eleven, played the viola in the theater and in the moving-picture house; when he was thirteen, he was a viola virtuoso, and he now plays in public his own concertos for that instrument. When he was twenty, he was first concert master of the Frankfort opera house. His teachers in composition were Arnold Mendelssohn and Bernhard Sekles at the Hoch Conservatory in Frankfort. He is the viola player in the Amar Quartet (Licco Amar, Walter Casper, Paul Hindemith, and Maurits Frank—in 1926 his brother Rudolf was the violoncellist).

Apropos of a performance of one of his works, in Berlin, the late Adolf Weissmann wrote in a letter to the *Christian Science Monitor:* "Promising indeed among the young German composers is Paul Hindemith. More than promising he is not yet. For the viola player Paul Hindemith, travelling with the Amar Quartet through half Europe, has seldom time enough to work carefully. The greater part of his compositions were created in the railway car. Is it, therefore, to be wondered at that their principal virtue lies in their rhythm? The rhythm of the rolling car is, apparently, blended with the rhythm springing from within. It is always threatening to outrun all the other values of what he writes. For that these values exist cannot be denied."

A foreign correspondent of the London *Daily Telegraph,* having heard one of his compositions, wrote: "It was all rather an exhilarating nightmare, as if Hindemith had been attempting to prove the theorem of Pythagoras in terms of parallelograms, which is amusing, but utterly absurd."

It has been said by A. Machabey that Hindemith has been influenced in turn by Wagner, Brahms—"an influence still felt"; Richard Strauss; Max Reger, who attracted him by his ingenuity and freedom from elementary technic; Stravinsky, who made himself felt after the war; and finally by the theatrical surroundings in which he lives. "He is opposed to post-romanticism. Not being able to escape from romanticism in his youth, today he seems to be completely stripped of it. Freed from the despotism of a text, from the preëstablished plan of programme music, from obedience to the caprices and emphasis of sentiment, music in itself suffices. . . . The reaction against romanticism is doubled by a democratic spirit which was general in Germany after the war." Therefore he has had many supporters, who welcomed, "besides this new spirit, an unexpected technic, unusual polyphony and instrumentation, in which one found a profound synthesis of primordial rhythms, tonalities enriched and extended by Schönberg and Hauer, economical and rational groupings of jazz." Then his compositions are so varied: chamber music for the ultra-fastidious; melodies for amateurs; dramatic works for opera-goers; orchestral pieces for frequenters of concerts; he has written for débutantes and children; for the cinema, marionettes, mechanical pianos, brass bands. Work has followed work with an amazing rapidity.

## ARTHUR
# HONEGGER

(Born at Havre, France, on March 10, 1892)

---

## "PACIFIC 231," ORCHESTRAL MOVEMENT

SOME SAY that Honegger had no business to summon a locomotive engine for inspiration. No doubt this music of Honegger's is "clever," but cleverness in music quickly palls. Louis Antoine Jullien years ago in this country excited wild enthusiasm by his *Firemen's Quadrille,* in which a conflagration, the bells, the rush of the firemen, the squirting and the shout of the foreman, "Wash her, Thirteen!" were graphically portrayed.

But there is majestic poetry in great machines, even in railway engines. One of Turner's most striking pictures is the one depicting a hare running madly across a viaduct with a pursuing locomotive in rain and mist. What was the most poetic thing of the Philadelphia exposition of 1876? The superb Corliss engine, epic in strength and grandeur. Walt Whitman, Kipling, and others have found inspiration in a locomotive; why reproach a composer for attempting to express "the visual impression and the physical sensation" of it? One may like or dislike *Pacific 231,* but it is something more than a musical joke; it was not merely devised for sensational effect.

When *Pacific 231* was first performed in Paris at Koussevitzky's concerts, May 8 and 15, 1924, Honegger made this commentary:

"I have always had a passionate love for locomotives. To me they

—and I love them passionately as others are passionate in their love for horses or women—are like living creatures.

"What I wanted to express in the *Pacific* is not the noise of an engine, but the visual impression and the physical sensation of it. These I strove to express by means of a musical composition. Its point of departure is an objective contemplation: quiet respiration of an engine in state of immobility; effort for moving; progressive increase of speed, in order to pass from the 'lyric' to the pathetic state of an engine of three hundred tons driven in the night at a speed of one hundred and twenty per hour.

"As a subject I have taken an engine of the 'Pacific' type, known as '231,' an engine for heavy trains of high speed."

Other locomotive engines are classified as "Atlantic," "Mogul." The number 231 here refers to the number of the "Pacific's" wheels 2—3—1.

"On a sort of rhythmic pedal sustained by the violins is built the impressive image of an intelligent monster, a joyous giant."

*Pacific 231* is scored for piccolo, two flutes, two oboes, English horn, two clarinets, bass clarinet, two bassoons, double bassoon, four horns, three trumpets, three trombones, bass tuba, snare drum, bass drum, cymbals, tam-tam, strings.

The locomotive engine has been the theme of strange tales by Dickens, Marcel Schwob, Kipling, and of Zola's novel, *La Bête humaine*. It is the hero of Abel Gance's film, *Roué* for which it is said Honegger adapted music, and the American film, *The Iron Horse*.

## PAUL MARIE THÉODORE
# VINCENT D'INDY

(Born at Paris, March 27, 1852;[1] died at Paris on December 2, 1931)

---

VINCENT D'INDY's music has often been charged with the atrocious crimes of austerity and aloofness; it has been called cerebral. It is true that d'Indy uses his head, not loses it, in composition; that his music will never be popular with the multitude; it lacks an obvious appeal to those who say, with an air of finality: "I know what I like." It is not sugary; it is not theatrical. To say that it is cold is to say that it is not effusive. D'Indy does not gush. Nor does he permit himself to run with a mighty stir and din to a blatant climax, dearly loved by those who think that noise shows strength. He respects his art and himself, and does not trim his sails to catch the breeze of popular favor. There is a nobility in his music; there is to those who do not wear their heart on their sleeve true warmth. There is a soaring of the spirit, not a drooping to court favor. And no one has ever questioned his constructive skill.

## SYMPHONY NO. 2, IN B FLAT MAJOR, OP. 57

*I. Extrêmement lent; très vif*
*II. Modérément lent*
*III. Modéré; très animé*
*IV. Introduction, fugue et finale*

THE MAJORITY of the pages in d'Indy's symphony contain music lofty and noble. Only the *finale* sinks below the prevailing high

[1]This year was given by the composer. The Catalogue of the Paris Conservatory gives 1851, the year also given by Adolphe Jullien.—P. H.

level, and there are fine moments in the introduction to this *finale*. It is natural that the influence of César Franck is shown especially in the two middle movements. So great was d'Indy's devotion to his master that he proudly admitted the influence; but d'Indy was no mere copyist; the greatest pages of the symphony are his own.

The Symphony in B flat major, composed in 1903–04, was produced at a Lamoureux concert, Paris, February 28, 1904. The score is dedicated to Paul Dukas. The symphony is scored for three flutes (and piccolo), two oboes, English horn, two clarinets, bass clarinet, three bassoons, four horns, small trumpet in E flat, two trumpets in C, three trombones, bass trombone, chromatic kettledrums, bass drum, cymbals, triangle, two harps, strings.

This symphony is without a programme of any sort. D'Indy wrote in an article published in the first number of *Musica* (Paris): "Symphonic music, unlike dramatic music, is developing toward complexity: the dramatic element is more and more introduced into absolute music, in such a way that form is here, as a rule, absolutely submissive to the incidents of a veritable action." Mr. Calvocoressi supplies a note to this remark: "To search for an action that is not purely musical in absolute music would be madness. There is, indeed, an action in this symphony, but it is wholly in the music: the putting into play of two principal themes, which present themselves at the beginning side by side, follow each other, war against each other, or, on the contrary, are each developed separately, associate with themselves new ideas which complete or serve as commentary, and at the end of the work are blended in an immense triumphal chant."[1] It would be idle, then, to attempt to characterize these themes as though they were dramatic motives. One can say, however, that two decided elements of musical expression are strongly opposed to each other.

The first movement is made up of two distinct parts: a slow introduction, in which the themes appear at first in the state of simple cells, and a lively movement.

I. *Extrêmement lent. Très vif.* B flat major, 4–2. Violoncellos and double basses, doubled by harps, announce an initial and somber theme

[1]*Le Guide musical,* May, 1904.

of almost sluggish rhythm. The flute replies with a phrase whose chief characteristic is an ascending leap of a seventh, a progression dear to the composer. This phrase is the second principal theme of the symphony. The phrase may be resolved in this instance into two distinct elements: the descending fourth—B flat to F sharp—which, with its own peculiar rhythm, is a cell that later on will assume great importance; the ascending seventh, which will play a dominating part and appear again throughout the work as a song of despair, a burst of the determined will. The second theme may then be considered as a sort of embryonic form which contains the chief elements of the symphony. The initial theme, on the contrary, will almost always keep a closer resemblance to itself; there will be numberless changes, melodic or rhythmic transformations, but its particular physiognomy will not be lost.

A *tutti* of some measures leads by a rapid *crescendo* to the main body, *très vif,* 3–4. A horn, accompanied by second violins and violas, announces a new theme, which belongs exclusively to this movement. The first two notes of this motive are the descending fourth, the first cell of the second chief theme. The second section of the new theme furnishes material for an abrupt and jerky figure, given soon afterwards to the wood-wind.

II. *Modérément lent.* D flat major, 6–4. The second movement begins with an announcement by the first violins of the second principal theme (descending fourth). The bass clarinet sings the rest of the motive, which is taken up by the strings. These first measures prepare the reëntrance of the same theme under a form (6–4) already used in the first movement. A new figure appears, which will be found in the *finale.* The development brings a modulation to E major, and harps give out a strongly rhythmed motive in that tonality. This motive will be employed in the *scherzo.* The dotted, characteristic rhythm is now kept up, while the oboe, then the clarinet, and also other instruments, sing in turn an expressive theme; on the conclusion of it is the first new theme of this movement, which in turn is a prolongation of the theme (6–4) of the first movement.

III. *Modéré,* D minor, 2–4. A solo viola chants a theme of archaic character, which reminds one of some old legend's air. The flute hints at the strongly rhythmed theme of the preceding movement, but the archaic tune is developed and interrupted suddenly by the horns proclaiming the initial theme, sadly changed and of greatly diminished importance. There is a fantastic whirlwind in the strings, and above it a bold theme is given out by the wood-wind. The strongly rhythmed theme appears almost immediately afterwards, and is added to the whirling triplets. There is a comparative lull, and the bold theme is now given out at length by the small trumpet, after which there is an orchestral explosion. Then the archaic tune appears, rhythmed curiously in 3–8, "after the manner of a pantomimic dance," and played by flutes and then bassoons; harp harmonics and the triangle give additional color to this episode.

IV. *Introduction, fugue, et finale.* The general form of this last movement is that of a rondo preceded by an introduction in two parts (introduction and fugue). In the introduction to the fugue all the chief thematic ideas of the preceding movements are recalled one by one, either by solo instruments or by groups of instruments.

The subject of the fugue is the expressive theme first sung by the oboe in the second movement, but now the theme is lengthened by an ascending arabesque. The final association of the two themes, already hinted at the beginning of the second movement by the appearance of a figure common to them both, is now frankly declared. This subject, persisting to the end of the fugue, brings in a lively movement, 5–4, the true *finale.* The oboe sings the first new theme of the second movement. The instrumental complications become more elaborate. The strongly rhythmed theme presents itself, and then a brand-new motive appears, interrupted by echoes of the archaic melody. This new theme prepares the return of the initial motive, which strengthens itself in canon form. The fugue subject creeps about the whole orchestra, while a more aggressive form of the often used theme of the second movement soars above. The brand-new theme returns, and once more ushers in the initial theme in the bass, while the second chief or cyclic theme is announced above. This is the final struggle of the two. The fugue subject soon reappears, and leads to a brilliant burst of the whole orchestra. The second chief or cyclic theme is then used as a broadly proportioned chorale, whose bass is the initial theme, now subdued and definitely associated with the triumph of the second theme. This triumph is thrice proclaimed in the peroration, and, between the proclamations, the archaic theme, with its characteristic initial fifth, is heard in the wood-wind.

## SYMPHONIC VARIATIONS, "ISTAR," OP. 42

*Istar,* the *Symphony on a Mountain Air,* and *A Summer Day on the Mountain* were composed in the period of d'Indy's life when he was concerned chiefly with making music, and not telling young composers how it should be made. Those three compositions, with the Symphony in B flat major, will represent him honorably in the years to come. One should not underrate his work as a teacher, his high ideals. His technic did not leave him in his later works, but his brain was more in evidence than any source of emotion. Maurice Boucher, speaking of Debussy being drawn instinctively toward the French poets contemporaneous with him (the poems of Rossetti and the dramas of Maeterlinck also attracted him) said that d'Indy "by his temperament was borne toward doctrinal discussions." In *Istar,* though his technical skill is brilliantly in evidence, there is pure music from the beginning to the end. It is true that the withholding of the theme in its full glory to the end might be called a "stunt," as Ravel's *Bolero* is a stunt, but d'Indy's is the legitimate, inevitable crowning of the work; Ravel's was designed chiefly to create curiosity with a final surprise, and the *Bolero* once known does not bear repeated hearings, for the effect, once known, is afterward discounted if not wholly lost.

This composition was first brought out in Brussels, and led by Eugène Ysaye, on January 10, 1897; it was performed in Chicago and led by Theodore Thomas on April 23, 1898. The variations—the work is practically a symphonic poem—are scored for piccolo, two flutes, two oboes, English horn, two clarinets and bass clarinet, three bassoons, four horns, three trumpets, three trombones, bass tuba, kettledrums, cymbals, triangle, two harps, and strings. They are dedicated to the Orchestral Society of the Ysaye Concerts.

William Foster Apthorp translated the verses on the title-page as follows:

*Toward the immutable land Istar, daughter of Sin, bent her steps, toward the abode of the dead, toward the seven-gated abode where He entered, toward the abode whence there is no return.*

. . . . . . . . . . . . . . . . . . .

*At the first gate, the warder stripped her; he took the high tiara from her head.*

*At the second gate, the warder stripped her; he took the pendants from her ears.*

*At the third gate, the warder stripped her; he took off the precious stones that adorn her neck.*

*At the fourth gate, the warder stripped her; he took off the jewels that adorn her breast.*

*At the fifth gate, the warder stripped her; he took off the girdle that encompasses her waist.*

*At the sixth gate, the warder stripped her; he took the rings from her feet, the rings from her hands.*

*At the seventh gate, the warder stripped her; he took off the last veil that covers her body.*

. . . . . . . . . . . . . . . . . . .

*Istar daughter of Sin went into the immutable land, she took and received the Waters of Life. She gave the sublime Waters, and thus, in the presence of all, delivered the Son of Life, her young lover.*

The variations begin *très lent,* F minor, 4–4, with a somber motive (first horn). The violas and clarinets, accompanied by wood-wind instruments in syncopated rhythm, answer with a second motive, and there is a modulation to F major. The variations, as Mr. Apthorp says, have one wholly original peculiarity: "The theme is not given out simply at the beginning, neither is it heard in its entirety until the last variation, in which it is sung by various groups of instruments in unison and octaves, and worked up later in full harmony. Each one of the variations represents one of the seven stages of Istar's being disrobed at the gates of the 'immutable land,' until in the last she stands forth in the full splendor of nudity. The composition is so free as to resent technical analysis; but by following the poem, and noting the garment or ornament taken off, the listener can appreciate the composer's poetic or picturesque suggestiveness in his music."

M. Lambinet, a professor at a Bordeaux public school, chose in 1905 the text "Pro Musica" for his prize-day speech. He told the boys that the first thing the study of music would teach them would be logic. "In symphonic development logic plays as great a part as sentiment. The theme is a species of axiom, full of musical truth, whence proceed deductions. The musician deals with sounds as the geometrician with lines and the dialectician with arguments." The master went on to remark: "A great modern composer, M. Vincent d'Indy, has reversed the customary process in his symphonic poem *Istar*. He by degrees unfolds from initial complexity the simple idea which was wrapped up therein, and appears only at the close, like Isis unveiled, like a scientific law discovered and formulated." The speaker found this happy definition for such a musical work—"an inductive symphony."

# FRANZ
# LISZT

(Born at Raiding, near Oedenburg, Hungary, October 22, 1811; died at Bayreuth, July 31, 1886)

---

LISZT SUFFERED as a composer from foolish adulation and still more absurd denunciation. It was not so many years ago that otherwise fair-minded musicians, professors in conservatories, composers of smug, respectable music, pianists and violinists of nimble fingers and lukewarm blood, would leave the concert hall with an air whenever one of Liszt's works was about to be performed. Liszt also suffered from admiring friends who helped themselves to his musical thoughts, to his new forms of musical expression, and using them for their own advantage, were applauded by the crowd, while Liszt himself was ignored or flouted. How much of Liszt there is in Richard Wagner's best!

Programme music has existed from the early days of the art. No doubt David's performance before Saul had some definite programme; but the symphonic poem as it is now known was invented and shaped by Liszt, and he has influenced in this respect composers of every nation. The modern Russians all hark back to Berlioz and Liszt. The more recent Germans and even the modern French were made possible by this Hungarian, who, in Paris, Weimar, or Rome, was first of all a citizen of the world. In the mass of his compositions there is mysticism that is vague and insignificant; there is affected simplicity that is as childish prattle; there is pathos that is bathos; eloquence sometimes degenerates into bombast; there is frequently the odor of tanbark, the vision of the ringmaster cracking his whip and the man in tights and spangles leaping through paper hoops or kissing his hand from the trapeze. Liszt was first famous as a virtuoso, and as Edward MacDowell once said, in every virtuoso there is the possibility of the rope dancer; it is in his blood.

The faults of Liszt as a composer are open to everyone. When they lie in the music for the piano they have been too often exaggerated by the "Liszt pupil." Nor have orchestral conductors always been fortunate in the interpretation of the greater works; they have been intoxicated by the pomp or fury and were unable to draw the line between sonority and vulgarity.

We are inclined to judge a master of years gone by as though he were a contemporary, and forgetting that he in his day was a daring innovator, a revolutionary, we cry out against his music as trite and moribund. Certain forms of Liszt's expression, forms that recall the reign of Rossini or Meyerbeer, are now distasteful to us, as are certain formulas of Wagner. Excessive modernity contains the seeds of early death. But the architecture that Liszt devised is still strong and beautiful, and is today a model for others who delight in strange ornamentation. The world of music owes Liszt a debt that it will be long in paying, and, as other debtors, it often forgets what it owes and abuses the creditor.

The years go by and the generosity, the loving-kindness, the nobility of Liszt, the man, are more and more clearly revealed. His purse, advice, assistance were ever ready. He would not cringe or flatter. His art was a religion. He was one of the very few composers that stood at ease in the presence of the mighty and were not snobbish toward the unfortunate, the misunderstood, the unappreciated. As a man in the world of his art he is therefore to be ranked with Handel and Hector Berlioz.

## FRANZ LISZT

# A "FAUST" SYMPHONY IN THREE CHARACTER PICTURES (AFTER GOETHE)

*I. Faust*
*II. Gretchen*
*III. Mephistopheles*

PERHAPS in the first movement there are a few passages that might be cut out or condensed, but no one would wish the movement "Gretchen" to be changed in any way; of all the music that is associated with the innocent maiden of Goethe's poem, this is surely the most expressive, the most beautiful. The remorseful, crazed Gretchen is not in Liszt's picture. We find her in the prison music of Boïto. And how paltry does the music of Mephistopheles conceived by Gounod seem in comparison with the ironical fiend of Liszt, mocking the doubts and the aspirations of the disillusionized philosopher!

Liszt told his biographer, Lina Ramann,[1] that the idea of this symphony came to him in Paris in the 'forties, and was suggested by Berlioz's *Damnation of Faust.* (Berlioz's work was produced at the Opéra-Comique, December 6, 1846.) Lina Ramann's biography is eminently unsatisfactory, and in some respects untrustworthy, but there is no reason to doubt her word in this instance. Some have said that Liszt was inspired by Ary Scheffer's pictures to illustrate Goethe's *Faust.* Peter Cornelius stated that Liszt was incited to his work by seeing the pictures "in which Scheffer had succeeded in giving a bodily form to the three leading characters in Goethe's poem." As a matter of fact, we believe, Scheffer did not portray Mephistopheles. Scheffer (1795–1858) was a warm friend of Liszt, and made a portrait of him in 1837, which is in the Liszt Museum at Weimar.

But Liszt made in the 'forties no sketches of his symphony. The

[1]Lina Ramann: *Franz Liszt als Kunstler und Mensch,* 1880; translated by E. Cowdrey, 1882.

music was composed in 1853–54; it was revised in 1857, when the final chorus was added. The *Faust* symphony is scored for three flutes (and piccolo), two oboes, two clarinets, two bassoons, four horns, three trumpets, three trombones, bass tuba, kettledrums, cymbals, triangle, harp, strings, and male chorus with tenor solo. In the revised and unpublished version the bass clarinet is used, but only for a few measures.

Miss Ramann admits frankly that the symphony is, without the final chorus, merely a series of musical "Faust pictures," as the pictures by Kaulbach, Kreling, and others, are in art; but without the chorus it does not reproduce the lyrical contents of the main idea of the poem itself.

I. "Faust." Some find in this movement five leading motives, each one of which portrays a characteristic of Faust or one of his fixed moods. The more conservative speak of first and second themes, subsidiary themes, and conclusion themes. However the motives are ticketed or numbered, they appear later in various metamorphoses.

The movement begins with a long introduction, *lento assai,* 4–4. "A chain of dissonances," with free use of augmented fifths (muted violas and violoncellos), has been described as the "Inquiry" theme, and the bold greater seventh (oboe) is also supposed to portray Faust, the disappointed philosopher. "These motives have here the expression of perplexed musing and painful regret at the vanity of the efforts made for the realization of cherished aspirations."

An *allegro impetuoso,* 4–4. Violins attack, and, after the interruption of reeds and horns, rush along and are joined by wind instruments. The "Inquiry" motive is sounded. The music grows more and more intense. A bassoon, *lento assai,* gives out the "Faust" motive and introduces the main body of the movement:

*Allegro agitato ed appassionato assai,* C minor, 4–4. The first theme, a violently agitated motive, is of kin in character to a leading theme of the composer's symphonic poem, *Prometheus,* which was composed in 1850 and revised in 1855. This theme comes here for the first time, except for one figure, a rising inflection at the end of the first phrase, which has been heard in the introduction. It is developed at length, and is repeated in a changed form by the whole orchestra. A new theme enters in passionate appeal (oboes and clarinets in dialogue with bassoons, violoncellos, and double basses), while the first violins bring back the sixteenth note figure of the first theme of the main section.

This second theme with subsidiary passage-work leads to an episode, *meno mosso, misterioso e molto tranquillo,* 6–4. The "Inquiry" theme in the introduction is developed in modulating sequence by clarinet and some of the strings, while there are sustained harmonies in wind instruments and ascending passages in muted violins and violas. But the "Inquiry" theme has not its original and gnarled form: it is calmer in line and it is more remote. Another theme comes in, *affettuoso poco andante,* E major, 7–4 (3–4, 4–4), which has been called the "Love" theme, as typical of Faust with Gretchen. This theme is based on the "Faust" motive heard near the beginning of the introduction from wind instruments. In this movement it is said to portray Gretchen, while in the "Gretchen" movement it portrays Faust; and this theme is burlesqued continually in the third movement, "Mephistopheles." The short theme given to wind instruments is interrupted by a figure for solo viola, which later in the symphony becomes a part of the theme itself. The "Faust-Gretchen" motive is developed in wood-wind and horns, with figures for violins and violas. Passage-work follows, and parts of the first theme appear, *allegro con fuoco,* 4–4. The music grows more and more passionate, and the rhythm of the wind instruments more pronounced. There is a transition section, and the basses allude to the last of the themes, the fifth according to some, the conclusion theme as others prefer, *grandioso, poco meno mosso,* which is given out *fortissimo* by the full orchestra. It is based on the initial figure of the violas and violoncellos in the introduction. The exposition section of the movement is now complete. The free fantasia, if the following section may be so called, begins with the return of *"tempo primo—allegro agitato assai,"* and the working out of thematic material is elaborate. There is a repetition section, or rather a recapitulation of the first, third, and fourth themes. The *coda* ends sadly with the "Faust" motive in augmentation.

II. "Gretchen." *Andante soave,* A flat major, 3–4. The movement has an introduction (flutes and clarinets), which establishes a mood. The chief theme, "characteristic of the innocence, simplicity, and contented happiness of Gretchen," may be called the "Gretchen" theme. It is sung (*dolce semplice*) by the oboe with only a solo viola accompaniment. The theme is then given to other instruments and with another accompaniment. The repeated phrase of flutes and clarinet, answered by violins, is supposed by some commentators to have reference to Gretchen's plucking the flower, with the words, "He loves me—loves me not," and at last, "He loves me!" The chief theme enters after this passage, and it now has a fuller expression and deeper significance. A second theme, typical of Gretchen, is sung by first violins, *dolce amoroso;* it is more emotional, more sensuous. Here there is a suggestion of a figure in the introduction. This theme brings the end to the first section, which is devoted exclusively to Gretchen.

Faust now enters, and his typical motive is heard (horn with agitated viola and violoncello accompaniment). The "Faust-Gretchen" motive of the first movement is used, but in a very different form. The restless theme of the opening movement is now one of enthusiastic love. The striking modulations that followed the first "Gretchen" theme occur again, but in different keys, and Faust soon leaves the scene. The third section of the movement is a much modified repetition of the first section. Gretchen now has memories of her love. A tender violin figure now winds about her theme. Naturally, the "He loves me—loves me not" music is omitted, but there is a reminiscence of the "Faust" motive.

III. "Mephistopheles." Mephistopheles is here the spirit of demoniacal irony. Mr. Apthorp, after saying that the prevalence of triple rhythms in the movement might lead one, but in vain, to look for something of the *scherzo* form in it, adds: "One may suspect the composer of taking Mephisto's *'Ich bin der Geist der stets verneint'* ('I am the spirit that denies') for the motto of this movement; somewhat in the sense of A. W. Ambros when he said of Jacques Offenbach in speaking of his opera-bouffes: 'All the subjects which artists have hitherto turned to account, and in which they have sought their ideals, must here be pushed *ad absurdum;* we feel as if Mephisto were ironically smiling at us in the elegant mask of "a man of the times," and asking us whether the whole baggage of the Antique and the Romantic were worth a rap.' "

It is not at all improbable that Liszt took the idea of Mephistopheles parodying the themes of Faust and Gretchen from the caricature of the motive of the fixed idea and from the mockery of the once loved one in the *finale* of Berlioz's *Episode in the Life of an Artist,* or *Fantastic* symphony.

There are no new themes introduced in the "Mephistopheles" movement.

As Miss Ramann says, Mephistopheles' character in this music is to be without character. His sport is to mock Faust as typified by his themes; but he has no power over the "Gretchen" themes, and they are left undisturbed.

Ernest Newman[2] finds the "Mephistopheles" section particularly ingenious. "It consists, for the most part, of a kind of burlesque upon the subjects of the *Faust* which are here passed, as it were, through a continuous fire of irony and ridicule. This is a far more effective way of depicting 'the spirit of denial' than making him mouth a farrago of pantomime bombast, in the manner of Boïto. The being who exists, for the purpose of the drama, only in endeavoring to frustrate every good impulse of Faust's soul, is really best dealt with, in music, not as a positive individuality, but as the embodiment of negation—a malicious, saturnine parody of all the good that has gone to the making of Faust. The 'Mephistopheles' is not only a piece of diabolically clever music, but the best picture we have of a character that in the hands of the average musician becomes either stupid, or vulgar, or both. As we listen to Liszt's music, we feel that we really have the Mephistopheles of Goethe's drama."

*Allegro vivace ironico,* C major, 2–4. There is a short pictorial introduction, an ascending chromatic run (violoncellos and double basses, chords for wood-wind, strings, with cymbals and triangle). There are ironical forms of the "Faust" and "Inquiry" motives, and the *sempre allegro* in which these themes appear leads to the main body of the movement, *allegro vivace,* 6–8, 2–4. The theme is the first of the first movement, and it now appears in a wildly excited form. Interrupted by the "Faust" motive, it goes on with still greater stress and fury. Transitional passages in the movement return in strange disguise. An episode *un poco animato* follows with an abrupt use of the "Faust" motive, and the "Inquiry" motive, reappearing, is greeted with jeers and fiendish laughter. The violas have a theme evolved from the "Faust" motive, which is then given to the violins and becomes the subject of fugal treatment. *Allegro animato;* the grandiose fifth, or conclusion, theme of the first movement is now handled most flippantly. There is a tempestuous *crescendo,* and then silence; muted horns sustain the chord of C minor, while strings *pizzicati* give out the "Inquiry" motive. "The passage is as a warning apparition." The hellish mockery breaks out again. Some find the music now inspired by an episode in Goethe's Walpurgis scene. In the midst of the din, wood-

[2]Ernest Newman: "Faust in Music," in *Musical Studies.*

wind instruments utter a cry, as when Faust exclaimed, "Mephistopheles, do you see yonder a pale, beautiful child, standing alone? . . . I must confess it seems to me that she looks like the good Gretchen." The music ascends in the violins, grows softer and softer. *Andante;* the oboe sings the "Gretchen" theme. The vision quickly fades. Again an outbreak of despair, and there is a recapitulation of preceding musical matter. In the *allegro non troppo* the "Faust" theme is chiefly used. "And then things grow more and more desperate, till we come to what we may call the transformation scene. It is like the rolling and shifting of clouds, and, indeed, transports us from the abode of mortal man to more ethereal spheres." The wild dissonances disappear; there is a wonderful succession of sustained chords. *Poco andante, ma sempre alla breve:* the "Gretchen" theme is colored mysteriously; trombones make solemn declaration. Gretchen is now Faust's redeemer. The male chorus, *Chorus mysticus,* accompanied by organ and strings, sings to the strain announced by the trombones, *andante mistico,* the lines of Goethe:

*Alles Vergängliche*
*Ist nur ein Gleichniss;*
*Das Unzulängliche,*
*Hier wird's Erreigniss;*
*Das Unbeschreibliche,*
*Hier ist's gethan;*
*Das Ewig-Weibliche*
*Zieht uns hinan.*

The solo tenor and chorus sing: *"Das Ewig-Weibliche zieht uns hinan"* (with the "Gretchen" motive rhythmically altered and with harp added to the accompaniment), and the work ends radiantly calm.

These lines have been Englished in prose: "All that is transitory is only a simile; the insufficient here becomes event; the indescribable is here done; the Ever feminine draws us onward." It was Liszt's intention, Brendel tells us, to have this chorus invisible at the first performance, but, inasmuch as it would have been necessary at Weimar to have it sung behind the lowered curtain, he feared the volume would be too weak.

## FRANZ LISZT

# SYMPHONIC POEM, NO. 3, "LES PRELUDES" (AFTER LAMARTINE)

According to statements of Richard Pohl, this symphonic poem was begun at Marseilles in 1834 and completed at Weimar in 1850. According to L. Ramann's chronological catalogue of Liszt's works, *The Preludes* was composed in 1854 and published in 1856.

Theodor Müller-Reuter says that the poem was composed at Weimar in 1849–50 from sketches made in earlier years, and this statement seems to be the correct one.

Ramann tells the following story about the origin of *The Preludes.* Liszt, it seems, began to compose at Paris, about 1844, choral music for a poem by Aubray, and the work was entitled *Les 4 Éléments* (*la Terre, les Aquilons, les Flots, les Astres*). The cold stupidity of the poem discouraged him, and he did not complete the cantata. He told his troubles to Victor Hugo, in the hope that the poet would take the hint and write for him; but Hugo did not or would not understand his meaning, so Liszt put the music aside. Early in 1854 he thought of using the abandoned work for a Pension Fund concert of the Court Orchestra at Weimar, and it then occurred to make the music, changed and enlarged, illustrative of a passage in Lamartine's *Nouvelles Méditations poétiques, XVme Méditation: "Les Préludes,"* dedicated to Victor Hugo.

The symphonic poem *Les Préludes* was performed for the first time in the Grand Ducal Court Theater, Weimar, at a concert for the Pension Fund of the widows and orphans of deceased members of the Court Orchestra on February 23, 1854. Liszt conducted from manuscript.

Liszt revised *Les Préludes* in 1853 or 1854. The score was published in May, 1856; the orchestral parts, in January, 1865.

The alleged passage from Lamartine that serves as a motto has thus been Englished:

"What is our life but a series of preludes to that unknown song, the first solemn note of which is sounded by death? Love forms the enchanted daybreak of every life; but what is the destiny where the first delights of happiness are not interrupted by some storm, whose fatal breath dissipates its fair illusions, whose fell lightning consumes its altar? and what wounded spirit, when one of its tempests is over, does not seek to rest its memories in the sweet calm of country life? Yet man does not resign himself long to enjoy the beneficent tepidity which first charmed him on Nature's bosom; and when 'the trumpet's loud clangor has called him to arms,' he rushes to the post of danger, whatever may be the war that calls him to the ranks, to find in battle the full consciousness of himself and the complete possession of his strength." There is little in Lamartine's poem that suggests this preface. The quoted passage beginning "The trumpet's loud clangor" is Lamartine's *"La trompette a jeté le signal des alarmes."*

*The Preludes* is scored for three flutes (and piccolo), two oboes, two clarinets, two bassoons, four horns, two trumpets, three trombones, bass tuba, kettledrums, snare drum, bass drum, cymbals, harp, and strings.

## PIANOFORTE CONCERTO, NO. 1, IN E FLAT

Liszt's E flat concerto, long the subject of scurrilous criticism because forsooth a triangle was indicated in the score, has long been the virtuoso concerto *par excellence*. But its virtuosity is of an unusual order. It does not display its innate quality to the precise and composed technician; it cannot be played complacently or casually. It demands an audacious, unhesitating bravura, large rhetorical phrases, bold accents, and a careless contempt for its difficulties. Its octave *cadenzas* suggest the remorseless dash of an eagle upon its prey.

This concerto was completed probably in 1848 or 1849, from sketches made in the early 'forties. According to a letter of Hans von Bülow's, the concerto was completed in June, 1849. Revised in 1853, it was published in 1857. The first performance was at Weimar, at a Court concert in the hall of the Grand Duke's palace (during the Berlioz week), on February 17, 1855; Liszt, pianist; Bülow, conductor. The concerto is dedicated to Henri Litolff. The orchestral part is scored for piccolo, two flutes, two oboes, two clarinets, two bassoons, two horns, two trumpets, three trombones, kettledrums, cymbals, triangle, and the usual strings.

The form is free. A few important themes are exposed, developed;

they undergo many transformations in rhythm and tempo. The first and leading theme is at once given out imperatively by the strings, with interrupting chords of wood-wind and brass. This is the theme to which Liszt used to sing: *"Das versteht ihr alle nicht!"*—according to Bülow and Ramann, *"Ihr Könnt alle nichts."* This theme may be taken as the motto of the concerto. *Allegro maestoso, tempo giusto,* 4–4. The second theme, B major, *quasi adagio,* 12–8, is first announced by muted violoncellos and double basses and then developed elaborately by the pianoforte. There are hints of this theme in the preceding section. The third theme, E flat minor, *allegretto vivace,* 3–4, in the nature of a *scherzo,* is first given to the strings, with preliminary warning and answers of the triangle, which, the composer says, should be struck with delicately rhythmic precision. The fourth theme is rather an answer to the chief phrase of the second than an individual motive. The *scherzo* tempo changes to *allegro animato,* 4–4, in which use is made chiefly of the motto theme. The final section is an *allegro marziale animato,* which quickens to a final *presto.*

The introduction of the triangle in the score caused great offense in Vienna. Hanslick damned the work by characterizing it as a " 'Triangle' concerto," when Pruckner played it there in the season of 1856–57. It was not heard again in that city until 1869, when Sophie Menter insisted on playing it. Liszt wrote a letter in 1857 describing the concerto and defending his use of the triangle.

# CHARLES MARTIN
# LOEFFLER

(Born at Mühlhausen [Alsace], January 30, 1861; died at Medfield, Mass., May 19, 1935)

---

## "A PAGAN POEM" (AFTER VIRGIL), OP. 14, FOR ORCHESTRA, PIANOFORTE, ENGLISH HORN, AND THREE TRUMPETS OBBLIGATI

THE MUSIC of the *Pagan Poem* is highly imaginative. Its pages are pages of beauty and passion. The strangeness of the opening is not forced or experimental. The composer himself first saw in his mind's eye the scene and heard the sorcerer's chant. And here is no love song of familiar type given to caterwauling 'cellos. There is no conventional lament of approved crape and tears. A dolorous theme, broadly and nobly thought, is sung by the English horn. The spell works. Daphnis now hastens toward the long empty and expectant arms. There is frantic and amorous exultation.

In this instance a rich and rare orchestral dress covers a well shaped and vigorous body.

This tone poem was suggested to Mr. Loeffler by certain verses in the eighth Eclogue of Virgil, which is sometimes known as "Pharmaceutria" (the Sorceress). The Eclogue, dedicated to Pollio, was written probably in 39 B.C. It consists of two love songs, that of Damon and that of Alphesibœus. Each song has ten parts, and these parts are divided by a recurring burden or refrain. Alphesibœus tells of the love incantation of a Thessalian girl, who by the aid of magical spells endeavors to bring back to her cottage her truant lover Daphnis. Virgil helped himself freely here from the second Idyll of Theocritus, "The Sorceress," in which Simaetha, a Syracuse maiden of middle rank, weaves spells to regain the love of Delphis.

Mr. Loeffler does not intend to present in this music a literal translation of Virgil's verse into tones. The poem is a fantasy, inspired by the verses.

The poem opens, *adagio,* 2–2, with a short motive, which, with an inversion of it, is much used throughout the work. The first chief theme is announced dolce, *mezzo-forte,* by viola solo and three flutes. It may be called the theme of invocation. The latter half of it may be divided into two motives, the first a phrase descending in whole tones, the second a rising and falling wail. These two motives are used separately and frequently in all sorts of ways. After the exposition of this theme the pianoforte enters *fortissimo* with a harmonized inversion of the introductory motive; a *crescendo* follows with use of the foregoing thematic material, and a *glissando* for the pianoforte leads to an *allegro,* in which now familiar thematic material is used until the second theme appears (first violins, harp, pianoforte). This theme is developed. A pianoforte *cadenza* built on thematic material leads to a *lento assai,* 6–4, with a dolorous theme (No. 3) for the English horn. The trumpets behind the scenes give out the burden of the sorceress. The *più vivo* section may suggest to some a chase of wolves ("I have often seen Moeris become a wolf and plunge into the forest"). *Tranquillo:* a fourth theme, 4–4, is given to the pianoforte. *Calando:* the refrain is heard again from behind the scenes. *Moderato:* the second chief theme, 6–4, now appears, and it is used extensively. *Largamente:* the trumpets, now on the stage, announce the coming of Daphnis, and there is the suggestion of the barking Hylax. The ending is a fanfare of frantic exultation.

This poem, dedicated to the memory of Gustave Schirmer, was written originally in 1901 for performance as chamber music.

In 1905 and 1906 the work was remoulded and treated much more symphonically. The first public performance was by the Boston Symphony Orchestra in Boston on November 23, 1907, Mr. Gebhard pianist.

The poem is scored for three flutes (and piccolo), two oboes, English horn, two clarinets, bass clarinet, two bassoons, four horns, three trumpets (and three trumpets off-stage), three trombones, bass tuba, kettledrums, glockenspiel, tam-tam, harp, pianoforte, strings.

# EDWARD
# MacDOWELL

(Born in New York, December 18, 1861;
died there, January 23, 1908)

---

## ORCHESTRAL SUITE NO. 2, IN E MINOR, "INDIAN," OP. 48

*I. Legend*
*II. Love Song*
*III. In War Time*
*IV. Dirge*
*V. Village Festival*

THE MUSIC has the characteristic force and tenderness of this composer when he was writing for himself and not directly for the general public. It is not necessary to lug in any question of whether this be distinctively American music, for the best pages of the suite are not parochial—they are not national.

They are universal in their appeal to sensitive hearers of any land. The movements that are the most poetically imaginative, that have the greatest distinction, are the "Legend," "In War Time," and above all the "Dirge." Music like this would honor any composer of whatever race he might be.

This lamentation might be that of the dying race. There is nothing of the luxury of woe; there is no conventional music for "threadbare crape and tears." There is the dignity of man who has been familiar with nature, who has known the voices of the day and of the night on lonely prairie and in somber forest. There is serene yielding to fate.

This suite was composed in 1891–92. The first performance in public was by the Boston Symphony Orchestra in the Metropolitan Opera House, New York, January 23, 1896.

The Indian themes used in the suite are as follows:

1. First theme, Iroquois. There is also a small Chippewa theme.
2. Iowa love song.
3. A well-known song among tribes of the Atlantic coast. There is a Dacota theme, and there are characteristic features of the Iroquois scalp dance.
4. Kiowa (woman's song of mourning for her absent son).
5. Women's dance, war song, both Iroquois.

The suite is scored for piccolo, two flutes, two oboes, two clarinets, two bassoons, four horns, two trumpets, three trombones, bass tuba, a set of three kettledrums, bass drum, cymbals, and strings.

I. "Legend": Not fast; with much dignity and character, E minor, 2–2. It has been said that this movement was suggested to the composer by Thomas Bailey Aldrich's Indian legend, "Miantowona"; but MacDowell took no pains to follow Aldrich's poem incident by incident, nor to tell any particular story; "the poem merely suggested to him to write something of a similar character in music."

II. "Love Song": Not fast; tenderly, A major, 6–8. One chief theme, which is announced immediately by the wood-wind, is developed, with the use of two subsidiary phrases, one a sort of response from the strings, the other a more assertive melody, first given out in D minor by wood-wind instruments.

III. "In War Time": With rough vigor, almost savagely, D minor, 2–4. The chief theme is played by two flutes, in unison, unaccompanied. Two clarinets, in unison and without accompaniment, answer in a subsidiary theme. This material is worked out elaborately in a form that has the characteristics of the *rondo*. The rhythm changes frequently towards the end from 2–4 to 6–8 and back again.

IV. "Dirge": Dirge-like, mournfully, in G minor, 4–4. The mournful chief theme is given out by muted violins in unison, which are soon strengthened by the violas, against repetitions of the tonic note G by piccolo, flutes, and two muted horns, one on the stage, the other behind the scenes, with occasional full harmony in groups of wind instruments. "The intimate relation between this theme and that of the first movement is not to be overlooked. It is answered by the horn behind the scenes over full harmony in the lower strings, the passage closing with a quaint concluding phrase of the oboe." The development of this theme fills the short movement.

V. "Village Festival": Swift and light, in E major, 2–4. Several related themes are developed. All of them are more or less derived from that of the first movement. There are lively dance rhythms. "But here also the composer has been at no pains to suggest any of the specific concomitants of Indian festivities; he has only written a movement in which merrymakings of the sort are musically suggested."

# GUSTAV MAHLER

(Born at Kalischt in Bohemia, on July 7, 1860; died at Vienna on May 18, 1911)

---

THOSE WHO without undue prejudice discuss Mahler the composer, admitting his faults, discussing them at length, dwelling on undeniable fine qualities, assert that his artistic life was greater than his own musical works, which, greatly planned, did not attain fulfillment and were often imitative. The sincerity of the composer was never doubted; the failure to secure that for which he strove is therefore the more pathetic.

He was of an intensely nervous nature. His life as a conductor—and he was a great conductor—the feverish atmosphere of the opera house, his going from city to city until his ability was recognized in Vienna and later at the Metropolitan, the death of a dearly loved child, the fact that he was a Jew, who had turned Catholic: these, with musical intrigues and controversies from which he suffered, gave him no mental or esthetic poise. It was his ambition to continue the work of men he revered, Beethoven and Wagner. In spite of his indisputable talent he was not the man to do this. In the nearer approaches to the ideal that was in his mind he was simply an imitator; not a convincing, not even a plausible one.

One has found through his symphonies restlessness that at times becomes hysterical; reminders of Wagner, Berlioz, Strauss; melodies in folk-song vein, often naïve, at times beautiful, but introduced as at random and quickly thrown aside; an overemployment of the wood-winds, used too often as solo instruments; passages for the brass which recall the fact that as a child Mahler delighted in military bands. Sudden changes from screaming outbursts to thin and inconsequential instrumentation; trivial moments when the hearer anticipates the movement of a country dance; diffuseness, prolixity that becomes boresome; an unwillingness to bring speech to an end; seldom genuine power or eloquence; yet here and there measures that linger in the memory.

## THE SYMPHONIES

No. 1. D major. Begun in December, 1883; completed at Budapest in 1888; produced at Budapest, Mahler, conductor, on November 20, 1889; published in 1898. The Budapest programme described it as a "symphonic poem in two parts." When it was performed at the Tonkünstler Fest at Weimar on June 3, 1894, through the insistence of Richard Strauss and Dr. Kretzschmar, it was known as *"Titan"* (after Jean Paul Richter's romance).

No. 2. C minor. Begun and completed in 1894. First performed at a Philharmonic Concert in Berlin, Richard Strauss, conductor, on March 4, 1895. Only the three instrumental movements were then performed. The second and third met with great favor; Mahler was called out five times after the *scherzo*. The majority of the Berlin critics distorted or suppressed this fact and represented the performance as a fiasco. The whole of the symphony was performed for the first time at Mahler's concert at Berlin on December 13, 1895. According to Ernst Otto Nodnagel, the critics again behaved "indecently"; took the purely orchestral movements for granted, and heard only the *finale* with the tenor and contralto solos. One of them spoke of "the cynical impudence of this brutal and very latest music maker." Nikisch and Weingartner were deeply impressed, and the greater part of the audience was wildly enthusiastic.

No. 3. F major, known as the *"Summer Morning's Dream,"* or *"Programme"* symphony. Sketched in 1895, completed in 1896. Produced piecemeal in 1896 at Berlin and Hamburg; in 1897 at Berlin. First performance of the whole symphony at a concert of the Allgemeiner Deutscher Musikverein at Krefeld in June, 1902. Published in 1898.

No. 4. G major. Composed in 1899–1900. First performance at Munich by the Kaim Orchestra on November 25, 1901. Mahler conducted. Published in 1900.

No. 5. C-sharp minor, known as *"The Giant"* Symphony. Completed in 1902. First performance at a Gürzenich concert in Cologne, October 18, 1904.

No. 6. A minor. Composed in 1903–04. Performed under Mahler's direction at the Tonkünstler Fest at Essen on May 27, 1906. Published in 1905.

No. 7. E minor. Composed in 1904–06. Produced at Prague on September 19, 1908. Mahler conducted. Published in 1908.

No. 8. In two parts, with soli and double chorus; first part, hymn, "Veni, Creator Spiritus," as a sonata first movement, with double fugue; second part, the last scenes of *Faust,* in form of an *adagio, scherzo,* and *finale.* Composition begun in 1906. First performance at Munich as *"Symphony of the Thousand"* on September 12, 1908, the year of publication.

No. 9. Begun in 1906. Produced at Vienna June 26, 1912, Bruno Walter, conductor. The last movement is an *adagio.*

No. 10. Composed in 1909–10; left unfinished by Mahler. First performance at Prague on June 6, 1924, Alex von Zemlinsky, conductor.

*"Das Lied von der Erde"* (Song of the Earth), a symphony in six parts for tenor and contralto soli with orchestra, the text taken from *The Chinese Flute,* a collection of Chinese lyrics by Hans Bethge. Composed in 1908, first produced at Munich November 20, 1911, Bruno Walter, conductor.

Some of Mahler's symphonies are described as programme music, but he was no friend of realism as it is understood by Richard Strauss. Mahler was reported as saying: "When I conceive a great musical picture, I always arrive at the point where I must employ the 'word' as the bearer of my musical idea. . . . My experience with the last movement of my second symphony was such that I ransacked the literature of the world, up to the Bible, to find the expository word." Though he differed with Strauss in the matter of realistic music, he valued him highly: "No one should think I hold myself to be his rival. Aside from the fact that, if his success had not opened a path for me, I should now be looked on as a sort of monster on account of my works, I consider it one of my greatest joys that my colleagues and I have found such a comrade in fighting and creating."

One reason why Mahler's symphonies were looked at askance by conductors was the enormous orchestra demanded. No. 2 called for as many strings as possible, two harps, four flutes (interchangeable with four piccolos), four oboes (two interchangeable with two English horns), five clarinets (one interchangeable with bass clarinet—and when it is possible the two in E flat should be doubled in *fortissimo* passages), four bassoons (one interchangeable with double bassoon), six horns (and four in the distance to be added in certain passages to the six), six trumpets (four in the distance, which may be taken from the six), four trombones, tuba, two sets of kettledrums, bass drum, snare drum (when possible several of them), cymbals, tam-tam of high pitch and one of low pitch, triangle, glockenspiel, three bells, a Ruthe (a bundle of rods to switch a drumhead), organ, two harps. In the distance a pair of kettledrums, bass drum, cymbals, triangle. Soprano solo, contralto solo, mixed chorus.

## SYMPHONY NO. 5, IN C SHARP MINOR IN THREE PARTS

*I.* 1. *Dead March—with measured step—like a funeral train Suddenly faster, passionately, wildly. A tempo*
2. *With stormy emotion. With utmost vehemence*

*II.* 3. *Scherzo. With force, but not too fast*

*III.* 4. *Adagietto, very slow*
5. *Rondo finale: allegro*

The symphony is like unto the great image that stood before Nebuchadnezzar in a vision. "And the form thereof was terrible. The image's head was of fine gold, his breast and his arms of silver, his belly and his thighs of brass; his legs of iron, his feet part of iron and part of clay."

There are musical thoughts that are lovely and noble. By their side are themes of a vulgarity that is masked only by adroit contrapuntal treatment or by the blare of instrumentation which gives a plausible and momentary importance. There is excessive reiteration of subjects and devices, and the skill displayed in embellishment and variation of orchestral color, color rather than nuance, does not relieve the monotony. The opening is imposing, but the chief theme of the Dead March disappoints. The first pages of the second section, "stormily restless," are a stroke of genius, the free expression of wild imagination. There are charming ideas in the *scherzo,* and there is also much that is only whimsical, as though Mahler had then written solely for his own amusement, and said to himself, "Let us try it this way. I wonder how it will sound." The *adagietto* is the most emotional portion of the work, and here Mahler employed simple means. Here the thought and the expression are happily wedded, nor does the ghost of Wagner, seen for a moment smiling, forbid this union. It may be that in the *finale* the composer could not help remembering the wondrous theme, D major, in the *adagio* of Beethoven's Ninth symphony; but the resemblance is after all only a suggestion, and this *finale* in *rondo* form, with the majestic peroration, is worked so that there is a steady *crescendo* of interest. As a whole Mahler's symphony, with its mixture of the grand and the common, with its spontaneity and its laborious artifice, is like unto the great image referred to above.

This symphony, known to some as *"The Giant"* symphony, was performed for the first time at a Gürzenich concert at Cologne, October 18, 1904. The composer conducted. There was a difference of opinion concerning the merits of the work. A visiting critic from Munich wrote that there was breathless silence after the first movement, "which proved more effectively than tremendous applause that the public was conscious of the presence of genius." It is stated that after the *finale* there was much applause; there was also hissing.

When the symphony was performed in certain German cities, as at Dresden, January 27, 1905, at a symphony concert of the Royal Orchestra, and at Berlin, February 20, 1905, at a Philharmonic concert, the programme books contained no analytical notes and no argument of any sort. The compilers thus obeyed the wish of the composer. Mr. Ludwig Schiedermair tells us, in his *Gustav Mahler: eine biographisch-kritische Würdigung,* of Mahler's abhorrence of all programme books for concert use, and he relates this anecdote. Mahler conducted a performance of his Symphony in C minor at a concert of the Munich Hugo Wolf Society. After the concert there was a supper, and in the course of the conversation someone mentioned programme books. "Then was it as though lightning flashed in a joyous, sunny landscape. Mahler's eyes were more brilliant than ever, his forehead wrinkled, he sprang in excitement from the table and exclaimed in passionate tones: 'Away with programme books, which breed false ideas! The audience should be left to its own thoughts over the work that is performing: it should not be forced to read during the performance; it should not be prejudiced in any manner. If a composer by his music forces on his hearers the sensations which streamed through his mind, then he reaches his goal. The speech of tones has then approached the language of words, but it is far more capable of expression and declaration.' And Mahler raised his glass and emptied it with *'Pereat den Programmen!'* "

Yet Mr. Mahler's enthusiastic admirer and partisan, Ernst Otto Nodnagel, of Darmstadt, contributed to "Die Musik" (second November number and first December number of 1904) a technical analysis of the Fifth symphony, an analysis of twenty-three large octavo pages, with a beautiful motto from Schiller. This analysis, published by Peters, and sold for the sum of thirty pfennig, is within reach of the humblest.

The symphony was completed in the spring of 1903. It was written in 1901–02 at his little country house near Maiernigg on Lake Wörther. Other works of this date are the *Kindertotenlieder* and other songs with Rückert's verses. The symphony is scored for four flutes (and piccolo), three oboes, three clarinets (and bass clarinet), two bassoons, one double bassoon, six horns (in third movement a horn obbligato), four trumpets, three trombones, tuba, kettledrums, snare drum, bass drum, cymbals, triangle, Glockenspiel, gong, harp, and strings.

Let us respect the wishes of the composer who looked on analytical or explanatory programmes as the abomination of desolation. Yet it may be said that in the *rondo finale,* after the second chief motive enters as the subject of a fugal section, one of the lesser themes used in the development is derived from Mahler's song, "Lob des hohen Verstands" (relating to the trial of skill between the nightingale and the cuckoo with the ass as judge).

## FELIX
# MENDELSSOHN-BARTHOLDY

(Born at Hamburg, February 3, 1809;
died at Leipsic, November 4, 1847)

---

MENDELSSOHN in his maturity wrote his music as he looks in his picture, smiling and with a stickpin in his ruffled shirt. When at seventeen he wrote his overture to *A Midsummer Night's Dream,* he was a romanticist. What might he not have accomplished if he had been poor and less respectable! He wrote this overture before he had been spoiled by flattery; before he became a composer of priggish formulas. Aubrey Beardsley pictured the later Mendelssohn in that forgotten magazine, the *Savoy.* There you see the man that was shocked by the resurrection of the nuns in *Robert the Devil,* by Terlina undressing in *Fra Diavolo,* by Hugo's *Ruy Blas,* although he condescended to write an overture for it. The spotless Mendelssohn who delighted Queen Victoria and her spouse by playing the organ to them. But the overture to Shakespeare's comedy is from another Mendelssohn, the composer of *The Hebrides,* portions of the *Walpurgis Night,* not the man of the oratorios and the sentimental *Songs without Words.*

## SYMPHONY IN A MAJOR, "ITALIAN," OP. 90

*I. Allegro vivace*
*II. Andante con moto*
*III. Con moto moderato*
*IV. Saltarello: presto*

HOW MUCH of Italy is there in this symphony of Mendelssohn? Suppose there were no title. The last movement might easily be recognized as a *saltarello;* but how about the other movements? The first is light and gay, but there is no geographical or national mood at once established, there is no authoritative characterization. I doubt whether even a tambourine would be of material assistance. It was not necessary for the composer to go to Naples to write the *andante.* As for the *scherzo,* the horns with their pleasant sentimentalism might represent today Germans in Rome, armed with red guide books, and now and then bursting out in songs of the Fatherland, something about the forest, or spring, or the blissfulness of sorrow and longing. The *saltarello* part was done much better by Berlioz. Compare this symphony, so far as local color is concerned, with a page of Bizet painting in tones a Southern scene, or with Richard Strauss' Italian suite, or with the suite of Charpentier, and Mendelssohn's music seems without marked distinction, rather tame and drab. Yet the first movement and the *finale* are amiable music, pages that may awaken a gentlemanlike joy, and there is no denying the clearness of the musical thought, the purity of expression, the sure and polished workmanship.

The symphony was completed in Berlin. Mendelssohn wrote to Pastor Bauer, "My work about which I recently had many misgivings is completed, and, looking it over, I now find that, contrary to my expectations, it satisfies me. I believe it has become a good piece. Be that as it may, I feel it shows progress, and that is the main point." The score bears the date, Berlin, March 13, 1833.

The first performance from manuscript and under the direction of the composer was at the sixth concert of the Philharmonic Society that season, May 13, 1833. "The concerts of the Society were this year, and onward, given in the Hanover Square Rooms, which had just been remodeled. The symphony made a great impression, and Felix electrified the audience by his wonderful performance of Mozart's Concerto in D minor, his *cadenzas* being marvels in design and execution. His new overture in C was produced at the last concert of the season."

Mendelssohn began to revise the symphony in June, 1834. On February 16, 1835, he wrote to Klingemann that he was biting his nails over the first movement and could not yet master it, but that in any event it should be something different—perhaps wholly new—and he had this doubt about every one of the movements. Towards the end of 1837 the revision was completed. Whether the symphony in its new form was played at a Philharmonic Society Concert in London, June 18, 1838, conducted by Moscheles, is doubtful, although Moscheles asked him for it. The first performance of the revised version on the European continent was at a Gewandhaus concert, Leipsic, November 1, 1849, when Julius Rietz conducted. The score and orchestral parts were not published until March, 1851.

Grove remarked of this work: "The music itself is better than any commentary. Let that be marked, learned, and inwardly digested."

Reismann found the first movement, *allegro vivace,* A major, 6–8, to be a paraphrase of the so-called "Hunting Song" in the first group of *Songs without Words.* The tonality is the same, and this is often enough to fire the imagination of a commentator. The chief subject begins with the violins in the second measure and is developed at length. The second subject, E major, is for clarinets. The development section begins with a new figure treated in imitation by the strings. The chief theme is then used, with the second introduced contrapuntally. In the recapitulation section the second theme is given to the strings.

The second movement, *andante con moto,* D minor, 4–4, sometimes called the "Pilgrims' March," but without any authority, is said "to have been a processional hymn, which probably gave the name of '*"Italian"* symphony' to the whole (!)." Lampadius remarks in connection with this: "I cannot discover that the piece bears any mark of a decided Catholic character, for, if I recollect rightly, I once heard Moscheles say that Mendelssohn had in his mind as the source of this second movement an old Bohemian folk song."[1] The two introductory measures suggested to Grove "the cry of a muezzin from his minaret," but, pray, what has this to do with Italy? The chief theme is given out by oboe, clarinet, and violas. The violins take it up with counterpoint for the flutes. There is a new musical idea for the clarinets. The first theme returns. The two introductory measures are used with this material in the remainder of the movement.

[1]Wilhelm Adolf Lampadius: *Felix Mendelssohn-Bartholdy,* 1848; translated by W. L. Gage, 1866.

The third movement is marked simply *"con moto moderato"* (A major, 3-4). "There is a tradition (said to originate with Mendelssohn's brother-in-law, Hensel, but still of uncertain authority) that it was transferred to its present place from some earlier composition. It is not, however, to be found in either of the twelve unpublished juvenile symphonies; and in the first rough draft of this symphony there is no sign of its having been interpolated. In style the movement is, no doubt, earlier than the rest of the work." The movement opens with a theme for first violins; the trio with a passage for bassoons and horns. The third part is a repetition of the first. In the coda there is at the end a suggestion of the trio.

The *finale* is a *saltarello, presto,* 4-4. There are three themes. The flutes, after six introductory measures, play the first. In the second, somewhat similar in character, the first and second violins answer each other. The third is also given to the first and second violins alternately, but now in the form of a continuously moving, not a jumping figure.

This *saltarello* was undoubtedly inspired by the Carnival at Rome, of which Mendelssohn gave a description in his letter of February 8, 1831. "On Saturday all the world went to the Capitol, to witness the form of the Jews' supplications to be suffered to remain in the Sacred City for another year, a request which is refused at the foot of the hill, but, after repeated entreaties, granted on the summit, and the Ghetto is assigned to them. It was a tiresome affair; we waited two hours, and after all, understood the oration of the Jews as little as the answer of the Christians. I came down again in very bad humor, and thought that the Carnival had begun rather unpropitiously. So I arrived in the Corso and was driving along, thinking no evil, when I was suddenly assailed by a shower of sugar comfits. I looked up; they had been flung by some young ladies whom I had seen occasionally at balls, but scarcely knew, and when in my embarrassment I took off my hat to bow to them, the pelting began in right earnest. Their carriage drove on, and in the next was Miss T——, a delicate young Englishwoman. I tried to bow to her, but she pelted me, too; so I became quite desperate, and clutching the confetti, I flung them back bravely. There were swarms of my acquaintances and my blue coat was soon as white as that of a miller. The B——s were standing on a balcony, flinging confetti like hail at my head; and thus pelting and pelted, amid a thousand jests and jeers and the most extravagant masks, the day ended with races."

It is a singular reflection on "local color" in music that Schumann mistook the *"Scotch"* symphony for the *"Italian,"* and wrote of the former: "It can, like the Italian scenes in *Titan,* cause you for a moment to forget the sorrow of not having seen that heavenly country." The best explanation of this Symphony No. 4, if there be need of any explanation, is found in the letters of Mendelssohn from Italy.

## OVERTURE AND INCIDENTAL MUSIC TO SHAKESPEARE'S PLAY, "A MIDSUMMER NIGHT'S DREAM"

Translations by Schlegel and Tieck of Shakespeare's plays were read by Mendelssohn and his sister Fanny in 1826. The overture, *A Midsummer Night's Dream,* was written in July and August of that year.

Klingemann tells us that part of the score was written "in the summer, in the open air, in the Mendelssohns' garden at Berlin, for I was present." This garden belonged to a house in the Leipziger Strasse (No. 3). It was near the Potsdam gate, and when Abraham Mendelssohn, the father, bought it, his friends complained that he was moving out of the world. There was an estate of about ten acres. In the house was a room for theatrical performances; and the center of the garden house formed a hall which held several hundred, and it was here that Sunday music was performed. In the time of Frederick the Great this garden was part of the Thiergarten. In the summer-houses were writing materials, and Felix edited a newspaper, called in summer *The Garden Times,* and in the winter *The Snow and Tea Times.*

Mendelssohn told Hiller that he had worked long and eagerly on the overture: "How in his spare time between the lectures at the Berlin University he had gone on extemporizing at it on the piano of a beautiful woman who lived close by; 'for a whole year, I hardly did anything else,' he said; and certainly he had not wasted his time."

It is said that Mendelssohn made two drafts of the overture, and discarded the earlier after he completed the first half. This earlier draft began with the four chords and the fairy figure; then followed a regular overture, in which use was made of a theme typical of the loves of Lysander and Hermia, and of kin to the "love melody" of the present version.

The overture was first written as a pianoforte duet, and it was first played to Moscheles in that form by the composer and his sister,

November 19, 1826. It was performed afterwards by an orchestra in the garden house. The first public performance was at Stettin in February, 1827, from manuscript, when Karl Löwe conducted. The critic was not hurried in those days, for an account of the concert appeared in the *Harmonicon* for December of that year. The critic had had time to think the matter over, and his conclusion was that the overture was of little importance.

The overture was performed in England for the first time on June 24 (Midsummer Day), 1829, at a concert given by Louis Drouet in the Argyll Rooms. Sir George Smart, who returned from the concert with Mendelssohn, left the score of the overture in a hackney coach. So the story is told; but is it not possible that the blameless Mendelssohn left it? The score was never found, and Mendelssohn rewrote it. The overture was played in England for the first time in connection with Shakespeare's comedy at London, in 1840, when Mme Vestris appeared in the performance at Covent Garden.

The orchestral parts were published in 1832; the score in April, 1835. The overture is dedicated to His Royal Majesty the Crown Prince of Prussia.

The overture opens *allegro di molto,* E major, 2-2, with four prolonged chords in the wood-wind. On the last of these follows immediately a *pianissimo* chord of E minor in violins and violas. This is followed by the "fairy music" in E minor, given out and developed by divided violins with some *pizzicati* in the violas. A subsidiary theme is given out *fortissimo* by full orchestra. The melodious second theme, in B major, begun by the wood-wind, is then continued by the strings and fuller and fuller orchestra. Several picturesque features are then introduced: the Bergomask dance from the fifth act of the play; a curious imitation of the bray of an ass in allusion to Bottom, who is, according to Maginn's paradox, "the blockhead, *the* lucky man on whom Fortune showers her favors beyond measure"; and the quickly descending scale passage for violoncellos, which was suggested to the composer by the buzzing of a big fly in the Schoenhauser Garten. The free fantasia is wholly on the first theme. The third part of the overture is regular, and there is a short *coda*. The overture ends with the four sustained chords with which it opened.

In 1843 King Frederick William the Fourth of Prussia wished Mendelssohn to compose music for the plays *Antigone, A Midsummer*

*Night's Dream, Athalie,* which should be produced in September. During March and April of that year Mendelssohn, who had written the overture in 1826, composed the additional music for Shakespeare's play. Tieck had divided the play into three acts and had said nothing to the composer about the change. Mendelssohn had composed with reference to the original division. The first performance was in the Royal Theater in the New Palace, Potsdam, October 14, 1843, on the eve of the festival of the King's birthday. Mendelssohn conducted.

The score was published in June, 1848; the orchestral parts in August of that year. The first edition for pianoforte was published in September, 1844.

Mendelssohn's music to the play consists of thirteen numbers: I. Overture; II. Scherzo (Entr'acte after Act I); III. Fairy March (in Act II); IV. "You spotted snakes," for two sopranos and chorus (in Act II); V. Melodrama (in Act II); VI. Intermezzo (Entr'acte after Act II); VII. Melodrama (in Act III); VIII. Notturno (Entr'acte after Act III); IX. *Andante* (in Act IV); X. Wedding March (after the close of Act IV); XI. *Allegro commodo* and *Marcia funebre* (in Act V); XII. Bergomask Dance (in Act V); XIII. *Finale* to Act V. Many of the themes in these numbers were taken from the overture.

The *scherzo* (entr'acte between Acts I and II) is an *allegro vivace* in G minor, 3–8. "Presumably Mendelssohn intended it as a purely musical reflection of the scene in Quince's house—the first meeting to discuss the play to be given by the workmen at the wedding—with which the first act ends. Indeed, there is a passing allusion to Nick Bottom's bray in it. But the general character of the music is bright and fairy-like, with nothing of the grotesque about it." The *scherzo* presents an elaborate development of two themes that are not sharply contrasted; the first theme has a subsidiary. The score is dedicated to Heinrich Conrad Schleinitz.

## CONCERT OVERTURE, "THE HEBRIDES," OR "FINGAL'S CAVE," OP. 26

In the *Hebrides* overture, Mendelssohn shook off his priggish formalism. He had been deeply affected by the sight of Staffa and Fingal's Cave; he was not ashamed to translate his emotions into music without obsequious obedience to the old pedagogic traditions. Here he is poetic, picturing the wildness of the far-off scene without too deliberate attempt at realism. Here is the suggestion—and with the small orchestra of the period!—as Mr. Apthorp put it, of screaming sea birds, whistling winds, the salty smell of the seaweed on the rocks. For once Mendelssohn showed himself more than a careful manufacturer of music when he revised his score, saying that the middle section smelt more of counterpoint than of train oil, sea gulls, and salt fish.

Mendelssohn saw Staffa and Fingal's Cave on August 7, 1829. He at once determined to picture the scenes in music. He wrote to his sister on that day: "That you may understand how extraordinarily the Hebrides affected me, the following came into my mind"; and he then noted down twenty-one measures in *alla breve,* which coincide for the first ten and a half measures with the later measures in 4–4. Ferdinand Hiller, who lived with Mendelssohn in Paris during the winter of 1831–32, tells how Mendelssohn brought to him the sketched score. "He told me how the thing came to him in its full form and color when he saw Fingal's Cave; he also informed me how the first measures, which contain the chief theme, had come into his mind. In the evening he was making a visit with his friend Klingemann on a Scottish family. There was a pianoforte in the room; but it was Sunday, and there was no possibility of music. He employed all his diplomacy to get at the pianoforte for a moment; when he had succeeded, he dashed off the theme out of which the great work grew. It was finished at Düsseldorf, but only after an interval of years." Hiller was mistaken about the place and time of completion.

The overture was first performed on May 14, 1832, from manuscript, in London, at the sixth concert of the Philharmonic Society at Covent Garden. Thomas Attwood conducted. The composer wrote: "It went splendidly, and sounded so droll amongst all the Rossini things." The *Athenæum* said that the overture as descriptive music was a failure. George Hogarth wrote in his History of the Philharmonic Society (1862): "It at once created a great sensation—a sensation, we need scarcely add, that has not been diminished by numberless repetitions. At a general meeting of the Society on the 7th of June, 1832,

Sir George Smart read a letter from Mendelssohn requesting the Society's acceptance of the score of this overture; and it was resolved to present him with a piece of plate in token of the Society's thanks, which was forthwith done." The *Harmonicon* praised the overture highly, and found the key of B minor well suited to the purpose.

## CONCERTO FOR VIOLIN, IN E MINOR, OP. 64

*I. Allegro molto appassionato*
*II. Andante*
*III. Allegretto non troppo; allegro molto vivace*

THE CONCERTO does not call for any true depth of emotional display. The sentiment is amiable and genteel, with a dash of becoming melancholy, and the strength is the conventional strength of a man who in music had little virility. Beautifully made, a polished piece of mechanism, the concerto always, under favorable circumstances, interests and promotes contagious good feeling.

Mendelssohn in his youth composed a violin concerto with accompaniment of stringed instruments, also a concerto for violin and pianoforte (1823) with the same sort of accompaniment. These works were left in manuscript. It was at the time that he was put into jackets and trousers. Probably these works were played at the musical parties at the Mendelssohn house in Berlin on alternate Sunday mornings. Mendelssohn took violin lessons first with Carl Wilhelm Henning and afterwards with Eduard Rietz, for whom he wrote this early violin concerto. When Mendelssohn played any stringed instrument, he preferred the viola.

As early as 1838 Mendelssohn conceived the plan of composing a violin concerto in the manner of the one in E minor, for on July 30 he wrote to Ferdinand David: "I should like to write a violin concerto for you next winter. One in E minor is running in my head, and the beginning does not leave me in peace." On July 24 of the next year he wrote from Hochheim to David, who had pressed him to compose the concerto: "It is nice of you to urge me for a violin concerto! I have the liveliest desire to write one for you, and if I have a few propitious days here, I'll bring you something. But the task is not an easy one. You demand that it should be brilliant, and how is such a one as I to do this? The whole of the first solo is to be for the E string!"

The concerto was composed in 1844 and completed on September 16 of that year at Bad Soden, near Frankfort-on-the-Main. David received the manuscript in November. Many letters passed between the composer and the violinist. David gave advice freely. Mendelssohn took time in revising and polishing. Even after the score was sent to the publishers in December, there were more changes. David is largely responsible for the *cadenza* as it now stands.

Mendelssohn played parts of the concerto on the pianoforte to his friends; the whole of it to Moscheles at Bad Soden.

The first performance was from manuscript at the twentieth Gewandhaus concert in Leipsic, March 13, 1845. Ferdinand David was the violinist. Niels W. Gade conducted.

The concerto is in three connected movements. The first, *allegro molto appassionato,* E minor, 2–2, begins immediately after an introductory measure with the first theme given out by the solo violin. This theme is developed at length by the solo instrument, which then goes on with *cadenza*-like passage-work, after which the theme is repeated and developed as a *tutti* by the full orchestra. The second theme is first given out *pianissimo* in harmony by clarinets and flutes over a sustained organpoint in the solo instrument. The chief theme is used in the development which begins in the solo violin. The brilliant solo *cadenza* ends with a series of *arpeggios,* which continue on through the whole announcement of the first theme by orchestral strings and wind. The conclusion section is in regular form. There is no pause between this movement and the *andante.*

The first section of the *andante,* C major, is a development of the first theme sung by the solo violin. The middle part is taken up with the development of the second theme, a somewhat agitated melody. The third part is a repetition of the first, with the melody in the solo violin, but with a different accompaniment. Mendelssohn originally intended the accompaniment (strings) to the first theme to be played *pizzicato.* He wrote to David, "I intended to write in this way, but something or other—I don't know what—prevented me."

The *finale* opens with a short introduction, *allegretto non troppo,* E minor, 4–4. The main body of the *finale, allegro molto vivace,*

E major, 4-4, begins with calls on horns, trumpets, bassoons, drums, answered by *arpeggios* of the solo violin and tremolos in the strings. The chief theme of the *rondo* is announced by the solo instruments. The orchestra has a second theme, B major; the violin one in G major. In the recapitulation section the *fortissimo* second theme appears again, this time in E major. There is a brilliant *coda.*

Mendelssohn used the following orchestration for the works discussed in this chapter (save for the addition of an ophicleide in the overture to *A Midsummer Night's Dream*): two flutes, two oboes, two clarinets, two bassoons, two horns, two trumpets, kettledrums, and strings.—EDITOR.

## MODESTE PETROVITCH
# MOUSSORGSKY

(Born at Karevo, district of Toropeta, in the government of Pskov, on March 21, 1839; died at St. Petersburg on March 28, 1881)

---

## "A NIGHT ON BALD MOUNTAIN" ("UNE NUIT SUR LE MONT-CHAUVE"); FANTASY FOR ORCHESTRA

### Posthumous Work Completed and Orchestrated by Rimsky-Korsakov

Moussorgsky's fantasy was composed in 1867 and was thus one of the few early Russian orchestral compositions of a fantastically picturesque nature. In the original form it was no doubt crude, for Moussorgsky had little technic for the larger forms of music; he despised "style," and believed that much knowledge would prevent him from attaining the realism that was his goal. That he himself was not satisfied with this symphonic poem is shown by the fact that he revised it two or three times. He died; Rimsky-Korsakov edited it and orchestrated it. The music was finally heard after Moussorgsky's death. Rimsky-Korsakov was a fastidious musician, a learned harmonist, a master of orchestrations. It is said that he sandpapered and polished *Boris Godounov* to the great detriment of Moussorgsky's opera; he chastened the wild spirit; he tamed the native savageness, so it is said. What did he do to this musical picture of a Witches' Sabbath on Bald Mountain?

Having heard several musical descriptions of these unholy Sabbaths, where reverence was paid Satan, exultantly ruling in the form of a he-goat, where there was horrid, obscene revelry, if we may believe well-instructed ancient and modern writers on Satanism and witchcraft, we wonder why any woman, young or old, straddled a broomstick and made her way hopefully and joyfully to a lonely mountain or barren plain. If we can put faith in the musical descriptions given by Berlioz, Boïto, Gounod, Satan's evening receptions were comparatively tame affairs, with dancing of a nature that would not have offended the selectmen and their wives and sisters of our little village in the sixties, when the waltz was frowned on as a sensual and ungodly diversion. Liszt's *Mephisto Waltz* is, indeed, sensuous, fleshly, but Satan in this instance only plays the fiddle; he is not master of sabbatic revels. In Moussorgsky's symphonic poem the *allegro* devoted to the worshipers of the devil is rather commonplace; its laborious wildness becomes monotonous in spite of the editor's instrumentation. Far more original and effective is the second section, in which a church bell puts the blasphemous revelers to flight.

In September, 1860, Moussorgsky wrote to Balakirev: "I have also been given a most interesting piece of work to do, which must be ready by next summer: a whole act of *The Bald Mountain* (after Megden's drama *The Witch*). The assembly of the witches, various episodes of witchcraft, the pageant of all the sorcerers, and a *finale,* the witch dance and homage to Satan. The libretto is very fine. I have already a few materials for the music, and it may be possible to turn out something very good." In September, 1862, he wrote to Balakirev, saying that his friend's attitude towards *The Witches* [*sic*] had embittered him. "I considered, still consider, and shall consider forever that the thing is satisfactory. . . . I come forth with a first big work. . . . I shall alter neither plan nor working-out; for both are in close relationship with the contents of the scene, and are carried out in a spirit of genuineness, without tricks or make-believes. . . . I have fulfilled my task as best I could. The one thing I shall alter is the percussion, which I have misused." A letter to Rimsky-Korsakov dated July, 1867, shows that he did rewrite *A Night on Bald Mountain,* but remained unwilling to make further alterations.

During the winter of 1871–72 the director of the opera at St. Petersburg planned that Moussorgsky, Borodin, Rimsky-Korsakov, and Cui should each write a portion of a fairy opera, *Mlada.* Moussorgsky was to write music for some folk scenes, a march for the procession of Slav princes and a great fantastical scene, "The Sacrifice to the Black Goat on Bald Mountain." This would give him the opportunity of using his symphonic poem. The project fell through on account of pecuniary reasons. Rimsky-Korsakov's *Mlada* was produced at St. Petersburg in 1892.

In 1877 Moussorgsky undertook to write an opera *The Fair at Sorotchinsi,* based on a tale by Gogol. He purposed to introduce in it *A Night on Bald Mountain,* and he revised the score.

It is said that the original version of the symphonic poem was for pianoforte and orchestra; that the revision for *Mlada* was for orchestra and chorus; that the work was to serve as a scenic interlude in the unfinished opera, *The Fair at Sorotchinsi.*

Rimsky-Korsakov as Moussorgsky's musical executor revised the score of the poem. He retained the composer's argument:

"Subterranean din of supernatural voices. Appearance of Spirits of Darkness, followed by that of the god Tchernobog. Glorification of Tchernobog. Black mass. Witches' Sabbath. At the height of the Sabbath there sounds far off the bell of the little church in a village which scatters the Spirits of Darkness. Daybreak."

The form is simple: a symphonic *allegro* is joined to a short *andante; allegro feroce; poco meno mosso.*

*A Night on Bald Mountain,* dedicated to Vladimir Stassov, is scored for piccolo, two flutes, two oboes, two clarinets, two bassoons, four horns, two trumpets, three trombones, bass tuba, kettledrums, bass drum, cymbals, tam-tam, bell in D, and strings.

The first performance was at a concert of the Russian Symphony Society at St. Petersburg on October 27, 1886. Rimsky-Korsakov conducted. The piece met with such success that it was played later in that season.

# WOLFGANG AMADEUS
# MOZART

(Born at Salzburg, January 27, 1756;
died at Vienna, December 5, 1791)

---

IN THIS LIFE that is "so daily," as Jules Laforgue complained, a life of tomorrow rather than of today, we are inclined to patronize the ancient worthies who in their own period were very modern, or to speak jauntily of them as bores, with their works of "only historical interest." Mozart has not escaped. Many concertgoers yawn at his name and wonder why such men as Richard Strauss or Vincent d'Indy could praise him with glowing cheeks. They suspect this attribute of worship to be a pose. Remind them of the fact that to such widely different characters as Rossini, Chopin, Tchaikovsky, Brahms, the musician of musicians was Mozart, and they say lightly, "There's no accounting for tastes; surely you do not pretend to maintain that Mozart is a man of this generation."

No, Mozart was neither a symbolist nor a pessimist. He was not a translator of literature, sculpture, or painting into music. His imagination was not fired by a metaphysical treatise. He simply wrote music that came into his head and disquieted him until it was jotted down on paper. He did not go about nervously seeking for ideas. His music is never the passionate cry, never the wild shriek of a racked soul. His music is never hysterical, it is never morbid. It is seldom emotional as we necessarily and unhappily understand that word today. Perhaps for these reasons it is still modern, immortal, and not merely on account of the long and exquisite melodic line, fitting, inevitable background, delicate coloring. Music that is only the true voice of a particular generation is moribund as soon as it is born.

His music, whether it vitalizes stage characters or is absolute, as in the three famous symphonies, and in the chamber works, is as the music on Prospero's isle: "Sounds and sweet airs that give delight and hurt not." The analyst may find pleasure in praising the unsurpassable workmanship, which is akin to the spontaneity of natural phenomena; he may marvel at the simplicity of plan and expression; the simplicity that is the despair of interpreters, for it is the touchstone of their own art or artificiality—and Mozart himself, when he told his emperor that his opera had just the right number of notes, anticipated the judgment of time—but he is still far from explaining the peculiar and ineffable tenderness of this music that soothes and caresses and comforts.

The serenity, the classic suggestion of emotion without the distortion that accompanies passion, would grace a tragedy of Sophocles or a comedy by Congreve. Mozart's music is essentially Grecian, yet now and then it reminds one of Watteau.

Hazlitt said of art that it should seem to come from the air and return to it. But he characterized it with finer appreciation when he said, without mention of Mozart's name, "Music is color without form; a soul without a body; a mistress whose face is veiled; an invisible goddess." And for this reason Debussy is the spiritual brother of Mozart, moderns both, yet classics.

## WOLFGANG AMADEUS MOZART

*Symphonies in E flat (Koechel No. 543), G minor (Koechel No. 550), C major ("Jupiter"), (Koechel No. 551)*

### SYMPHONY IN E FLAT MAJOR (KOECHEL NO. 543)

I. *Adagio; allegro*
II. *Andante*
III. *Minuetto; trio*
IV. *Finale: allegro*

Mozart wrote his symphony when in a condition of distress, but who would know from the music of the composer's poverty and gloom? The iteration of the chief theme of the second movement soon frets the nerves, not from any poignancy of emotion, but from its very placidity. And how seldom in Mozart's music is there any emotional burst as we understand emotion today! There are a few passages in the first movement of the G minor symphony, pages in certain chamber works, and in the *Requiem,* and there are the two great scenes in *Don Giovanni,* the trio between the Don, the Commander, and Leporello after the duel, and the scene between the blaspheming rake and the Stone Man. As a rule the emotion of Mozart is that of the classic frieze or urn. Beauty with him is calm and serene, and emotion, he believed, should always be beautiful.

The symphony in E flat induced A. Apel to attempt a translation of the music into poetry that should express the character of each movement. It excited the fantastical E. T. A. Hoffmann to an extraordinary rhapsody: "Love and melancholy are breathed forth in purest spirit tones; we feel ourselves drawn with inexpressible longing toward the forms which beckon us to join them in their move with the spheres in the eternal circles of the solemn dance." So explained Johannes Kreisler in the *Phantasiestücke in Callots Manier.*

## SYMPHONY IN G MINOR (KOECHEL NO. 550)

*I. Allegro molto*
*II. Andante*
*III. Minuetto; trio*
*IV. Finale: allegro assai*

IT SEEMS as if Mozart lost his classic serenity whenever he chose the key of G minor. In the immortal symphony there is, except in the beautiful, characteristically Mozartian *andante,* a feverishness, an intensity not to be found in his other symphonies; and so in the perfect flower of his chamber music there is a direct, passionate appeal of one theme (G minor again) that reminds one of the terribly earnest Verdi of the 'fifties.

Some years ago, a prominent writer about music, a wild-eyed worshiper of Liszt and Wagner, published the statement that this symphony is interesting only in a historical sense. His idols would have been the first to laugh at him. There are few things in art that are perfect. The G minor symphony is one of them. Its apparent simplicity is an adorable triumph of supreme art.

## SYMPHONY IN C MAJOR, "JUPITER" (KOECHEL NO. 551)

*I. Allegro vivace*
*II. Andante cantabile*
*III. Minuetto: allegretto; trio*
*IV. Finale: allegro molto*

HEARING the *andante,* the *minuet,* and the wonderful *finale,* one no longer questions the famous and subtle saying of Rossini. When asked who was the greatest composer, he answered "Beethoven"; he then said, "But Mozart is the only one."

Let the first movement pass with its second theme that reminds one of charming music in *The Marriage of Figaro*. The *andante* could have been written only by Mozart. There is spiritualized sensuousness; there is perfect form, exquisite proportion, and euphony.

Has there not too much been said about the marvelous display of science in the construction of the *finale?* The wonder of it is that the display does not impress the hearer unduly. To him it is merely gay and charming music. It ravishes his ear without his taking interest in the technical devices, even if he could recognize and understand them. If the title should be "Symphony in C major with the Fugue," the word "fugue" would not fill his soul with dismal foreboding. There has been only one Mozart, as there has been only one Handel.

It is not known who gave the title "Jupiter" to the symphony. There is nothing in the music that reminds one of Jupiter Tonans, Jupiter Fulgurator, Jupiter Pluvius; or of the god who, assuming various disguises, came down to earth, where by his adventures with women semi-divine or mortals of common clay he excited the jealous rage of Juno. The music is not of an Olympian mood. It is intensely human in its loveliness and its gayety.

It is possible that the *"Jupiter"* symphony was performed at the concert given by Mozart in Leipsic. The two that preceded the great three were composed in 1783 and 1786. The latter of the two (D major) was performed at Prague with extraordinary success. Publishers were not slow in publishing Mozart's compositions, even if they were as conspicuous niggards as Joseph II himself. The two symphonies played at Leipsic were probably of the three composed in 1788, but this is only a conjecture.

Some say the title "Jupiter" was applied to the symphony by J. B. Cramer, to express his admiration for the loftiness of ideas and nobility of treatment. Some maintain that the triplets in the first measure suggest the thunderbolts of Jove. Some think that the "calm, godlike beauty" of the music compelled the title. Others are satisfied with the belief that the title was given to the symphony as it might be to any masterpiece or any impressively beautiful or strong or big thing. To them "Jupiter" expresses the power and brilliançe of the work.

The eulogies pronounced on this symphony are familiar to all—from Schumann's "There are things in the world about which nothing can be said, as Mozart's C major symphony with the fugue, much of Shakespeare, and pages of Beethoven," to Bülow's "I call Brahms' First symphony the Tenth, not because it should be placed after the Ninth: I should put it between the Second and the *Eroica,* just as I think the first not the symphony of Beethoven but the one composed by Mozart and known by the name of 'Jupiter.'" But there were decriers early in the nineteenth century. Thus Hans Georg Nägeli (1773–1836) attacked this symphony bitterly on account of its well-defined and long-lined melody, "which Mozart mingled and confounded with a free instrumental play of ideas, and his very wealth of fancy and emotional gifts led to a sort of fermentation in the whole province of art, and caused it to retrograde rather than to advance." He found fault with certain harmonic progressions which he characterized as trivial. He allowed the composer originality and a certain power of combination, but he found him without style, often shallow and confused. He ascribed these qualities to the personal qualities of the man himself: "He was too hasty, when not too frivolous, and he wrote as he himself was." Nägeli was not the last to judge a work according to the alleged morality or immorality of the maker.

Mozart wrote his three greatest symphonies in 1788. The one in E flat is dated June 26; the one in G minor, July 25; the one in C major with the *fugue-finale,* August 10.

His other works of that year are of little importance with the exception of a piano concerto in D major which he played at the coronation festivities of Leopold II at Frankfort in 1790. Why is this? 1787 was the year of *Don Giovanni;* 1790, the year of *Cosi fan tutte.* Was Mozart, as some say, exhausted by the feat of producing three symphonies in such a short time? Or was there some reason for discouragement and consequent idleness?

The Ritter Gluck, composer to the Emperor Joseph II, died November 15, 1787, and thus resigned his position with a salary of 2,000 florins. Mozart was appointed his successor, but the thrifty Joseph cut down the salary to 800 florins. And Mozart at this time was sadly in need of money, as his letters show. In a letter of June, 1788, he tells of his new lodgings, where he could have better air, a garden, quiet. In another, dated June 27, he says: "I have done more work in the ten days that I have lived here than in two months in my other lodgings, and I should be much better here, were it not for dismal thoughts that often come to me. I must drive them resolutely away; for I am living comfortably, pleasantly, and cheaply." We know that he borrowed from Puchberg, a merchant with whom he became acquainted at a Masonic lodge, for the letter with Puchberg's memorandum of the amount is in the collection edited by Nohl.

Mozart could not reasonably expect help from the Emperor. The composer of *Don Giovanni* and the *"Jupiter"* symphony was unfortunate in his emperors.

The Emperor Joseph was in the habit of getting up at five o'clock; he dined on boiled bacon at 3.15 P. M.; he preferred water as a beverage, but would drink a glass of Tokay; he was continually putting chocolate drops from his waistcoat pocket into his mouth; he gave gold coins to the poor; he was unwilling to sit for his portrait; he had remarkably fine teeth; he disliked sycophantic fuss; he patronized the English, who introduced horse-racing; and Michael Kelly, who tells us many things, says that Joseph was "passionately fond of music and a most excellent and accurate judge of it." We know that he did not like the music of Mozart.

Joseph commanded from his composer Mozart no opera, cantata, symphony, or piece of chamber music, although he was paying him 800 florins a year. He did order dances, for the dwellers in Vienna were dancing mad. Kelly, who knew Mozart and sang in the first performance of *Le Nozze di Figaro* in 1786, says in his memoirs (written by Theodore Hook): "The ridotto rooms, where the masquerade took place, were in the palace; and, spacious and commodious as they were, they were actually crammed with masqueraders. I never saw or indeed heard of any suite of rooms where elegance and convenience were more considered, for the propensity of the Vienna ladies for dancing and going to carnival masquerades was so determined that nothing was permitted to interfere with their enjoyment of their favorite amusement. . . . The ladies of Vienna are particularly celebrated for their grace and movements in waltzing, of which they never tire. For my own part, I thought waltzing from ten at night until seven in the morning a continual whirligig, most tiresome to the eye and ear, to say nothing of any worse consequences."[1] Mozart wrote for these dances, as did Haydn, Hummel, Beethoven.

We know little or nothing concerning the first years of the three symphonies. Gerber's *"Lexicon der Tonkünstler"* (1790) speaks appreciatively of him: the erroneous statement is made that the Emperor fixed his salary in 1788 at 6,000 florins; the varied ariettas for piano are praised especially; but there is no mention whatever of any symphony.

The enlarged edition of Gerber's work (1813) contains an extended notice of Mozart's last years, and we find in the summing up of his career: "If one knew only one of his noble symphonies, as the overpoweringly great, fiery, perfect, pathetic, sublime symphony in C." And this reference is undoubtedly to the *"Jupiter,"* the one in C major.

Mozart gave a concert at Leipsic in May, 1789. The programme was made up wholly of pieces by him, and among them were two symphonies in manuscript. At a rehearsal for this concert Mozart took the first *allegro* of a symphony at a very fast pace, so that the orchestra soon was unable to keep up with him. He stopped the players and began again at the same speed, and he stamped the time so furiously that his steel shoe buckle flew into pieces. He laughed, and, as the players still dragged, he began the *allegro* a third time. The musicians, by this time exasperated, played to suit him. Mozart afterwards said to some who wondered at his conduct, because he had on other occasions protested against undue speed: "It was not caprice on my part. I saw that the majority of the players were well along in years. They would have dragged everything beyond endurance if I had not set fire to them and made them angry, so that out of sheer spite they did their best." Later in the rehearsal he praised the orchestra, and said that it was unnecessary for it to rehearse the accompaniment to the pianoforte concerto: "The parts are correct, you play well, and so do I." This concert, by the way, was poorly attended, and half of those who were present had received free tickets from Mozart, who was generous in such matters.

Mozart also gave a concert of his own works at Frankfort, October 14, 1790. Symphonies were played in Vienna in 1788, but they were by

[1]Michael Kelly: *Reminiscences,* 1826; written by Theodore Hook, from material furnished by Kelly.

Haydn; and one by Mozart was played in 1791. In 1792 a symphony by Mozart was played at Hamburg.

The early programmes, even when they have been preserved, seldom determine the date of a first performance. It was the custom to print: *"Symphonie von Wranitsky," "Sinfonie von Mozart," "Sinfonia di Haydn."* Furthermore, it should be remembered that *Sinfonie* was then a term often applied to any work in three or more movements written for strings, or strings and wind instruments.

## OVERTURE TO THE OPERA, "THE MARRIAGE OF FIGARO"

*Le Nozze di Figaro: dramma giocoso in quadro atti; poesia di Lorenzo Da Ponte, aggiustata dalla commedia del Beaumarchais, "Le Mariage de Figaro"; musica di W. A. Mozart,* was composed at Vienna in 1786 and produced there on May 1 of the same year.

The overture opens (*presto,* D major, 4-4) immediately with the first theme; the first part of it is a running passage of seven measures in eighth notes (strings and bassoons in octaves), and the second part is given for four measures to wind instruments, with a joyous response of seven measures by full orchestra. This theme is repeated. A subsidiary theme follows, and the second theme appears in A major, a gay figure in the violins, with bassoon, afterward flute. There is no free fantasia. There is a long *coda.*

Mozart saw in the play of Beaumarchais an excellent libretto for an opera. Da Ponte tells the story in his amusing *Memoirs:* "Talking one day with him [Mozart], he asked me if I could turn Beaumarchais's *Noces de Figaro* into an opera. The proposition was to my taste, and the success was immediate and universal. A little before, this piece had been forbidden by the Emperor's command, on account of its immorality. How then to propose it anew? Baron Vetzlar [Wezlar] offered me with his customary generosity a reasonable price for my libretto and assured me that he would see to its production at London or in France, if it were refused in Vienna. I did not accept the offer, and I secretly began work. I waited the opportune moment to propose the poem either to the Intendant or, if I had the courage, to the Emperor himself. Martin alone was in my confidence, and he was so generous, out of deference to Mozart, to give me time to finish my piece before I began work on one for him. As fast as I wrote the words, Mozart wrote the music, and it was all finished in six weeks. The lucky star of Mozart willed an opportune moment and permitted me to carry my manuscript directly to the Emperor.

" 'How's this?' said Joseph to me. 'You know that Mozart, remarkable for his instrumental music, has with one exception never written for song, and the exception is not good for much.'

"I answered timidly, 'Without the kindness of the Emperor, I should have written only one drama in Vienna.'

" 'True: but I have already forbidden the German company to play this piece *Figaro*.'

" 'I know it; but, in turning it into an opera, I have cut out whole scenes, shortened others, and been careful everywhere to omit anything that might shock the conventionalities and good taste; in a word, I have made a work worthy of the theater honored by His Majesty's protection. As for the music, as far as I can judge, it seems to me a masterpiece.'

" 'All right; I trust to your taste and prudence. Send the score to the copyists.'

"A moment afterward I was at Mozart's. I had not yet told him the good news, when he was ordered to go to the palace with his score. He obeyed, and the Emperor thus heard several *morceaux* which delighted him. Joseph II had a very correct taste in music, and in general for everything that is included in the fine arts. The prodigious success of this work throughout the whole world is a proof of it. The music, incredible to relate, did not obtain a unanimous vote of praise. The Viennese composers crushed by it, Rosenberg and Casti especially, never failed to run it down."[2]

Did Da Ponte show himself the courtier when he spoke of the Emperor's "very correct taste in music"?

There was a cabal from the start against the production of Mozart's opera. Kelly says in his *Reminiscences:* "Every one of the opera company took part in the contest. I alone was a stickler for Mozart, and naturally enough, for he had a claim on my warmest wishes. . . . Of all the performers in this opera at that time, but one survives—myself. [This was written in 1826.] It was allowed that never was opera stronger cast. I have seen it performed at different periods in other countries, and well too, but no more to compare with its original performance than light is to darkness. All the original performers had the

[2]Lorenzo da Ponte: *Memoirs,* translated by Elizabeth Abbott, 1929.

advantage of the instruction of the composer, who transfused into their minds his inspired meaning. I never shall forget his little animated countenance, when lighted up with the glowing rays of genius; it is as impossible to describe as it would be to paint sunbeams."

## OVERTURE TO THE OPERA "THE MAGIC FLUTE"

EMANUEL JOHANN SCHIKANEDER, the author of the libretto of *Die Zauberflöte* (The Magic Flute), was a wandering theater director, poet, composer, and play actor. Vain, improvident, shrewd, a bore, he nevertheless had good qualities that won for him the friendship of Mozart. In 1791 Schikaneder was the director of the Auf der Wieden, a little theater where comic operas were performed. He no doubt would have made a success of his venture, had he curbed his ambition. On the verge of failure, he made a fairy drama out of *Lulu, or the Enchanted Flute,* Liebeskind's story in a collection of fairy tales published by Wieland. He asked Mozart to write the music for it. Mozart, pleased with the scenario, accepted the offer and said: "If I do not bring you out of your trouble, and if the work is not successful, you must not blame me; for I have never written magic music." Schikaneder had followed closely Wieland's text; but he learned that Marinelli, a rival manager, the director of the Leopoldstadt Theater thought of putting upon the stage a piece with the same subject; so he hurriedly, and with the assistance of an actor named Gieseke, modified the plot, and substituted for the evil genius of the play the high priest Sarastro, who appears to be the custodian of the secrets and the executor of the wishes of the Masonic order.

Schikaneder knew the ease with which Mozart wrote. He also knew that it was necessary to keep watch over him, that he might be ready at the appointed time. Mozart's wife was then in Baden. Schikaneder therefore put Mozart in a little pavilion which was in the midst of a garden near his theater. The music of *The Magic Flute* was written in this pavilion and in a room of the casino of Josephdorf. Mozart was deep in doleful dumps when he began his task, so Schikaneder surrounded him with members of his company. It was long believed that the composer was then inspired by the beautiful eyes of the singing woman, Gerl, but the story may rest on no better foundation than the one of the Mme Hofdaemmel tragedy, which even Otto Jahn thought worthy of his investigation.

Schikaneder made his proposal early in March, 1791. The overture, with the Priests' March, was composed September 28, 1791. On September 30 of that year *Die Zauberflöte,* a grand opera in two acts, was produced at the Auf der Wieden Theater.

Schikaneder's name was in large type on the bill; Mozart's name was in small type underneath the cast. Johann Schenk (1753–1836), who made money and won fame by the popularity of his operas—*Der Dorfbarbier* (1796) was long a favorite—Schenk gave Beethoven lessons in counterpoint at Vienna in 1793–94—sat in one of the orchestra seats. At the end of the overture, he went to Mozart and kissed his hand. Mozart stroked his admirer's cheek. But the first act was not well received. Mozart went behind the scenes and saw Schikaneder in his costume of a bird. He reassured Mozart, but the opera disappointed the Viennese at first, and Mozart was cut to the quick. The cool reception was not due to the character of the subject; for "magic plays" with music of Viennese composers, as Wenzel Müller, were very popular, and *The Magic Flute* was regarded as a *Singspiel,* a "magic farce," with unusually elaborate music. The report from Vienna that was published in Kunzen and Reichardt's music journal, *Studien fur Tonkünstler und Musikfreunde* (Berlin, 1793, p. 79), tells the story: "The new machine comedy, *The Magic Flute,* with music by our *Kapellmeister* Mozard [*sic*], which was given at great expense and with such sumptuousness, did not meet with the expected success, for the contents and dialogue of the piece are utterly worthless." Schikaneder was obstinate in his faith; the opera soon became the fashion. The two hundredth representation was celebrated at Vienna in October, 1795. *The Magic Flute* made its way over the continent. The libretto was translated into Dutch, Swedish, Danish, Polish, Italian. Paris knew the opera in 1801 (August 23) as *Les Mystères d'Isis.* The first performance in London was on May 25, 1819, in Italian.

Mozart died shortly after the production of *The Magic Flute,* in deep distress. This opera, with the music of his *Requiem,* was in his mind until the final delirium. While the opera was performing he would take his watch from under his pillow and follow the performance in imagination: "We are now at the end of the act," or "Now comes the grand aria for the Queen of Night." The day before he died, he sang with his weak voice the opening measures of "Der Vogelfänger bin ich ja," and endeavored to beat the time with his hands. The frivolous and audacious Schikaneder, "sensualist, parasite, spendthrift," filled his purse by this opera: in 1798 he built the Theater an der Wien. On the roof he put his own statue, clothed in the feather costume of Papageno. His luck was not constant; in 1812 he died in poverty.

## CONCERTOS FOR VIOLIN

*No. 1, in B flat major* *(Koechel No. 207)*
*No. 2, in D major* *(Koechel No. 212)*
*No. 3, in G major* *(Koechel No. 216)*
*No. 4, in D major* *(Koechel No. 218)*
*No. 5, in A major* *(Koechel No. 219)*
*No. 6, in E flat major* *(Koechel No. 268)*

Mozart composed five violin concertos at Salzburg in 1775. The accompaniment of the five concertos is scored for the same instruments: two oboes, two horns, strings. In 1776 Mozart wrote a sixth concerto—E flat major—with an accompaniment scored for flute, two oboes, two bassoons, two horns, and strings. A seventh was discovered by Dr. Kopfermann in 1907. There is some doubt as to its genuineness.

These concertos were undoubtedly written for Mozart's own use. As a child, he played the violin as well as the forerunners of the pianoforte, and on his tour in 1763 he played the violin in public. His first published composition was a sonata in C major for pianoforte and violin (K. No. 6). This, and one in D major, were composed in 1763 at Paris. They are dedicated to the Princess Victoire of France. In 1775 Mozart was practicing diligently the violin to please his father. It was one of Wolfgang's duties at the Court to play the violin. He disliked to do it. His father, an excellent violinist, encouraged his son: "You have no idea how well you play the violin; if you would only do yourself justice, and play with boldness, spirit, and fire, you would be the first violinist in Europe." This was in answer to a letter from Munich in which Mozart had written: "I played as though I were the greatest fiddler in Europe." In 1777 the father reproached him for neglecting the violin (in Vienna Wolfgang preferred to play the viola in quartets). And it was in 1777 that Mozart wrote of one Franzl whom he heard playing a violin concerto at Mannheim: "You know I am no great lover of difficulties. He plays difficult things, but one does not recognize the difficulties and imagines that one could do the same thing at once: that is true art. He also has a beautiful round tone —not a note is missing, one hears everything; everything is well marked. He has a fine *staccato* bow, up as well as down; and I have never heard so good a double shake as his. In a word, though he is no wizard, he is a solid violinist."

The characteristics of the Salzburg violin concertos are the same. They are in three movements, *allegro, andante* or *adagio,* and *rondo.* The first movement is the one most developed, although it might be considered as in aria form rather than the form befitting a first movement of a symphony. There is the customary alternation between *tutti* and solo passages. The structure is more compact than that of the aria; it has more life. The "passage" measures grow out of the themes, play about them, or are closely related to them. The second movement requires expressive playing of sustained melody and is of a cheerful character. The *finale* is in rondo form and joyful mood.

## MOZART AS PIANIST

From Mozart's letters, one learns something about his own manner of playing the piano:

"Herr Stein sees and hears that I am more of a player than Beecke—that without making grimaces of any kind I play so expressively that, according to his own confession, no one shows off his pianoforte as well as I. That I always remain strictly in time surprises everyone; they cannot understand that the left hand should not in the least be concerned in a *tempo rubato.* When they play, the left hand always follows" (1777).

About Nannette Stein's playing: "She sits opposite the treble instead of in the middle of the instrument, so that there may be greater opportunities for swaying about and making grimaces. Then she rolls up her eyes and smirks. If a passage occurs twice, it is played slower the second time; if three times, still slower. When a passage comes, up goes the arm, and, if there is to be an emphasis it must come from the arm, heavily and clumsily, not from the fingers. But the best of all is that when there comes a passage (which ought to flow like oil) in which there necessarily occurs a change of fingers, there is no need of taking care: when the time comes you stop, lift the hand and nonchalantly begin again. This helps one the better to catch a false note, and the effect is frequently curious" (1777). Nannette was then eight years old.

At Aurnhammer's: "The young woman is a fright, but she plays ravishingly, though she lacks the true singing style in her *cantabile;* she is too jerky" (1781).

"Whenever I played for him [Richter, a pianist], he looked immovably at my fingers, and one day he said, 'My God! how I am obliged to torment myself and sweat, and yet without obtaining applause; and for you, my friend, it is mere play!' 'Yes,' said I, 'I had to labor once in order not to show labor now' " (1784).

"It is much easier to play rapidly than slowly; you can drop a few notes in passages without anyone noticing it. But is it beautiful? At such speed you can use the hands indiscriminately; but is that beautiful?" (1778.)

"Give me the best clavier in Europe and at the same time hearers who understand nothing or want to understand nothing, and who do not feel what I play with me, and all my joy is gone" (1778).

"The *andante* is going to give us the most trouble, for it is full of expression and must be played with taste . . . If I were her [Rose Cannabich's] regular teacher, I would lock up all her music, cover the keyboard with a handkerchief, and make her practice on nothing but passages, trills, mordents, etc., until the difficulty with the left hand was remedied."

Saint-Saëns, lover of irony and paradox, wrote a preface to his edition of Mozart's pianoforte sonatas, published at Paris in 1915, in which, after a discussion of the ornaments, he has this to say:

"One is accustomed in modern editions to be prodigal with *liaisons,* to indicate constantly *legato, molto legato, sempre legato.* There is nothing of this in the manuscripts and the old editions. Everything leads us to believe that this music should be performed lightly, that the figures should produce an effect analogous to that obtained on the violin by giving a stroke to each note without leaving the string. When Mozart wished the *legato,* he indicated it. In the middle of the last century, pianists were still found whose playing was singularly leaping (as one may say). The old non-*legato,* being exaggerated, became a *staccato.* This exaggeration brought a reaction in the contrary sense, and this was pushed too far. . . .

"This music of Mozart during his early years is destitute of nuances;

occasionally a *piano* or a *forte;* nothing more. The reason for this abstinence is because these pieces were written for the clavecin, and its sonority could not be modified by a pressure of the finger. Clavecins with two keyboards could alternate with *forte* and *piano,* but nuances, properly speaking, were unknown to them.

"In the 18th century, one lived more quietly than today, nor were there in music our modern habits of speed, which is often inflicted on ancient compositions to their great injury. It is necessary to shun in the case of Mozart this tendency to hurry the movements, as too often happens. His *presto* corresponds to our *allegro;* his *allegro* to our *allegro moderato.* His *adagios* are extremely slow, as is shown by the multiplicity of notes sometimes contained in a single beat. The *andante* is not very slow.

"It was the rule, in his time, not to put the thumb on a black key except from absolute necessity. This method of fingering gives to the hand great restfulness, precious for the performance of old music that demands perfect equality of the fingers.

"The first pianofortes were far from having the powerful sonority of the great modern instruments. Therefore, it is not always necessary to take Mozart's *forte* literally; it is often the equivalent of our *mezzo forte.*"

## SERGE SERGIEVICH
# PROKOFIEFF

(Born at Sontsovka, Russia, April 23, 1891)

---

## SCYTHIAN SUITE, "ALA AND LOLLI," OP. 20

*I. The Adoration of Veles and Ala*
*II. The Enemy God and the Dance of the Black Spirits*
*III. Night*
*IV. The Glorious Departure of Lolli and the Procession of the Sun*

THE ANCIENT Scythians, wildly savage, had horrid manners and customs. Herodotus tells us at pleasing length how they sacrificed one in a hundred of their enemies to Mars; how in battle they scalped their foes and drank their blood; how they burned false prophets among their many soothsayers; how they strangled servants of their dead king and seated them upon horses stuffed with chaff to place about the monument. Truly a splendidly barbarous folk.

And in his Scythian suite, Prokofieff has written superbly barbaric music.

This music is something more than roaring, blaring dissonance; something more than eccentric experimentation in harmonic schemes and daring orchestration. The suite is deftly planned; broadly conceived; carried out with rare dramatic intensity.

No matter how wild this music is, there is admirable method in the madness; there is a refreshing mastery in the development of the composer's purpose. He knew what he wanted; he gained his effects. They are not episodic, spasmodic, but skillfully continuous. The third movement, "Night," is perhaps the most remarkable in the revelation of poetically dramatic feeling. There is "the blackness of darkness"—a night in which Nature herself shudders and is afraid; a night when the Demon is master, and strange, sinister deeds are wrought. Compare this movement with the magnificent *finale* with its amazing climax.

This suite was composed in 1914. The first performance was at the Imperial Maryinski Theater, Petrograd, on January 29, 1916. The composer conducted.

The suite is scored for piccolo, three flutes, three oboes, English horn, three clarinets, bass clarinet, three bassoons, double bassoon, eight horns, four trumpets, four trombones, bass tuba, kettledrums, bass drum, side drum, tambourine, cymbals, triangle, celesta, xylophone, bells, two harps, pianoforte, and strings.

The four movements have this programme:

I. Invocation to Veles and Ala. *Allegro feroce,* 4-4 time. The music describes an invocation to the sun, worshiped by the Scythians as their highest deity, named Veles. This invocation is followed by the sacrifice to the beloved idol, Ala, the daughter of Veles.

II. The Evil-God and dance of the pagan monsters. *Allegro sostenuto,* 4-4 time. The Evil-God summons the seven pagan monsters from their subterranean realms and, surrounded by them, dances a delirious dance.

III. Night. *Andantino,* 4-4 time. The Evil-God comes to Ala in the darkness. Great harm befalls her. The moon rays fall upon Ala, and the moon-maidens descend to bring her consolation.

IV. Lolli's pursuit of the Evil-God and the sunrise. *Tempestuoso,* 4-4 time. Lolli, a Scythian hero, went forth to save Ala. He fights the Evil-God. In the uneven battle with the latter, Lolli would have perished, but the Sun-God rises with the passing of night and smites the evil deity. With the description of the sunrise the suite comes to an end.

Scythia is a name that has been applied to different countries at different times. The Scythia described by Herodotus comprised the southeastern parts of Europe between the Carpathian Mountains and the river Tanaïs (now Don). Herodotus gives a graphic and singularly interesting account of these wild, barbaric nomads in the fourth book of his history. We are interested here only with what he has to say about their religion:

"They propitiate the following gods only: Vesta, most of all; then Jupiter, deeming the Earth to be the wife of Jupiter; after these, Apollo, and Venus Urania, and Hercules and Mars. All the Scythians acknowledge these, but those who are called Royal Scythians sacrifice also to Neptune. Vesta in the Scythian language is named Tabiti; Jupiter is, in my opinion, very rightly called Papæus; the Earth, Apia; Apollo, Œtosyrus; Venus Urania, Artimposa; and Neptune, Thamimasadas. They are not accustomed to erect images, altars, and temples, except to Mars; to him they are accustomed." Then follows a minute description of the manner in which they sacrificed cattle and enemies taken prisoners, the latter to Mars. "Swine they never use, nor suffer them to be reared in their country."

## CLASSICAL SYMPHONY, OP. 25

*I. Allegro*
*II. Larghetto*
*III. Gavotte*
*IV. Finale*

Prokofieff's symphony is a delightful little work, fresh, melodious, vivacious, with significant themes; masterly, not pedantic treatment of them; charming orchestration achieved by apparently simple means, but showing consummate skill. The first movement and the *finale* are in many measures truly Mozartean in mood, the *larghetto* and the gavotte are more modern but in no way agressively contradictory.

This symphony, begun in 1916, was completed in 1917. The first performance was at Leningrad by the orchestra now known as the

State Orchestra. The first performance in the United States was at a concert of the Russian Symphony Orchestra in New York, in December, 1918.

The symphony, scored for two flutes, two oboes, two clarinets, two bassoons, two horns, two trumpets, kettledrums, and strings, is dedicated to Boris Assafieff, who, as Igor Gleboff, has written much about music. "The composer's idea in writing this work was to catch the spirit of Mozart and to put down that which, if he were living now, Mozart might put into his scores."[1]

I. *Allegro,* D major, 4–4 time. The chief theme is given to the first violins. A transitional passage has material for the flutes. Development follows. The second theme is for first violins. The development begins with use of the first subject. The transitional measures are taken up, later the second theme. The recapitulation opens in C major (strings). Then follows the transitional passage (D major) for the flute. The second theme is again for the strings. There is a short *coda.*

II. *Larghetto,* A major, 2–2 time. First violins announce the chief theme. There are episodes.

III. *Gavotta: Non troppo allegro,* D major, 4–4 time. The subject is given at once to strings and wood-wind. The trio is in G major (flutes and clarinets above an organ point for violoncellos and double basses). This subject is repeated by the strings.

IV. *Finale: Molto vivace,* D major, 2–2 time. The first theme is for the strings; the second, A major, for wood-wind.

[1]Felix Borowski, Chicago Orchestra Programme.

## SERGEI VASSILIEVICH
# RACHMANINOFF

(Born at Onega in the government of Novgorod, April 1, 1873)

---

## SYMPHONY NO. 2, IN E MINOR, OP. 27

*I. Largo; allegro moderato*
*II. Allegro molto*
*III. Adagio*
*IV. Allegro vivace*

THE COMPOSITION is a long one; it lasts about an hour. The first two movements seem by far the strongest, architecturally and emotionally. The third movement seems insufferably long drawn out and sentimental. The fourth movement gains on a second hearing —has a more decided profile, and seems less episodic.

The reasons for the popularity of this symphony are not far to seek. The themes are eminently melodious, and some of them are of singular beauty; there is rich coloring; there are beautiful nuances in color; there is impressive sonority; there are frequent and sharp contrasts in sentiment, rhythm, expression; there is stirring vitality. Mr. Rachmaninoff in this symphony is romantic in the old and accustomed forms. He does not surprise or perplex by experiments in harmony; his form is essentially academic and traditional. Here is another case of new wine in old leather bottles, but first of all the bottles were put in thorough order, patched, strengthened, cleaned.

Instantaneous popularity often indicates some weakness in a composition. It will be interesting to watch the life of this symphony. There was a time when Raff's *Lenore* was as rapturously applauded. The most extravagant things were said about it. Raff too had uncommon contrapuntal skill; he too was a fecund melodist; he too had a pretty sense of color in his day. And what, pray, has become of Raff's *Lenore?* It is in the great cemetery of orchestral compositions buried snugly with its heroine and her Wilhelm.

Let us enjoy, however, the gifts the gods give us and not indulge ourselves in gloomy thoughts. Mr. Rachmaninoff has written beautiful and eloquent music in this symphony. He has shown technical skill and revealed an emotional side that he has concealed in other compositions. Whether he would show inspiration outside of traditional forms; whether he has imagination in sufficient degree to shape wondrous thoughts in a freer form and be a law not only to himself but to his hearers—these questions we shall call unnecessary.

This symphony, composed at Dresden, was played at Moscow at a concert of the Imperial Russian Music Society in the course of the season of 1908–09. The composer conducted.

The symphony, dedicated to S. Tanéïev, is scored for three flutes (and piccolo), three oboes, English horn, two clarinets, bass clarinet, two bassoons, four horns, three trumpets, three trombones, bass tuba, kettledrums, snare drum, bass drum, cymbals, glockenspiel, and the usual strings.

There is an introduction, *largo,* 4–4, to the first movement. Violoncellos and double basses give an indication of the chief motive. Sustained chords of wind instruments follow, and over them appears the leading thought of the symphony (violins). The solo for the basses is repeated a third lower, and again chords for wind instruments follow. (These passages for wind instruments are used reminiscently in the second movement.) The violin theme is now more broadly developed, and after a short *crescendo* a phrase for the English horn leads to the main portion of the first movement, *allegro moderato,* E minor, 2–2.

The first theme, *molto espressivo,* of the first movement, enters after four measures of prelude and is given to the violins. A motive in triplets for basses, *poco a poco più vivo,* is added. This leads to a section, *moderato,* in which, after preluding, a theme in G major is sung by violins. This becomes more passionate, and leads to a close in G major with a melody for violoncellos. The chief theme of the symphony is developed in the working out, by solo violin, by the rest of the strings and by wood-wind instruments. There is a noticeable rhythmic figure for violas, and this slackening of the pace brings the return of the chief theme of the movement with an elaborate *crescendo.* There are fanfares for the brass, and a horn-call is freely used. There is an agitated *coda.*

Second movement, *allegro molto,* A minor, 2–2. The theme begins with horns and is carried out by violins, while there are characteristic figures for wood-wind instruments. The first section is constructed simply and clearly from portions of this theme. There is a melodious section, *moderato* (violins in octaves, violas, and violoncellos *cantabile*), and then the energetic rhythmic figure brings in the repetition of the first portion of the movement. The trio, *meno mosso,* begins with a design for second violins, and its development includes march-like harmonies for the brass. There is a free repetition of the *scherzo* portion, and at the end a reminiscence of the theme for brass in the introduction.

The third movement, *adagio,* A major, 4–4, is in song form, and there are three leading melodies in succession. The chief one is given to the first violins; the clarinet has an expressive air; the third melody is for oboes and violins. In the middle section there is a return to the chief theme of the symphony. It occurs in dialogue form, and it also appears at the end of the repetition of the first section.

The *finale, allegro vivace,* begins with a lively introduction which is rhythmically developed out of the first jubilant motive for full orchestra. There is a march theme for wind instruments. The second theme is for strings, D major, and is in lyric mood. Many of the melodic figures heard before enter in the *finale.* The climax of passion is reached when the brass sounds forth the bass motive of the introductory *largo,* and at the end the *adagio* theme is sung against the dance motive of the *finale.*

## CONCERTO NO. 2, IN C MINOR, FOR PIANOFORTE WITH ORCHESTRA, OP. 18

*I. Moderato*
*II. Adagio sostenuto*
*III. Allegro scherzando*

THE CONCERTO is of uneven worth. The first movement is labored and has little marked character. It might have been written by any German, technically well-trained, who was acquainted with the music of Tchaikovsky. The *adagio* and the *finale* have more racial spirit and are well designed to win the favor of the crowd; the *adagio* by its agreeable sentiment, the *finale* by the sharply defined themes, the hustle and rush, the *crescendo* of excitement, with the apotheosis, full vigor of the orchestra with a long, sweeping *cantilena,* an obvious tune—truly an *ad captandum finale.*

This concerto was performed for the first time at a concert of the Philharmonic Society of Moscow, October 14, 1901, when the composer was the pianist. The concerto gained for the composer, in 1904, the Glinka prize of 500 roubles, founded by the publisher Belaïev. Published in 1901, it is dedicated to N. Dahl.

The orchestral portion of the concerto is scored for two flutes, two oboes, two clarinets, two bassoons, four horns, two trumpets, three trombones and bass tuba, kettledrums, bass drum, cymbals, and the usual strings.

Rachmaninoff has composed four pianoforte concertos: No. 1, F sharp minor, Op. 1, was written in 1890–91 and revised in 1917; No. 2, in C minor, 1900; No. 3, in D minor, 1909; No. 4, in G minor, 1927.

There follows a description of the Second concerto:

I. *Moderato,* C minor, 2–2. Introductory chords for the pianoforte lead to the exposition of the first theme, which is given to the strings while the pianoforte has an *arpeggio* figure in accompaniment. There is a short orchestral interlude, and the second theme, E flat major, is announced by the pianoforte. The presentation of this subject ends with a *coda* in which there is passage-work for the pianoforte while there is a suggestion of the first theme in the brass choir. The section of development begins with a working out of the first motive, at first in the orchestra. In the recapitulation, *maestoso, alla marcia,* the chief theme is given to the strings, while there are chords for the brass and a counter theme for the solo instrument. The horns take the second theme in augmentation, *moderato,* A flat major. The material for the *coda, meno mosso,* is taken from the chief theme, and the pianoforte has passage-work.

II. *Adagio sostenuto,* E major, 4–4. There is a short introduction with sustained harmonies for strings. These harmonies are soon reinforced by wind instruments. The pianoforte enters with a figure over which the flute and then the clarinet announce the theme on which the movement is built. The opening phrase for the clarinet has much significance in this respect. The pianoforte now has the theme, and the accompaniment of a broken chord figure is given to violins (*pizzicato*) and clarinets. The pace is quickened for the working out of the subject and for episodic material. There is a *cadenza* for the pianoforte, after which there is a repetition in part of the opening section. The *coda* contains a new musical thought for the pianoforte: a progression of chords in the upper part is accompanied by a broken chord figure in the left, and wood-wind instruments play against this in triplets.

III. *Allegro scherzando,* C minor, 4–4. There are introductory measures, and the first motive is for the pianoforte. This motive is developed. The second motive is for oboe and violoncellos, and is taken up later by the pianoforte and leads to figuration in triplets, *meno mosso,* for the same instrument. Then comes a section *allegro scherzando, moto primo,* in which the chief theme is further developed. There is a *fugato:* the first violins are answered by pianoforte and lower strings. In the recapitulation section there is a suggestion of the chief theme, but the second motive is in the orchestra, this time for violins and flute, and it is taken up later, as it was before, by the solo instrument. The triplet figuration returns. *Allegro scherzando:* the chief theme is treated in imitation by the orchestra. There is an increase in speed with a *crescendo,* and, when the climax is reached, there is a *cadenza* for the pianoforte. The second theme is announced by the full orchestra *maestoso,* with chords for the solo instrument. There is a brilliant *coda.*

## JOSEPH MAURICE
# RAVEL

(Born at Ciboure, Basses Pyrénées, March 7, 1875; died at Paris, December 28, 1937)

---

## "MA MERE L'OYE" (MOTHER GOOSE), FIVE CHILDREN'S PIECES

I. *Pavane de la Belle au Bois Dormant (Pavane of Sleeping Beauty)*
II. *Petit Poucet (Hop o' my Thumb)*
III. *Laideronnette, Impératrice des Pagodes (Laideronnette, Empress of the Pagodas)*
IV. *Les Entretiens de la Belle et de la Bête (Conversations of Beauty and the Beast)*
V. *Le Jardin Féerique (The Fairy Garden)*

RAVEL'S MUSIC is of the most delicate texture, lacework with exquisite thoughts orchestrated as for the little orchestra of ivory instruments imagined by Jules Laforgue. Although to the eye the structure of the score is simple, the performance demands the utmost skill on the part of the players and the finest taste of an imaginative conductor. It would be hard to say which of the five movements is the most beautiful in fancy. The "Pavane" has a subtle, melancholy charm. "Hop o' my Thumb" is curiously rhythmed and strangely effective by means of orchestration. "Laideronnette" in the movement of a march is delightful, and with the movement that follows, in the time of a slow waltz and with a solo for the double bassoon representing the Beast, wins immediate popularity. In the ballet the Apotheosis was the "Fairy Garden," and this movement, too, is most poetic.

These pieces were originally composed in 1908 for pianoforte (four hands), and for the pleasure of the children, Mimie and Jean Godebski, to whom they were dedicated when the pieces were published in 1910. They were first performed at a concert of the Société Musicale Independante, Salle Gaveau, Paris, on April 20, 1910. The pianists were Christine Verger, six years old, and Germaine Duramy, ten years old.

I. "Pavane of the Sleeping Beauty." *Lent,* A minor, 4–4. This movement is only twenty measures long. It is based on the opening phrase for flute, horns, and violas.

II. "Hop o' my Thumb." Ravel has quoted in the score this passage from Perrault's tale: "He believed that he would easily find his path by means of his bread crumbs which he had scattered wherever he had passed; but he was very much surprised when he could not find a single crumb: the birds had come and eaten everything up."

III. "Laideronnette, Empress of the Pagodas." The French give the name *pagode* to a little grotesque figure with a movable head, and thus extend the meaning, which was also found in English for pagoda, "an idol or image." This latter use of the word is now obsolete in the English language. A *laideron* is any ugly young girl or young woman. There is this quotation from "Serpentin Vert" by the Countess Marie Catherine d'Aulnoy (about 1655–1705) who wrote romances and also fairy tales in imitation of Perrault. "She undressed herself and went into the bath. The pagodes and pagodines began to sing and play on instruments; some had theorbos made of walnut shells; some had viols made of almond shells; for they were obliged to proportion the instruments to their figure." Laideronnette, in the story, the daughter of a king and queen, was cursed in her cradle by Magotine, a wicked fairy, with the curse of the most horrible ugliness. When the princess grew up, she asked that she might dwell far away in a castle where no one could see her. In the forest near by she met a huge green serpent, who told her that he was once handsomer than she was. Laideronnette had many adventures. In a little boat, guarded by the serpent, she went out to sea and was wrecked on the coast of a land inhabited by pagodes, a little folk whose bodies were formed from porcelain, crystal, diamonds, emeralds, etc. The ruler was an unseen monarch—the green snake who also had been enchanted by Magotine. Finally, he was changed into human shape, and he married Laideronnette, whose beauty was restored.

IV. "The Conversations of Beauty and the Beast." Quotations from Mme Leprince de Beaumont are given:

" 'When I think how good-hearted you are, you do not seem to me so ugly.'

" 'Yes, I have, indeed, a kind heart; but I am a monster.'

" 'There are many men more monstrous than you.'

" 'If I had wit, I would invent a fine compliment to thank you, but I am only a beast.'

. . . . . . . . . . . . . . . . .

" 'Beauty, will you be my wife?'

" 'No, Beast!'

" 'I die content since I have the pleasure of seeing you again.'

" 'No, my dear Beast, you shall not die; you shall live to be my husband!' "

The Beast had disappeared, and she saw at her feet only a prince more beautiful than Love, who thanked her for having broken his enchantment.

*"Mouvement de valse très modéré,"* F major, 3-4. This movement is based chiefly on a melody for the clarinet, which begins in the second measure. There is a middle section with a subject suggesting the Beast and given to the double bassoon. The two subjects are combined. At the end, a solo violin plays the theme of the middle section.

V. "The Fairy Garden." *Lent et grave,* C major, 3-4. The movement is based on the opening theme for strings.

The orchestration is as follows: two flutes (and piccolo), two oboes (and English horn), two clarinets, two bassoons, double bassoon, two horns, kettledrums, triangle, cymbals, bass drum, tam-tam, xylophone, glockenspiel, celesta, harp and strings.

MAURICE RAVEL

## "DAPHNIS ET CHLOÉ," BALLET IN ONE ACT, ORCHESTRAL FRAGMENTS, SECOND SERIES "DAYBREAK," "PANTOMIME," "GENERAL DANCE"

Ravel's cunningly and gorgeously orchestrated ballet bears separation from the stage and stage effects, the dancers and the mimes. Nor is it necessary for one's enjoyment to be concerned with the adventures of Daphnis and Chloe. Here is something more than purple patches of instrumental color and dexterous juggling with surprising combinations of timbres. There is form, there is melody, there are ravishing harmonic devices; there is, above all, poetic imagination.

Ravel composed his ballet, *Daphnis and Chloe,* expecting that it would be performed by the Russian Ballet at Paris in 1911. Jacques Durand, the publisher, says that Ravel was asked by Diaghilev in 1911 to write this ballet. Others give the year 1910. Durand also says Diaghilev was not at first satisfied with the ballet and hesitated to produce it, but Durand finally persuaded him; that Diaghilev's first unfavorable impression was due to his knowing the music only by the arrangement for piano. At the rehearsals there were violent scenes between Fokine and Diaghilev, which led to the rupture which became "official" after that season of the Ballet Russe. It was not performed until June 5, 1912. The performances were at the Châtelet. Nijinsky mimed Daphnis; Mme Karsavina, Chloe. Messrs. Bolm and Cechetti also took leading parts. The conductor was Mr. Monteux. The score, however, was published in 1911. Two concert suites were drawn from it. The first—"Nocturne," "Interlude," "Danse Guerrière"—was performed at a Châtelet concert conducted by Gabriel Pierné on April 2, 1911.

The second suite is scored for two flutes (and piccolo), a flute in G, two oboes, English horn, a clarinet in E flat, two clarinets in B flat, bass clarinet in B flat, three bassoons, double bassoon, four horns, four trumpets, three trombones, bass tuba, kettledrums, bass drum, cymbals, triangle, tambourine, two side drums, castanets, celesta, glockenspiel, two harps, strings (double basses with the low C), chorus of mixed voices. This chorus, which sings without words, can be replaced by variants inserted for this purpose in the orchestral parts.

The following argument is printed in the score of the suite to illustrate the significance of the sections in succession:

"No sound but the murmur of rivulets fed by the dew that trickles from the rocks. Daphnis lies stretched before the grotto of the nymphs. Little by little the day dawns. The songs of birds are heard. Afar off a shepherd leads his flock. Another shepherd crosses the back of the stage. Herdsmen enter, seeking Daphnis and Chloe. They find Daphnis and awaken him. In anguish he looks about for Chloe. She at last appears, encircled by shepherdesses. The two rush into each other's arms. Daphnis observes Chloe's crown. His dream was a prophetic vision: the intervention of Pan is manifest. The old shepherd Lammon explains that Pan saved Chloe, in remembrance of the nymph Syrinx, whom the god loved.

"Daphnis and Chloe mime the story of Pan and Syrinx. Chloe impersonates the young nymph wandering over the meadow. Daphnis as Pan appears and declares his love for her. The nymph repulses him; the god becomes more insistent. She disappears among the reeds. In desperation he plucks some stalks, fashions a flute, and on it plays a melancholy tune. Chloe comes out and imitates by her dance the accents of the flute.

"The dance grows more and more animated. In mad whirlings, Chloe falls into the arms of Daphnis. Before the altar of the nymphs he swears on two sheep his fidelity. Young girls enter; they are dressed as Bacchantes and shake their tambourines. Daphnis and Chloe embrace tenderly. A group of young men come on the stage.

"Joyous tumult. A general dance. Daphnis and Chloe."

The scenario of the ballet was derived by Michel Fokine from the charming romance of Longus. There are stage pictures of Chloe carried away by robbers, rescued by Pan at the prayer of Daphnis, and of the lovers miming together the story of Pan and Syrinx. There are scenes in the grove of Pan and in the pirate camp, besides those mentioned above. The scenery and costumes were designed by Leon Bakst.

MAURICE RAVEL

## BOLERO

*Bolero* does not fare the better by repetition. It is the clever trick of a super-refined composer. The trick is amazingly well performed, but it is only a trick. The surprise of a first performance does not affect one a second time. Still, there is the expectation of something going to happen, of a final, thunderous proclamation of the inherently negligible tune. According to the old saw, surprise is the chief element of wit. Perhaps—but honest laughter follows the first cracking of a joke. After that, the laughter is only courteous.

This *Bolero,* dedicated to Ida Rubinstein, was brought out by her and danced by her at Paris November 22, 1928. Alexandre Benois designed the settings and the costumes to represent a scene that Goya might have painted: a Spanish inn, with the dancer on a trestle table, men surrounding it. At first calm, the actors on the Parisian stage were little by little excited to frenzy as the dancer became more and more animated. Knives were drawn—the woman was tossed from arms to arms, until her partner intervened; they danced until quiet was restored. So was the scene described by French and English reporters.

The first performance in the United States of this Bolero as a concert piece was by the Philharmonic Society of New York, Mr. Toscanini conductor, on November 14, 1929.

*Tempo di ballo, moderato assai,* 3-4. A drum gives the dance rhythm, which is maintained throughout; a flute announces the theme, which is taken up by the wind instruments in turn; then by groups of instruments. There is a *crescendo* for about twenty minutes, until there is an explosive modulation—brass and percussion instruments swell the din until at last there is what has been described as a "tornado of sound."

M. Prunières called attention to the fact that Ravel was not the first to repeat a simple, common theme until by the monotony of tune and rhythm the hearer was excited (as are Oriental hearers by the same method). Padilla, the composer of *Valencia,* had worked this obsession by the repetition of a tune for at least twenty times.

Ravel's *Bolero* calls for these instruments: two flutes (and piccolo), two oboes, oboe d'amour, English horn, two clarinets, one E flat clarinet, two bassoons, double bassoon, four horns, four trumpets, three trombones, bass tuba, high saxophone in F, soprano and tenor saxophones in B flat, kettledrums, side drums, cymbal, tam-tam, celesta, harp, and the usual strings.

# OTTORINO
# RESPIGHI

(Born on July 9, 1879, at Bologna, Italy;
died at Rome, April 18, 1936)

---

## SYMPHONIC POEM, "PINES OF ROME"

*I. The Pines of the Villa Borghese*
*II. The Pines near a Catacomb*
*III. The Pines of the Janiculum*
*IV. The Pines of the Appian Way*

RESPIGHI wrote *Pines of Rome* as a companion piece to his *Fountains of Rome*. He may yet write *"Hills of Rome,"* but it would have to be in seven movements. In the *Fountains of Rome* he set no bird a-singing. In the third section [of the Pines of Rome] "Pines of the Janiculum," he introduces a nightingale. Perhaps he had in mind the reply of the good King Agesilaus, who, when a man was recommended to him as a skillful imitator of that justly famous bird, replied: "I have heard the nightingale itself." So Respighi obtained a gramophone record of a nightingale which he heard singing. The movement would not suffer if there were no nightingale in the orchestra.

In the "Pines of the Villa Borghese," where children are supposed to be playing games, darting to and fro, shrieking, emitting loud squeals of joy, the instrumentation is unusually brilliant, effective, original. One finds more poetic feeling, more imagination in "Pines near a Catacomb," with the somber opening, the solemnity of the double basses, the mysterious song which swells and dies away. Yes, there is more poetic feeling in this movement than in "Pines of the Janiculum," with the moon full and the gramophone turned on for the faint voice of the nightingale. At first in the *finale* there is the rhythm of innumerable steps that De Quincey might have heard at the beginning of his "Dream Fugue" in "The Vision of Sudden Death." There is the vision of past glories, of soldiers victorious making their clashing and blaring way to the Capitol; with the huzzaing crowd "to see Great Pompey pass the streets of Rome." This march is exciting by reason of its rhythmic and dynamic increasing intensity and its overpowering climax.

But if one takes the work poem as a whole, the composer is revealed as a supreme master of orchestral color rather than a man of fine, entrancing, impressive ideas.

This symphonic poem was composed in 1924. It was performed at a concert in the Augusteum, Rome, in the season of 1924–25. The score calls for 3 flutes (and piccolo), 2 oboes, English horn, 2 clarinets, bass clarinet, 2 bassoons, double bassoon, 4 horns, 1 trumpet off stage, 3 trumpets, 3 trombones and bass tuba, 6 buccine (the bucina was the war trumpet of ancient Rome): 2 flicorni (Fluegelhorn) soprani, 2 flicorni tenori, 2 flicorni bassi—replaced if necessary by horns; kettledrums, bass drum, cymbals, 2 small cymbals, tambourine, rattle, triangle, tam-tam, harp, bells, celesta, gramophone (No. R. 6105 of the Concert Record Gramophone—the "Song of the Nightingale"), pianoforte, organ, and strings.

The piece is in four connected sections. They are based upon this programme, printed as preface to the score:

"1. The Pines of the Villa Borghese. *Allegretto vivace,* 2–8. Children are at play in the pine grove of the Villa Borghese, dancing the Italian equivalent of 'Ring Around a-Rosy'; mimicking marching soldiers and battles; twittering and shrieking like swallows at evening; and they disappear. Suddenly the scene changes to—

"2. The Pines near a Catacomb. *Lento,* 4–4; beginning with muted and divided strings, muted horns, *piano.* We see the shadows of the pines which overhang the entrance to a catacomb. From the depths rises a chant which reëchoes solemnly, sonorously, like a hymn, and is then mysteriously silenced.

"3. The Pines of the Janiculum. *Lento* 4–4; *piano cadenza;* clarinet solo. There is a thrill in the air. The full moon reveals the profile of the pines of Gianicolo's Hill. A nightingale sings (represented by a gramophone record of a nightingale's song heard from the orchestra).

"4. The Pines of the Appian Way. *Tempo di marcia.* Misty dawn on the Appian Way. The tragic country is guarded by solitary pines. Indistinctly, incessantly, the rhythm of innumerable steps. To the poet's phantasy appears a vision of past glories; trumpets blare, and the army of the consul advances brilliantly in the grandeur of a newly risen sun toward the sacred way, mounting in triumph the Capitoline Hill."

Mr. Ernest Newman was facetious, hearing the symphonic poem at a concert of the London Symphony Orchestra in October, 1925: "The tame nightingale in the last movement (a gramophone record, 'kindly lent,' as the programme informed us, 'by the Gramophone Company, Hayes') did not communicate the expected thrill. Perhaps the captive bird does not sing with the rapture of the free one. Perhaps the proper romantic associations were lacking; it might have been better had the lights been put out and we had all held hands. But I fancy the explanation is that realism of this sort is a trifle too crude to blend with music. We all remember Mr. Arnold Bennett's 'Card,' who, having bought in the days of his prosperity a painting of a Swiss scene with a church tower in it, and still having enough of the Five Towns left in him to want to fortify the beautiful with the useful, had a real clock face inserted in the tower to tell him and the world the time. Since then we have read of Mr. Harry Leon Wilson's little boy, who used to gaze with a blend of fascination and terror on a picture of a lion in a cage, the bars of the cage being real, inserted in the frame; the great thing was to put your fingers behind the bars and half hope, half fear that the lion would go for them. Musical realism of the Respighi type has the same queer attractiveness and the same drawbacks. Of course, if the public likes it, it can be extended indefinitely. We may yet live to see the evening when the *Pastoral* symphony will be given with real running water in the slow movement, nightingale by the Gramophone Company, quail by Messrs. Fortnum and Mason."

## NICOLAS ANDREJEVITCH
# RIMSKY-KORSAKOV

(Born at Tikhvin, in the government of Novgorod, March 18, 1844; died at St. Petersburg, June 21, 1908)

---

## SYMPHONIC SUITE, "SCHEHERAZADE" (AFTER "THE THOUSAND NIGHTS AND A NIGHT"), OP. 35

*I. The Sea and Sindbad's Ship*
*II. The Story of the Kalandar Prince*
*III. The Young Prince and the Young Princess*
*IV. Festival at Baghdad. The Sea. The Ship Goes to Pieces against a Rock Surmounted by a Bronze Warrior. Conclusion*

RIMSKY-KORSAKOV wrote an argument for his score. The music is in illustration of *Sindbad the Sailor,* the storm at sea, the shipwreck, the tale of one of the three Kalandars, a tale of a prince and a princess. The argument is not wholly clear, and probably this was the composer's intention. What prince and what princess? There are so many in *The Thousand Nights and a Night.* Who will be so rash as to name the one of the three Kalandars? In the last movement there is a festival at Baghdad, and lo, suddenly Sindbad's ship sails to its fate.

In the ballet all this music is wedded to the story that is the prelude to the wondrous tales: the story of the two rulers, their wanton wives, and the resolve of one of the Kings to kill a spouse every morning, until Scheherazade by her charm as a narrator softens his heart. What then becomes of the graphic sea music; or that illustrative of Kalandar, prince and princess? It is not necessary to insist on the incongruity.

Unless a conductor can feel in this music the spirit of *The Thousand Nights and a Night,* unless he is himself a rhapsodist with admiration for the wild fancy, the humor now grotesque, now cruel, now Rabelaisian, for the sensuousness that is at times sensuality; unless there is understanding, with appreciation of the imagination that peopled the air with slaves of King Solomon's ring, hideous afreets and space-annihilating genii, his interpretation will be that of a man who complains of endless repetitions without contrapuntal development. The music is not for the academic.

Grant that *Scheherazade* reeks at times of benzoin and the pastils of the harem; that it suggests:

> *Lucent syrops, tinct with cinnamon;*
> *Manna and dates in argosy transferred*
> *From Fez; and spiced dainties, every one*
> *From silken Samarcand to cedared Lebanon—*

grant all this: there remains the superb sea music with the rolling billows, the tossing, laboring vessel, the final crash and wild farewell. There is more than a constant display of fancy or imagination. The wonder is, as a matter of technic, how Rimsky-Korsakov succeeds in casting his spell with analogous themes constantly varied. Nor is this due solely to the surprising, masterly, and entrancing instrumentation.

*Scheherazade,* with the *Easter Overture,* was composed in the summer of 1881 at Neyzhgovitsy on the shore of Lake Cheryemenyetskoye. It was produced at St. Petersburg in the course of the following concert season.

The suite, dedicated to Vladimir Stassov, is scored for piccolo, two flutes, two oboes (and English horn), two clarinets, two bassoons, four horns, two trumpets, three trombones, bass tuba, kettledrums, snare drum, bass drum, tambourine, cymbals, triangle, tam-tam, harp, and strings.

The following programme is printed in Russian and French on a fly-leaf of the score:

"The Sultan Schahriar, persuaded of the falseness and the faithlessness of women, has sworn to put to death each one of his wives after the first night. But the Sultana Scheherazade saved her life by interesting him in tales which she told him during one thousand and one nights. Pricked by curiosity, the Sultan put off his wife's execution from day to day, and at last gave up entirely his bloody plan.

"Many marvels were told Schahriar by the Sultana Scheherazade. For her stories the Sultana borrowed from poets their verses, from folk songs their words; and she strung together tales and adventures."

Rimsky-Korsakov has this to say about *Scheherazade* in *My Musical Life,* translated into English by J. A. Joffe:

"The programme I had been guided by in composing *Scheherazade* consisted of separate, unconnected episodes and pictures from *The Arabian Nights:* the fantastic narrative of the Prince Kalandar, the Prince and the Princess, the Baghdad festival, and the ship dashing against the rock with the bronze rider upon it. The unifying thread consisted of the brief introductions to Movements I, II, and IV, and the *intermezzo* in Movement III, written for violin solo, and delineating Scheherazade herself as telling her wondrous tales to the stern Sultan. The conclusion of Movement IV serves the same artistic purpose.

"In vain do people seek in my suite leading motives linked always and unvaryingly with the same poetic ideas and conceptions. On the contrary, in the majority of cases, all these seeming leitmotives are nothing but purely musical material, or the given motives for symphonic development. These given motives thread and spread over all the movements of the suite, alternating and intertwining each with the other. Appearing as they do each time under different moods, the self-same motives and themes correspond each time to different images, actions and pictures.

"Thus, for instance, the sharply outlined fanfare motive of the muted trombone and trumpet, which first appears in the Kalandar's

Narrative (Movement II) appears afresh in Movement IV, in the delineation of the doomed ship, though this episode has no connection with the Kalandar's Narrative. The principal theme of the Kalandar's Narrative (B minor, 3–4) and the theme of the Princess in Movement III (B flat major, 6–8, clarinet) in altered guise and quick tempo appear as the secondary themes of the Baghdad festival; yet nothing is said in *The Arabian Nights* about these persons taking part in the festivities. The unison phrase, as though depicting Scheherazade's stern spouse, at the beginning of the suite, appears in the Kalandar's Narrative, where there cannot, however, be any thought of Sultan Schahriar.

"In this manner, developing quite freely the musical data taken as a basis of the composition, I had in view the creation of an orchestral suite in four movements, closely knit by the community of its themes and motives, yet presenting, as it were, a kaleidoscope of fairy-tale images and designs of Oriental character—a method that I had to a certain degree made use of in my *Skazka* (Fairy Tale), the musical data of which are as little distinguishable from the poetic as they are in *Scheherazade*.

"In composing *Scheherazade* I meant these hints to direct but slightly the hearer's fancy on the path which my own fancy had traveled, and to leave more minute and particular conceptions to the will and mood of each listener. All I had desired was that the hearer, if he liked my piece *as symphonic music,* should carry away the impression that it is beyond doubt an Oriental narrative of some numerous and varied fairy-tale wonders, and not merely four pieces played one after the other and composed on the basis of themes common to all the four movements. Why, then, if that be the case, does this name and the subtitle ('After *The Thousand and One Nights*') connote in everybody's mind the East and fairy-tale wonders; besides, certain details of the musical exposition hint at the fact that all of these are various tales of some one person (which happens to be Scheherazade) entertaining therewith her stern husband."

A characteristic theme, the typical theme of *Scheherazade,* keeps appearing in the four movements. This theme, that of the Narrator, is a florid melodic phrase in triplets, and it ends generally in a free *cadenza.* It is played, for the most part, by a solo violin; sometimes by a woodwind instrument. "The presence in the minor cadence of the characteristic seventh, G, and the major sixth, F sharp—after the manner of the Phrygian mode of the Greeks or the Doric church tone—might illustrate the familiar beginning of all folk tales, 'Once upon a time.'"

I. The Sea and Sindbad's Ship. *Largo e maestoso,* E minor, 2–2. The chief theme of this movement, proclaimed frequently and in many transformations, has been called by some the "Sea" motive, by others the "Sindbad" motive. It is proclaimed immediately and heavily in fortissimo unison and octaves. Soft chords of wind instruments—chords not unlike the first chords of Mendelssohn's "Midsummer Night's Dream" overture in character—lead to the "Scheherazade" motive, lento, 4–4, played by solo violin against chords of the harp. Then follows the main body of the movement, allegro non troppo, E major, 6–4, which begins with a combination of the chief theme, the "sea" motive, with a rising and falling arpeggio figure, the "wave" motive. There is a crescendo. A modulation leads to C major. Wood-wind instruments and violoncellos pizzicato introduce a motive that has been called the "ship," at first for solo flute, then oboe, lastly, clarinet. A reminiscence of the "sea" motive is heard from the horn between the phrases. A solo violoncello continues the "wave" motive, which in one form or another persists almost throughout the whole movement. The "Scheherazade" motive soon enters (solo violin). There is a long period that at last reëstablishes the chief tonality, E major. The "sea" motive is sounded by full orchestra. The development is easily followed. There is an avoidance of contrapuntal use of thematic material. The style of the composer in this suite is homophonous, not polyphonic. He prefers to produce his effects by melodic, harmonic, rhythmic transformations and by most ingenious and highly colored orchestration. The movement ends tranquilly.

II. The Story of the Kalandar Prince. The second movement opens with a recitative-like passage, *lento,* B minor, 4–4. A solo violin accompanied by the harp gives out the "Scheherazade" motive, with a different *cadenza.* There is a change to a species of *scherzo* movement, *andantino,* 3–8. The bassoon begins the wondrous tale, *capriccioso quasi recitando,* accompanied by the sustained chords of four double basses. The beginning of the second part of this theme occurs later and transformed. The accompaniment has the bagpipe drone. The oboe then takes up the melody, then the strings with quickened pace, and at last the wind instruments, *un poco piu animato.* The chief motive of the first movement is heard in the basses. A trombone sounds a fanfare, which is answered by the trumpet; the first fundamental theme is heard, and an *allegro moto* follows, derived from the preceding fanfare, and leads to an orientally colored *intermezzo*. "There are curious episodes in which all the strings repeat the same chord over and over again in rapid succession—very like the responses of a congregation in church—as an accompaniment to the 'Scheherazade' motive, now in the clarinet, now in the bassoon." The last interruption leads to a return of the Kalandar's tale, *con moto*, 3–8, which is developed, with a few interruptions from the "Scheherazade" motive. The whole ends gayly.

III. The Young Prince and the Young Princess. Some think from a similarity of the two themes typical of prince and princess that the composer had in mind the adventures of Kamar al-Zaman (Moon of the Age) and the Princess Budur (Full Moons). "They were the likest of all folk, each to other, as they were twins or an only brother and sister," and over the question which was the more beautiful, Maymunah, the Jinniyah, and Dabnash, the Ifrit, disputed violently.

This movement is in simple *romanza* form. It consists in the long but simple development of two themes of folk-song character. The first is sung by the violins, *andantino quasi allegretto*, G major, 6–8. There is a constant recurrence of songlike melody between phrases in this movement, of quickly rising and falling scale passages, as a rule in the clarinet, but also in the flute or first violins. The second theme, *pochissimo piu mosso*, B flat major and G minor, 6–8, introduces a section characterized by highly original and daringly effective orchestration. There are piquant rhythmic effects from a combination of triangle, tambourine, snare drum, and cymbals, while violoncellos (later the bassoon) have a sentimental counter phrase.

IV. Festival at Baghdad. The Sea. The Ship Goes to Pieces Against a Rock Surmounted by a Bronze Warrior. Conclusion. *Allegro molto*, E minor, 6–8. The *finale* opens with a reminiscence of the "sea" motive of the first movement, proclaimed in unisons and octaves. Then follows the "Scheherazade" motive (solo violin), which leads to the fête in Baghdad, *Allegro molto e frenetico*, E minor, 6–8. The musical portraiture, somewhat after the fashion of a tarantelle, is based on a version of the "sea" motive, and it is soon interrupted by Scheherazade and her violin. In the movement *vivo*, E minor, there is a combination of 2–8, 6–16, 3–8 times, and two or three new themes, besides those heard in the preceding movements, are worked up elaborately. The festival is at its height—"This is indeed life; O sad that 'tis fleeting"—

when there seems to be a change of festivities, and the jollification to be on shipboard. In the midst of the wild hurrah the ship strikes the magnetic rock.

The trombones roar out the "sea" motive against the billowy "wave" motive in the strings, *Allegro non troppo e maestoso,* C major, 6–4; and there is a modulation to the tonic, E major, as the tempest rages. The storm dies. Clarinets and trumpets scream one more cry on the march theme of the second movement. There is a quiet ending with development of the "sea" and "wave" motives. The tales are told. Scheherazade, the narrator, who lives with Shahryar "in all pleasance and solace of life and its delights till there took them the Destroyer of delights and the Severer of societies, the Desolator of dwelling places and Garnerer of graveyards, and they were translated to the ruth of Almighty Allah," fades with the vision and the final note of her violin.

## CAPRICE ON SPANISH THEMES, OP. 34

*I. Alborada*
*II. Variations*
*III. Alborada*
*IV. Scene and Gypsy Song*
*V. Fandango of the Asturias*
*(Played without pause)*

Rimsky-korsakov's *Capriccio Espagnol* was performed for the first time in St. Petersburg at a Russian Symphony concert, October 31, 1887. The composer conducted. The caprice was published in 1887, yet we find Tchaikovsky writing to Rimsky-Korsakov in 1886 (November 11): "I must add that your *Spanish Caprice* is a colossal masterpiece of instrumentation, and you may regard yourself as the greatest master of the present day." Rimsky-Korsakov wrote in his *Autobiography:* "The opinion formed by both critics and public, that the *capriccio* is a magnificently orchestrated piece, is wrong. The *capriccio* is a brilliant composition for the orchestra. The change of timbres, the felicitous choice of melodic designs and figuration patterns, exactly suiting each instrument, brief virtuoso *cadenzas* for instrument solo, the rhythm of the percussion instruments, etc., constitute here the very essence of the composition and not its garb or orchestration. All in all, the *capriccio* is a purely external piece, but vividly brilliant for all that."

The caprice is dedicated to the artists of the orchestra of the Imperial Russian Opera House of St. Petersburg. The names, beginning with M. Koehler and R. Kaminsky, are given, sixty-seven in all, on the title-page of the score. The caprice is scored for piccolo, two flutes, two oboes (and English horn), two clarinets, two bassoons, four horns, two trumpets, three trombones, bass tuba, kettledrums, side drum, bass drum, cymbals, triangle, tambourine, castanets, harp, and strings.

It was in the summer of 1887 that Rimsky-Korsakov, purposing at first to use Spanish dance themes for a virtuoso violin piece, sketched instead this caprice. He thought the third section, the "Alborada" in B flat major, to be a little less successful than the other sections, on account of the brass somewhat drowning the melodic designs of the wood-wind, but this fault could be remedied by a careful conductor. Rimsky-Korsakov tells how, at the rehearsal in St. Petersburg, the orchestra applauded vigorously after the first movement, and in fact after those succeeding, and the composer was so pleased that he dedicated the *capriccio* to the players. He also says that the first performance was extraordinarily brilliant, more so than when it was later led by others, even by Arthur Nikisch.

The movements, according to the direction of the composer, are to be played without intervening pauses.

I. Alborada. *Vivo e strepitoso.* This serenade opens with the wild, tempestuous chief theme, which is given to the full orchestra. There is a subsidiary theme for the wood-wind instruments. Both themes are repeated twice by solo clarinet, accompanied by horns and bassoons, and strings *pizzicato.* A delicate *cadenza* for solo violin brings the close, *pianissimo.*

II. Variations. *Andante con moto,* F major, 3–8. The horns give out the theme with a rocking accompaniment for strings. Before this theme is ended, the strings have the first variation. The second variation, *poco meno mosso,* is a dialogue between English horn and horn. The third variation is for full orchestra. The fourth, *tempo primo,* E major, organ-point on B, is for wood-wind, two horns, and two violoncellos, accompanied by sixteenth notes for clarinet and violins. The fifth, F major, is for full orchestra. A *cadenza* for solo flute brings the end.

III. Alborada. *Vivo e streptoso,* B flat major, 2–4. This movement is a repetition of the first, transposed to B flat major and with different orchestration. Clarinets and violins have now exchanged their parts. The solo that was originally for clarinet is now for solo violin; the *cadenza* that was originally for the solo violin is now for the solo clarinet.

IV. Scene and Gypsy Song. *Allegro,* D minor, 6–8. This dramatic scene is a succession of five *cadenzas.* The movement begins abruptly with a roll of side drum, with a fanfare, quasi-*cadenza,* in syncopated rhythm, gypsy fashion, for horns and trumpets. The drum roll continues, now *pianississimo.* The second *cadenza,* which is for solo violin, introduces the chief theme. This is repeated by flute and clarinet. The third *cadenza,* freer in form, is for flute over a kettledrum roll; the fourth, also free, for clarinet over a roll of cymbals. The fifth *cadenza* is for harp with triangle.

The gypsy song begins after a harp *glissando.*

The song is attacked savagely by the violins and is punctuated by trombone and tuba chords and cymbal strokes. The *cadenza* theme enters, full orchestra, with a characteristic figure for accompaniment. The two themes are alternated. There is a side theme for solo violoncello. Then the strings, in guitar fashion, hint at the fandango rhythm of the *finale,* and accompany the gypsy song, which is now blown *staccato* by wood-wind instruments. The *cadenza* theme is enwrapped in triplets for strings alternating with harmonics *pizzicato.* The pace grows more and more furious, *animato,* and leads into the *finale.*

V. Fandango of the Asturias. A major, 3–4.

The chief theme of the fandango in this *Spanish Caprice* is announced immediately by the trombones, and a related theme for wood-wind instruments follows. Both themes are repeated by oboes and violins, while flutes and clarinets have figured in accompaniment. There is a variation in dance form for solo violin. The chief theme in a modified version is given to bassoons and violoncellos. The clarinet has a solo with fandango accompaniment, and the dance grows more and more furious until the chief theme is heard again from the trombones. The *fandango* suddenly is changed into the "Alborada" of the first movement, *Coda, vivo.* There is a short closing *presto.*

# CHARLES CAMILLE SAINT-SAËNS

(Born at Paris, October 9, 1835;
died at Algiers, December 16, 1921)

---

An enemy of Saint-Saëns—and Saint-Saëns made enemies by his barbed words—might have applied to him the lines of Juvenal:

*Grammaticus, rhetor, geometres, pictor, aliptes,*
*Augur, Schoenobates, medicus, magus, omnia novit.*
*Graeculus esuriens in coelum, jusseris, ibit*—[1]

for Saint-Saëns was not satisfied with the making of music or the career of a virtuoso. Organist, pianist, caricaturist, dabbler in science, enamored of mathematics and astronomy, amateur comedian, feuilletonist, critic, traveler, archæologist—he was a restless man.

He was of less than average height, thin, nervous, sick-faced; with great and exposed forehead, hair habitually short, beard frosted. His eyes were almost level with his face. His eagle-beak would have excited the admiration of Sir Charles Napier, who once exclaimed: "Give me a man with plenty of nose." Irritable,

[1] *"Grammarian, painter, augur, rhetorician,*
*Rope-dancer, conjuror, fiddler, and physician,*
*All trades his own, your hungry Greekling counts;*
*And bid him mount the sky—the sky he mounts!"*
Gifford's Translation.

Compare Dr. Johnson's lines:
*All sciences the hungry Monsieur knows,*
*And bid him go to hell—to hell he goes!*

whimsical, ironical, paradoxical, indulging in sudden changes of opinion, he was faithful to friends, appreciative of certain rivals, kindly disposed toward young composers, zealous in practical assistance as well as in verbal encouragement. A man that knew the world and sparkled in conversation; fond of society; at ease and on equal terms with leaders in art, literature, fashion. A man whose Monday receptions were long famous in Paris, eagerly anticipated by *Tout Paris;* yet never so happy as when acting Calchas to Bizet's or Regnault's Helen in Offenbach's delightful *La Belle Hélène,* or impersonating in an extraordinary costume Gounod's Marguerite surprised by the casket of jewels. An indefatigable student of Bach, he parodied the Italian opera of the 'thirties, 'forties, 'fifties in *Gabriella di Vergi.*

Then there is his amusing *Carnival des Animaux,* which was written, as his *Gabriella di Vergi,* without intention of publication. A Parisian from crown of head to sole of foot; yet a nomad.

In 1867 Berlioz called Saint-Saëns "one of the greatest musicians of our epoch." In 1878 Bülow lamented in a letter to Hans von Bronsart that there was no musician in Germany like Saint-Saëns "except you and me." Liszt's admiration for Saint–Saëns is well known. In 1918 there were some, even in this country, who applauded him as the greatest living composer. On the other hand, there have been critics who said that he was too much of a musician to be a great composer or creator. The praise of Gounod —"Saint-Saëns will write at will a work *à la Rossini, à la Verdi, à la Schumann, à la Wagner*"—was counted by them a reproach; it was regarded as a courteous manner of saying, "Saint-Saëns has the unfortunate faculty of assimilation." Hugues Imbert, discussing him, admitted that there is no graver censure than to say of an artist, "He is incapable of being himself."

So far as an intimate knowledge of music as a science is concerned, so far as fluency and ease of expression are concerned, Saint-Saëns was beyond a doubt a remarkable musician.

## CHARLES CAMILLE SAINT-SAENS

An extraordinary man and musician. Possessing an uncommon technical equipment as composer, pianist, organist; French in clearness of expression, logic, exquisite taste; a master of rhythm, with a clear appreciation of tonal color and the value of simplicity in orchestration, he is seldom warm and tender; seldom does he indulge himself in sentiment, passion, imagination. With him orthodox form must always be kept in mind. Hence perhaps the reactionary attitude of his later years; his sharp criticism of the more modern school of French composers, including César Franck. His wit and brilliancy are indisputable. He seldom touches the heart or sweeps away the judgment. He was not a great creator, yet his name is ever to be mentioned with respect. Without consideration of his many admirable compositions, one should bear this in mind: In the face of difficulties, discouragement, misunderstanding, sneers, he worked steadily from his youth up, and always to the best of his ability, for righteousness in absolute music; he endeavored to introduce into French music thoughtfulness and sincerity for the advantage and the glory of the country that he dearly loved.

## SYMPHONY NO. 3, IN C MINOR (WITH ORGAN), OP. 78

*I. Adagio; allegro moderato; poco adagio*
*II. Allegro moderato; presto; maestoso; allegro*

SAINT-SAËNS' Symphony in C minor has the finest and most characteristic qualities of the best French music: logical construction, lucidity, frankness, euphony. The workmanship is masterly. There is no hesitation. The composer knew exactly what he wanted and how to express himself. A few of the themes that when first exposed might seem to some insignificant assume importance and even grandeur in the development. The chief theme of the *adagio,* the theme for strings, is very French in its sustained suavity, in a gentle, emotional quality that never loses elegance, and the preparation for the entrance of this *adagio* is worthy of the greatest masters. It is not necessary to speak of the many beautiful or stirring pages; of the consummate skill of the technician; of the unerring instrumentation.

This symphony was composed for the London Philharmonic Society and first performed at a concert of that society in London, May 19, 1886, when the composer conducted. It was performed at Aix-la-Chapelle in September of that year under the direction of the composer.

For the first performance in London, Saint-Saëns prepared the following analysis, which was translated into English:

"This symphony is divided into two parts, after the manner of Saint-Saëns' Fourth concerto for piano and orchestra and Sonata for piano and violin. Nevertheless, it includes practically the traditional four movements: the first, checked in development, serves as an introduction to the *adagio,* and the *scherzo* is connected, after the same manner, with the *finale.* The composer has thus sought to shun in a certain measure the interminable repetitions which are more and more disappearing from instrumental music.

"The composer thinks that the time has come for the symphony to benefit by the progress of modern instrumentation, and he therefore establishes his orchestra as follows: three flutes, two oboes, English horn, two clarinets, bass clarinet, two bassoons, double bassoon, four horns, three trumpets, three trombones, tuba, three kettledrums, organ, pianoforte (now for two hands and now for four), triangle, a pair of cymbals, bass drum, and the usual strings.

"After an introduction *adagio* of a few plaintive measures the string quartet exposes the initial theme, which is somber and agitated (*allegro moderato*). The first transformation of this theme leads to a second motive, which is distinguished by greater tranquillity; after a short development, in which the two themes are presented simultaneously, the motive appears in a characteristic form, for full orchestra, but only for a short time. A second transformation of the initial theme includes now and then the plaintive notes of the introduction. Varied episodes bring gradually calm, and thus prepare the *adagio* in D flat.

Tne extremely peaceful and contemplative theme is given to the violins, violas, and violoncellos, which are supported by organ chords. This theme is then taken by clarinet, horn, and trombone, accompanied by strings divided into several parts. After a variation (in arabesques) performed by the violins, the second transformation of the initial theme of the *allegro* appears again, and brings with it a vague feeling of unrest, which is enlarged by dissonant harmonies. These soon give way to the theme of the *adagio,* performed this time by some of the violins, violas, and violoncellos, with organ accompaniment and with a persistent rhythm of triplets presented by the preceding episode. This first movement ends in a *coda* of mystical character, in which are heard alternately the chords of D flat major and E minor.

"The second movement begins with an energetic phrase (*allegro moderato*), which is followed immediately by a third transformation of the initial theme in the first movement, more agitated than it was before, and into which enters a fantastic spirit that is frankly disclosed in the *presto*. Here arpeggios and scales, swift as lightning, on the pianoforte, are accompanied by the syncopated rhythm of the orchestra, and each time they are in a different tonality (F, E, E flat, G). This tricky gayety is interrupted by an expressive phrase (strings). The repetition of the *allegro moderato* is followed by a second *presto,* which at first is apparently a repetition of the first *presto;* but scarcely has it begun before a new theme is heard, grave, austere (trombone, tuba, double basses), strongly contrasted with the fantastic music. There is a struggle for the mastery, and this struggle ends in the defeat of the restless, diabolical element. The phrase rises to orchestral heights, and rests there as in the blue of a clear sky. After a vague reminiscence of the initial theme of the first movement, a *maestoso* in C major announces the approaching triumph of the calm and lofty thought. The initial theme of the first movement, wholly transformed, is now exposed by divided strings and the pianoforte (four hands), and repeated by the organ with the full strength of the orchestra. Then follows a development built in a rhythm of three measures. An episode of a tranquil and pastoral character (oboe, flute, English horn, clarinet) is twice repeated. A brilliant *coda,* in which the initial theme by a last transformation takes the form of a violin figure, ends the work; the rhythm of three measures becomes naturally and logically a huge measure of three beats; each beat is represented by a whole note, and twelve quarters form the complete measure."

This symphony is dedicated to the memory of Franz Liszt.

Liszt died at Bayreuth, July 31, 1886. The symphony was performed at London before his death. When Liszt was in Paris in March of 1886 to hear the performance of his *Graner Messe* at St. Eustache, the symphony was nearly completed, and Saint-Saëns gave Liszt an idea of it by playing it on the pianoforte. The statement that Saint-Saëns intended the symphony to be "a funereal memorial and an apotheosis of the glorious master" is nonsensical. The dedication was a posthumous tribute.

## ARNOLD
# SCHOENBERG

(Born at Vienna, September 13, 1874)

---

## "VERKLÄRTE NACHT" (RADIANT NIGHT), ARRANGED FOR STRING ORCHESTRA, OP. 4

SCHOENBERG'S music, to be enjoyed, does not need either the original verse or the paraphrase. Indeed, it would be better if the argument were not printed for the concertgoer. As it is, he may be too anxious to discover the emancipated woman and the good, easy-going, complaisant man in the music, and be oblivious of the strains of beauty and passion. For this music, on the whole prolix, has beautiful and passionate pages of compelling eloquence. Other pages are a sandy, dreary waste. The impression would be still stronger, the music still more significant, if the composition were much shorter. Whether the music itself gains by the revision and enlargement, is a question that admits of discussion.

This piece, originally a sextet, was published in 1905; the arrangement for string orchestra was published in 1917. The sextet was composed in 1899.

An excerpt from Richard Dehmel's poem, "Weib und die Welt," is printed on a flyleaf of the score. When the sextet was first performed in New York by the Kneisel Quartet, Mr. Krehbiel paraphrased this poetic fragment as follows:

"Two mortals walk through a cold, barren grove. The moon sails over the tall oaks, which send their scrawny branches up through the unclouded moonlight. A woman speaks. She confesses a sin to the man at her side: she is with child, and he is not its father. She had lost belief in happiness, and, longing for life's fullness, for motherhood and mother's duty, she had surrendered herself, shuddering, to the embraces of a man she knew not. She had thought herself blessed, but now life had avenged itself upon her, by giving her the love of him she walked with. She staggers onward, gazing with lack-lustre eye at the moon which follows her. A man speaks. Let her not burden her soul with thoughts of guilt. See, the moon's sheen enwraps the universe. Together they are driving over chill waters, but a flame from each warms the other. It, too, will transfigure the little stranger, and she will bear the child to him. For she has inspired the brilliant glow within him and made him too a child. They sink into each other's arms. Their breaths meet in kisses in the air. Two mortals wander through the wondrous moonlight."

FRANZ PETER
# SCHUBERT

(Born at Lichtenthal, near Vienna, January 31, 1797; died at Vienna, November 19, 1828)

---

SCHUBERT was a clumsy man, short, round-shouldered, tallow-faced, with a great shock of black hair, with penetrating though spectacled eyes, strong-jawed, stubby-fingered. He shuffled in his walk, and he expressed himself in speech with difficulty. He described himself as unhappy, miserable; but his practical jokes delighted tavern companions, and he was proud of his performance of *The Erlking* on a comb. He kept a diary and jotted down platitudes. He had little taste for literature, painting, sculpture, travels; he was not interested in politics or in questions of sociology. He went with his own kind. Unlike Beethoven, he could not impose on the aristocracy of Vienna. He loved the freedom of the tavern, the dance in the open air or late at night, when he would play pretty tunes for the dancers. Handel was the superb personage of music. Gluck was a distinguished person at the Court of Marie Antoinette; Sarti pleased the mighty Catherine of Russia; Rossini, the son of a strolling horn player, was at ease with royalty and worshiped by women. There is little in the plain life of Schubert to fire the zeal of the anecdotical or romantic biographer. No Grimm, no Diderot, relished his conversation. There is no gossip of noble and perfumed dames looking on him favorably. There is a legend that he was passionately in love with Caroline of the House of Esterhazy; but his passion followed a spell of interest in a pretty housemaid. He sang love in immortal strains; but women were not drawn towards him as they were towards Haydn, Mozart, Beethoven—the list is a long one. He was not a spectacularly heroic figure. His morbidness has not the inviting charm of Schumann's torturing introspection. We sympathize more deeply with the sufferings of Mozart, and yet the last years of Schubert were perhaps as cruel. Dittersdorf is close to us by his autobiography. Smug Blangini amuses by his vanity and by his indiscreet defence of Pauline Bonaparte, his pupil. No one can imagine Schubert philosophizing in books after the fashion of Wagner, Gounod, Saint-Saëns. It would have been easier for him to write a dozen symphonies than a feuilleton in the manner of Hector Berlioz. Schubert was a simple, kindly, loving, honest man, whose trade, whose life, was music.

Schubert thought in song even when he wrote for the pianoforte, string quartet, or orchestra. The songs which he wrote in too great number were composed under all sorts of conditions, almost always hurriedly, in the fields, in the tavern, in bed. There were German songs before Schubert—folk songs, songs of the church, set songs for home and concert; but Schubert created a new lyric—the emotional song. Plod your weary way through the ballads of Zumsteeg, the songs of J. A. Hiller, Reichardt, Zelter, and the others: how cold, formal, precise they are! They are like unto the cameo brooches that adorn the simpering women in old tokens or keepsakes; as remote and out of fashion as the hair jewelry of the early 'sixties. Take away "The Violet," and what interest is there in Mozart's book of songs? There is Haydn's famous *Canzonet;* there is perhaps Beethoven's "In Questa Tomba" with a few of the songs addressed to the *"Ferne Geliebte";* but Beethoven knew the voice best as an orchestral instrument. The modern song was invented by Franz Schubert.

The striking characteristics of Schubert's songs, spontaneity, haunting melody, a birthright mastery over modulation, a singular good fortune in finding the one inevitable phrase for the prevailing sentiment of the poem and in finding the fitting descriptive figure for salient detail, are also found in the best of his instrumental works.

There is the spontaneous simplicity, the simplicity praised by Walt Whitman: "The art of art, the glory of expression is simplicity. To speak with the perfect rectitude and insouciance of the movements of animals and the unimpeachableness of the sentiment of trees in the woods and grass by the roadside is the flawless triumph of art. The greatest poet swears to his art: 'I will not be meddlesome. I will not have in my writing any elegance or effect or originality to hang in the way between me and the rest like curtains. What I tell, I tell for precisely what it is. Let who may exalt or startle or fascinate or soothe, I will have purposes as health or heat or snow has, and be as regardless of observation. What I experience or portray shall go from my composition without a shred of my composition. You shall stand by my side and look in the mirror with me."

Then there is the ineffable melancholy that is the dominating note. There is gayety such as was piped naïvely by William Blake in his *Songs of Innocence;* there is the innocence that even Mozart hardly reached in his frank gayety; yet in the gayety and innocence is a melancholy—despairing, as in certain songs of "The Winter Journey," when Schubert smelled the mould and knew the earth was impatiently looking for him—a melancholy that is not the titanic despair of Beethoven, not the whining or shrieking pessimism of certain German and Russian composers; it is the melancholy of an autumnal sunset, of the ironical depression due to a burgeoning noon in spring, the melancholy that comes between the lips of lovers.

*The sunniest things throw sternest shade,*
*And there is even a happiness*
*That makes the heart afraid!*

*There is no music in the life*
*That sounds with idiot laughter solely;*
*There's not a string, attuned to mirth,*
*But has its chord in melancholy.*

No one has treated the passion of love more purely. Love with the modern French composer is too often merely a pronounced phase of eroticism, or it is purely, or impurely, cerebral. With Wagner it is as a rule heroically sensuous if not sensual. Is there one page of Schubert's music that is characterized first of all by sensuousness? A few measures are played or sung; the music may be unknown to the hearer, but he says to himself "Schubert," and not merely because he recognizes restless changes from major to minor and from minor to major, tremulous tonalities, surprising ease in modulation, naïve, direct melody. The sedulous ape may sweat in vain; there is no thought of Schubert, whose mannerisms are his whole individuality.

This individuality defies analysis. It was finely said by Walt Whitman that all music is "what awakens from you when you are reminded by the instruments"; the hearer's thoughts are sweeter and purer, his soul is cheered or soothed, when he is reminded by the music of Schubert.

Pompous eulogies have been paid this homely, human, inspired man, who knew poverty and distress, who was ignored by the mob while he lived his short life, who never heard some of his most important works, whose works were scattered.

"Schubert, turning round, clutched at the wall with his poor, tired hands, and said in a slow voice, 'Here, here is my end.' At three in the afternoon of Wednesday, November 19, 1828, he breathed his last, and his simple, earnest soul took its flight from the world. There never has been one like him, and there will never be another." When you read these words of Sir George Grove, something chokes you; they outweigh the purple phrases and dexterously juggled sentences of the rhetorician.

## SYMPHONY NO. 8, IN B MINOR ("UNFINISHED")

*I. Allegro moderato*
*II. Andante con moto*

Let us be thankful that Schubert never finished the work. Possibly the lost arms of the Venus of Milo might disappoint if they were found and restored. The few measures of the *scherzo* that are in the manuscript furnish but slight hope that here at last Schubert would not, as in so many of his works of long breath, maintain a steady *decrescendo* of interest.

Surely, no one would deny the melancholy beauty of the first movement of Schubert's symphony, with its lyricism that is appealingly feminine, with its melancholy that is without touch of peevishness and without taint of pessimism; and the second movement has the serenity—that is, Schubert's romantic serenity, which is another thing than the classic serenity of Mozart.

The symphony is eminently Schubertian in its beauty and in its weakness. In the first movement there are measures of a grandeur that is seldom found in Schubert's compositions. In these measures we recognize the Schubert that conceived the "Doppelgänger," the "Gruppe aus dem Tartarus," and a few other songs in which dramatic force comes before charming lyricism.

Two brothers, Anselm and Joseph Hüttenbrenner, were fond of Schubert. Their home was in Graz, Styria, but they were living at Vienna. Anselm was a musician; Joseph was in a government office. Anselm took Schubert to call on Beethoven, and there is a story that the sick man said, "You, Anselm, have my mind; but Franz has my soul." Anselm closed the eyes of Beethoven in death. These brothers were constant in endeavor to make Schubert known. Anselm went so far as to publish a set of *Erlking Waltzes,* and assisted in putting Schubert's opera, *Alfonso and Estrella* (1822), in rehearsal at Graz, where it would have been performed if the score had not been too difficult for the orchestra. In 1822 Schubert was elected an honorary member of musical societies of Linz and Graz. In return for the compliment from Graz, he began the Symphony in B minor, No. 8 (October 30, 1822). He finished the *allegro* and the *andante,* and he wrote nine measures of the *scherzo.* Schubert visited Graz in 1827, but neither there nor elsewhere did he ever hear his unfinished work.

Anselm Hüttenbrenner went back to his home about 1820. It was during a visit to Vienna that he saw Beethoven dying. Joseph remained at Vienna. In 1860 he wrote from the office of the Minister of the Interior a singular letter to Johann Herbeck, who then conducted the concerts of the Gesellschaft der Musikfreunde. He begged permission to sing in concerts as a member of the society, and urged him to look over symphonies, overtures, songs, quartets, choruses by Anselm. He added towards the end of the letter, "He [Anselm] has a treasure in Schubert's B minor symphony, which we put on a level with the great Symphony in C, his instrumental swan song, and any one of the symphonies by Beethoven."

Herbeck was inactive and silent for five years, although he visited Graz several times. Perhaps he was afraid that if the manuscript came to light he could not gain possession of it, and the symphony, like the one in C, would be produced elsewhere than in Vienna. Perhaps he thought the price of producing one of Anselm Hüttenbrenner's works in Vienna too dear. There is reason to believe that Joseph insisted on this condition.[1]

In 1865 Herbeck was obliged to journey with his sister-in-law, who sought health. They stopped in Graz. On May 1 he went to Ober-Andritz, where the old and tired Anselm, in a hidden little one-story cottage, was awaiting death. Herbeck sat down in a humble inn. He talked with the landlord, who told him that Anselm was in the habit of breakfasting there. While they were talking, Anselm appeared. After a few words, Herbeck said, "I am here to ask permission to produce one of your works at Vienna." The old man brightened, he shed his indifference, and after breakfast took him to his home. The work-

[1]See *Johann Herbeck,* by L. Herbeck, Vienna, 1885, page 165.

room was stuffed with yellow and dusty papers, all in confusion. Anselm showed his own manuscripts, and finally Herbeck chose one of the ten overtures for performance. "It is my purpose," he said, "to bring forward three contemporaries, Schubert, Hüttenbrenner, and Lachner, in one concert before the Viennese public. It would naturally be very appropriate to represent Schubert by a new work." "Oh, I have still a lot of things by Schubert," answered the old man; and he pulled a mass of papers out of an old-fashioned chest. Herbeck immediately saw on the cover of a manuscript *"Symphonie in H moll,"* in Schubert's handwriting. Herbeck looked the symphony over. "This would do. Will you let me have it copied immediately at my cost?" "There is no hurry," answered Anselm. "Take it with you."

The symphony was first played at a Gesellschaft concert, Vienna, December 17, 1865, under Herbeck's direction. It was played at the Crystal Palace, Sydenham, in 1867.

## SYMPHONY NO. 7, IN C MAJOR

*I. Andante; allegro non troppo*
*II. Andante con moto*
*III. Scherzo: allegro vivace; trio*
*IV. Finale: allegro vivace*

THERE are some who are not persuaded by Schumann and Weingartner into enjoying the extreme length of the symphony. They would fain have the work undergo some process of condensation, and yet it would be difficult for them to indicate the measures or sections that should be omitted.

It is still a marvelous work in certain respects. The Hungarian dash in the second theme of the first movement; the wonderful trombone passage; the melodic charm of the *andante* and the infinite beauty of the detail—but when one begins to speak of this movement he might vie with Schubert in length; the expressive trio of the *scherzo;* the rush of the *finale*—these place the symphony high on the list; and yet, and yet—but Schubert was not a severe critic of his own compositions. He wrote at full speed, and he had not the time to revise, to condense.

The manuscript of this symphony, numbered 7 in the Breitkopf & Härtel list and sometimes known as No. 10, bears the date March, 1828. In 1828 Schubert composed besides this symphony the songs "Die Sterne" and "Der Winterabend"; the oratorio, *Mirims Siegesgesang;* the song "Auf dem Strom"; the *Schwanengesang* cycle; the string quintet, Op. 163, and the Mass in E flat. On November 14 he took to his bed. It is said that Schubert gave the work to the Musikverein of Vienna for performance; that the parts were distributed; that it was even tried in rehearsal; that its length and difficulty were against it, and it was withdrawn on Schubert's own advice in favor of his earlier Symphony in C, No. 6 (written in 1817). All this has been doubted; but the symphony is entered in the catalogue of the society under the year 1828, and the statements just quoted have been fully substantiated. Schubert said, when he gave the work to the Musikverein, that he was through with songs and should henceforth confine himself to opera and symphony.

It has been said that the first performance of the symphony was at Leipsic in 1839. This statement is not true. Schubert himself never heard the work; but it was performed at a concert of the Gesellschaft der Musikfreunde, Vienna, December 14, 1828, and repeated March 12, 1829. It was then forgotten until Schumann visited Vienna in 1838 and looked over the mass of manuscripts then in the possession of Schubert's brother Ferdinand. Schumann sent a transcript of the symphony to Mendelssohn for the Gewandhaus concerts, Leipsic. It was produced at the concert of March 21, 1839, under Mendelssohn's direction, and repeated three times during the following season—December 12, 1839, March 12 and April 3, 1840. Mendelssohn made some cuts in the work for these performances. The score and parts were published in January, 1850.

The manuscript is full of alterations. As a rule Schubert made few changes or corrections in his score. In this symphony, alterations are found at the very beginning. The subject of the introduction and that of the *allegro* were materially changed; the tempo of the opening movement was altered from *allegro vivace* to *allegro ma non troppo.*

Only the *finale* seems to have satisfied him as originally conceived, and this *finale* is written as though at headlong speed.

The symphony[2] is scored for two flutes, two oboes, two clarinets, two bassoons, two horns, two trumpets, three trombones, kettledrums, strings. There is a story that Schubert was afraid he had made too free use of trombones and asked advice of Franz Lachner.

The second theme of the first movement has a decidedly Slav-Hungarian character, and this character colors other portions of the symphony both in melody and general mood. The rhythm of the *scherzo* theme had been used by Schubert as early as 1814 in his Quartet in B flat. It may also be remarked that the *scherzo* is not based on the old minuet form, and that there is more thematic development than was customary in such movements at that period.

There is a curious tradition—a foolish invention is perhaps the better phrase—that the *finale* illustrates the story of Phaëton and his justly celebrated experience as driver of Apollo's chariot. Others find in the *finale* a reminiscence of the terrible approach of the Statue towards the supper table of Don Giovanni.

[2]The *Unfinished* symphony has the same orchestration.—EDITOR.

# ROBERT ALEXANDER SCHUMANN

(Born at Zwickau, Saxony, June 8, 1810; died at Endenich, near Bonn, July 29, 1856)

---

IT HAS BEEN URGED against Schumann that his symphonies were thought for the pianoforte and then orchestrated crudely, as by an amateur. This, however, is not the fatal objection. He had his own orchestral speech. Good, bad, or indifferent, it was his own. He could not have otherwise expressed himself through the orchestral instruments. His speech is to be accepted or rejected as the hearer is impressed chiefly by ideas, or by the manner of expression.

A more serious objection is this: the genius of Schumann was purely lyrical, although occasionally there is the impressive expression of a wild or melancholy mood, as in the chords of unearthly beauty soon after the beginning of the overture to *Manfred*. Whether the music be symphonic, chamber, a pianoforte piece or a song, the beauty, the expressive force lies in the lyric passages. When Schumann endeavored to build a musical monument, to quote Vincent d'Indy's phrase, he failed; for he had not architectonic imagination or skill.

His themes in symphonies, charming as they often are, give one the impression of fragments, of music heard in sleep-chasings. Never a master of contrapuntal technique, he repeated these phrases over and over again instead of broadly developing them, and his filling in is generally amateurish and perfunctory.

## ROBERT SCHUMANN

The best of Schumann's music is an expression of states and conditions of soul. This music is never spectacular; it is never objective. Take, for instance, his music to Goethe's *Faust.* The episodes that attracted the attention of Berlioz, Liszt, Gounod, were not to Schumann a source of inspiration. It was the mysticism in the poem that led him to musical interpretation. His music, whether for voice or instruments, is first of all *innig,* and this German word is not easily translated into English. Heartfelt, deep, ardent, fervent, intimate; no one of these words conveys exactly the idea contained in *innig*. There is the intimacy of personal and shy confession.

Schumann in his life was a reticent man. He dreamed dreams. He was lost in thought when others, in the beerhouse or at his home, were chattering about art. He put into his music what he would with difficulty have said aloud to his Clara. As a critic he was bold in praise and blame. As a composer he was often not assertive as one on a platform. He told his dreams, he wove his romantic fabric for a few sympathetic souls. It is true that in his days of wooing he was orchestrally jubilant, as in the first movement of the Symphony in B flat, but in this movement the anticipation aroused by the first measures is not realized. The thoughts soared above the control of the thinker; there was not the mastery over them that allowed no waste material, that gives golden expression without alloy.

In his own field, Schumann is lonely, incomparable. No composer has whispered such secrets of subtle and ravishing beauty to a receptive listener. The hearer of Schumann's music must in turn be imaginative and a dreamer. He must often anticipate the composer's thought. This music is not for a garish concert hall; it shrinks from boisterous applause.

## SYMPHONY NO. 1, IN B FLAT MAJOR, OP. 38

*I. Andante un poco maestoso; allegro molto vivace*
*II. Larghetto*
*III. Scherzo: molto vivace. Trio (1): molto più vivace; Trio (2)*
*IV. Allegro animato e grazioso*

THE OPENING is imposing with need of re-orchestration. Charming is the lyric passage in the *scherzo* that puts one in mind of Schubert's "Hark, Hark, the Lark"; but for the most part there is rhythmic uniformity and boresome repetition that no change in the instrumentation could redeem. As the thick orchestration stands, if the music is played according to Schumann's directions, Weingartner says, it is impossible to produce a true *forte* or an expressive *pianissimo.*

Schumann was married to Clara Wieck, September 12, 1840, after doubts, anxieties, and opposition on the part of her father; after a nervous strain of three or four years. His happiness was great, but to say with some that this joy was the direct inspiration of the First symphony would be to go against the direct evidence submitted by the composer. He wrote Ferdinand Wenzel: "It is not possible for me to think of the journal" (the *Neue Zeitschrift für Musik,* founded by Schumann, Wieck, Schunke, and Knorr in 1834, and edited in 1841 by Schumann alone). "I have during the last days finished a task (at least in sketches) which filled me with happiness, and almost exhausted me. Think of it, a whole symphony—and, what is more, a Spring symphony; I myself can hardly believe that it is finished." And he said in a letter (November 23, 1842) to Spohr: "I wrote the symphony toward the end of the winter of 1841, and, if I may say so, in the vernal passion that sways men until they are very old, and surprises them again with each year. I do not wish to portray, to paint; but I believe firmly that the period in which the symphony was produced influenced its form and character, and shaped it as it is." He wrote to Wilhelm Taubert, who was to conduct the work in Berlin: "Could you infuse into your orchestra in the performance a sort of longing for the Spring, which I had chiefly in mind when I wrote in February, 1841? The first entrance of trumpets, this I should like to have sounded as though it were from high above, like unto a call to awakening; and then I should like reading between the lines, in the rest of the introduction, how everywhere it begins to grow green, how a butterfly takes wing; and, in the *allegro,* how little by little all things come, that in any way belong to Spring. True, these are fantastic thoughts, which came to me after my work was finished; only I tell you this about the *finale,* that I thought it as the good-bye of Spring."

(It may here be noted that the symphony was fully sketched in four days, and that Schumann now speaks of composing the work in February, 1841, and now of writing it towards the end of that year.)

Berthold Litzmann, in the second volume of his *Clara Schumann* (Leipsic, 1906), gives interesting extracts from the common diary of Schumann and his wife, notes written while Schumann was composing this symphony.

Towards the end of December, 1840, she complained that Robert had been for some days "very cold toward her, yet the reason for it is a delightful one." On January 17–23, 1841, she wrote that it was not her week to keep the diary, "but, if a man is composing a symphony, it is not to be expected that he will do anything else. . . . The symphony is nearly finished. I have not yet heard a note of it, but I am exceedingly glad that Robert at last has started out in the field where, on account of his great imagination, he belongs." January 25: "Today, Monday, Robert has nearly finished his symphony; it was composed chiefly at night—for some nights my poor Robert has not slept on account of it. He calls it 'Spring symphony.' . . . A spring poem by [Boettger] gave him the first impulse toward composition."

According to the diary Schumann completed the symphony on Tuesday, January 26. "Begun and finished in four days. . . . If there were only an orchestra for it right away. I must confess, my dear husband, I did not give you credit for such dexterity." Schumann began to work on the instrumentation January 27; Clara impatiently waited to hear a note of the symphony. The instrumentation of the first movement was completed February 4, that of the second and third movements on February 13, that of the fourth on February 20, in the year 1841. Not till February 14 did Schumann play the symphony to her. E. F. Wenzel, later a teacher at the Leipsic Conservatory, and E. Pfundt, a kettledrum player of the Gewandhaus orchestra, were present. "I should like," she wrote in her diary, "to say a little something about the symphony, yet I should not be able to speak of the little buds, the perfume of the violets, the fresh green leaves, the birds in the air. . . . Do not laugh at me, my dear husband! If I cannot express myself poetically, nevertheless the poetic breath of this work has stirred my very soul." The instrumentation was completed on February 20.

Clara wrote to Emilie Liszt after the performance: "My husband's symphony achieved a triumph over all cabals and intrigues. . . . I never heard a symphony received with such applause."

Robert wrote in the diary some days before that his next symphony should be entitled "Clara; and I shall paint her therein with flutes, oboes, and harps."

The first movement opens with an introduction, *andante un poco maestoso,* B flat major, 4-4, which begins with a virile phrase in the horns and trumpets, answered by the full orchestra *fortissimo.* There are stormy accents in the basses, with full chords in the brass and other strings, and each chord is echoed by the wood-wind. Flute and clarinet notes over a figure in the violas lead to a gradual *crescendo ed accelerando,* which introduces the *allegro molto vivace,* B flat major, 2-4. This begins at once with a brilliant first theme. The chief figure is taken from the initial horn and trumpet call as Schumann originally wrote it. The development of the theme leads finally to a modulation to the key of C major, and there is the thought, naturally, of F major as the tonality of the second theme, but this motive given out by the clarinets and bassoons is in no definite tonality; it is in a mode which suggests A minor and also D minor; the second section ends, however, in F major, and the further development adheres to this key. The first part of the movement is repeated. The free fantasia is long and elaborately worked out. The first movement does not return in the shape it has at the beginning of the *allegro,* but in the broader version heard at the opening of the introduction. The long *coda* begins *animato, poco a poco stringendo,* on a new theme in full harmony in the strings, and it is developed until horns and trumpets sound the familiar call.

The second movement, *larghetto,* E flat major, 3-8, opens with a *romanza* developed by the violins. The second theme, C major, is of a more restless nature, and its phrases are given out alternately by the wood-wind and violins. The melodious first theme is repeated, B flat major, by the violoncellos against an accompaniment in second violins and violas and syncopated chords in the first violins and the woodwind. There is a new episodic theme. The first motive appears for the third time, now in E flat major. It is sung by the oboe and horn, accompanied by clarinets and bassoons, with passages in the strings. Near the close of the short *coda* are solemn harmonies in bassoons and trombones. This movement is enchained with the *scherzo.*

The *scherzo, molto vivace,* D minor, 3–4, begins in G minor. The first trio, *molto più vivace,* D major, 2–4, includes harmonic interplay between strings and wind instruments. It is developed at some length, and the *scherzo* is repeated. There is a second trio, B flat major, 3–4, with imitative contrapuntal work, and it is followed by a second repetition of the *scherzo.* A short *coda* has the rhythm of the first trio and brings the end.

*Finale: allegro animato e grazioso,* B flat major, 2–2. It begins with a *fortissimo* figure which is used hereafter. The first theme, a cheerful, tripping dance melody, enters and is developed by strings and woodwind. The second theme, equally blithe, is in G major, and the impressive initial figure of the full orchestra at the beginning of the movement, now given out by the strings, is in the second phrase. The two motives are worked up alternately. The free fantasia opens quietly. Trombones sound the rhythm of the first theme of the first movement. There is a long series of imitations on the first theme of the *finale.* This series leads to some horn calls and a *cadenza* for the flute. The third section of the movement is regular, and there is a brilliant *coda.*

## SYMPHONY NO. 2, IN C MAJOR, OP. 61

*I. Sostenuto assai; allegro ma non troppo*
*II. Scherzo: allegro vivace. Trio (1); Trio (2)*
*III. Adagio espressivo*
*IV. Allegro molto vivace*

WITH THE EXCEPTION of the introduction to the first movement and the *adagio,* in which the romantic dreamer Schumann is revealed, the symphony has aged. And in this symphony, more than the other three, the orchestration seems hopelessly crude, ineffective, distressing to the ear, while the musical contents are seldom worthy of a more tasteful dress.

Yet there are few *adagios* to be compared with this dramatic song of Schumann. If he had only had the courage to cut out that meaningless and incongruous little episode, too deliberately contrapuntal.

In October, 1844, Schumann left Leipsic, where he had lived for about fourteen years. He had in July given up the editorship of the *Neue Zeitschrift;* he had been a teacher of pianoforte playing and composition at the Leipsic Conservatory from April, 1843. A singularly reserved man, hardly fitted for the duties of a teacher and without pupils, he was in a highly nervous state, so that a physician recommended a change of scene and told him he should not hear too much music. Schumann therefore moved back to Dresden. "Here," he wrote in 1844, "one can recover the old lost longing for music, there is so little to hear. This suits my condition, for I still suffer very much from my nerves, and everything affects and exhausts me immediately." He saw few people; he talked little. In the early 'eighties they still showed in Dresden a restaurant frequented by him, where, seated in a room with his head against a wall, he would sit for hours at a time, dreaming daydreams. In 1846 he was very sick, mentally and bodily. "He observed that he was unable to remember the melodies that occurred to him when he was composing; the effort of invention fatigued his mind to such an extent that it impaired his memory." When he did work, he applied himself to contrapuntal problems.

The Symphony in C major, known as No. 2, but really the third—for the one in D minor, written first, was withdrawn after performance, remodeled, and finally published as No. 4—was composed in the years 1845 and 1846. The symphony was published, score and parts, in November, 1847. The symphony was first played at the Gewandhaus, Leipsic, under Mendelssohn's direction, on November 5, 1846.

Schumann wrote from Dresden on April 2, 1849, to Otten, a writer and conductor at Hamburg, who had brought about the performance of the symphony in that city: "I wrote the symphony in December, 1845, when I was still half sick. It seems to me one must hear this in the music. In the *finale* I first began to feel myself; and indeed I was much better after I had finished the work. Yet, as I have said, it recalls to me a dark period of my life. That, in spite of all, such tones of pain can awaken interest, shows me your sympathetic interest. Everything you say about the work also shows me how thoroughly you know music; and that my melancholy bassoon in the *adagio,* which I introduced in that spot with especial fondness, has not escaped your notice, gives me the greatest pleasure." In the same letter he expressed the opinion that Bach's Passion according to John was a more powerful and poetic work than his Passion according to Matthew.

And yet, when Jean J. H. Verhulst of The Hague (1816–91) visited Schumann in 1845 and asked him what he had written that was new and beautiful, Schumann answered he had just finished a new symphony. Verhulst asked him if he thought he had fully succeeded. Schumann then said, "Yes, indeed, I think it's a regular Jupiter."

There is a dominating motive, or motto, which appears more or less prominently in three of the movements. This motto is proclaimed at the very beginning, *sostenuto assai,* 6–4, by horns, trumpets, alto trombone, *pianissimo,* against flowing counterpoint in the strings. This motto is heard again in the *finale* of the following *allegro,* near the end of the *scherzo,* and in the concluding section of the *finale.* (It may also be said here that relationship of the several movements is further founded by a later use of other fragments of the introduction and by the appearance of the theme of the *adagio* in the *finale.*) This motto is not developed: its appearance is episodic. It is said by one of Schumann's biographers that the introduction was composed before the symphony was written, and that it was originally designed for another work. The string figure is soon given to the wood-wind instruments. There is a *crescendo* of emotion and an acceleration of the pace until a *cadenza* for the first violins brings in the *allegro, ma non troppo,* 3–4. The first theme of this *allegro* is exposed frankly and *piano* by full orchestra with the exception of trumpets and trombones. The rhythm is nervous, and accentuation gives the idea of constant syncopation. The second theme, if it may be called a theme, is not long in entering. The exposition of this movement, in fact, is uncommonly short. Then follows a long and elaborate development. In the climax the motto is sounded by the trumpets.

The *scherzo, allegro vivace,* C major, 2–4, has two trios. The *scherzo* proper consists of first violin figures in sixteenth notes, rather simply accompanied. The first trio, in G major, 2–4, is in marked contrast. The first theme, in lively triplet rhythm, is given chiefly to wood-wind and horns; it alternates with a quieter, flowing phrase for strings. This trio is followed by a return of the *scherzo*. The second trio, in A minor, 2–4, is calm and melodious. The simple theme is sung at first in full harmony by strings (without double basses) and then developed against a running contrapuntal figure. The *scherzo* is repeated, and, towards the close, trumpets and horns loudly sound the motto.

The third movement, *adagio espressivo*, 2–4, is the development of an extended *cantilena* that begins in C minor and ends in E flat major. Violins first sing it; then the oboe takes it, and the song is more and more passionate in melancholy until it ends in the wood-wind against violin trills. This is followed by a contrapuntal episode, which to some is incongruous in this extremely romantic movement. The melodic development returns, and ends in C major.

The *finale, allegro molto vivace,* C major, 2–2, opens after two or three measures of prelude with the first theme of vigorous character (full orchestra except trombones). This is lustily developed until it reaches a transitional passage, in which the violins have prominent figures. All this is in *rondo* form. The second theme is scored for violas, violoncellos, clarinets, and bassoons, while violins accompany with the figures mentioned. This theme recalls the opening song of the *adagio*. A new theme, formed from development of the recollection, long hinted at, finally appears in the wood-wind and is itself developed into a *coda* of extraordinary length. Figures from the first theme of the *finale* are occasionally heard, but the theme itself does not appear in the *coda,* although there is a reminiscence of a portion of the first theme of the first movement. The motto is sounded by the brass. There is a second exultant climax, in which the introductory motive is of great importance.

## SYMPHONY NO. 3, IN E FLAT MAJOR, "RHENISH," OP. 97

*I. Vivace*
*II. Moderato assai*
*III. Allegro non troppo*
*IV. Maestoso*
*V. Vivace*

This music has not the buoyancy and exciting rush of the First symphony, or the romantic spirit of the one in D minor. Nor are there pages equal in sheer beauty to those of the *adagio* in the Second symphony. One wishes that the first movement was not in so continuously heroic, exultant vein; that there was at least a breathing spell. The second movement expresses a sort of clumsy joviality. The third might be a pretty piano piece that had been orchestrated. The fourth movement, the "cathedral scene," is the most impressive portion of the symphony. Here we have lofty ideas and a solemn, ecstatical mood befitting a gorgeous ceremony of the holy church.

Schumann's symphony was intended by him to be a glorification of Rhenish scenes and Rhenish life. It was composed first of all for Düsseldorf, the city where he met with many disappointments, many vexations. He was temperamentally unfitted for the position of city conductor. He did not have a firm control over the players—in a word he was a composer—a man of dreams and visions—not an interpreter of works by others, not even of his own works. It was received coldly when it was first heard. The compositions that followed showed his failing powers. There were intrigues that vexed him. Little by little his mind gave way. There was the attempt at suicide; then madness. But the Schumann of this symphony was still the composer to be reckoned with.

The symphony was sketched and orchestrated at Düsseldorf between November 2 and December 9, 1850. Clara Schumann wrote in her diary, November 16, 1850: "Robert is now at work on something, I do not know what; for he has said nothing to me about it." It was on December 9 that he surprised her with the symphony. Sir George Grove, for some reason or other, thought Schumann began to work on it before he left Dresden to accept the position of City Conductor at Düsseldorf; that he wished to compose an important work for production at the Lower Rhine Festival.

The first performance of this symphony was in Geisler Hall, Düsseldorf, at the sixth concert of Der Allgemeine Musikverein, February 6,

1851. Schumann conducted from manuscript. The reception was cold. Mme Schumann wrote after the performance that the "creative power of Robert was again ever new in melody, harmony, and form. . . . I cannot say which one of the five movements is my favorite. The fourth is the one that at present is the least clear to me; that it is most artistically made—that I hear—but I cannot follow it so well, while there is scarcely a measure in the other movements that remains unclear to me; and indeed to the layman is this symphony, especially in its second and third movements, easily intelligible."

Schumann wrote (March 19, 1851) to the publisher, Simrock, at Bonn: "I should have been glad to see a greater work published here on the Rhine, and I mean this symphony, which perhaps mirrors here and there something of Rhenish life." It is known that the solemn fourth movement was inspired by the recollection of the ceremony at Cologne Cathedral at the installation of the Archbishop of Geissel as Cardinal, at which Schumann was present (November 12, 1850). Wasielewski quotes the composer as saying that his intention was to portray in the symphony as a whole the joyful folk life along the Rhine, "and I think," said Schumann, "I have succeeded." Yet he refrained from writing even explanatory mottoes for the movements. The fourth movement originally bore the inscription, "In the character of the accompaniment to a solemn ceremony"; but Schumann struck this out and said: "One should not show his heart to people; for a general impression of an art work is more effective; the hearers then, at least, do not institute any absurd comparison." The symphony was very dear to him. He wrote (July 1, 1851) to Carl Reinecke, who made a four-handed arrangement at Schumann's wish and to his satisfaction: "It is always important that a work which cost so much time and labor should be reproduced in the best possible manner."

The first movement, *lebhaft* (lively, animated), E flat major, 3–4, begins immediately with a strong theme, announced by full orchestra. The basses take the theme, and violins play a contrasting theme, which is of importance in the development. The complete statement is repeated; and the second theme, which is of an elegiac nature, is introduced by oboe and clarinet and answered by violins and wood-wind. The key is G minor, with a subsequent modulation to B flat. The fresh rhythm of the first theme returns. The second portion of the movement begins with the second theme in the basses, and the two chief themes are developed with more impartiality than in the first section, where Schumann is loath to lose sight of the first and more heroic motive. After he introduces towards the end of the development the first theme in the prevailing tonality, so that the hearer anticipates the beginning of the reprise, he makes unexpected modulations, and finally the horns break out with the first theme in augmentation in E flat major. Impressive passages in syncopation follow, and trumpets answer, until in an ascending chromatic climax the orchestra with full force rushes to the first theme. There is a short *coda.*

The second movement is a *scherzo* in C major, *sehr mässig* (very moderately), in 3–4. William Foster Apthorp found the theme to be "a modified version of the so-called 'Rheinweinlied,'" and this theme of "a rather ponderous joviality" well expresses "the drinkers' *'Uns ist ganz cannibalisch wohl, als wie fünf hundert Säuen!'* (As 'twere five hundred hogs, we feel so cannibalic jolly!) in the scene in Auerbach's cellar in Goethe's *Faust.*" This theme is given out by the violoncellos and is followed by a livelier contrapuntal counter theme, which is developed elaborately. In the trio horns and other wind instruments sing a *cantilena* in A minor over a long organ-point on C. There is a pompous repetition of the first and jovial theme in A major; and then the other two themes are used in combination in their original form. Horns are answered by strings and wood-wind, but the ending is quiet.

The third movement, *nicht schnell* (not fast), in A flat major, 4–4, is really the slow movement of the symphony, the first theme, clarinets and bassoons over a viola accompaniment, reminding some of Mendelssohn; others of *"Tu che a Dio spiegasti l' ali,"* in *Lucia di Lammermoor.* The second theme is a tender melody, not unlike a refrain heard now and then. On these themes the *romanza* is constructed.

The fourth movement, *feierlich,* E flat minor, 4–4, is often described as the "Cathedral scene." Three trombones are added. The chief motive is a short figure rather than a theme, which is announced by trombones and horns. This appears augmented, diminished, and afterwards in 3–2 and 4–2. There is a departure for a short time to B major, but the tonality of E flat minor prevails to the end.

*Finale: lebhaft,* E flat major, 2–2. This movement is said to portray a Rhenish festival. The themes are of a gay character. Towards the end the themes of the "Cathedral scene" are introduced, followed by a brilliant *stretto.* The *finale* is lively and energetic. The music, as a rule, the free development of thematic material of the same unvaried character.

## SYMPHONY NO. 4, IN D MINOR, OP. 120

*I. Andante; allegro*
*II. Romanza*
*III. Scherzo*
*IV. Largo; finale*
*(Played without pause.)*

WEINGARTNER regards the D minor symphony of Schumann as inferior to the first and second of the same composer. I fail to see why. Surely this symphony does not fall behind its companions; it is the one of Schumann's four that can be heard with full enjoyment. The middle movements breathe a romantic spirit that Schumann himself never surpassed as expressions of gentle, dreamy melancholy. I know of few more haunting pages in orchestral music than those of the trio in the *scherzo.*

This symphony was composed in 1841, immediately after the Symphony in B flat major, No. 1. According to the composer's notes it was "sketched at Leipsic in June, 1841, newly orchestrated at Düsseldorf in 1851. The first performance of the original version was at the Gewandhaus, Leipsic, under David's direction. December 6, 1841." Clara Schumann wrote in her diary on May 31 of that year: "Robert began yesterday another symphony, which will be in one movement, and yet contain an *adagio* and a *finale.* I have heard nothing about it, yet I see Robert's bustle, and I hear the D minor sounding wildly from a distance, so that I know in advance that another work will be fashioned in the depths of his soul. Heaven is kindly disposed toward us: Robert cannot be happier in the composition than I am when he shows me such a work." A few days later she wrote: "Robert composes steadily; he has already completed three movements, and I hope the symphony will be ready by his birthday."

Their first child, Marie, was born on September 1, 1841. On the thirteenth of the month, his wife's birthday, Marie was baptized and the mother received from her husband the D minor symphony: "which I have quietly finished," he said.

Schumann was not satisfied with the symphony, and he did not publish it. In December, 1851, he revised the manuscript. During the years between 1841 and 1853 Schumann had composed and published the Symphony in C (No. 2) and the Symphony in E flat (No. 3); the one in D minor was published therefore as No. 4. In its first form the one in D minor was entitled *"Symphonische Phantasie."*

The symphony in the revised and present form was played for the first time at the seventh concert of the Allgemeine Musikverein at Düsseldorf on March 3, 1853, in Geisler Hall. Schumann conducted from manuscript. At this concert selections from the Mass were performed for the first time.

The concert master, Ruppert Becker, made these entries in his diary concerning the rehearsals and the first performance of this symphony in Düsseldorf:

"Tuesday, evening of March 1. Rehearsal for 7th Concert. Symphony by Schumann for the first time; a somewhat short but thoroughly fresh and vital piece of music. Wednesday, 2. 9 o'clock in the morning, 2 rehearsal for concert. Thursday, 3. 7th concert: Program.

"Of Schumann compositions these were new: Symphony D minor, which he had already composed 12 years ago, but had left lying till now. 2 excerpts from a Mass: both full of the most wonderful harmonies, only possible with Schumann. I liked the symphony especially on account of its swing."

The symphony was dedicated to Joseph Joachim. On the title-page of the manuscript was this inscription: "When the first tones of this symphony were awakened, Joseph Joachim was still a little fellow; since then the symphony and still more the boy have grown bigger, wherefore I dedicate it to him, although only in private. Düsseldorf, December 23, 1853. Robert Schumann."

The parts were published in November, 1853. The score was published the next month.

It was stated for many years that the only changes made by Schumann in this symphony were in the matter of instrumentation, especially in the wood-wind. Some time after the death of Schumann the first manuscript passed into the possession of Johannes Brahms, who finally allowed the score to be published, edited by Franz Wüllner. It was then found that the composer had made important alterations in thematic development. He had cut out elaborate contrapuntal work to gain a broader, simpler, more rhythmically effective treatment, especially in the last movement. He had introduced the opening theme of the first movement "as a completion of the melody begun by the three exclamatory chords which make the fundamental rhythm at the beginning of the last movement." And, on the other hand, some thought the instrumentation of the first version occasionally preferable on account of clearness to that of the second.

It was Schumann's wish that the symphony should be played without pauses between the movements. Mendelssohn expressed the same wish for the performance of his *"Scotch"* symphony, which was produced nearly four months after the first performance of this Symphony in D minor.

The first movement begins with an introduction, *ziemlich langsam (un poco lento),* D minor, 3–4. The first motive is used later in the "Romanze." The orchestra gives out an A which serves as background for this motive in sixths in the second violins, violas, and bassoons. This figure is worked up contrapuntally. A dominant organ-point appears in the basses, over which the first violins play an ascending figure; the time changes from 3–4 to 2–4.

The main body of this movement, *lebhaft (vivace),* in D minor, 2–4, begins *forte* with the development of the violin figure just mentioned. This theme prevails, so that in the first section there is no true second theme. The characteristic trombone figure reminds one of a passage in Schumann's piano Quartet in E flat, Op. 47. There is a heroic figure in the wood-wind instruments. After the repetition comes a long free fantasia. The true second theme, sung in F major by first violins, appears. The development is now perfectly free. There is no third part.

The "Romanze," *ziemlich langsam (un poco lento),* in D minor—or, rather, A minor plagal—opens with a mournful melody said to be familiar in Provence. Schumann intended originally to accompany the song of oboe and first violoncellos with a guitar. This theme is followed by the dreamy motive of the introduction. Then the first phrases of the "Romanze" are sung again by oboe and violoncellos, and there is a second return of the contrapuntal work—now in D major—with embroidery by a solo violin. The chief theme brings the movement to a close on the chord of A major.

The *scherzo, lebhaft (vivace),* in D minor, 3–4, presents the development of a rising and falling scale-passage of a few notes. The trio, in B flat major, is of a peculiar and beautiful rhythmic character. The first beat of the phrase falls constantly on a rest in all the parts. The melody is almost always in the wood-wind, and the first violins are used in embroidery. The *scherzo* is repeated after the trio, which returns once more as a sort of *coda.*

The *finale* begins with a short introduction, *langsam (lento),* in B flat major, and it modulates to D minor, 4–4. The chief theme of the first movement is worked up against a counter figure in the trombones to a climax. The main body of the movement *lebhaft (vivace),* in D major, 4–4, begins with the brilliant first theme, which has the character of a march, and it is not unlike the theme of the first movement with its two members transposed. The figure of the trombones in the introduction enters. The *cantabile* second theme begins in B minor, but it constantly modulates in the development. The free fantasia begins in B minor, with a G (strings, bassoons, trombones), which is answered by a curious ejaculation by the whole orchestra. There is an elaborate contrapuntal working out of one of the figures in the first theme. The third part of the movement begins irregularly with the return of the second theme in F sharp minor. The second theme enters in the tonic. The *coda* begins in the manner of the free fantasia, but in E minor; but the ejaculations are now followed by the exposition and development of a passionate fourth theme. There is a free closing passage, *schneller (più moto),* in D major, 2–2.

## CONCERTO IN A MINOR, FOR PIANOFORTE AND ORCHESTRA, OP. 54

*I. Allegro*
*II. Adagio*
*III. Allegro non troppo*

After Schumann heard for the first time Mendelssohn play his own Concerto in G minor, he wrote that he would never dream of composing a concerto in three movements, each one complete in itself. It is said that he began to write a pianoforte concerto when he was only seventeen and ignorant of musical form; that in 1836 he sketched a concerto in F major when he was living at Heidelberg. In January,

1839, he wrote from Vienna to Clara Wieck, his betrothed: "My concerto is a compromise between a symphony, a concerto, and a huge sonata. I see I cannot write a concerto for the virtuosos: I must plan something else." The key was not mentioned.

The first movement of the Concerto in A minor was written at Leipsic in the summer of 1841—it was begun in May. It was then called *"Phantasie"* in A minor, and was not intended for the movement of a concerto. It was played for the first time by Clara Schumann, on August 13, 1841, at a private rehearsal in the Gewandhaus, Leipsic. This rehearsal was for the changes made in Schumann's First symphony. Schumann wished in 1843 or 1844 to publish the work as an *allegro affettuoso,* also as *Concert Allegro,* for pianoforte with orchestral accompaniment, "Op. 48," but he could not find a publisher. The *intermezzo* and *finale* were composed at Dresden, May–July, 1845. Clara wrote in her diary on July 31, 1845: "Robert has finished his concerto and given it to the copyists."

The whole concerto was played for the first time by Clara Schumann at her concert, December 4, 1845, in the Hall of the Hôtel de Saxe, Dresden, from manuscript. The second performance was at Leipsic, January 1, 1846, when Clara Schumann was the pianist and Mendelssohn conducted. Verhulst attended a rehearsal, and said that the performance was rather poor; the passage in the *finale* with the puzzling rhythms "did not go at all."

I. *Allegro affettuoso,* A minor, 4–4. After a short pianoforte prelude, the first period of the first theme is announced by wind instruments. The antithesis, which is almost an exact repetition of the thesis, is for the pianoforte. The second theme is practically a new version of the first and may be considered as a new development of it. The free fantasia begins *andante espressivo,* A flat major, 6–4. The recapitulation section is almost a repetition of the first. There is an elaborate *cadenza* for the pianoforte before the *coda,* which is an *allegro molto,* A minor, 2–4.

II. *Intermezzo: andante grazioso,* F major, 2–4. The movement is in simple *romanza* form. Dialogue between solo instrument and orchestra; then more emotional phrases for violoncellos, violins, etc. (accompanied by pianoforte *arpeggios*). At the close there are hints at the first theme of the first movement, which lead directly to the *finale.*

III. *Allegro vivace,* A major, 3–4. The movement is in sonata form. The pianoforte gives out the chief theme. After a modulation to E major, the second theme is for the pianoforte. This theme is distinguished by constantly syncopated rhythm. A contrasting theme is developed in florid fashion by the pianoforte. The free fantasia begins with a short orchestral *fugato* on the first theme. The third part begins irregularly in D major, with the first theme as an orchestral *tutti*. There is a long *coda*.

In each of his four symphonies Schumann used two flutes, two oboes, two clarinets, two bassoons, four horns (two horns sufficed for the Second symphony), two trumpets, three trombones, kettledrums, and strings. For the piano concerto, he used the same orchestration, with two horns, and omitting the trombones.—EDITOR.

# ALEXANDER NICOLAIEVITCH SCRIABIN

(Born at Moscow on January 6, 1872; died there on April 27, 1915)

---

## "THE POEM OF ECSTASY" (LE POÈME DE L'EXTASE), OP. 54

A SINGULAR and at times interesting composition. Victor Hugo has said that agony when at its height is mute. Some, on hearing Scriabin's score, have wished, no doubt, that this were true of ecstasy. Is the music really ecstatic? There are anthropological sociologists who find extreme voluptuousness in physical pain. Mantegazza has a chapter on this subject, a chapter that is not for the *jeune fille*. We are told that Scriabin in this music wished to express the ecstasy of untrammeled action, the joy in creative activity. Let the poem he wrote, and the title, be put aside; there are fine and original passages in the composition, and there is certainly untrammeled action. The themes themselves are not important, not expressive, not significant enough to warrant the extravagant development and the polyphonic complexity. There is also irritating repetition.

*"Le Poème de l'Extase"* was performed for the first time by the Russian Symphony Society of New York in New York, December 10, 1908. Modeste Altschuler conducted. We were indebted to Mr. Altschuler in 1910 for the following information about *The Poem of Ecstasy:*

"While I was in Switzerland during the summer of 1907 at Scriabin's villa, he was all taken up with the work, and I watched its progress with keen interest. The composer of the *Poème de l'Extase* has sought to express therein something of the emotional (and therefore musically communicable) side of his philosophy of life. Scriabin is neither a pantheist nor a theosophist, yet his creed includes ideas somewhat related to each of these schools of thought. There are three divisions in his poem: 1. His soul in the orgy of love; 2. The realization of a fantastical dream; 3. The glory of his own art."

Mr. Modeste Altschuler has interesting letters written by Scriabin covering the period of his sojourn in the United States and Mr. Altschuler's journey to Russia in 1907, the aim of which was to secure a subsidy from the Russian government for the Russian Symphony Orchestra in New York. Scriabin was very anxious to assist Mr. Altschuler in his mission. The letters plainly indicate his anxiety. Those letters will appear in Mr. Altschuler's *Memoirs,* which a Russian historian was taking down in November, 1930, when Mr. Altschuler was conductor of the Hollywood Symphony Orchestra.

Scriabin wrote from Paris in the spring of 1907 that he had finished The Poem of Ecstasy. The revised instrumentation now in use was made that summer (1907) by the composer and Modeste Altschuler together, in Switzerland, where they spent two weeks together.

It has been said that the subject of *Le Poème de l'Extase* begins where that of *Le divin Poème* leaves off. The three divisions of the latter symphony, movements joined together without a pause, are "Luttes," "Voluptés," "Jeu divin" (creative force consciously exercised).

*Le Poème de l'Extase* was completed in January, 1908, in Switzerland, the month of the Fifth sonata, which, it is said, was written in three or four days. It is scored for these instruments: piccolo, three flutes, three oboes, English horn, three clarinets, bass clarinet, three bassoons, double bassoon, eight horns, five trumpets, three trombones, bass tuba, kettledrums, bass drum, cymbals, triangle, tam-tam, bells, deep chime in C, celesta, two harps, organ, and the usual strings.

Scriabin wrote a poem in Russian for this orchestral composition. The poem was published at Geneva, Switzerland, 1906. Mr. Altschuler kindly lent his copy of it. A literal translation into English was made by Mrs. Lydia L. Pimenov-Noble of Boston expressly for the Boston Symphony Programme Book of October 22, 1910. The poem is very long, too long for reprinting. There are verses that recur like a refrain, especially the first lines:

*The Spirit,*
*Winged by the thirst for life,*
*Takes flight*
*On the heights of negation.*
*There in the rays of his dream*
*Arises a magic world*
*Of marvelous images and feelings.*
*The Spirit playing,*
*The Spirit longing,*
*The Spirit with fancy creating all,*
*Surrenders himself to the bliss of love.*

The poem ends with a rhapsodic invocation of the poet to the world he has created:

*"O pure aspirations,*
*I create thee,*
*A complex entity.*
*A feeling of bliss*
*Embracing all of you.*
*I am a moment illuminating eternity.*
*I am affirmation,*
*I am ecstasy."*
*By a general conflagration*
*The universe is embraced.*
*The Spirit is at the height of being.*
*And he feels*
*The tide unending*
*Of the divine power,*
*Of free will.*
*He is all-daring,*
*What menaced—*

*Now is excitement,*
*What terrified*
*Is now delight;*
*And the bites of panthers and hyenas have become*
*But a new caress,*
*A new pang,*
*And the sting of the serpent*
*But a burning kiss.*
*And the universe resounded*
*With a joyful cry,*
*"I am."*

# JEAN JULIUS CHRISTIAN
# SIBELIUS

(Born at Tavastehus, Finland, December 8, 1865)

---

SOME, JUDGING the music of Sibelius or rhapsodizing over it, have laid great stress on the fact that Finland is a wild and desolate country. They therefore argue that the music of Sibelius must be bleak and grim. They are also convinced that Sibelius himself must be a stern-visaged man, something of a Berserk, savage and unapproachable, to write as he does. But travelers assure us that in Finland there are smiling landscapes, and we know from personal acquaintance that Mr. Sibelius, like Baptista Minola in the comedy, is "an affable and courteous gentleman." We doubt if climatic conditions, the constitutional qualities or the passive mood of a man necessarily affect his music. Beethoven was in doleful dumps when he wrote one of his most cheerful symphonies. We have heard music by contemporaneous Italian composers that is more barbaric, gloomier than the great majority of that by Scandinavian or Russian musicians.

## SYMPHONY NO. 1, IN E MINOR, OP. 39

*I. Andante ma non troppo; allegro energico*
*II. Andante ma non troppo lento*
*III. Allegro*
*IV. Finale (quasi una fantasia): andante; allegro molto*

THERE IS a marked difference between the mood and the orchestral expression of this First symphony and those of the composer's Fifth and Seventh. Sibelius was not young in years when he wrote the First—he was thirty-four—but this symphony was the work of one musically young. It is seldom that a first symphony con-rests on firm foundations architectonically planned, logically continuous in flow of musical thought, as is the First symphony of Brahms, who had written much chamber music before he ventured into the symphonic field.

The musical thoughts of a symphonic composer meditating his first work of long breath are many; they are often yeasty in their exuberance. There is not yet in the joy of composing the ability to eliminate. There is so much to say; all of it is thought important, essential.

Yet this exuberance when it expresses itself in a fantastical manner is not displeasing. Better wild irregularity, barbaric force than the smug aping of orthodox and approved predecessors. In the first symphony he did not escape the influence of Tchaikovsky, an influence shown particularly in the second movement. But the voice of Sibelius himself speaks in no uncertain tones: a virile voice that has new things to say; is not ashamed of screaming outbursts, sudden contrasts; not a whining egoist, not a despairing pessimist; a strong soul not disturbed by the sensuous charm of woman.

And so this symphony is more than conventionally interesting. It is dramatic, as if Sibelius had had a drama in his mind, perhaps one of his own life. The music is free, outspoken. It is without fear of the learned professor at the conservatory. One might say of the symphony, one hears this music and is in the mighty presence of a man.

The First symphony was composed in 1899 and published in 1902. The first performance was at Helsingfors on April 26, 1899. The symphony was played in Berlin at a concert of Finnish music, led by Robert Kajanus, in July, 1900.

I. Introduction: *andante ma non troppo,* E minor, 2-2. Over a drum roll that rises and falls in intensity a clarinet sings a mournful melody, which is of much importance in the *finale* of the symphony.

The first violins, after the short introduction, give out the first theme with imitative passages for violas and violoncellos, *allegro energico,* E minor, 6–4. There are two subsidiary motives: one for wind instruments, and one, derived from this last, for strings. A *crescendo* leads to a climax, with the proclamation of the first chief theme by full orchestra with a furious drum roll. The second and contrasting chief motive is given to the flutes, *piano ma marcato,* against tremulous violins and violas and delicate harp chords. The conclusion of this theme is developed and given to the flutes with syncopated rhythm for the strings. The pace is quickened, and there is a *crescendo,* which ends in B minor. The free fantasia is of a passionate nature with passages that suggest mystery; heavy chords for wind instruments are bound together with chromatic figures for the strings; wood-wind instruments shriek out cries with the interval of a fourth; cries that are taken from one in the introduction; the final section of the second theme is sung by two violins with strange figures for the strings, *pianissimo,* and with rhythms taken from the second chief theme. These rhythms in the course of a powerful *crescendo* dominate at last. The first chief theme endeavors to assert iself, but it is lost in descending chromatic figures. Again there is a crescendo, and the strings have the second subsidiary theme, which is developed until the wild entrance of the first chief motive. The orchestra rages until, after a great outburst and with clash of cymbals, a diminuendo leads to gentle echoes of the conclusion of the second theme. Now the second theme tries to enter, but without the harp chords that first accompanied it. Rhythms that are derived from it lead to defiant blasts of the brass instruments. The movement ends in this mood.

II. *Andante, ma non troppo lento,* E flat major, 2–2.

"The *adagio (andante)* is steeped in his proper pathos, the pathos of brief, bland summers, of light that falls for a moment, gentle and mellow, and then dies away. Something like a memory of a girl sitting amid the simple flowers in the white Northern sunshine haunts the last few measures."[1]

"The *andante* is purest folk melody; and it is strange how we know this, though we do not know the special tune."[2]

[1]Paul Rosenfeld: *Musical Portraits,* 1920.

[2]Philip H. Goepp.

III. *Allegro,* C major, 3-4. The chief theme of the *scherzo* may be said to have the characteristically national humor, which seems to Southern nations wild and heavily fantastical. The second theme is of a lighter and more graceful nature. The trio, E major, is of a somewhat more tranquil nature.

IV. *Finale (quasi una fantasia),* E minor. The *finale* begins with the melody of the introduction of the first movement. It is now of an epic, tragic nature, and not merely melancholy. There are hints in the lower strings at the chief theme, which at last appears, 2-4, in the wood-wind. This theme has a continuation which later has much importance. The prevailing mood of the *finale* is one of wild and passionate restlessness, but the second chief theme, *andante assai,* is a broad, dignified, melodious motive for violins.

"The substratum [of the symphony] is national; in fact, one may say that if the principal subjects are predominantly Slavonic in character, the subsidiary ones are often distinctly Finnish, and the atmosphere of storm and conflict which pervades the entire work is largely the outcome of a kind of revolt on the part of this thematic rank and file against their lords and masters. In this way the symphony presents a symbolical picture of Finnish insurrection against Russian tyranny and oppression. Not that I would suggest for a moment that the composer had any such purpose in mind while writing it, but there would be nothing surprising if there were an unconscious correspondence between the state of mind of the composer and the position of his unhappy country at the time when the symphony was conceived, at the very height of the Tsarist persecution. On the contrary, it would be surprising if there were not."[3]

## SYMPHONY NO. 2, IN D MAJOR, OP. 43

*I. Allegretto*
*II. Tempo andante ma rubato*
*III. Vivacissimo; lento e suave*
*IV. Finale: allegro moderato*

MR. PAUL ROSENFELD, who writes about certain modern composers as if he had summered and wintered with them and been

[3]*Sibelius,* by Cecil Gray, London, 1931.

through them with a dark lantern, finds this symphony of a "pastoral" nature, full of "home sounds, of cattle." The music reveals a "pale, evanescent sunlight," and through the music sounds "the burden of a lowly tragedy." This is entertaining reading, to be sure, but to be charged with these impressions Mr. Rosenfeld must have heard a tea-table performance of the symphony. There is almost continually the tragic note in the music, but the tragedy is hardly "lowly."

This music is extremely Northern, at times bleak and windswept. Arresting and impressive music; and lo, suddenly Sibelius drops into Tchaikovskian mood, and even speaks the self-torturing Russian's speech. Yet Sibelius is generally in the foreground, and his speech is generally his own. It is when he would touch the heart of the public that Tchaikovsky pushes him aside. There is much of interest in the symphony besides the peculiar esthetic and racial quality: there are qualities of the orchestration that hold the attention and excite admiration, as the long *pizzicato* figure for the double basses.

This symphony, composed in 1901–02, was produced at Helsingfors, March 8, 1902, at a concert given by the composer.

According to Georg Schneevoight, an intimate friend of Sibelius, the composer's intention was to depict in the first movement the quiet, pastoral life of the Finns undisturbed by thought of oppression. The second movement is charged with patriotic feeling, but the thought of a brutal rule over the people brings with it timidity of soul. The third, in the nature of a *scherzo,* portrays the awakening of national feeling, the desire to organize in defense of their rights, while in the *finale* hope enters their breasts and there is comfort in the anticipated coming of a deliverer.

I. *Allegretto,* D major, with various rhythms, that of 6–4 predominating. The movement begins with an accompaniment figure for strings, which reappears in the course of the development. The quaint first theme is announced by oboes and clarinets. This theme is worked, and secondary motives are introduced, to be used again later. A passage for strings *pizzicato* leads to a theme given out by flutes, oboes, and clarinets in octaves; bassoons and brass instruments sustain, and the strings have the characteristic strumming heard at the beginning. After the free fantasia a prolonged tremolo of strings leads to the recapitulation. The quaint first theme appears again in the wood-wind, but the accompaniment is more elaborate. The second theme is again announced by wind instruments, and at the end there is the initial figure of accompaniment.

II. *Tempo andante ma rubato,* D minor, 4-4, 3-8, 4-4. On a roll of kettledrums, double basses begin *pizzicato,* a figure which is finally taken up by violoncellos, and serves as an accompaniment for a mournful theme sung by the bassoons in octaves. The movement becomes more animated and more dramatic. After a climax *fortississimo, molto largamente,* the second and expressive theme is sung by some of the first violins, violas, violoncellos (F sharp major, *andante sostenuto*), accompanied at first by strings and then by running passages in flutes and bassoons. This theme, now in wood-wind instruments, is accompanied by running passages for violins. The first theme returns in F sharp minor, and is developed to another climax, after which the second theme enters in D minor, and toward the close there are hints at the first motive.

III. *Vivacissimo,* B flat major, 6-8. The movement begins with a nimble theme for violins. There is a short development, and flute and bassoon announce the second theme, against the rhythm of the first, which returns against a *tremolo* of wood-wind instruments supported by brass and kettledrums. *Lento e suave,* G flat major, 12-4. The oboe has the theme over sustained chords for bassoons and horns. This section, which serves here as a trio to a *scherzo,* is short. There is a repetition, with changes of the opening section. The oboe sounds again the theme of the trio, and there is a free transition to the *finale* without any pause.

IV. *Finale: allegro moderato,* D major, 3-2. The movement is fashioned after the general style of a *rondo* on a short and simple theme announced immediately by violins, violas, and violoncellos. There are less important motives which serve as thematic material, and there are modifications of tonality and tempo. The movement ends in a sonorous apotheosis, *molto largamente.*

## SYMPHONY NO. 4, IN A MINOR, OP. 63

*I. Tempo molto moderato quasi adagio*
*II. Allegro molto vivace*
*III. Il tempo largo*
*IV. Allegro*

THE FOURTH SYMPHONY is strangely different in character from those that precede and follow it. Was Sibelius experimenting, endeavoring to strike out a new path? Was he dissatisfied with the result? When it was performed in New York as a new piece, Mr. Henderson, the most sympathetic of those reviewing the symphony, thought that Sibelius had "parted company with himself and joined the futurists." One of the critics went so far as to describe the work as "inconsequential as the ravings of a drunken man." This was an absurd opinion, for, whatever may be said of the symphony, it is not "inconsequential"; it was planned deliberately; one might say, from the lack of emotional quality, planned in cold blood.

Perhaps there was an argument in his mind. Perhaps he had been hearing *Parsifal,* for there are times in the symphony when one is reminded of Amfortas with his complaining voice. Not that Sibelius was obliged to borrow phrases; but the mood of the composer and that of the wounded knight are at times alike. There is also the suggestion of similar harmonic and orchestral, but not melodic expression.

The thematic material is for the most part cool, contemplative, often fragmentary, or purposely incomplete. The melancholy that drips from the pages is almost without relief. Nor does one find the symphony of "baffling simplicity" as a London reviewer found it a few years ago. The "simplicity" was carefully contrived. There is little real beauty, frank or subtle—there is little that impresses by loftiness of thought, or nobility of expression. There is prevailing sobriety. Sibelius might say, "That is the way I felt when I wrote it. I could not write otherwise any more than I could then feel differently." Is it not a significant fact that Sibelius soon left this path that he had found?

This symphony, dated 1911, was performed at Helsingfors in that year. The score is dedicated to Eero Järnefelt.

The reviewer for the London *Times* noted (February 28, 1921) that there was moderate applause after a performance, and added: "After all, what was there to make a fuss about? No accumulation of energy, no building to a climax, no display of rhetoric; just a number of ideas, each dwelt on as long as it showed capacity for growth, each left as soon as it had generated another; there is just enough relevance to defeat the charge of inconsequence, not enough arrangement to suggest a moment's tautology. The fineness of this symphony is of the ascetic type which refuses the luxuries of sound and finds a miracle in the simplest relations of notes. From these relations the tunes grow naturally as folk tunes grow. From the intonation of two notes at the outset comes the whole of the first movement; a perfect fifth is the source of the most expansive melody which crowns the third movement. There is nothing abstruse about it; people only fail to understand it because they cannot believe that any man could be so simple and so real as Sibelius shows himself to be."

Mr. Fox Strangways wrote (February 21, 1932): "Sibelius has, what only the best composers have, the flair for the phrase that will repay investigation. His phrase on paper impresses no one; when you hear it, spaced out, set in relief, debated upon, it grows life size. He seems to go on for minutes together in an ordinary tone of voice, and then suddenly an idea stings him, and he is afire, and the whole room hanging on his lips."

"The complete absence of sensuous appeal in this work," writes Cecil Gray, "coupled with the exacting demands it makes upon the intelligence of audiences, will always prevent it from being popular. For the few, however, it probably constitutes Sibelius's greatest achievement; he has certainly never written anything to surpass it."

## SYMPHONY NO. 5, IN E FLAT MAJOR, OP. 82

*I. Tempo molto moderato; allegro moderato*
*II. Andante mosso, quasi allegretto*
*III. Allegro molto: un pochettino largamente*

THERE IS not a sensuous note, not a single bid for immediate popularity; but there is something in the symphony that will be permanent. It is skillfully constructed in a new manner; skillfully scored with most ingenious effects not too laboriously contrived, and with a comparatively small orchestra. The young composer of today, looking at the score, will rub his eyes in wonder and exclaim: "What! No English horn, no bass clarinet, only four horns, no celesta, xylophone, harp, tam-tam? What's the man thinking about?"

But Sibelius has ideas. He feels deeply; he pours out his emotions; he snaps his fingers at decorations, at sensational effects, at sugared pages sure to please. When he is in lighter mood it is only for a moment; the eternal questions asked since the beginning of time are ever in his mind; yet serious, he is not dull, he does not sermonize. He writes music first of all to free himself of what is in his heart and brain and must out.

This man of the North knows the exciting effect of oriental repetition in phrase and rhythm, and on these repetitions he rears imposing musical structures. There are measures to which dervishes might whirl, rays of the sun break through the clouds, yet we prefer Sibelius when the sky is leaden.

---

(The biography of Sibelius by Karl Ekman, published since these notes were written, has divulged new information about this symphony, information partly derived from the composer. It was composed in the last months of 1914, and first performed at Helsingfors, December 8, 1915. Sibelius made a revision in 1916. Still he was not satisfied with it, and revealed in a letter of May, 1918, that he was recasting the Fifth Symphony, while plans for a sixth and seventh were also taking shape. The second and final revision was performed at Helsingfors, November 24, 1919.—EDITOR)

The first two movements are played as one.

When the symphony was performed in London the *Daily Telegraph* had this to say: "It is true that this symphony is designed on broader lines than its predecessor; it contains more positive statement of its ideas, many of which are of the simplest melodic kind, that the coloring is richer and fuller, with more use of the effects of orchestral masses. . . .

"The first two movements are closely linked together by a four-note motto theme which pervades the greater part of the subject matter of both; they are distinguished by contrast of mood. The first is a dreaming fantasy in which many motives and forces contend; the second unifies them in a more closely knit *scherzo* rhythm. Through both of them the strings supply in an uneasy background of shimmering sound, while the voices of the wind instruments are more closely articulated.

"The third movement is *andante quasi allegretto*. The rather dry rhythmic pattern of the chief theme is discussed among the instruments in a way which is strangely Mozart-like, and marks more definitely Sibelius's abstracted devotion to pure beauty of design. The *finale* launches out into a franker expression of feeling. Its second subject makes an almost passionate appeal on its first revival, and this appeal is intensified in the long development of it which leads to the *coda*. Yet somehow this ending left the feeling that the composer had not allowed himself to say all that he meant, or the thing which he meant most of all. This may have been partly in the playing, for Sibelius is a difficult conductor to follow.

"Sibelius, both as composer and conductor, stands apart, a lonely figure seeking with difficulty to bring the ideals which are intensely real to him into touch with other minds. Possibly it is his struggle for expression which sometimes recalls Beethoven as one listens to him."

## SYMPHONY NO. 7, OP. 105

### (*In one movement*)

MR. LAWRENCE GILMAN was right in characterizing Sibelius' Seventh symphony as "enigmatic, puissant." Is it also, as he says, "strangely moving"? It is not a symphony for an afternoon's careless pleasure.

The music of Sibelius seldom accepts the canons of obvious beauty. His musical soul is proud, regardless of popular applause. In his latest works he seems to be writing for himself; to be absorbed in introspection and the expression of what he finds that is dear and important to himself alone. There are noble ideas, fleeting and haunting passages, in this symphony, but the plan and the conclusion of the whole are not easily grasped.

It has been said that this symphony, published in 1925, was composed with the view of producing it under the direction of the composer at an English music festival. Sickness prevented his going to England. The symphony was performed in Philadelphia by the Philadelphia Orchestra, Mr. Stokowski conductor, on April 3, 1926.

There is no designation of key. The opening measures are in A minor; the ending is in C major.

The first section is a somber *adagio*. It opens with an ascending scale, 3–2 time for the strings. This is the basic theme of the symphony, appearing as a whole, in fragments, or inverted. A lyric theme follows, C major, for violas (divided) and violoncellos. The violins join later. There is a melody, somewhat like a chant for a solo trombone. This later assumes marked importance. The pace grows faster, until it is *vivacissimo,* C minor. Mr. Gilman, in his lucid notes for the Philadelphia Programme Book, finds that the subject now announced by the strings "recalls the mood of the *scherzo* of Beethoven's '*Eroica.*'" The *adagio* tempo recurs, as does the trombone theme, which the brass section enlarges. Change in tempo: *allegro molto moderato.* There is a new motive, C major, 6–4, simple, in folk manner; still another motive with wood-wind "doubled in pairs, playing in thirds, fifths and sixths." The development is for strings and wind. *Vivace,* E flat major. Antiphonal measures for strings and wood-wind. "The tempo becomes *presto,* the key C major. The strings, divided in eight parts, begin a mysteriously portentous passage, at first *pianississimo,* with the violas and violoncellos defining an urgent figure against a reiterated pedal G of the violins, basses, and tympani. A *crescendo, rallentando,* is accompanied by a fragment of the basic scale passage, in augmentation, for the horns. The tempo is again *adagio;* and now the chant-like C major theme is heard once more from the brass choir, against mounting figurations of the strings. There is a climax *fortissimo,* for the whole orchestra. The strings are heard alone, *largamente molto,* in an *affettuoso* of intense expression. Flute and bassoon in octaves, supported by soft string tremolos, sing a plaint. The strings, *dolce,* in syncopated rhythm, modulate through seventh chords in A flat and G to a powerful suspension, *fortissimo,* on the tonic chord of C major; and this brings to a close the enigmatic, puissant, and strangely moving work."[4]

The instrumentation which Sibelius calls for in his Seventh symphony is typical of the severely "classical" orchestration which was the basis of his symphonies in general: two flutes, two oboes, two clarinets, two bassoons, four horns, three trumpets, three trombones, kettledrums, and strings. This was also the instrumentation of the Third, Fourth, Fifth, and Sixth (although, for episodic purposes, a glockenspiel was added to the Fourth, and a bass clarinet and harp to the Sixth). The First symphony had a richer bass and percussion—bass tuba, bass drum, cymbals, triangle, and harp were used (compare the orchestration of *Finlandia* and *The Swan of Tuonela* of the same early period). When he wrote his Second symphony, Sibelius dropped all these instruments of percussion. The tuba he kept for the Second, but he did not use it again in his symphonies.—EDITOR.

## "FINLANDIA," SYMPHONIC POEM FOR ORCHESTRA, OP. 26, NO. 7

It is said that *Finlandia,* although it was composed as far back as 1894, evokes such enthusiasm in the composer's native land that performance of it was forbidden by the oppressing Russian. The question is, does *Finlandia* evoke enthusiasm in Madrid, Dresden, Boston? For after all it is something more than a national document. It is picturesque, with suggestions of prayers and hymns, revolts and revolutions.

There is more of Finland in the symphonies, the violin concerto, and *A Saga* of Sibelius than in his *Finlandia,* which is hot with the

[4] Lawrence Gilman, Philadelphia Orchestra Programme Notes.

spirit of revolt. No doubt he wrote this music with a patriotic heart, but patriotism is not an essential quality in a musical work of art.

*Finlandia: Tondight for orkester,* Op. 26, No. 7, was composed in 1894. It is not a fantasia on genuine folk tunes. The composer is the authority for this statement. Mrs. Newmarch says: "Like Glinka, Sibelius avoids the crude material of the folk song; but like this great national poet, he is so penetrated by the spirit of his race that he can evolve a national melody calculated to deceive the elect. On this point the composer is emphatic, "There is a mistaken impression among the press abroad," he has assured me, "that my themes are often folk melodies. So far I have never used a theme that was not of my own invention. Thus the thematic material of *Finlandia* and *En Saga* is entirely my own."

The following note is from a programme of the Russian Symphony Society:

"*Finlandia,* though without explanatory subtitle, seems to set forth an impression of the national spirit and life. . . . The work records the impressions of an exile's return home after a long absence. An agitated, almost angry theme for the brass choir, short and trenchant, begins the introduction, *andante sostenuto* (*alla breve*). This theme is answered by an organ-like response in the wood-wind, and then a prayerful passage for strings, as though to reveal the essential earnestness and reasonableness of the Finnish people, even under the stress of national sorrow. This leads to an *allegro moderato* episode, in which the restless opening theme is proclaimed by the strings against a very characteristic rhythmic figure, a succession of eight beats, the first strongly accented. . . . With a change to *allegro* the movement, looked at as an example of the sonata form, may be said to begin. A broad, cheerful theme by the strings in A flat, against the persistent rhythm in the brass, is followed by a second subject, introduced by the wood-wind and taken up by the strings, then by the 'cello and first violin. This is peaceful and elevated in character, and might be looked upon as prophetic of ultimate rest and happiness. The development of these musical ideas carries the tone poem to an eloquent conclusion."

*Finlandia* is scored for two flutes, two oboes, two clarinets, two bassoons, four horns, three trumpets, three trombones, bass tuba, kettle-drums, bass drum, cymbals, triangle and strings.

## "THE SWAN OF TUONELA" ("TUONELAN JOUTSEN"), LEGEND FROM THE FINNISH FOLK EPIC "KALEVALA"

HERE IS no swan, singing before death, a fable that suggested to Villiers de l'Isle-Adam one of his cruelest tales, and served Anna Pavlowa for an entrancing, memorable dance-pantomime to Saint-Saëns' familiar music. This is the swan that glides and sings on the river of black water around Tuonela, the Kingdom of Death. Sibelius, to whom the Finnish epic *Kalevala* furnished subjects for several of his earlier compositions, by economic means, by an unerring choice of his instruments, portrays the scene and gives the song—after the hearer is acquainted with the explanatory note in the score. Suppose that the hearer had no knowledge of the legend, had never read of Lemminkainen's adventures; how, to win the maid Pohjola, he set out to accomplish certain tasks, among them to shoot a swan on this River of Death. How would the hearer then be impressed? Surely he would be moved by the strangeness of the music, by the mysterious first measures, by the unearthly melancholy of the song, by the quiet intensity of it all. He would find in the music a tragic mood, simply but unmistakably expressed. To us this legend of Sibelius, for itself, is commanding music.

*The Swan of Tuonela* is the third section of a symphonic poem *Lemminkainen,* in four parts, Op. 22, 1. "Lemminkainen and the Maidens"; 2. "His Sojourn in Tuonela"; 3. "The Swan of Tuonela"; 4. "Lemminkainen Homefaring." These pieces are drawn from the Finnish epic *Kalevala.* A note on the score of *The Swan of Tuonela* runs thus: "Tuonela, the Kingdom of Death, the Hades of Finnish mythology, is surrounded by a broad river of black water and rapid current, in which the Swan of Tuonela glides in majestic fashion and sings.

Lemminkainen is one of the four principal heroes of the *Kalevala*. Mr. W. F. Kirby, in his translation of the epic, describes him as a "jovial, reckless personage, always getting into serious scrapes, from which he escapes either by his own skill in magic or by his mother's. His love for his mother is the redeeming feature in his character. One of his names is Kaukomieli, and he is, in part, the original of Longfellow's 'Pau-Puk-Keewis.'"

In the thirteenth and fourteenth Runos, it is told how Lemminkainen asks the old woman of Pohja for her daughter Pohjola. She demands that he should first accomplish certain tasks: to capture on snowshoes the elk of Hiisi; to bridle fire-breathing steeds. Succeeding in these adventures, he is asked to shoot a swan on the river of Tuonela.

*I will only give my daughter,*
*Give the youthful bride you seek for,*
*If the river swan you shoot me,*
*Shoot the great bird on the river;*
*There on Tuoni's murky river,*
*In the sacred river's whirlpool,*
*Only at a single trial,*
*Using but a single arrow.*

Lemminkainen came to the river. A cowherd, Märkähattu, old and sightless, who had long waited for him, slew him there by sending a serpent "like a reed from out the billows" through the hero's heart, and cast the body into the stream. Lemminkainen floated on to Tuonela's dread dwelling. The son of Tuoni cut the body into pieces. The hero's mother, learning of his fate, raked the water under the cataract till she found all the fragments. She joined them together and restored her son to life by charms and magic salves, so that he could return home with her.

The piece is written in A minor, *andante molto sostenuto* 9–4 time. Mrs. Rosa Newmarch *(Jean Sibelius)* says of it:

"The majestic but intensely sad, swan-like melody is heard as a solo for *cor-anglais,* accompanied at first by muted strings and the soft roll of drums. Now and then this melody is answered by a phrase given to first violoncello or viola, which might be interpreted as the farewell sigh of some soul passing to Tuonela. For many bars the brass is silent, until suddenly the first horn (muted) echoes a few notes of the swan melody with the most poignant effect. Gradually the music works up to a great climax, indicated *con gran suono,* followed by a treble *pianissimo,* the strings playing with the back of the bow. To this accompaniment, which suggests the faint flapping of pinions, the swan's final phrases are sung. The strings return to the natural bowing and the work ends in one of the characteristic, sighing phrases for violoncello."

The second theme is given out by the strings to a slow but rhythmed accompaniment of wood-wind, brass, and drums.

The score calls for oboe, English horn (solo), bass clarinet, two bassoons, four horns, three trombones, kettledrums, bass drum, harp, and the usual strings.

# RICHARD STRAUSS

(Born at Munich, June 11, 1864)

## "DON JUAN," TONE POEM (AFTER NICOLAUS LENAU), OP. 20

SOME OF STRAUSS's wild-eyed worshipers, not content with the quotations that serve as mottoes, have invented ingenious analyses in which we are told the precise meaning of each theme in *Don Juan,* and how this section represents his passion for a widow and that for a maiden. But did not Strauss himself say that the theme which represents, according to an analyst, Don Juan rushing off to new triumphs was intended as his drunken entrance into a ballroom? And is it not possible that when Strauss wrote down this theme he attached no specific and minute significance to it? No, there is no need of the showman with blackboard and rod while this music is playing. "Don Juan—after Lenau's poem" is enough; and merely *Don Juan* might serve.

A daring, brilliant composition: one that paints the hero as might a master's brush on canvas. How expressive the themes! How daring the treatment of them! What fascinating, irresistible insolence, glowing passion, and then the taste of Dead Sea fruit!

*Don Juan,* composed at Munich 1887–88, is known as the first of Strauss's symphonic or tone poems, but *Macbeth,* Op. 23, was composed at Munich, 1886–87 (revised in 1890 at Weimar), and published later (1891). *Don Juan* was published in 1890. The first performance of *Don Juan* was at the second subscription concert of the Grand Ducal Court Orchestra of Weimar in the fall of 1889.

The work is scored for three flutes (and piccolo), two oboes, English horn, two clarinets, two bassoons, double bassoon, four horns, three trumpets, three trombones, tuba, kettledrums, triangle, cymbals, glockenspiel, harp, strings. The score is dedicated "To my dear friend, Ludwig Thuille," a composer and teacher, born at Bozen in 1861, who was a fellow student at Munich. Thuille died in 1907.

Strauss's hero is Lenau's, in search of the ideal woman. Not finding one reaching his standard, disgusted with life, he practically commits suicide by dropping his sword when fighting a duel with a man whose father he had killed. Before this Don Juan dies, he provides in his will for the women he had seduced and forsaken.

Lenau wrote his poem in 1844. It is said that his third revision was made in August and September of that year at Vienna and Stuttgart. After September he wrote no more, for he went mad, and he was mad until he died in 1850. The poem, "Eitel nichts," dedicated in the asylum at Winnenthal, was intended originally for *Don Juan. Don Juan* is of a somewhat fragmentary nature. The quotations made by Strauss paint well the hero's character.

L. A. Frankl, a biographer of the morbid poet, says that Lenau once spoke as follows concerning his purpose in this dramatic poem: "Goethe's great poem has not hurt me in the matter of *Faust* and Byron's 'Don Juan' will here do me no harm. Each poet, as every human being, is an individual ego. My Don Juan is no hot-blooded man eternally pursuing woman. It is the longing in him to find a woman who is to him incarnate womanhood, and to enjoy in the one, all the women on earth, whom he cannot as individuals possess. Because he does not find her, although he reels from one to another, at last Disgust seizes hold of him, and this Disgust is the Devil that fetches him."

It has been said that the "emotional phases of the story" appealed to Strauss:

1. The fiery ardor with which Don Juan pursues his ideal;
2. The charm of woman; and
3. The selfish idealist's disappointment and partial atonement by death.

There are two ways of considering this tone poem: to say that it is a fantasia, free in form and development—the quotations from the poem are enough to show the mood and the purposes of the composer; or to discuss the character of Lenau's hero, and then follow foreign commentators who give significance to every melodic phrase and find deep, esoteric meaning in every modulation. No doubt Strauss himself would be content with the verses of Lenau and his own music, for he is a man not without humor, and on more than one occasion has slyly smiled at his prying or pontifical interpreters.

Strauss has particularized his hero among the many that bear the name of Don Juan, from the old drama of Gabriel Tellez, the cloistered monk who wrote, under the name of "Tirso de Molina," *El Burlador de Sevilla y el Convidado de Piedra* (first printed in 1634). Strauss's hero is specifically the Don Juan of Lenau, not the rakehelly hero of legend and so many plays, who at the last is undone by the Statue invited by Juan to supper.

## "TOD UND VERKLÄRUNG" (DEATH AND TRANSFIGURATION) TONE POEM, OP. 24

"Death and transfiguration" is now more old-fashioned than the G minor symphony of Mozart. The anguish of the dying man, who does not make the graceful and gracious apology of Charles II on his deathbed, no longer moves us. His recollections seem sentimental and vapid, while the trombone passages once considered as terrific, awe-inspiring, are not so significant as the single horn of Charon in Gluck's *Alceste*. *Don Juan,* on the other hand, holds its own by its defiant spirit, expressing the arrogance of the Don on his triumphant way—by its dramatic translation into music of the words put by Lenau into his mouth:

*Exhausted is the fuel;*
*And on the hearth, the cold is fiercely cruel.*

The superb horn phrase should have accompanied the entrance of Lovelace into the ballroom, one of the most powerful scenes in Richardson's long-winded romance.

## RICHARD STRAUSS

This tone poem was composed at Munich in 1888–89.

Hans von Bülow wrote to his wife from Weimar, November 13, 1889: "Strauss is enormously beloved here. His *Don Juan* evening before last had a wholly unheard-of success. Yesterday morning Spitzweg and I were at his house to hear his new symphonic poem *Tod und Verklärung*—which has again inspired me with great confidence in his development. It. is a very important work in spite of sundry poor passages, and it is also refreshing."

The first performance was from manuscript, under the direction of the composer, at the fifth concert of the 27th Musicians' Convention of the Allgemeine Deutscher Musikverein in the City Theater of Eisenach, June 21, 1890.

The poem is dedicated to Friedrich Rösch, and is scored for three flutes, two oboes, English horn, two clarinets, bass clarinet, two bassoons, double bassoon, four horns, three trumpets, three trombones, tuba, a set of three kettledrums, two harps, gong, and strings.

On the flyleaf of the score is a poem in German.

The following literal translation is by William Foster Apthorp:

"In the necessitous little room, dimly lighted by only a candle end, lies the sick man on his bed. But just now he has wrestled despairingly with Death. Now he has sunk exhausted into sleep, and one hears only the soft ticking of the clock on the wall in the room, whose awful silence gives a foreboding of the nearness of death. Over the sick man's pale features plays a sad smile. Dreams he, on the boundary of life, of the golden time of childhood?

"But death does not long grant sleep and dreams to his victim. Cruelly he shakes him awake, and the fight begins afresh. Will to live and power of Death! What frightful wrestling! Neither bears off the victory, and all is silent once more!

"Sunk back tired of battle, sleepless, as in fever-frenzy the sick man now sees his life pass before his inner eye, trait by trait and scene by scene. First the morning red of childhood, shining bright in pure innocence! Then the youth's saucier play—exerting and trying his strength—till he ripens to the man's fight, and now burns with hot lust after the higher prizes of life. The one high purpose that has led him through life was to shape all he saw transfigured into a still more transfigured form. Cold and sneering, the world sets barrier upon barrier in the way of his achievement. If he thinks himself near his goal, a 'Halt!' thunders in his ear. 'Make the barrier thy stirrup! Ever higher and onward go!' And so he pushes forward, so he climbs, desists not from his sacred purpose. What he has ever sought with his heart's deepest yearning, he still seeks in his death sweat. Seeks—alas! and finds it never. Whether he comprehends it more clearly or it grows upon him gradually, he can yet never exhaust it, cannot complete it in his spirit. Then clangs the last stroke of Death's iron hammer, breaks the earthly body in twain, covers the eye with the night of death.

"But from the heavenly spaces sounds mightily to greet him what he yearningly sought for here: deliverance from the world, transfiguration of the world."

The poem by Ritter is, after all, the most satisfactory explanation of the music to those that seek eagerly a clew and are not content with the title. The analysts have been busy with this tone poem as well as the others of Strauss. Wilhelm Mauke wrote a pamphlet of twenty pages with twenty-one musical illustrations, and made a delicate distinction between "Fever" theme No. 1 and "Fever" theme No. 2. Reimann and Brandes have been more moderate. *Death and Transfiguration* may be divided into sections, closely joined, and for each one a portion of the poem may serve as a motto.

I. *Largo,* C minor, D flat major, 4–4. The chief "Death" motive is a syncopated figure, *pianissimo,* given to the second violins and violas. A sad smile steals over the sick man's face (wood-wind accompanied by horns and harps), and he thinks of his youth (a simple melody, the childhood motive, announced by the oboe). These three motives establish the mood of the introduction.

II. *Allegro molto agitato,* C minor. Death attacks the sick man. There are harsh double blows in quick succession. What Mauke characterizes as the "Fever" motive begins in the basses, and wildly dissonant chords shriek at the end of the climbing motive. There is a mighty *crescendo,* the chief "Death" motive is heard, the struggle begins (full orchestra, *fortississimo*). There is a second chromatic and feverish motive, which appears first in sixteenths, which is bound to a contrasting and ascending theme that recalls the motive of the struggle. This second feverish theme goes canonically through the instrument groups. The sick man sinks exhausted (*ritenuto*). Trombones, violoncellos, and violas intone even now the beginning of the "Transfiguration" theme, just as Death is about to triumph. "And again all is still!" The mysterious "Death" motive knocks.

III. And now the dying man dreams dreams and sees visions (*meno mosso, ma sempre alla breve*). The "Childhood" motive returns (G major) in freer form. There is again the joy of youth (oboes, harp, and, bound to this motive of "Hope" that made him smile before the struggle, the motive now played by solo viola). The fight of manhood with the world's prizes is waged again (B major, full orchestra, *fortissimo*), waged fiercely. "Halt!" thunders in his ears, and trombones and kettledrums sound the dread and strangely rhythmed motive of "Death" (drums beaten with wooden drumsticks). There is contrapuntal elaboration of the "Life Struggle" and "Childhood" motives. The "Transfiguration" motive is heard in broader form. The chief "Death" motive and the feverish attack are again dominating features. Storm and fury of orchestra. There is a wild series of ascending fifths. Tam-tam and harp knell the soul's departure.

IV. The "Transfiguration" theme is heard from the horns; strings repeat the "Childhood" motive. A *crescendo* leads to the full development of the "Transfiguration" theme (*moderato,* C major), "World deliverance, world transfiguration."

The scoring is as follows: three flutes, two oboes, English horn, two clarinets, bass clarinet, two bassoons, double bassoon, four horns, three trumpets, three trombones and bass tuba, kettledrums, tam-tam, two harps, and strings.

## "TILL EULENSPIEGEL'S MERRY PRANKS, AFTER THE OLD-FASHIONED ROGUISH MANNER —IN RONDO FORM," OP. 28

*Till Eulenspiegel* disputes with *Don Juan* the first position among the symphonic poems of Strauss. The opening of *Thus Spake Zarathustra* is colossal in its elemental grandeur; the death music in *Don Quixote* is incomparably beautiful; there are a few pages in *A Hero's Life* that remind one of Beethoven at his best; the love music in the *Domestic symphony* is memorable; but *Till Eulenspiegel* and *Don Juan* are continuously impressive, each in its way, and are free from the suspicion of effects made for the sake of effect, designed deliberately to make the bourgeois stare.

The story is medieval and Rabelaisian, and the music is quite as broad as the tale. Clear motives typify Till, who can be traced from beginning to end. He "bobs up" (no other term can describe it) through every kind of repression and persecution; he is saucy and insouciant; he is comically repentant when at the last he is hanged, and his last faint squeak is very mock-pathetic.

This hanging is a deviant from the old story in which Till evades his doom and cheats the executioner. For some time the reviewers were in doubt as to whether Strauss had given warrant for the execution—which shows the weak point of "programme music," for no one ought to have had any doubts upon the subject after hearing the change of style from glibness to utter dejection at the end.

*Till Eulenspiegel's lustige Streiche, nach alter Schelmenweise—in Rondoform, für grosses Orchester gesetzt, von Richard Strauss,* was produced at a Gürznich concert at Cologne, November 5, 1895. It was composed in 1894–95 at Munich, and the score was completed there, May 6, 1895. The score and parts were published in September, 1895.

There has been dispute concerning the proper translation of the phrase, *nach alter Schelmenweise,* in the title. Some, and Apthorp was one of them, translate it "after an old rogue's tune." Others will not have this at all, and prefer "after the old—or old-fashioned—roguish manner," or, as Krehbiel suggested, "in the style of old-time waggery," and this view is in all probability the sounder. It is hard to twist *Schelmenweise* into "rogue's tune." *Schelmenstück,* for instance, is "a knavish trick," a "piece of roguery." As Krehbiel well said: "The reference [*Schelmenweise*] goes, not to the thematic form of the phrase, but to its structure. This is indicated, not only by the grammatical form of the phrase but also by the parenthetical explanation: '*in Rondoform.*' What connection exists between roguishness, or waggishness, and the rondo form it might be difficult to explain. The roguish wag in this case is Richard Strauss himself, who, besides putting the puzzle into his title, refused to provide the composition with even the smallest explanatory note which might have given a clue to its contents." It seems to us that the puzzle in the title is largely imaginary. There is no need of attributing any intimate connection between "roguish manner" and *"rondo* form."

Till (or Tyll) Eulenspiegel is the hero of an old *Volksbuch* of the fifteenth century attributed to Dr. Thomas Murner (1475–1530). Till is supposed to be a wandering mechanic of Brunswick, who plays all sorts of tricks, practical jokes—some of them exceedingly coarse—on everybody, and he always comes out ahead. In the book, Till (or Till Owlglass, as he is known in the English translation) goes to the gallows, but he escapes through an exercise of his ready wit and dies peacefully in bed, playing a sad joke on his heirs, and refusing to lie still and snug in his grave. Strauss kills him on the scaffold. The German name is said to find its derivation in an old proverb: "Man sees his own faults as little as a monkey or an owl recognizes his ugliness in looking into a mirror."

When Dr. Franz Wüllner, who conducted the first performance at Cologne, asked the composer for an explanatory programme of the "poetical intent" of the piece, Strauss replied: "It is impossibie for me to furnish a programme to *Eulenspiegel;* were I to put into words the thoughts which its several incidents suggest to me, they would seldom suffice, and might give rise to offense. Let me leave it, therefore, to my hearers to crack the hard nut which the Rogue has prepared for them. By way of helping them to a better understanding, it seems sufficient to point out the two 'Eulenspiegel' motives, which, in the most manifold disguises, moods, and situations, pervade the whole up to the catastrophe, when, after he has been condemned to death, Till is strung up to the gibbet. For the rest, let them guess at the musical joke which a Rogue has offered them." Strauss indicated in notation three motives—the opening theme of the introduction, the horn theme that follows almost immediately, and the descending interval expressive of condemnation and the scaffold.

The rondo, dedicated to Dr. Arthur Seidl, is scored for piccolo, three flutes, three oboes, English horn, small clarinet in E flat, two clarinets, bass clarinet, three bassoons, double bassoon, four horns (with the addition of four horns *ad lib.*), three trumpets (with three additional trumpets *ad lib.*), three trombones, bass tuba, kettledrums, snare drum, bass drum, cymbals, triangle, a watchman's rattle, strings.

## "THUS SPAKE ZARATHUSTRA," TONE POEM (FREELY AFTER FRIEDRICH NIETZSCHE), OP. 30

STRAUSS's huge "machine" has aged. The opening measures are still stupendous. The "Grave Song" and "Night Song" are not without compelling beauty, but on the whole, Nietzschian philosophy and music do not dwell together in harmony. Dismiss the thought of Nietzsche; consider the music as absolute music, and there is much that is boresome and inherently cheap, if not vulgar, in spite, or by reason of the bombast and pretentiousness.

The full title of this composition is *Also sprach Zarathustra, Tondichtung (frei nach Friedrich Nietzsche) für grosses Orchester*. Composition was begun at Munich, February 4, 1896, and completed there August 24, 1896. The first performance was at Frankfort-on-the-Main, November 27 of the same year. The composer conducted, and also at Cologne, December 1.

Friedrich Nietzsche conceived the plan to his *Thus Spake Zarathustra: A Book for All and None,* in August, 1881, as he was walking through the woods near the Silvaplana Lake in the Engadine and saw a huge tower-like crag. He completed the first part in February, 1883, at Rapallo, near Genoa; he wrote the second part in Sils Maria in June and July, the third part in the following winter at Nice, and the fourth part, not then intended to be the last, but to serve as an interlude, from November, 1884, till February, 1885, at Mentone. Nietzsche never published this fourth part; it was printed for private circulation and not publicly issued till after he became insane. The whole of *Zarathustra* was published in 1892.

Nietzsche's Zarathustra is by no means the historical or legendary Zoroaster, mage, leader, warrior, king. The Zarathustra of Nietzsche is Nietzsche himself, with his views on life and death. Strauss's opera *Guntram* (1894) showed the composer's interest in the book. Before the tone poem was performed, this programme was published: "First movement: Sunrise, Man feels the power of God. *Andante religioso.* But man still longs. He plunges into passion (second movement) and finds no peace. He turns towards science, and tries in vain to solve life's problem in a fugue (third movement). Then agreeable dance tunes sound and he becomes an individual, and his soul soars upward while the world sinks far beneath him." But Strauss gave this explanation to Otto Florsheim: "I did not intend to write philosophical music or to portray in music Nietzsche's great work. I meant to convey by means of music an idea of the development of the human race from its origin, through the various phases of its development, religious and scientific, up to Nietzsche's idea of the Superman. The whole symphonic poem is intended as my homage to Nietzsche's genius, which found its greatest exemplification in his book, *Thus Spake Zarathustra*."

*Thus Spake Zarathustra* is scored for piccolo, three flutes (one interchangeable with a second piccolo), three oboes, English horn, two clarinets in B flat, clarinet in E flat, bass clarinet, three bassoons, double bassoon, six horns, four trumpets, three trombones, two bass tubas, kettledrums, bass drum, cymbals, triangle, glockenspiel, a low bell in E, two harps, organ, sixteen second violins, twelve violas, twelve violoncellos, eight double basses.

On a flyleaf of a score is printed the following excerpts from Nietzsche's book, the first section of "Zarathustra's Introductory Speech":

"Having attained the age of thirty, Zarathustra left his home and the lake of his home and went into the mountains. There he rejoiced in his spirit and his loneliness, and for ten years did not grow weary of it. But at last his heart turned—one morning he got up with the dawn, stepped into the presence of the Sun and thus spake unto him: 'Thou great star! What would be thy happiness, were it not for those on whom thou shinest? For ten years thou hast come up here to my cave. Thou wouldst have got sick of thy light and thy journey but for me, mine eagle and my serpent. But we waited for thee every morning and receiving from thee thine abundance, blessed thee for it. Lo! I am weary of my wisdom, like the bee that hath collected too much honey; I need hands reaching out for it. I would fain grant and distribute until the wise among men could once more enjoy their folly, and the poor once more their riches. For that end I must descend to the depth; as thou dost at even, when sinking behind the sea, thou givest light to the lower regions, thou resplendent star! I must, like thee, go down, as men say—men to whom I would descend. Then bless me, thou impassive eye, that canst look without envy even upon overmuch happiness. Bless the cup which is about to overflow, so that the water golden-flowing out of it may carry everywhere the reflection of thy rapture. Lo! this cup is about to empty itself again, and Zarathustra will once more become a man.'—Thus Zarathustra's going down began."

This prefatory note in Strauss's tone poem is not a "programme" of the composition itself. It is merely an introduction. The sub-captions of the composer in the score indicate that the music after the short musical introduction begins where the quotation ends.

"The scene of *Thus Spake Zarathustra,"* says Dr. Tille, "is laid, as it were, outside of time and space, and certainly outside of countries and nations, outside of this age, and outside of the main condition of all that lives—the struggle for existence. . . . There appear cities and mobs, kings and scholars, poets and cripples, but outside of their realm there is a province which is Zarathustra's own, where he lives in his cave amid the rocks, and whence he thrice goes to men to teach them his wisdom. This Nowhere and Nowhen, over which Nietzsche's imagination is supreme, is a province of boundless individualism, in which a man of mark has free play, unfettered by the tastes and inclinations of the multitude. . . . *Thus Spake Zarathustra* is a kind of summary of the intellectual life of the nineteenth century, and it is on this fact that its principal significance rests. It unites in itself a number of mental movements which, in literature as well as in various sciences, have made themselves felt separately during the last hundred years, without going far beyond them. By bringing them into contact, although not always into uncontradictory relation, Nietzsche transfers them from mere existence in philosophy, or scientific literature in general, into the sphere or the creed of *Weltanschauung* of the educated classes, and thus his book becomes capable of influencing the views and strivings of a whole age."

Zarathustra teaches men the deification of Life. He offers not joy of life, for to him there is no such thing, but fullness of life, in the joy of the senses, "in the triumphant exuberance of vitality, in the pure, lofty naturalness of the antique, in short, in the fusion of God, world, and ego."

There is a simple but impressive introduction, in which there is a solemn trumpet motive, which leads to a great climax for full orchestra and organ on the chord of C major. There is this heading, "Von den

Hinterweltlern" (Of the Dwellers in the Rear World). These are they who sought the solution in religion. Zarathustra too had once dwelt in this rear world. (Horns intone a solemn Gregorian *Credo*.)

The next heading is "Von der grossen Sehnsucht" (Of the Great Yearning). This stands over an ascending passage in B minor in violoncellos and bassoons, answered by wood-wind instruments in chromatic thirds.

The next section begins with a pathetic *cantilena* in C minor (second violins, oboes, horn), and the heading is: "Von den Freuden und Leidenschaften" (Of Joys and Passions).

"Grablied" (Grave Song). The oboe has a tender *cantilena* over the Yearning motive in violoncellos and bassoons.

"Von der Wissenschaft" (Of Science). The fugued passage begins with violoncellos and double basses (divided). The subject of this *fugato* contains all the diatonic and chromatic degrees of the scale, and the real responses to this subject come in successively a fifth higher.

Much farther on a passage in the strings, beginning in the violoncellos and violas, arises from B minor. "Der Genesende" (The Convalescent).

"Tanzlied." The dance song begins with laughter in the wood-wind.

"Nachtlied" (Night Song).

"Nachtwanderlied" (The Song of the Night Wanderer, though Nietzsche in later editions changed the title to "The Drunken Song"). The song comes after a *fortissimo* stroke of the bell, and the bell, sounding twelve times, dies away softly.

The mystical conclusion has excited much discussion. The ending is in two keys—in B major in the high wood-wind and violins, in C major in the basses, *pizzicato*. "The theme of the Ideal sways aloft in the higher regions in B major; the trombones insist on the unresolved chord of C, E, F sharp; and in the double basses is repeated C, G, C, the World Riddle." This riddle is unsolved by Nietzsche, by Strauss, and even by Strauss's commentators.

## "DON QUIXOTE," FANTASTIC VARIATIONS ON A THEME OF KNIGHTLY CHARACTER, OP. 35

## INTRODUCTION, THEME WITH VARIATIONS, AND FINALE

Don quixote, a virtuoso tone poem, shows Strauss at his best and at his worst. Composers have laid violent hands on the world-famous novel of Cervantes. The Knight has figured in both serious and comic operas. It occurred to Strauss that Don Quixote might be portrayed by one instrument, Sancho Panza by another. Strauss undoubtedly rubbed his hands with glee at the thought of the musical representation of ba-a-a-ing sheep and the opportunity of introducing a wind machine with a man turning a crank for the variation, "The Ride through the Air." But there are fine passages in the work. When Don Quixote speaks nobly of the ideal, Strauss gives him noble music, and Strauss has seldom written more charming music than for the last speech of Sancho Panza. One might ask, however, if this music is in Sancho Panza's character as Cervantes describes it. And in the final music—the disillusionment of Don Quixote and his death—Strauss attains, without straining and exaggeration, an emotional height that is seldom found in his instrumental compositions that follow. Hearing these emotional sections one almost forgets the imitative and pictorial passages of the work, which seem too long, with much music that is of little worth and interest.

*Don Quixote (Introduzione, Tema con Variazioni, e Finale): Fantastische Variationen uber ein Thema ritterlichen Charakters,* was composed at Munich in 1897 (the score was completed on December 29th of that year). It was played for the first time at a Gürzenich Concert, Cologne, from manuscript, Franz Wüllner conductor, March 8, 1898. Friedrich Grützmacher was the solo violoncellist. Strauss conducted his composition on March 18, 1898, at a concert of the Frankfort Museumgesellschaft, when Hugo Becker was the violoncellist. It is said that Becker composed an exceedingly piquant *cadenza* for violoncello on the "Quixote" motive for his own enjoyment at home.

The work is scored for piccolo, two flutes, two oboes, English horn, two clarinets, bass clarinet, three bassoons, double bassoon, six horns, three trumpets, three trombones, tenor tuba, bass tuba, kettledrums, snare drum, bass drum, cymbals, triangle, tambourine, wind machine, harp, sixteen first violins, sixteen second violins, twelve violas, ten violoncellos, eight double basses. It is dedicated to Joseph Dupont.

Much has been written in explanation of this work, which followed *Also sprach Zarathustra,* Op. 30 (1896), and preceded *Ein Heldenleben,* Op. 40 (1898). As the story goes, at a music festival in Düsseldorf in 1899 an acquaintance of Strauss complained bitterly before the rehearsal that he had no printed "guide" to *Don Quixote,* with which he was unfamiliar. Strauss laughed, and said for his consolation, "Get out! you do not need any." Arthur Hahn wrote a pamphlet of twenty-seven pages in elucidation. In this pamphlet are many wondrous things. We are told that certain queer harmonies introduced in an otherwise simple passage of the introduction "characterize admirably the well-known tendency of Don Quixote toward false conclusions."

There is no programme attached to the score of this work. The arrangement for pianoforte gives certain information concerning the composer's purposes.

Max Steinitzer declares in his *Richard Strauss* (Berlin and Leipsic, 1911) that with the exception of some details, as the "Windmill" episode, the music is intelligible and effective as absolute music; that the title is sufficiently explanatory. "The introduction begins immediately with the hero's motive and pictures with constantly increasing liveliness by other themes of knightly and gallant character life as it is mirrored in writings from the beginning of the seventeenth century. 'Don Quixote, busied in reading romances of chivalry, loses his reason—and determines to go through the world as a wandering knight.'" It is easy to recognize the hero's theme in its variations, because the knight is always represented by the solo violoncello. The character of Sancho Panza is expressed by a theme first given to bass clarinet and tenor tuba; but afterward and to the end by a solo viola. *Don Quixote* is divided into an introduction, a theme with variations, and a *finale*. The sections are connected without a break. Each variation portrays an incident in the novel.

## Introduction

*Mässiges Zeitmass* (*moderato*), D major, 4–4. Don Quixote plunged himself deeply in his reading of books of knighthood, "and in the end, through his little sleep and much reading, he dried up his brains in such sort, as he lost wholly his judgment. His fantasy was filled with those things that he read, of enchantments, quarrels, battles, challenges, wounds, wooings, loves, tempests, and other impossible follies."[1] The first theme (wind instruments) foreshadows the typical Don Quixote motive, and is here typical of knight-errantry in general. The next section (strings) represents the idea of knightly gallantry, and the whole theme ends with the passages that include the strange harmonies and portray his madness. These strange progressions recur frequently throughout the work. "He does not dream," says Mr. H. W. Harris, "that his reasoning is at fault or that he is the victim of self-delusion; on the contrary, he ascribes all such discrepancies to magic, by which he believes himself to be persecuted, which is clearly being employed to make things appear otherwise than his judgment assures him they really should be."

The first section of the first theme is ornamented (violas). Don Quixote grows more and more romantic and chivalric. He sees the Ideal Woman, his lady-love (oboe). The trumpets tell of a giant attacking her and her rescue by a knight. "In this part of the Introduction, the use of mutes on all the instruments—including the tuba, here so treated for the first time—creates an indescribable effect of vagueness and confusion, indicating that they are mere phantasms with which the Knight is concerned, which cloud his brain." A Penitent enters (muted violas *fortissimo*). Don Quixote's brain grows more and more confused. The orchestral themes grow wilder. An augmented version of the first section of the theme (brass), followed by a harp *glissando,* leads to shrill discord—the Knight is mad. "The repeated use of the various sections of the first theme shows that his madness has something to do with chivalry." Don Quixote has decided to be a knight-errant.

[1]Quotations from the novel itself are here taken from the translation into English by Thos. Shelton (1612–20.)

## Theme

"Don Quixote, the knight of the sorrowful countenance; Sancho Panza." *Moderato,* D minor, 4–4. The Don Quixote theme is announced by solo violoncello. It is of close kin to the theme of the introduction. Sancho Panza is typified by a theme given first to bass clarinet and tenor tuba; but afterward the solo viola is the characteristic instrument of Sancho.

## Variation I

The Knight and the Squire set out on their journey. "In a leisurely manner," D minor, 12–8. The beautiful Dulcinea of Toboso inspires the Knight (a version of the "Ideal Woman" theme), who soon sees some windmills (brass) and prepares to attack. A breeze arises (wood-wind and strings), and the Knight, angry at the challenge, attacks, and is knocked down by the sails (run in wood-wind, harp *glissando,* heavy drum-beats).

## Variation II

The Victorious Battle against the Host of the Great Emperor Alifanfaron. "Warlike," D major, 4–4. There is a cloud of dust; surely a great army approaches; the Knight rushes to fight, in spite of the warnings of Sancho, who sees the sheep. There is a pastoral figure (wood-wind), and out of the dust cloud (strings) comes a chorus of "Ba-a-a-a" (muted brass). Don Quixote charges and puts the foes to confusion.

## Variation III

The Dialogues of the Knight and the Squire. *Moderato,* 4–4. Sancho questions the worth of such a life. Don Quixote speaks of honor and glory (first theme), but Sancho sees nothing in them. The dispute waxes hot. Don Quixote speaks nobly of the ideal. Sancho prefers the easy, comfortable realities of life. At last his master is angry and bids him hold his tongue.

## Variation IV

The Adventure with the Penitents. "Somewhat broader," D minor, 4–4. A church theme (wind instruments) announces the approach of a band of pilgrims. Don Quixote sees in them shameless robbers, desperate villains. He attacks them. They knock him senseless and go on their prayerful way. Sancho, sorely disturbed, rejoices when his master shows signs of life, and after he has helped him, lies down by his side and goes to sleep (bass tuba, double bassoon).

## Variation V

The Knight's Vigil. "Very slow," 4–4. Don Quixote, ashamed to sleep, holds watch by his armor. Dulcinea, answering his prayers, appears in a vision (the "Ideal Woman" theme, horn). A *cadenza* for harp and violins leads to a passage portraying his rapture.

## Variation VI

The Meeting with Dulcinea. G major, 2–4, 3–4. A common country wench comes along (wood-wind, tambourine), and Sancho by way of jest points her out to his master as Dulcinea. The Knight cannot believe it. Sancho swears it is so. The Knight suddenly knows that some magic has worked this transformation, and he vows vengeance.

## Variation VII

The Ride through the Air. D minor, 8–4. Knight and Squire sit, blindfolded, on a wooden horse, which, they have been made to believe, will bear them through the air. Their respective themes soar skyward. The wind whistles about them (chromatic flute passages, harp, drum roll, wind machine). They stop suddenly (long-held bassoon note), and, looking about them, they think themselves still on the ground. "The persistent *tremolo* of the double basses on one note may be taken to mean that the two did not really leave the solid earth."

## Variation VIII

The Journey in the Enchanted Bark. Don Quixote sees an empty boat, and he is sure it is sent by some mysterious power, that he may do a glorious deed. He and Sancho embark. His typical theme is changed into a barcarolle. The boat upsets, but they succeed in gaining the shore; and they give thanks for their safety (wind instruments *religioso*).

## Variation IX

The Combat with Two Magicians. "Quickly and stormily," D minor, 4-4. Don Quixote is again on his famous horse, eager for adventure. Two peaceable monks are jogging along on their mules, and the Knight sees in them the base magicians who have worked him harm. He charges them and puts them to flight. The two themes are a version of the Don Quixote motive and an ecclesiastical phrase for the bassoons.

## Variation X

Don Quixote, defeated by the Knight of the White Moon, returns home and resolves to be a shepherd. "Know, sir," said the Knight of the White Moon, "that I am styled the Bachelor Samson Carrasco, and am one of Don Quixote's town; whose wild madness hath moved as many of us as know him to compassion, and me amongst the rest most; and believing that the best means to procure his health is to keep him quiet, and so to have him in his own house, I thought upon this device." So said this knight after the furious battle which is thus described:

"They both of them set spurs to their horses, and the Knight of the White Moon's being the swifter, met Don Quixote ere he had run a quarter of his career so forcibly (without touching him with his lance, for it seemed he carried it aloft on purpose) that he tumbled horse and man both to the ground, and Don Quixote had a terrible fall; so he got straight on the top of him; and, clapping his lance's point upon his visor, said, 'You are vanquished, Knight, and a dead man, if you confess not, according to the conditions of our combat.' Don Quixote, all bruised and amazed, without heaving up his visor, as if he had spoken out of a tomb, with a faint and weak voice, said, 'Dulcinea del Toboso is the fairest woman in the world, and I the unfortunatest Knight on earth; and it is not fit that my weakness defraud this truth; thrust your lance into me, Knight, and kill me, since you have bereaved me of my honor.' 'Not so truly,' quoth he of the White Moon, 'let the fame of my Lady Dulcinea's beauty live in her entireness; I am only contented that the grand Don Quixote retire home for a year, or till such time as I please, as we agreed, before we began the battle.' And Don Quixote answered that, so nothing were required of him in prejudice of his Lady Dulcinea, he would accomplish all the rest, like a true and punctual knight." The variation portrays the fight. The pastoral theme heard in the second variation—the battle with the sheep—reappears. Don Quixote loses one by one his illusions.

## Finale

The Death of Don Quixote. "Very peacefully," D major, 4-4. The typical theme of the Knight takes a new form. The queer harmonies in a section of this theme are now conventional, commonplace. "They stood all gazing one upon another, wondering at Don Quixote's sound reasons, although they made some doubt to believe them. One of the signs which induced them to conjecture that he was near unto death's door was that with such facility he was from a stark fool become a wise man. For, to the words already alleged, he added many more so significant, so Christian-like, and so well couched, that without doubt they confidently believed that Don Quixote was become a right wise man. . . . These heavy news opened the sluices of the tears-ful and swollen-blubbering eyes of the maid, of the niece, and of his good Squire Sancho Panza; so that they showered forth whole fountains of tears and fetched from the very bottom of their aggrieved hearts a thousand groaning sighs. For in effect (as we have already declared elsewhere) whilst Don Quixote was simply the good Alonso Quixano, and likewise when he was Don Quixote de la Mancha, he was ever of a mild and affable disposition and of a kind and pleasing conversation: and therefore was he not only beloved of all his household, but also of all those that knew him. . . . He had no sooner ended his discourse and signed and sealed his will and testament, but a swooning and faintness surprising him, he stretched himself the full length of his bed. All the company were much distracted and moved thereat, and ran presently to help him; and during the space of three days, that he lived after he had made his will, he did swoon and fall into trances almost every hour. All the house was in a confusion and uproar; all which notwithstanding the niece ceased not to feed very devoutly: the maidservant to drink profoundly, and Sancho to live merrily. For, when a man is in hope to inherit anything, that hope doth deface or at least moderate in the mind of the inheritor the remembrance or feeling of the sorrow and grief which of reason he should have a feeling of the testator's death. To conclude, the last day of Don Quixote came, after he had received all the sacraments; and had by many and godly reasons made demonstration to abhor all the books of errant chivalry. The notary was present at his death and reporteth how he had never read or found in any book of chivalry that any errant knight died in his bed so mildly, so quietly, and so Christianly as did Don Quixote. Amidst the wailful plaints and blubbering tears of the bystanders, he yielded up the ghost, that is to say, he died."

"Tremolos in the strings indicate the first shiver of a deadly fever." The Knight feels his end is near. Through the violoncello he speaks his last words. He remembers his fancies; he recalls the dreams and the ambitions; he realizes that they were all as smoke and vanity; he is, indeed, ready to die.

## "EIN HELDENLEBEN" (A HERO'S LIFE), TONE POEM, OP. 40

We doubt if *Ein Heldenleben* will be ranked among Strauss's important works, though some of the sections, notably "The Hero's Escape from the World, and Conclusion" are impressive, having emotional depth, being the baring of a soul. No man is perhaps a hero to his valet; but Strauss is evidently a hero to himself. He is autobiographical in this tone poem, as in his *Domestic* symphony. There is a certain presumption in asking one to hear musical descriptions of a composer's struggles, his feelings at being adversely criticized by wretched Philistines, who do not appreciate him, his sulking and withdrawal, like Achilles to his tent. And why drag Frau Strauss into the musical story and typify her, capricious, coquettish, by whimsical measures for the violin? This tone poem, in spite of the sections just referred to, might be justly entitled "A Poseur's Life," and a blustering poseur at that.

Still, in *Ein Heldenleben* there is the peaceful, contemplative ending, pages that Strauss has seldom surpassed, only in the recognition scene of *Elektra* and the presentation of the rose by the cavalier.

*Ein Heldenleben,* a *Tondichtung,* was first performed at the eleventh concert of the Museumsgesellschaft, Frankfort-on-the-Main, March 3,

1899, when Strauss conducted from manuscript and Alfred Hess played the violin solo.

Strauss began the composition of this tone poem at Munich, August 2, 1898; he completed the score December 27, 1898, at Charlottenburg. The score and parts were published at Leipsic in March, 1899.

The score calls for these instruments: sixteen first and second violins, twelve violas, twelve violoncellos, eight double basses, two harps, a piccolo, three flutes, three or four oboes, an English horn, clarinet in E flat, two clarinets in B flat, bass clarinet, three bassoons, double bassoon, eight horns, five trumpets, three trombones, a tenor tuba, a bass tuba, kettledrums, bass drum, snare drum, side drum, cymbals. It is dedicated to Willem Mengelberg and his orchestra in Amsterdam. Strauss has said that he wrote *A Hero's Life* as a companion work to his *Don Quixote,* Op. 35: "Having in this later work sketched the tragi-comic figure of the Spanish Knight whose vain search after heroism leads to insanity, he presents in *A Hero's Life* not a single poetical or historical figure, but rather a more general and free ideal of great and manly heroism—not the heroism to which one can apply an everyday standard of valor, with its material and exterior rewards, but that heroism which describes the inward battle of life, and which aspires through effort and renouncement towards the elevation of the soul."

There are many descriptions and explanations of *Ein Heldenleben.* One of the longest and deepest—and thickest—is by Friedrich Rösch. This pamphlet contains seventy thematical illustrations, as well as a descriptive poem by Eberhard König. Romain Rolland quotes Strauss as saying: "There is no need of a programme. It is enough to know there is a hero fighting his enemies."

The work is in six sections:

## The Hero

The chief theme, which is typical of the hero, the whole and noble man, is announced at once by horn, violas and violoncellos, and the violins soon enter. This theme, E flat major, 4-4, is said to contain within itself four distinct motives, which collectively illustrate the will power and self-confidence of the hero, and their characteristic features are used throughout the work in this sense. Further themes closely related follow. They portray various sides of the hero's character—his pride, emotional nature, iron will, richness of imagination, "inflexible and well-directed determination instead of low-spirited and sullen obstinacy," etc. This section closes with pomp and brilliance, with the motive thundered out by the brass; and it is the most symphonic section of the tone poem. "A pause is made on a dominant seventh: 'What has the world in store for the young dreamer?'"

## The Hero's Antagonists

They are jealous, they envy him, they sneer at his aims and endeavors, they are suspicious of his sincerity, they see nothing except for their own gain; and through flute and oboe they mock and snarl. They are represented by about a half-a-dozen themes, of which one is most important. Diminutions of the preceding heroic themes show their belittlement of his greatness. (It has been said that Strauss thus wished to paint the critics who had not been prudent enough to proclaim him great.) "Fifths in the tubas show their earthly, sluggish nature." The hero's theme appears in the minor; and his amazement, indignation, and momentary confusion are expressed by "a timid, writhing figure." Finally the foes are shaken off.

## The Hero's Helpmate

This is an amorous episode. The hero is shy. The solo violin represents the loved one, who at first is coy, coquettish, and disdains his humble suit. There is a love theme, and there are also two "thematic illustrations of feminine caprice" much used later on. At last she rewards him. The themes given to the solo violin, and basses, violoncellos, and bassoon, are developed in the love duet. A new theme is given to the oboe, and a theme played by the violins is typical of the crowning of happiness. The clamorous voices of the world do not mar the peacefulness of the lovers.

## The Hero's Battlefield

There is a flourish of trumpets without. The hero rushes joyfully to arms. The enemy sends out his challenge. The battle rages. The typical heroic theme is brought into sharp contrast with that of the challenger, and the theme of the beloved one shines forth amid the din and the shock of the fight. The foe is slain. The themes lead into a song of victory. And now what is there for the hero? The world does not rejoice in his triumph. It looks on him with indifferent eyes.

## The Hero's Mission of Peace

This section describes the growth of the hero's soul. The composer uses thematic material from *Don Juan, Also sprach Zarathustra, Tod und Verklärung, Don Quixote, Till Eulenspiegel's lustige Streiche, Guntram, Macbeth,* and his song, "Traum durch die Dämmerung." Jean Marnold claims that there are twenty-three of these reminiscences, quotations, which Strauss introduces suddenly, or successively, or simultaneously, "and the hearer that has not been warned cannot at the time notice the slightest disturbance in the development. He would not think that all these themes are foreign to the work he hears, and are only souvenirs."

## The Hero's Escape from the World, and Conclusion

The world is still cold. At first the hero rages, but resignation and content soon take possession of his soul. The bluster of nature reminds him of his old days of war. Again he sees the beloved one, and in peace and contemplation his soul takes flight. For the last time the hero's theme is heard as it rises to a sonorous, impressive climax. And then is solemn music, such as might serve funeral rites.

## IGOR FEDOROVITCH
# STRAVINSKY

(Born at Oranienbaum, near St. Petersburg, on June 17, 1882)

---

As for Stravinsky, we personally prefer the Stravinsky of the *Sacre du Printemps* to the Stravinsky who of late has been attempting to compose in the manner of Bach. To begin with, we do not hear music now with the ears of the earlier centuries, and the old idiom today has no pertinence except when it has been handed down to us by a master of it, who broke through the idiom and made a universal language of it for many years to come. Stravinsky's feeble echo is simply dull, boresome. His "Muscovism" is greatly to be preferred.

## SUITE FROM "L'OISEAU DE FEU" (THE FIRE-BIRD)
### A Danced Legend

*I. Introduction: Kastcheï's Enchanted Garden and Dance of the Fire-Bird*
*II. Supplication of the Fire-Bird*
*III. The Princesses Play with the Golden Apples*
*IV. Dance of the Princess*
*IVa. Berceuse*
*V. Infernal Dance of All the Subjects of Kastcheï*
*VI. Finale*

In the summer of 1909 Diaghilev asked Stravinsky to write a ballet founded on the old Russian legend of the Fire-Bird. The score was ready in May, 1910. The scenario was the work of Fokine.

The first performance of *L'Oiseau de Feu*, a *Conte dansé*, in two scenes, was at the Paris *Opéra* on June 25, 1910. The Fire-Bird, Tamara Karsavina; The Beautiful Tsarevna, Mme Fokina; Ivan Tsarevitch, Fokine; Kastcheï, Boulgakov. Gabriel Pierné conducted. The stage settings were by Golovine and Bakst. Balakirev had sketched an opera in which the Fire-Bird was the central figure, but nothing came of it. Kastcheï (or Kostcheï) is the hero of Rimsky-Korsakov's opera *Kastcheï the Immortal: an Autumn Legend*, produced at the Private Opera, Moscow, in 1902. He also figures as "the man-skeleton" in Rimsky-Korsakov's *Mlada*, a fairy opera-ballet (St. Petersburg, 1893) and, by implication, Moussorgsky's symphonic poem, *A Night on Bald Mountain.*

Mr. Montagu-Nathan[1] says in his sketch of Stravinsky: "In identifying the literary basis of *The Fire-Bird* with that of Korsakov's *Kastcheï*, it should be pointed out that the latter work is but a *pastiche* of episodes derived from legendary lore, with the monster as a central figure. In Stravinsky's ballet, the ogre is an accessory character, so far as concerns the dramatic action, but his presence in the scheme is nevertheless vital to it."

"Ivan Tsarevich, the hero of many tales, wandering in the night, espies the Fire-Bird attempting to pluck the golden fruit from a silver tree, and, after a chase, succeeds in capturing her. But receiving the gift of a glowing feather he consents to forego his prize. As the darkness of night lifts, Ivan discovers that he is in the grounds of an old castle, from which thirteen maidens presently emerge. They are observed by the concealed youth to make play with the tree and its fruit. Disclosing himself, he obtains possession of a golden apple. With the approaching dawn the maidens withdraw into the castle, which Ivan now recognizes as that of the fearsome Kastcheï, captor of decoyed travelers, over whom he tyrannously wields his magic power. Ivan resolves upon entering Kastcheï's abode, but on opening the gate he is confronted first by a motley horde of freakish monsters and then by the ogre himself, to whose court they belong. Kastcheï seeks to bewitch the young adventurer and to turn him to stone, but Ivan is protected by the glowing feather. Presently the bird comes to his aid and nullifies Kastcheï's threatened spell, and, after demonstrating its power by causing the frightful company of courtiers to break into a frenzied dance, reveals the casket in which Kastcheï's 'death' is

[1]M. Montagu-Nathan: *Contemporary Russian Composers*, 1917.

hidden. From the casket Ivan takes an egg, which he dashes to the ground; the death it contains unites itself with its owner, and the dread wizard dies. His castle vanishes, his victims are liberated, and Ivan receives the hand of the most beautiful of the maidens."

The score, which was later revised with a smaller orchestration, calls for piccolo, three flutes (one interchangeable with a second piccolo), three oboes, English horn, three clarinets in A (one interchangeable with a small clarinet in D), bass clarinet, three bassoons (one interchangeable with a second double bassoon), double bassoon, four horns, three trumpets, three trombones, bass tuba, kettledrums, bass drum, cymbals, triangle, bells, tambourine, xylophone, celesta, pianoforte, three harps, sixteen first violins, sixteen second violins, fourteen violas, eight violoncellos, six double basses.

## SUITE FROM THE BALLET, "PETROUCHKA"

*Carnival—The Magician—Russian Dance—Petrouchka—The Arab —Dance of the Ballerina—Carnival—Nurses' Dance—The Bear and the Peasant Playing a Hand-Organ—The Merchant and the Gypsies—The Dance of the Coachmen and Grooms—The Masqueraders—The Quarrel of the Arab and Petrouchka, and the Death of Petrouchka.*

THE BALLET *Petrouchka: Scènes burlesques en 4 Tableaux,* scenario by Alexandre Benois, was completed by Stravinsky at Rome in May (13–26), 1911. It was produced by Diaghilev at the Châtelet, Paris, on June 13, 1911. The chief dancers were Mme Tamar Karsavina, La Ballerine; Nijinsky, Petrouchka. Mr. Monteux conducted; Mr. Fokine was the ballet master. The scenery and costumes were designed by Benois; the scenery was painted by Anisfeld.

"This ballet depicts the life of the lower classes in Russia, with all its dissoluteness, barbarity, tragedy, and misery. Petrouchka is a sort of Polichinello, a poor hero always suffering from the cruelty of the police and every kind of wrong and unjust persecution. This represents symbolically the whole tragedy in the existence of the Russian people, a suffering from despotism and injustice. The scene is laid in the midst of the Russian carnival, and the streets are lined with booths in one of which Petrouchka plays a kind of humorous rôle. He is killed, but he appears again and again as a ghost on the roof of the booth to frighten his enemy, his old employer, an allusion to the despotic rules in Russia."

The following description of the ballet is taken from *Contemporary Russian Composers,* by Mr. Montagu-Nathan:

"The 'plot' of *Petrouchka* owes nothing to folklore, but retains the quality of the fantastic. Its chief protagonist is a lovelorn doll; but we have still a villain in the person of the *focusnik,* a showman who for his own ends prefers to consider that a puppet has no soul. The scene is the Admiralty Square, St. Petersburg; the time 'Butter-Week,' somewhere about the eighteen-thirties. . . . Prior to the raising of the first curtain the music has an expectant character and the varied rhythmic treatment of a melodic figure which has a distinct folk-tune flavor has all the air of inviting conjecture as to what is about to happen. Once the curtain goes up we are immediately aware that we are in the midst of a carnival, and are prepared for some strange sights. The music describes the nature of the crowd magnificently, and in his orchestral reproduction of a hurdy-gurdy, whose player mingles with the throng, Stravinsky has taken pains that his orchestral medium shall not lend any undue dignity to the instrument. . . . Presently the showman begins to attract his audience, and, preparatory to opening his curtain, plays a few mildly florid passages on his flute. With his final flourish he animates his puppets. They have been endowed by the showman with human feelings and passions. Petrouchka is ugly and consequently the most sensitive. He endeavors to console himself for his master's cruelty by exciting the sympathy and winning the love of his fellow doll, the Ballerina, but in this he is less successful than the callous and brutal Moor, the remaining unit in the trio of puppets. Jealousy between Petrouchka and the Moor is the cause of the tragedy which ends in the pursuit and slaughter of the former. The Russian Dance which the three puppets perform at the bidding of their taskmaster recalls vividly the passage of a crowd in Rimsky-Korsakov's *Kitezh.*

"When at the end of the dance the light fails and the inner curtain falls, we are reminded by the roll of the side drum which does duty as entr'acte music that we have to do with a realist, with a composer who is no more inclined than was his precursor Dargomijsky to make concessions; he prefers to preserve illusions, and so long as the drum continues its slow fusillade the audience's mind is kept fixed upon the doll it has been contemplating. The unsuccessful courtship is now enacted and then the scene is again changed to the Moor's apartment, where, after a monotonous droning dance, the captivation of the Ballerina takes place. There are from time to time musical figures recalling the showman's flute flourishes, apparently referring to his dominion over the doll. . . . The scene ends with the summary ejection of that unfortunate (Petrouchka), and the drum once more bridges the change of scene.

"In the last tableau the Carnival, with its consecutive common chords, is resumed. The nurses' dance, which is of folk origin, is one of several items of decorative music, some of them, like the episode of the man with the bear, and the merchant's accordion, being fragmentary. With the combined dance of the nurses, coachmen, and grooms, we have again a wonderful counterpoint of the melodic elements.

"When the fun is at its height, it is suddenly interrupted by Petrouchka's frenzied flight from the little theater. He is pursued by the Moor, whom the cause of their jealousy tries vainly to hold in check. To the consternation of the spectators, Petrouchka is slain by a stroke of the cruel Moor's sword, and a tap on the *tambour de Basque*.

"The showman, having demonstrated to the satisfaction of the gay crowd that Petrouchka is only a doll, is left alone with the corpse, but is not allowed to depart in absolute peace of mind. To the accompaniment of a ghastly distortion of the showman's flute music the wraith of Petrouchka appears above the little booth. There is a brief reference to the carnival figure, then four concluding *pizzicato* notes, and the drama is finished. From his part in outlining it we conclude that Stravinsky is an artist whose lightness of touch equals that of Ravel, whose humanity is as deep as Moussorgsky's."

The ballet calls for these instruments: four flutes (two interchangeable with piccolo), four oboes (one interchangeable with English horn), four clarinets (one interchangeable with bass clarinet), four bassoons (one interchangeable with double bassoon), four horns, two trumpets (one interchangeable with little trumpet, in D), two *cornets-à-pistons,* three trombones, bass tuba, kettledrums, snare drum, *tambour de Provence,* bass drum, tambourine, cymbals, triangle, glockenspiel, xylophones, tam-tam, celesta (two and four hands), pianoforte, two harps, strings. The score, dedicated to Alexandre Benois, was published in 1912.

## "LE SACRE DU PRINTEMPS" ("THE RITE OF SPRING"), PICTURES OF PAGAN RUSSIA

### I. The Adoration of the Earth

*Introduction—Harbingers of Spring—Dance of the Adolescents—Abduction—Spring Rounds—Games of the Rival Cities—The Procession of the Wise Men—The Adoration of the Earth (The Wise Man)—Dance of the Earth.*

### II. The Sacrifice

*Introduction—Mysterious Circles of the Adolescents—Glorification of the Chosen One—Evocation of the Ancestors—Ritual of the Ancestors—The Sacrificial Dance of the Chosen One.*

*The Rite of Spring,* or more literally according to the Russian *Spring Consecration,* scenery and costumes designed by Nicolas Roerich, choreography by W. Nijinsky, was produced at the Théâtre des Champs Élysées on May 29, 1913, by the Diaghilev Ballet Russe. Mr. Monteux conducted. The chief dancers were M. Nijinsky and Mlle Piltz. The performance, while it delighted some, incited howls of protest. The hissing was violent, mingled with counter cheers, so that M. Astruc ordered the lights turned up. The late Alfred Capu wrote a bitter article published in *Le Figaro,* in which he said:

"Bluffing the idle rich of Paris through appeals to their snobbery is a delightfully simple matter. . . . The process works out as follows: Take the best society possible, composed of rich, simple-minded, idle people. Then submit them to an intense régime of publicity. By pamphlets, newspaper articles, lectures, personal visits and all other appeals to their snobbery, persuade them that hitherto they have seen only vulgar spectacles, and are at last to know what is art and beauty. Impress them with cabalistic formulæ. They have not the slightest notion of music, literature, painting, and dancing; still, they have heretofore seen under these names only a rude imitation of the real thing. Finally assure them that they are about to see real dancing and hear real music.

It will then be necessary to double the prices at the theater, so great will be the rush of shallow worshipers at this false shrine."

Mr. Carl Van Vechten describes the scene in his book: *Music after the Great War:*

"I attended the first performance in Paris of Stravinsky's anarchistic (against the canons of academic art) ballet, *The Rite of Spring,* in which primitive emotions are both depicted and aroused by a dependence on barbarous rhythm in which melody and harmony, as even so late a composer as Richard Strauss understands them, do not enter. A certain part of the audience, thrilled by what it considered to be a blasphemous attempt to destroy music as an art, and swept away with wrath, began very soon after the rise of the curtain to whistle, to make cat-calls, and to offer audible suggestions as to how the performance should proceed. Others of us, who liked the music and felt that the principles of free speech were at stake, bellowed defiance. It was war over art for the rest of the evening, and the orchestra played on unheard, except occasionally when a slight lull occurred. The figures on the stage danced in time to music that they had to imagine they heard, and beautifully out of rhythm with the uproar in the auditorium. I was sitting in a box, in which I had rented one seat. Three ladies sat in front of me, and a young man occupied the place behind me. He stood up during the course of the ballet to enable himself to see more clearly. The intense excitement under which he was laboring, thanks to the potent force of the music, betrayed itself presently when he began to beat rhythmically on the top of my head with his fists. My emotion was so great that I did not feel the blows for some time. They were perfectly synchronized with the beat of the music. When I did, I turned around. His apology was sincere. We had both been carried beyond ourselves."

There were five performances in Paris that season.

When this ballet was brought out at Drury Lane, London, on July 11, 1913, with Mr. Monteux conductor, it was thought advisable to send a lecturer, Mr. Edwin Evans, in front of the curtain, to explain the ideas underlying the ballet. At the end of the performance there was greater applause than hissing.

The music of this ballet was performed for the first time in concert form by an orchestra conducted by Mr. Monteux at one of his concerts at the Casino de Paris in Paris on April 5, 1914, when it was enthusiastically applauded.

And now *The Rite of Spring* is acclaimed by many as Stravinsky's "greatest work."

The orchestration is as follows: piccolo, 3 flutes (the third interchangeable with a second piccolo), bass flute; five oboes (the fourth interchangeable with English horn); small clarinet in E flat, three clarinets and bass clarinet; three bassoons, two double bassoons; eight horns (two interchangeable with tenor tubas); small trumpet in D, three trumpets in C, bass trumpet; three trombones; two bass tubas; kettledrums, bass drum, two antique cymbals, tam-tam, scratcher, and strings.

## JOSEPH DEEMS
# TAYLOR

(Born at New York, December 22, 1885)

---

## "THROUGH THE LOOKING GLASS," SUITE, FIVE PICTURES FROM LEWIS CARROLL, OP. 12

*Ia. Dedication*
*Ib. The Garden of Live Flowers*
*II. Jabberwocky*
*III. Looking-Glass Insects*
*IV. The White Knight*

It is a pleasure to find an American composer of talent who is willing to write music that is cheerful, not portentous; whose fancy is delicate; who uses a large orchestra discreetly, not chiefly to make a thunderous noise. Mr. Taylor for his inspiration went to a book that for years has pleased children from the tender age to that of white hair; he did not ransack the Grecian or the Scandinavian mythology; he had no thesis, no exposition of colors; he did not attempt to portray in music cave life and the rude rites of primitive man. Nor did he strive painfully to be ultra-modern in the French, Italian, or German manner. He remembered Lewis Carroll's story. Pleasant and amusing musical thoughts came into his head, and he expressed them musically, without laboring after transliteration. Even his narration of the Jabberwock's fate is not too realistic, and in this movement the measures that may be taken to picture the peaceful scene while the hero waited "with vorpal sword" in hand by the Tumtum tree the approach of the fearful monster are charged with poetic beauty. Charming also is the "Dedication." The whole work shows genuine fancy, a gift of expression in an individual manner. Whether without titles the music would identify this or that episode is not to the point. The suite is frankly programme music, but of the better kind; natural, not pretentious; amusing, but as a man of talent amuses first himself, then those who are privileged to be with him.

This suite, inspired by *Through the Looking-Glass,* by Lewis Carroll (Charles Lutwidge Dodgson, 1832–98), was written in 1917–19 for flute, oboe, clarinet, bassoon, horn, pianoforte, and strings. It was produced in this form at a concert of the New York Chamber Music Society in New York on February 18, 1919. The suite was then in three movements. In September, 1921, Mr. Taylor began to revise the suite for full orchestra. He added "The Garden of Live Flowers." The first performance of the revised work was by the New York Symphony Orchestra in Brooklyn, March 10, 1923. The performance was repeated in New York the following afternoon.

The score, dedicated "To Katharine Moore Taylor from a difficult son," calls for these instruments: three flutes (and piccolo), two oboes, English horn, two clarinets, bass clarinet, two bassoons, double bassoon, four horns, three trumpets, three trombones, tuba, a set of three kettledrums, snare drum, tambourine, cymbals, triangle, glockenspiel, xylophone, pianoforte, and strings.

When the suite was produced by the Symphony Society of New York, the programme contained a description by Mr. Taylor:

"The suite needs no extended analysis. It is based on Lewis Carroll's immortal nonsense fairy tale, *Through the Looking-Glass and What Alice Found There,* and the five pictures it presents will, if all goes well, be readily recognizable to lovers of the book. There are four movements, the first being subdivided into two connected parts."

### Ia. Dedication

Carroll precedes the tale with a charming poetical foreword, the first stanza of which the music aims to express. It runs:

*Child of the pure, unclouded brow*
*And dreaming eyes of wonder!*
*Though time be fleet, and I and thou*
*Are half a life asunder,*
*Thy loving smile will surely hail*
*The love gift of a fairy tale.*

A simple song theme, briefly developed, leads to

### IB. THE GARDEN OF LIVE FLOWERS

(The score contains this extract from the book:

" 'O Tiger Lily,' said Alice, addressing herself to one that was waving gracefully about in the wind, 'I wish you could talk.'

" 'We can talk,' said the Tiger-Lily, 'when there's anybody worth talking to.'

" 'And can the flowers talk?'

" 'As well as you can,' said the Tiger-Lily, 'and a great deal louder.' ")

Shortly after Alice had entered the looking-glass country she came to a lovely garden in which the flowers were talking—in the words of the Tiger-Lily, "as well as you can, and a great deal louder." The music, therefore, reflects the brisk chatter of the swaying, bright-colored denizens of the garden.

### II. JABBERWOCKY

This is the poem that so puzzled Alice, and which Humpty-Dumpty finally explained to her. The theme of that frightful beast, the Jabberwock, is first announced by the full orchestra. The clarinet then begins the tale, recounting how on a "brillig" afternoon, the "slithy toves did gyre and gimble in the wabe." Muttered imprecations by the bassoon warn us to "beware the Jabberwock, my son." A miniature march signalizes the approach of our hero, taking "his vorpal sword in hand." Trouble starts among the trombones—the Jabberwock is upon us. The battle with the monster is recounted in a short and rather repellent fugue, the double basses bringing up the subject and the hero fighting back in the interludes. Finally his vorpal blade (really a xylophone) goes "snicker-snack" and the monster, impersonated by the solo bassoon, dies a lingering and convulsive death. The hero returns to the victorious strains of his own theme—"O frabjous day! Callooh! Callay!" The whole orchestra rejoices—the church bells are rung—alarums and excursions.

Conclusion. Once more the "slithy toves" perform their pleasing evolutions, undisturbed by the uneasy ghost of the late Jabberwock.

## III. Looking-Glass Insects

(The score contains extracts from the dialogue of Alice and the gnat "about the size of a chicken" about various insects, among them the bread-and-butter-fly.

" 'And what does it live on?'

" 'Weak tea with cream in it.'

" 'Supposing it couldn't find any?'

" 'Then it would die, of course.'

" 'But that must happen very often,' said Alice thoughtfully.

" 'It always happens,' said the gnat.")

Here we find the vociferous diptera that made such an impression upon Alice—the Bee-elephant, the Gnat, the Rocking-horse-fly, the Snap-dragon-fly, and the Bread-and-butter-fly. There are several themes, but there is no use trying to decide which insect any one of them stands for.

## IV. The White Knight

(The score contains extracts from the conversation of the White Knight, and an account of his leave-taking.)

He was a toy Don Quixote, mild, chivalrous, ridiculous, and rather touching. He carried a mouse-trap on his saddle-bow, "because, if they do come, I don't choose to have them running about." He couldn't ride very well, but he was a gentle soul, with good intentions. There are two themes: the first, a sort of instrumental prance, being the Knight's own conception of himself as a slashing, dare-devil fellow. The second is bland, mellifluous, a little sentimental—much more like the Knight as he really was. The first theme starts off bravely, but falls out of the saddle before very long, and has to give way to the second. The two alternate, in various guises, until the end, when the Knight rides off, with Alice waving her handkerchief—he thought it would encourage him if she did.

# PETER ILITCH TCHAIKOVSKY

(Born at Votkinsk, in the government of Viatka, Russia, May 7, 1840; died at St. Petersburg, November 6, 1893)

---

IT IS TRUE that in more than one page of his symphonies Tchaikovsky narrowly escapes the reproach of vulgarity; but the earnestness, the sincerity of the speech makes its way even before the development and the amplification make them seem inevitable. The heart of Tchaikovsky was that of a little child; the brain was that of a man weary of the world and all its vanities. And so we have the singular phenomenon of naïveté, accompanied by a superrefined skill—and all this in the body and mind of a man fundamentally oriental in his tastes and especially in his love of surprising or monotonous rhythms and gorgeous colors. The very modernity of Tchaikovsky, his closeness to us as the spokesman of the things we think and dare not say—these qualities may war against his lasting fame; but in our day and generation he is the supreme interpreter by music of elemental and emotional thought. The emptiness of life obsessed him, and in the expression of his thought he is again the man of his period. When faith returns again to the world, his music may be studied with interest and curiosity as an important document in sociology. But in the present we are under his mighty spell.

## SYMPHONY NO. 4, IN F MINOR, OP. 36

*I. Andante sostenuto; moderato con anima in movimento di valse*
*II. Andantino in modo di canzona*
*III. Scherzo: "pizzicato ostinato"; allegro*
*IV. Finale: allegro con fuoco*

IF TCHAIKOVSKY had a programme in mind when he composed his Fifth and Sixth symphonies, he never published it to the world; but for the Fourth he wrote an elaborate one. Does the music gain by it? To us the Fourth symphony is interesting because it seems nearer to the Russian spirit and life as portrayed by Dostoivsky than the later ones. Even the ornamentation, the arabesques, that in another's music would seem as so many excrescences, perhaps frivolous, are here in place. The neurotic, self-torturing Tchaikovsky was for years obsessed by the thought of death and the charnel house. Fate was to him not a word to be associated only with the story of Œdipus or Pelop's line. The Fourth symphony is a personal document, revealing the man, as his letters revealed him. It is easy to pick flaws in it; to dismiss it as a suite, not a symphony; to complain of this or that; but the music with its deep-rooted melancholy, its noisy attempt to forget the inevitable end, its drunken hilarity, its dark and sinister sadness, is not easily to be put aside, not easily to be forgotten.

Tchaikovsky composed this symphony during the winter of 1877–78. He had lost interest in an opera, *Othello,* for which a libretto at his own wish had been drafted by Stassov. The first draft was finished in May, 1877. He began the instrumentation on August 23 of that year, and finished the first movement September 24. He began work again towards the end of November. The *andantino* was finished on December 27, the *scherzo* on January 1, 1878, and the *finale* on January 7, 1878.

The first performance was at a symphony concert of the Russian Musical Society, Moscow, February 22, 1878. Nicholas Rubinstein conducted.

The dedication of this symphony is as follows: *"À mon meilleur ami"* (To my best friend), and thereby hangs a tale.

This best friend was the widow Nadejda Filaretovna von Meck. Her maiden name was Frolovsky. Born in the village Snamensk, government of Smolensk, February 10, 1831, she married in 1848 an engineer, and for some years knew poverty. Her courage did not give way; she was a helpmeet for her husband, who finally became famous and successful. In 1876 her husband died. She was left with eleven children and a fortune of "many millions of rubles." Dwelling at Moscow, fond of music, she admired beyond measure certain works by Tchaikovsky. Inquiring curiously concerning his character as a man and about his worldly circumstances, she became acquainted with Kotek, a pupil of Tchaikovsky in composition. Through him she gave Tchaikovsky commissions for transcriptions for violin and pianoforte of some of his works. There was an interchange of letters. In the early summer of 1877 she learned that he was in debt. She sent him 3,000 rubles; in the fall of the same year she determined to give him yearly the sum of 6,000 rubles, that he might compose free from pecuniary care and vexation; but she insisted that they should never meet. They never spoke together; their letters were frequent and intimate. Tchaikovsky poured out his soul to this woman, described by his brother Modeste as proud and energetic, with deep-rooted principles, with the independence of a man; a woman that held in disdain all that was petty and conventional; pure in thought and action; a woman that was compassionate, not sentimental.

The composer wrote to her on May 13, 1877, that he purposed to dedicate this symphony to her. "I believe that you will find in it echoes of your deepest thoughts and feelings. At this moment any other work would be odious to me; I speak only of work that presupposes the existence of a determined mood. Added to this I am in a very nervous, worried, and irritable state, highly unfavorable to composition, and even my symphony suffers in consequence." In August, 1877, writing to her, he referred to the symphony as "yours." "I hope it will please you, for that is the main thing." He wrote in August from Kamenka: "The first movement has cost me much trouble in scoring it. It is very complicated and long; but it seems to me it is also the most important. The other movements are simple, and it will be fun to score them. There will be a new effect of sound in the *scherzo,* and I expect much from it. At first the strings play alone and *pizzicato* throughout. In the trio the wood-wind instruments enter and play alone. At the end all three choirs toss short phrases to each other. I believe that the effects of sound and color will be most interesting." He wrote to her in December from Venice that he was hard at work on the instrumentation: "No one of my orchestral pieces has cost me so much labor, but on no one have I worked with so much love and with such devotion. At first I was led on only by the wish to bring the symphony to an end, and then I grew more and more fond of the task, and now I cannot bear to leave it. My dear Nadejdna Filaretovna, perhaps I am mistaken, but it seems to me that this symphony is no mediocre piece; that it is the best I have yet made. How glad I am that it is *our* work, and that you will know when you hear it how much I thought about you in every measure! If you were not, would it ever have been finished? When I was in Moscow and thought that my end was about to come [There is a reference here to the crazed condition of Tchaikovsky after his amazing marriage to Antonina Ivanovna Milioukov. The wedding was on July 18, 1877. He left his wife at Moscow, October 6, of that year.] I wrote on the first draft: 'If I should die, please send this manuscript to N. F. von Meck.' I wished the manuscript of my last composition to be in your possession. Now I am not only well, but, thanks to you, in the position to give myself wholly to work, and I believe that I have written music which cannot fall into oblivion. Yet it is possible that I am wrong; it is the peculiar habit of all artists to wax enthusiastic over the youngest of their productions." Later he had chills as well as fever over the worth of the symphony.

## SYMPHONY NO. 5, IN E MINOR, OP. 64

*I. Andante; Allegro con anima*
*II. Andante cantabile, con alcuna licenza*
*III. Valse (Allegro moderato)*
*IV. Finale (Andante maestoso; allegro vivace)*

Tchaikovsky was singularly reticent in his letters concerning the Fifth symphony, but who can refrain from thinking with Ernest

Newman that this symphony was written to a programme; that the work "embodies an emotional sequence of some kind"? There is the tread of inexorable fate; this tread disturbs the beauty of the *andante;* it checks the forced gayety of the dancers in the waltz, and is the triumphant spirit in the *finale* something more than a heroic defiance of the inevitable, a brave stand before the approach of death?

We are interested in the woe of Canio or of the Navarraise; we are moved by the infinite sadness of Mélisande; we understand the tragedy in the humble home on Montmartre and the agony of Rigoletto. We endure the spectacle of the anguish of these men and women on the stage, applaud and go comfortably to bed. Tchaikovsky's music awakens in the breast the haunting, unanswerable questions of life and death that concern us directly and personally.

About the end of April, 1888, Tchaikovsky took possession of his country house at Frolovskoe, which had been made ready for him, when he was at Paris and London, by his servant Alexis. Frolovskoe is a picturesque place on a wooded hill on the way from Moscok to Klin. The house was simple. "Here he [Tchaikovsky] could be alone,"—we quote from Mrs. Newmarch's translation into English of Modeste Tchaikovsky's life of Peter,—"free from summer excursionists, to enjoy the little garden (with its charming pool and tiny islet) fringed by the forest, behind which the view opened out upon a distant stretch of country—upon that homely, unassuming landscape of Central Russia which Tchaikovsky preferred to all the sublimities of Switzerland, the Caucasus, and Italy. Had not the forest been gradually exterminated, he would never have quitted Frolovskoe, for, although he only lived there for three years, he became greatly attached to the place. A month before his death, traveling from Klin to Moscow, he said, looking out at the churchyard of Frolovskoe: 'I should like to be buried there.'"

On June 22 he wrote to Mme von Meck: "Now I shall work my hardest. I am exceedingly anxious to prove to myself, as to others, that I am not played out as a composer. . . . Have I told you that I intend to write a symphony? The beginning was difficult; but now inspiration seems to have come. However, we shall see."

In July, Tchaikovsky received a letter from an American manager who offered him 25,000 dollars for a concert tour of three months. The sum seemed incredible to the composer: "Should this tour really take place, I could realize my long-cherished wish to become a landowner." On August 6 he wrote to Mme von Meck: "When I am old and past composing, I shall spend the whole of my time in growing flowers. I have been working with good results. I have orchestrated half the symphony. My age—although I am not very old [he was then forty-eight]—begins to tell on me. I become very tired, and I can no longer play the pianoforte or read at night as I used to do." On August 26 he wrote to her: "I am not feeling well, . . . but I am so glad that I have finished the symphony that I forget my physical troubles. . . . In November I shall conduct a whole series of my works in St. Petersburg, at the Philharmonic, and the new symphony will be one of them."

The Fifth symphony was performed for the first time at St. Petersburg, November 17, 1888. The composer conducted. The audience was pleased, but the reviews in the newspapers were not very favorable. On November 24 of the same year, Tchaikovsky conducted the symphony again at a concert of the Musical Society.

In December, 1888, he wrote to Mme von Meck: "After two performances of my new symphony in St. Petersburg and one in Prague, I have come to the conclusion that it is a failure. There is something repellent, something superfluous, patchy, and insincere, which the public instinctively recognizes. It was obvious to me that the ovations I received were prompted more by my earlier work, and that the symphony itself did not really please the audience. The consciousness of this brings me a sharp twinge of self-dissatisfaction. Am I really played out, as they say? Can I merely repeat and ring the changes on my earlier idiom? Last night I looked through *our* symphony [No. 4]. What a difference! How immeasurably superior it is! It is very, very sad!" He was cheered by news of the success of the symphony in Moscow.

At the public rehearsal in Hamburg, the symphony pleased the musicians; there was real enthusiasm.

Tchaikovsky wrote after the concert to Davidov: "The Fifth symphony was magnificently played and I like it far better now, after having held a bad opinion of it for some time. Unfortunately, the Russian press continues to ignore me. With the exception of my nearest and dearest, no one will ever hear of my successes."

Modeste Tchaikovsky is of the opinion that the Fifth symphony was a long time in making its way chiefly on account of his brother's inefficiency as a conductor.

The *andante,* E minor, 4–4 theme of the symphony, which occurs in the four movements, typical of fate, "the eternal note of sadness," of what you will, is given at the very beginning to the clarinets, and the development serves as an approach to the *allegro.* The principal theme of the first movement, *allegro con anima,* 6–8, is announced by clarinet and bassoon. It is developed elaborately and at great length. This theme is said to have been derived from a Polish folk song. The second theme in B minor is given to the strings. The recapitulation begins with the restatement of the principal theme by the bassoon. There is a long *coda,* which finally sinks to a *pianissimo* and passes to the original key.

The second movement has been characterized as a romance, firmly knit together in form, and admitting great freedom of interpretation, as the qualification, *"con alcuna licenza,"* of the *andante cantabile* indicates. After a short introduction in the deeper strings, the horn sings the principal melody. The oboe gives out a new theme, which is answered by the horn, and this theme is taken up by violins and violas. The principal theme is heard from the violoncellos, after which the clarinet sings still another melody, which is developed to a climax, in which the full orchestra thunders out the chief theme of the symphony, the theme of bodement. The second part of the movement follows in a general way along the lines already established. There is another climax, and again is heard the impressive theme of the symphony.

The third movement is a waltz *allegro moderato,* A major, 3–4. The structure is simple, and the development of the first theme, *dolce con grazia,* given to violins against horns, bassoons, and string instruments, is natural. Toward the very end clarinets and bassoons sound, as afar off, the theme of the symphony: the gayety is over.

There is a long introduction, *andante maestoso,* E major, 4–4, to the *finale,* a development of the somber and dominating theme. This *andante* is followed by an *allegro vivace,* E minor, with the first theme given to the strings, and a more tuneful theme assigned first to the wood-wind and afterward to the violins. The development of the second theme contains illusions to the chief theme of the symphony.

Storm and fury; the movement comes to a halt; the *coda* begins in E major, the *allegro vivace* increases to a *presto.* The second theme of the *finale* is heard, and the final climax contains a reminiscence of the first theme of the first movement.

Some find pleasure in characterizing Tchaikovsky's symphonies as suites; Dvořák is said to have made this criticism. But the Fifth symphony escapes this charge, for objectors admit that in this work the composer made his nearest approach to true symphonic form—in spite of the fact that there is no repetition of the first part of the first *allegro,* and a waltz movement takes the place of the *scherzo.*

## SYMPHONY NO. 6, IN B MINOR, "PATHETIC," OP. 74

*I. Adagio; allegro non troppo*
*II. Allegro con grazia*
*III. Allegro molto vivace*
*IV. Finale: adagio lamentoso*

We well remember the sensation the Sixth symphony made in Boston when Mr. Paur brought it out. When the late William Foster Apthorp described the music as "obscene," a singular word to apply to it, indignant denunciatory letters were sent to the *Evening Transcript,* written by persons who, as Charles Reade once said of letter writers to newspapers, had no other waste-pipe for their intellect.

This symphony was at the first so popular that some predicted its life would be short. It is still an amazing human document. The Fifth may for some reasons be preferred as a purely musical composition; the Fourth has more of the Russian folk-spirit; but the somber eloquence of the *Pathetic,* its pages of recollected joys fled forever, its wild gayety quenched by the thought of the inevitable end, its mighty lamentation—these are overwhelming and shake the soul.

## PETER ILITCH TCHAIKOVSKY

The first mention of the *Pathetic* symphony is in a letter from Tchaikovsky to his brother Anatol, dated Klin, February 22, 1893: "I am now wholly occupied with the new work (a symphony) and it is hard for me to tear myself away from it. I believe it comes into being as the best of my works. I must finish it as soon as possible, for I have to wind up a lot of affairs and I must also soon go to London. I told you that I had completed a symphony which suddenly displeased me, and I tore it up. Now I have composed a new symphony *which I certainly shall not tear up."*

Returning in August from a trip to London, Peter wrote to Modeste that he was up to his neck in his symphony. "The orchestration is the more difficult, the farther I go. Twenty years ago I let myself write at ease without much thought, and it was all right. Now I have become cowardly and uncertain. I have sat the whole day over two pages; that which I wished came constantly to naught. In spite of this, I make progress." He wrote to Davidov, August 15: "The symphony which I intended to dedicate to you—I shall reconsider this on account of your long silence—is progressing. I am very well satisfied with the contents, but not wholly with the orchestration. I do not succeed in my intentions. It will not surprise me in the least if the symphony is cursed or judged unfavorably; 'twill not be for the first time. I myself consider it the best, especially the most open-hearted of all my works. I love it as I never have loved any other of my musical creations. My life is without the charm of variety; evenings I am often bored; but I do not complain, for the symphony is now the main thing, and I cannot work anywhere so well as at home." He wrote Jurgenson, his publisher, on August 24, that he had finished the orchestration: "I give you my word of honor that never in my life have I been so contented, so proud, so happy, in the knowledge that I have written a good piece." It was at this time that he thought seriously of writing an opera with a text founded on *The Sad Fortunes of the Reverend Mr. Barton,* by George Eliot, of whose best works he was an enthusiastic admirer.

Tchaikovsky left Klin forever on October 19. He stopped at Moscow to attend a funeral, and there with Kashkin he talked freely after supper. Friends had died; who would be the next to go? "I told Peter," said Kashkin, "that he would outlive us all. He disputed the likelihood, yet added that never had he felt so well and happy." Peter told him that he had no doubt about the first three movements of his new symphony, but that the last was still doubtful in his mind; after the performance he might destroy it and write another *finale*. He arrived at St. Petersburg in good spirits, but he was depressed because the symphony made no impression on the orchestra at the rehearsals. He valued highly the opinion of players, and he conducted well only when he knew that the orchestra liked the work. He was dependent on them for the finesse of interpretation. "A cool facial expression, an indifferent glance, a yawn—these tied his hands; he lost his readiness of mind, he went over the work carelessly, and cut short the rehearsal, that the players might be freed from their boresome work." Yet he insisted that he never had written and never would write a better composition than this symphony.

The Sixth symphony was performed for the first time at St. Petersburg, October 28, 1893. Tchaikovsky conducted. The symphony failed. "There was applause," says Modeste, "and the composer was recalled, but with no more enthusiasm than on previous occasions. There was not the mighty, overpowering impression made by the work when it was conducted by Napravnik, November 18, 1893, and later, wherever it was played." The critics were decidedly cool.

The morning after, Modeste found Peter at the tea-table with the score of the symphony in his hand. He regretted that, inasmuch as he had to send it that day to the publisher, he had not yet given it a title. He wished something more than "No. 6," and did not like "Programme symphony." "What does Programme symphony mean when I will give it no programme?" Modeste suggested "Tragic," but Peter said that would not do. "I left the room before he had come to a decision. Suddenly I thought, 'Pathetic.' I went back to the room,—I remember it as though it were yesterday,—and I said the word to Peter. 'Splendid, Modi, bravo, "Pathetic"!' and he wrote in my presence the title that will forever remain."

On November 1, Tchaikovsky was in perfect health. He dined with an old friend and went to the theater. In the cloakroom there was talk about spiritualism. Varlamov objected to all talk about ghosts and anything that reminded one of death. Tchaikovsky laughed at Varlamov's manner of expression and said: "There is still time enough to become acquainted with this detestable snub-nosed one. At any rate, he will not have us soon. I know that I shall live for a long time." He then went with friends to a restaurant, where he ate macaroni and drank white wine with mineral water. When he walked home about 2 A.M., Peter was well in body and in mind.

There are some who find pleasure in the thought that the death of a great man was in some way mysterious or melodramatic. For years some insisted that Salieri caused Mozart to be poisoned. There was a rumor after Tchaikovsky's death that he took poison or sought deliberately the cholera. When Mr. Alexander Siloti, a pupil of Tchaikovsky, first visited Boston, in 1898, he did not hesitate to say that there might be truth in the report, and, asked as to his own belief, he shook his head with a portentous gravity that Burleigh might have envied. We have been assured by other Russians who knew Tchaikovsky that he killed himself, nor was the reason for his so doing withheld. Peter's brother Modeste gives a circumstantial account of Peter's death from natural causes. Peter awoke November 2 after a restless night, but he went out about noon to make a call; he returned to luncheon, ate nothing, and drank a glass of water that had not been boiled. Modeste and others were alarmed, but Peter was not disturbed, for he was less afraid of the cholera than of other diseases. Not until night was there any thought of serious illness, and then Peter said to his brother: "I think this is death. Good-bye, Modi." At eleven o'clock that night it was determined that his sickness was cholera.

Modeste tells at length the story of Peter's ending. Their mother had died of cholera in 1854, at the very moment that she was put into a bath. The physicians recommended as a last resort a warm bath for Peter, who, when asked if he would take one, answered: "I shall be glad to have a bath, but I shall probably die as soon as I am in the tub—as my mother died." The bath was not given that night, the second night after the disease had been determined, for Peter was too weak. He was at times delirious, and he often repeated the name of Mme von Meck in reproach or in anger, for he had been sorely hurt by her sudden and capricious neglect after her years of interest and devotion. The next day the bath was given. A priest was called, but it was not possible to administer the Communion, and he spoke words that the dying man could no longer understand. "Peter Ilitch suddenly opened his eyes. There was an indescribable expression of unclouded consciousness. Passing over the others standing in the room, he looked at the three nearest him, and then toward heaven. There was a certain light for a moment in his eyes, which was soon extinguished, at the same time with his breath. It was about three o'clock in the morning."

What was the programme in Tchaikovsky's mind? Kashkin says that, if the composer had disclosed it to the public, the world would not have regarded the symphony as a kind of legacy from one filled with a presentiment of his own approaching end; that it seems more reasonable "to interpret the overwhelming energy of the third movement and the abysmal sorrow of the *finale* in the broader light of a national or historical significance rather than to narrow them to the expression of an individual experience. If the last movement is intended to be predictive, it is surely of things vaster and issues more fatal than are contained in a mere personal apprehension of death. It speaks rather of a '*lamentation large et souffrance inconnue,*' and seems to set the seal of finality on all human hopes. Even if we eliminate the purely subjective interest, this autumnal inspiration of Tchaikovsky, in which we hear 'the ground whirl of the perished leaves of hope, still remains the most profoundly stirring of his works.' . . ."

## "ROMEO AND JULIET," OVERTURE FANTASIA (AFTER SHAKESPEARE)

THE *Romeo and Juliet* overture would be worth a journey if only to hear Tchaikovsky's love music. Here is the incomparable expression in tones of the Southern passion of Juliet, and it is strangely Shakespearean. The remainder of the overture is rather rank Russian, with the exception of the music of Friar Laurence and the noble requiem at the end.

This overture fantasia was begun and completed in 1869. The first performance was at a concert of the Musical Society, Moscow, on March 16, 1870; Nicholas Rubinstein conducted. The work was revised in the summer of 1870 during a sojourn in Switzerland; it was published in 1871. Tchaikovsky, not satisfied with it, made other changes, and, it is said, shortened the overture. The second edition, published in 1881, contains these alterations.

The first performance in the United States was in New York, by the Philharmonic Society, George Matzka, conductor, on April 22, 1876.

The overture begins *andante non tanto, quasi moderato,* F sharp minor, 4-4. Clarinets and bassoons sound the solemn harmonies, which, according to Kashkin, characterize Friar Laurence; and yet Hermann Teibler finds this introduction symbolical of "the burden of fate." A short theme creeps among the strings. There is an organ-point on D flat, with modulation to F minor (flutes, horns, harp, lower strings). The Friar Laurence theme is repeated (flutes, oboes, clarinets, English horn, with *pizzicato* bass). The ascending cry of the flutes is heard in E minor instead of F minor, as before.

*Allegro giusto,* B minor, 4-4. The two households from "ancient grudge break to new mutiny." Wood-wind, horn, and strings picture the hatred and fury that find vent in street brawls. A brilliant passage for strings is followed by a repetition of the strife music. Then comes the first love theme, D flat major (muted violas and English horn, horns in syncopated accompaniment, with strings *pizzicato*). This motive is not unlike in mood, and at times in melodic structure, Tchaikovsky's famous melody, *Nur wer die Sehnsucht kennt* (Op. 6, No. 6), which was composed in December, 1869. In the "Duo from Romeo and Juliet," found among Tchaikovsky's sketches and orchestrated by S. Taneiev, this theme is the climax, the melodic phrase which Romeo sings to *"O nuit d'extase, arrête-toi! O nuit d'amour, étends ton voile noir sur nous!"* O tarry, night of ecstasy! O night of love, stretch thy dark veil over us!). Divided and muted violins, with violas *pizzicato,* play delicate, mysterious chords (D flat major), which in the duet above mentioned serve as accompaniment to the amorous dialogue of Romeo and Juliet in the chamber scene. Flutes and oboes take up the first love theme.

There is a return to tumult and strife. The theme of dissension is developed at length; the horns intone the Friar Laurence motive. The strife theme at last dominates *fortissimo,* until there is a return to the mysterious music of the chamber scene (oboes and clarinets, with murmurings of violins and horns). The song grows more and more passionate, until Romeo's love theme breaks out, this time in D major, and is combined with the strife theme and the motive of Friar Laurence in development. A burst of orchestral fury; there is a descent to the depths; violoncellos, basses, bassoons, alone are heard; they die on low F sharp, with roll of kettledrums. Then silence.

*Moderato assai,* B minor. Drum beats, double basses *pizzicato.* Romeo's song in lamentation. Soft chords (wood-wind and horns) bring the end.

## CONCERTO FOR PIANOFORTE NO. 1, IN B FLAT MINOR, OP. 23

*I. Allegro non troppo e molto maestoso; allegro con spirito*
*II. Andantino semplice; allegro vivace assai*
*III. Allegro con fuoco*

THERE WAS an old Grecian gentleman who apologized for the sumptuous funeral provided for his little child. There are men who have built a lordly portico for a dwelling place, and then, for some reason or other, lack of funds or through caprice, contented themselves with a tasteless, shabbily furnished mansion. The opening section of Tchaikovsky's piano concerto has a compelling melodic sentence, treated gorgeously, and with magnificent breadth and sweep. What follows is a curious mixture of engrossing measures and wild vulgarity.

Perhaps Nicholas Rubinstein was right, after all, in his bitter, almost venomous tirade when Tchaikovsky played it to him in private. When the concerto was brought out in Boston by Bülow, in October, 1875—it was the very first performance—a critic of this city shrewdly discovered that the first movement was "not in the classical concerto spirit." Tchaikovsky himself was amused by American reviews sent to him by Bülow. Peter wrote: "The Americans think that the first movement of my concerto 'suffers in consequence of the absence of a central idea'—and in the *finale* this reviewer has found 'syncopation in trills, spasmodic pauses in the theme, and disturbing octave passages!' Think what healthy appetites these Americans must have: each time Bülow was obliged to repeat the whole *finale* of my concerto! Nothing like this happens in our country!"

In 1874 Tchaikovsky was a teacher of theory at the Moscow Conservatory. (He began his duties at that institution in 1866 at a salary of thirty dollars a month.) On December 13, 1874, he wrote to his brother Anatol: "I am wholly absorbed in the composition of a pianoforte concerto, and I am very anxious that Rubinstein [Nicholas] should play it in his concert. I make slow progress with the work, and without real success; but I stick fast to my principles, and cudgel my brain to subtilize pianoforte passages: as a result I am somewhat nervous, so that I should much like to make a trip to Kiev for the purpose of diversion."

The orchestration of the concerto was finished on February 21, 1875, but before that date he played the work to Nicholas Rubinstein. The episode is one of the most singular in the history of this strangely sensitive composer. He described it in a letter written to Nadeshda Filaretovna von Meck. This letter is dated San Remo, February 2, 1878. It has been published in Modeste Tchaikovsky's Life of his famous brother.

"In December, 1874, I had written a pianoforte concerto. As I am not a pianist, I thought it necessary to ask a virtuoso what was technically unplayable in the work, thankless, or ineffective. I needed the advice of a severe critic who at the same time was friendly disposed toward me. Without going too much into detail, I must frankly say that an interior voice protested against the choice of Nicholas Rubinstein as a judge over the mechanical side of my work. But he was the best pianist in Moscow, and also a most excellent musician. I was told that he would take it ill from me if he should learn that I had passed him by and shown the concerto to another; so I determined to ask him to hear it and criticize the pianoforte part.

"On Christmas Eve, 1874, we were all invited to Albrecht's, and Nicholas asked me, before we should go there, to play the concerto in a classroom of the Conservatory. We agreed to it. I took my manuscript, and Nicholas and Hubert came. Hubert is a mighty good and shrewd fellow, but he is not a bit independent; he is garrulous and verbose; he must always make a long preface to 'yes' or 'no'; he is not capable of expressing an opinion in decisive, unmistakable form; and he is always on the side of the stronger, whoever he may chance to be. I must add that this does not come from cowardice, but only from natural instability.

"I played through the first movement. Not a criticism, not a word. You know how foolish you feel, if you invite one to partake of a meal provided by your own hands, and the friend eats and—is silent! 'At least say something, scold me good-naturedly, but for God's sake speak, only speak, whatever you may say.' Rubinstein said nothing. He was preparing his thunderstorm; and Hubert was waiting to see how things would go before he should jump to one side or the other. The matter was right here: I did not need any judgment on the artistic form of my work: there was question only about mechanical details. This silence of Rubinstein said much. It said to me at once: 'Dear friend, how can I talk about details when I dislike your composition as a whole?' But I kept my temper and played the concerto through. Again silence.

" 'Well?' I said, and stood up. Then burst forth from Rubinstein's mouth a mighty torrent of words. He spoke quietly at first; then he waxed hot, and at last he resembled Zeus hurling thunderbolts. It appeared that my concerto was utterly worthless, absolutely unplayable; passages were so commonplace and awkward that they could not be improved; the piece as a whole was bad, trivial, vulgar. I had stolen this from that one and that from this one; so only two or three pages were good for anything, while the others should be wiped out or radically rewritten. 'For instance, that! What is it, anyhow?' (And then he caricatured the passage on the pianoforte.) 'And this? Is it possible?' and so on, and so on. I cannot reproduce for you the main thing, the tones in which he said all this. An impartial bystander would necessarily have believed that I was a stupid, ignorant, conceited note-scratcher, who was so impudent as to show his scribble to a celebrated man.

"Hubert was staggered by my silence, and he probably wondered how a man who had already written so many works and was a teacher of composition at the Moscow Conservatory could keep still during such a moral lecture or refrain from contradiction—a moral lecture that no one should have delivered to a student without first examining carefully his work. And then Hubert began to annotate Rubinstein; that is, he incorporated Rubinstein's opinions, but sought to clothe in milder words what Nicholas had harshly said."

Tchaikovsky erased the name of Nicholas Rubinstein from the score and inserted in the dedication the name of Hans von Bülow, whom he had not yet seen; but Klindworth had told him of Bülow's interest in his works and his efforts to make them known in Germany. Bülow acknowledged the compliment, and in a warm letter of thanks praised the concerto, which he called the "fullest" work by Tchaikovsky yet known to him: "The ideas are so original, so noble, so powerful; the details are so interesting, and though there are many of them they do not impair the clearness and the unity of the work. The form is so mature, ripe, distinguished for style, for intention and labor are everywhere concealed. I should weary you if I were to enumerate all the characteristics of your work—characteristics which compel me to congratulate equally the composer as well as all those who shall enjoy actively or passively (respectively) the work."

For a long time Tchaikovsky was sore in heart, wounded by his friend. In 1878 Nicholas had the manliness to confess his error; as a proof of his good-will he studied the concerto and played it often and brilliantly in Russia and beyond the boundaries, as at the Paris Exhibition of 1878.

## CONCERTO FOR VIOLIN, IN D MAJOR OP. 35

*I. Allegro moderato*
*II. Canzonetta: andante*
*III. Finale: allegro vivacissimo*

HANSLICK's volumes of collected reviews and essays are many. It is possible that in the days to come he will be remembered only by the fact that he said, apropos of Tchaikovsky's violin concerto, that it stank in the ear. In spite of Hanslick's dictum, the concerto still lives, whatever its obvious faults: its endless repetitions, its measures of sheer padding. Why cannot someone arrange *Gems from Tchaikovsky's Concerto* after the manner of various anthologies (including *Crumbs of Comfort*)? Long-winded, tedious at times as it is, the concerto, by reason of melodic charm and demoniacal spirit, is still heard by the people gladly.

The concerto, dedicated at first to Leopold Auer, but afterwards to Adolf Brodsky—and thereby hangs a tale—was performed for the first time at a Philharmonic concert, Vienna, December 4, 1881. Brodsky was the solo violinist. An interesting letter from him to Tchaikovsky after the first performance, is published in Modeste's Life of his brother

(Vol. II, p. 177): "I had the wish to play the concerto in public ever since I first looked it through. That was two years ago. I often took it up and often put it down, because my laziness was stronger than my wish to reach the goal. You have, indeed, crammed too many difficulties into it. I played it last year in Paris to Laroche, but so badly that he could gain no true idea of the work; nevertheless, he was pleased with it. That journey to Paris which turned out unluckily for me—I had to bear many rude things from Colonne and Pasdeloup—fired my energy (misfortune always does this to me, but when I am fortunate then am I weak) so that, back in Russia, I took up the concerto with burning zeal. It is wonderfully beautiful. One can play it again and again and never be bored; and this is a most important circumstance for the conquering of its difficulties. When I felt myself sure of it, I determined to try my luck in Vienna. Now I come to the point where I must say to you that you should not thank me: I should thank you; for it was only the wish to know the new concerto that induced Hans Richter and later the Philharmonic Orchestra to hear me play and grant my participation in one of these concerts. The concerto was not liked at the rehearsal of the new pieces, although I came out successfully on its shoulders. It would have been most unthankful on my part, had I not strained every nerve to pull my benefactor through behind me. Finally we were admitted to the Philharmonic concert. I had to be satisfied with one rehearsal, and much time was lost there in the correction of the parts, that swarmed with errors. The players determined to accompany everything *pianissimo,* not to go to smash; naturally, the work, which demands many nuances, even in the accompaniment, suffered thereby. Richter wished to make some cuts, but I did not allow it."

The concerto came immediately after a *divertimento* by Mozart. According to the account of the Viennese critics and of Brodsky there was a furious mixture of applause and hissing after the performance. The applause prevailed, and Brodsky was thrice recalled, which showed that the hissing was directed against the work, not the interpreter. Out of ten critics only two, and they were the least important, reviewed the concerto favorably. The review by Eduard Hanslick, who was born hating programme music and the Russian school, was extravagant in its bitterness, and caused Tchaikovsky long-continued distress, although Brodsky, Carl Halir, and other violinists soon made his concerto popular. Tchaikovsky wrote from Rome, December 27, 1881, to Jurgenson: "My dear, I saw lately in a café a number of the *Neue Freie Presse* in which Hanslick speaks so curiously about my violin concerto that I beg you to read it. Besides other reproaches he censures Brodsky for having chosen it. If you know Brodsky's address, please write to him that I am moved deeply by the courage shown by him in playing so difficult and ungrateful a piece before a most prejudiced audience. If Kotek, my best friend, were so cowardly and pusillanimous as to change his intention of acquainting the St. Petersburg public with this concerto, although it was his pressing duty to play it, for he is responsible in the matter of ease of execution of the piece; if Auer, to whom the work is dedicated, intrigued against me, so am I doubly thankful to dear Brodsky, in that for my sake he must stand the curses of the Viennese journals."

The review of Hanslick is preserved in the volume of his collected *feuilletons* entitled, *Concerte, Componisten, und Virtuosen der Letzten fünfzehn Jahre, 1870–1885,* pp. 295, 296 (Berlin, 1886). The criticism in its fierce extravagance now seems amusing. Here are extracts: "For a while the concerto has proportion, is musical, and is not without genius, but soon savagery gains the upper hand and lords it to the end of the first movement. The violin is no longer played: it is yanked about, it is torn asunder, it is beaten black and blue. I do not know whether it is possible for anyone to conquer these hair-raising difficulties, but I do know that Mr. Brodsky martyrized his hearers as well as himself. The *adagio,* with its tender national melody, almost conciliates, almost wins us. But it breaks off abruptly to make way for a *finale* that puts us in the midst of the brutal and wretched jollity of a Russian *kermess.* We see wild and vulgar faces, we hear curses, we smell bad brandy. Friedrich Vischer once asserted in reference to lascivious painting that there are pictures which 'stink in the eye.' Tchaikovsky's violin concerto brings to us for the first time the horrid idea that there may be music that stinks in the ear." Modeste Tchaikovsky tells us that this article disquieted Peter till he died; that he knew it by heart, as he did an adverse criticism written by César Cui in 1866.

The concerto was dedicated first to Leopold Auer. Tchaikovsky, in the Diary of his tour in 1888, wrote: "I do not know whether my dedication was flattering to Mr. Auer, but in spite of his genuine friendship he never tried to conquer the difficulties of this concerto. He pronounced it impossible to play, and this verdict, coming from such an authority as the St. Petersburg virtuoso, had the effect of casting this unfortunate child of my imagination for many years to come into the limbo of hopelessly forgotten things." The composer about seven years before this wrote to Jurgenson from Rome (January 16, 1882) that Auer had been "intriguing against him." Peter's brother Modeste explains this by saying: "It had been reported to Peter that Auer had dissuaded Emile Sauret from playing the concerto in St. Petersburg; but Modeste also adds that Auer changed his opinion many years later, and became one of the most brilliant interpreters of the concerto.

The following orchestration was used by Tchaikovsky in his last three symphonies (with no percussion but timpani in the Fifth): piccolo, two flutes, two oboes, two clarinets, two bassoons, four horns, two trumpets, three trombones, bass tuba, kettledrums, bass drum, cymbals, triangle, and strings. In the *Romeo and Juliet* overture, the English horn and harp were added for color, and the bass drum (with the customary kettledrums) sufficed for percussion. In the piano and violin concertos there was the same scheme of orchestration (without the additional percussion).—EDITOR.

# RICHARD
# WAGNER

(Born at Leipsic, May 22, 1813;
died at Venice, February 13, 1883)

---

IT IS NOT EASY for anyone who did not live through the period of the Wagnerian excitement to understand the fierceness of the controversy. The younger generation reads at its ease accounts of protests against compositions by Strauss, Reger, Schönberg; how this or that piece was hissed by some in a concert hall and applauded by others; it reads and is amused, but it regards the discussion as academic. The Wagner question, like the Beecher trial, like the Ibsen controversy in Norway, divided households.

The world has moved since 1876. Much water has flowed under the bridge. Wagner is still one of the most commanding figures in the temple, but it is no longer an act of irreverence to discuss him as Verdi, Gluck, Richard Strauss are discussed. It is now generally agreed that this towering genius was after all a mortal; that he was often verbose, that he could be dull in his musical speech, as other geniuses were before him.

The great public today cares nothing about Wagner's philosophy, or the "metaphysics" of his *Ring*. Wotan, Mime, Siegfried, and the rest of them, heroic or shabby characters, are as Radames, Salome, Mélisande, Edgardo, Leonora, Manrico in the tower; they are persons in a drama who sing, and do not speak the dialogue. We have the heartiest admiration for the great scenes in the *Ring*, and yet find Wotan long-winded and tiresome in his reminiscences and narrations. Mime is like Artemus Ward's kangaroo, "an amoozin' little cuss." Alberich with his gibbering and his jumping about is also amusing. The Dragon and the Bird do not excite our ridicule. We accept them and find their singing no more surprising than the vocal endurance of Tristan on his deathbed or the moving scenery in the first act of *Parsifal.* The dragon is a familiar figure in art, and we should not rub our eyes more than once if we should see one in the wilds of New Jersey. We enjoy seeing him in his proper place in *Siegfried* and do not wish to be told what he represents or typifies.

Enemies of Wagner, esthetic enemies, used to reproach him for the "immorality" of his librettos. In *Tannhäuser* there is the Venusberg. In *Die Walküre* there is the incestuous and adulterous pair whose amorous shoutings shocked Arthur Schopenhauer. Reading the story of *Tristan,* these rigid moralists held the nose and called for civet. Fie on Kundry's case!

We now hear little about the "immorality" of the music dramas. King Mark's long harangue is more immoral than the rapturous duet of the lovers; the Landgrave is more immoral than Venus; for Mark and the Landgrave, by reason of their long-winded platitudes, make Virtue boresome and Respectability a monster.

And in the expression of certain emotions and passions, in the expression of amorous ecstasy and the mystery of death, Wagner reached a height of eloquence that has seldom been attained by makers of music. Hearing the announcement by Brünnhilde of Siegmund's fate, the love song of Tristan and Isolde under the cloak of the conniving night, the rustle and murmur of Siegfried's forest, we marvel at the genius of the man who first heard these things and had the ability to let the world hear them with him.

## RICHARD WAGNER

# OVERTURE TO "RIENZI, THE LAST OF THE TRIBUNES"

THE OVERTURE to *Rienzi* is at the best mere circus music. It is a good thing to hear it once in a while, for it shows that Wagner, on occasion, could be more vulgar than Meyerbeer, whom he so cordially disliked.

Wagner left Königsberg in the early summer of 1837 to visit Dresden, and there he read Bärmann's translation into German of Bulwer's *Rienzi*. And thus was revived his long-cherished idea of making the last of the Tribunes the hero of a grand opera. "My impatience with a degrading plight now amounted to a passionate craving to begin something grand and elevating, no matter if it involved the temporary abandonment of any practical goal. This mood was fed and strengthened by a reading of Bulwer's *Rienzi*. From the misery of modern private life, whence I could nohow glean the scantiest material for artistic treatment, I was wafted by the image of a great historico-political event in the enjoyment whereof I needs must find a distraction lifting me above cares and conditions that to me appeared nothing less than absolutely fatal to art." The overture to *Rienzi* was completed October 23, 1840. The opera was produced at the Royal Saxon Court Theater, Dresden, October 20, 1842.

The overture is scored for piccolo, two flutes, two oboes, two clarinets, two bassoons, serpent (third bassoon), two valve horns, two plain horns, two valve trumpets, two plain trumpets, three trombones, one ophicleide, kettledrums, two snare drums, bass drum, triangle, cymbals, and strings. The serpent mentioned in the score is replaced by the double bassoon, and the ophicleide by the bass tuba.

All the themes of the overture are taken from the opera itself. The overture begins with a slow introduction, *molto sostenuto e maestoso,* D major, 4-4. It opens with "a long-sustained, swelled and diminished A on the trumpet," in the opera, the agreed signal for the uprising of the people to throw off the tyrannical yoke of the nobles. The majestic *cantilena* of the violins and the violoncellos is the theme of Rienzi's prayer in the fifth act. The last prolonged A leads to the main body of the overture. This begins *allegro energico,* D major, 2-2, in the full orchestra on the first theme, that of the chorus, *"Gegrüsst sei hoher Tag!"* at the beginning of the first *finale* of the opera. The first subsidiary theme enters in the brass, and it is the theme of the battle hymn ("Santo spirito cavaliere") of the revolutionary faction in the third act. A transitional passage in the violoncellos leads to the entrance of the second theme—Rienzi's prayer, already heard in the introduction of the overture—which is now given, *allegro,* in A major, to the violins. The "Santo spirito cavaliere" theme returns in the brass, and leads to another and joyful theme, that of the *stretto* of the second *finale,* "Rienzi, dir sei Preis," which is developed with increasing force. In the *coda, molto più stretto,* the "Santo spirito cavaliere" is developed in a most robust manner.

## OVERTURE TO "DER FLIEGENDE HOLLÄNDER" ("THE FLYING DUTCHMAN")

THE OVERTURE to *The Flying Dutchman* gives the condensed and essential drama. We are relieved of the avaricious father who is delighted at the thought of handing his daughter to the mysterious stranger; nor does one have to hear the bleatings of the saphead lover. No wonder Senta preferred the Dutchman.

Wagner's overture is a stormy seascape. The Dutchman knew no calm seas. The music that typifies him is one of Wagner's happiest inventions. Poor Vanderdecken sings nothing so compelling, not even in his monologue. One hears enough of Senta's ballad in the overture; one is not tempted to laugh at the operatic spinning wheels that stick when they should revolve; one does not find Wagner trying to write with Italian melodiousness.

The overture was sketched at Meudon near Paris in September, 1841, and completed and scored at Paris in November of that year. In 1852, Wagner changed the ending. In 1860 he wrote another ending for the Paris concerts.

It opens *allegro con brio* in D minor, 6–4, with an empty fifth, against which horns and bassoons give out the "Flying Dutchman" motive. There is a stormy development, through which this motive is kept sounding in the brass. There is a hint at the first theme of the main body of the overture, an *arpeggio* figure in the strings, taken from the accompaniment of one of the movements in the Dutchman's first air in Act I. The storm section over, there is an episodic *andante* in F major in which wind instruments give out phrases from Senta's ballad of the Flying Dutchman (Act II). The episode leads directly to the main body of the overture, *allegro con brio* in D minor, 6-4, which begins with the first theme. This theme is developed at great length with chromatic passages taken from Senta's ballad. The "Flying Dutchman" theme comes in episodically in the brass from time to time. The subsidiary theme in F major is taken from the sailors' chorus, "Steuermann, lass' die Wacht!" (Act III). The second theme, the phrase from Senta's ballad already heard in the *andante* episode, enters *fortissimo* in the full orchestra, F major, and is worked up brilliantly with fragments of the first theme. The "Flying Dutchman" motive reappears *fortissimo* in the trombones. The *coda* begins in D major, 2-2. A few rising *arpeggio* measures in the violins lead to the second theme, proclaimed with the full force of the orchestra. The theme is now in the shape found in the *allegro* peroration of Senta's ballad. It is worked up energetically.

The overture is scored for piccolo, two flutes, two oboes, English horn, two clarinets, four horns, two bassoons, two trumpets, three trombones, bass tuba, kettledrums, harp, strings.

## OVERTURE TO TANNHÄUSER

*Tannhäuser und der Sängerkrieg auf Wartburg,* Romantic Opera in three acts, book and music by Wagner, was produced at the Royal Opera House in Dresden, under the direction of the composer, on October 19, 1845.

The overture was written in Dresden, probably in March–April, 1845. The first performance of it as a concert piece was at a concert at Leipsic for the benefit of the Gewandhaus Orchestra Pension Fund, February 12, 1846. Mendelssohn conducted it from manuscript.

Wagner's own programme of the overture was published in the *Neue Zeitschrift* of January 14, 1853. It was written at the request of orchestral players who were rehearsing the overture for performance at Zurich. The translation into English is by William Ashton Ellis.

"To begin with, the orchestra leads before us the Pilgrims' Chant alone; it draws near, then swells into a mighty outpour, and passes finally away.—Evenfall; last echo of the chant. As night breaks, magic sights and sounds appear, a rosy mist floats up, exultant shouts assail our ears, the whirlings of a fearsomely voluptuous dance are seen. These are the Venusberg's seductive spells, that show themselves at dead of night to those whose breast is fired by daring of the senses. Attracted by the tempting show, a shapely human form draws nigh; 'tis Tannhäuser, Love's minstrel. . . . Venus, herself, appears to him. . . . As the Pilgrims' Chant draws closer, yet closer, as the day drives farther back the night, that whir and soughing of the air—which had erewhile sounded like the eerie cries of souls condemned—now rises, too, to ever gladder waves; so that when the sun ascends at last in splendor, and the Pilgrims' Chant proclaims in esctasy to all the world, to all that lives and moves thereon, Salvation won, this wave itself swells out the tidings of sublimest joy. 'Tis the carol of the Venusberg itself, redeemed from curse of impiousness, this cry we hear amid the hymn of God. So wells and leaps each pulse of Life in chorus of Redemption; and both dissevered elements, both soul and senses, God and Nature, unite in the atoning kiss of hallowed Love."

The overture is scored for piccolo, two flutes, two oboes, two clarinets, two bassoons, four horns, three trumpets, three trombones, bass tuba, kettledrums, cymbals, triangle, tambourine, and strings.

## PRELUDE TO "LOHENGRIN"

WE REMEMBER how at one of Theodore Thomas's concerts at Central Park Garden in New York—it was in the 'seventies—when this prelude was played we heard strong hissing from many who would not have "the music of the future." And so today there are "lovers of music" who cannot endure the music of the present and swear it cannot be the music of future, for they have ears but they do not and will not hear.

"Ephraim is joined to idols; let him alone."

*Lohengrin,* an opera in three acts, was performed for the first time at the Court Theater, Weimar, August 28, 1850. Liszt conducted.

Liszt described the prelude as "a sort of magic formula which, like a mysterious initiation, prepares our souls for the sight of unaccustomed things, and of a higher signification than that of our terrestrial life."

Wagner's own explanation has been translated into English as follows:

"Love seemed to have vanished from a world of hatred and quarreling; as a lawgiver she was no longer to be found among the communities of men. Emancipating itself from barren care for gain and possession, the sole arbiter of all worldly intercourse, the human heart's unquenchable love-longing again at length craved to appease a want, which, the more warmly and intensely it made itself felt under the pressure of reality, was the less easy to satisfy, on account of this very reality. It was beyond the confines of the actual world that man's ecstatic imaginative power fixed the source as well as the outflow of this incomprehensible impulse of love, and from the desire of a comforting sensuous conception of this supersensuous idea invested it with a wonderful form, which, under the name of the 'Holy Grail,' though conceived as actually existing, yet unapproachably far off, was believed in, longed for, and sought for. The Holy Grail was the costly vessel out of which, at the Last Supper, our Saviour drank with His disciples, and in which His blood was received when out of love for His brethren He suffered upon a cross, and which till this day has been preserved with lively zeal as the source of undying love; albeit, at one time this cup of salvation was taken away from unworthy mankind, but at length was brought back again from the heights of heaven by a band of angels, and delivered into the keeping of fervently loving, solitary men, who, wondrously strengthened and blessed by its presence, and purified in heart, were consecrated as the earthly champions of eternal love.

"This miraculous delivery of the Holy Grail, escorted by an angelic host, and the handing of it over into the custody of highly favored men, was selected by the author of *Lohengrin,* a knight of the Grail, for the introduction of his drama, as the subject to be musically portrayed; just as here, for the sake of explanation, he may be allowed to bring it forward as an object for the mental receptive power of his hearers.

"The prelude is scored for three flutes, two oboes, English horn, two clarinets, bass clarinet, four horns, three trumpets, three trombones, bass tuba, kettledrums, cymbals, and strings."

## PRELUDE AND LIEBESTOD FROM "TRISTAN UND ISOLDE"

THE SUBJECT of *Tristan und Isolde* was first mentioned by Wagner in a letter to Liszt in the latter part of 1854; the poem was written at Zürich in the summer of 1857, and finished in September of that year. The composition of the first act was completed at Zürich, December 31, 1857 (some say, but only in the sketch); the second act was completed at Venice in March, 1859; the third act at Lucerne in August, 1859.

Wagner himself frequently conducted the prelude and Love-Death, arranged by him for orchestra alone, in the concerts given by him in 1863. At those given in Carlsruhe and Löwenberg the programme characterized the prelude as *Liebestod* and the latter section, now known as *Liebestod,* as *Verklärung* (Transfiguration).

The prelude, *langsam und schmachtend* (slow and languishingly), in A minor, 6–8, is a gradual and long-continued *crescendo* to a most sonorous *fortissimo;* a shorter *decrescendo* leads back to *pianissimo.* It is free in form and of continuous development. There are two chief themes: the first phrase, sung by violoncellos, is combined in the third measure with a phrase ascending chromatically and given to the oboes.

These phrases form a theme known as the "Love Potion" motive, or the motive of "Longing"; for passionate commentators are not yet agreed about the terminology. The second theme, again sung by the violoncellos, a voluptuous theme, is entitled "Tristan's Love Glance."

The prelude is scored for three flutes (and piccolo), two oboes, English horn, two clarinets, bass clarinet, three bassoons, four horns, three trumpets, three trombones, bass tuba, kettledrums, harp, and the usual strings.

Wagner wrote this explanatory programme:

"A primitive old love poem, which, far from having become extinct, is constantly fashioning itself anew, and has been adopted by every European language of the Middle Ages, tells us of Tristan and Isolde. Tristan, the faithful vassal, woos for his king her for whom he dares not avow his own love, Isolde. Isolde, powerless to do otherwise than obey the wooer, follows him as bride to his lord. Jealous of this infringement of her rights, the Goddess of Love takes her revenge. As the result of a happy mistake, she allows the couple to taste of the love potion which, in accordance with the custom of the times, and by way of precaution, the mother had prepared for the husband who should marry her daughter from political motives, and which, by the burning desire which suddenly inflames them after tasting it, opens their eyes to the truth and leads to the avowal that for the future they belong only to each other. Henceforth, there is no end to the longings, the demands, the joys and woes of love. The world, power, fame, splendor, honor, knighthood, fidelity, friendship, all are dissipated like an empty dream. One thing only remains: longing, longing, insatiable longing, forever springing up anew, pining and thirsting. Death, which means passing away, perishing, never awakening, their only deliverance. . . . Powerless, the heart sinks back to languish in longing, in longing without attaining; for each attainment only begets new longing, until in the last stage of weariness the foreboding of the highest joy of dying, of no longer existing, of the last escape into that wonderful kingdom from which we are furthest off when we are most strenuously striving to enter therein. Shall we call it death? Or is it the hidden wonder-world from out of which an ivy and vine, entwined with each other, grew up upon Tristan's and Isolde's grave, as the legend tells us?"

## PRELUDE TO "DIE MEISTERSINGER VON NÜRNBERG"

THE IDEA of the opera occurred to Wagner at Marienbad in 1845. He then sketched a scenario which differed widely from the one finally adopted. It is possible that certain scenes were written while he was at work on *Lohengrin;* there is a legend that the quintet was finished in 1845. Some add to this quintet the songs of Sachs and Walther. Wagner wrote to a friend on March 12, 1862: "Tomorrow I hope at least to begin the composition of *Die Meistersinger*"—the libretto was completed at Paris in 1861. He worked at Biebrich on the Rhine in 1862 on the music. The prelude was sketched in February of that year. The instrumentation was completed in the following June.

He wrote to his friend Dr. Anton Pusinelli from Penzing near Vienna on March 14, 1864: "I have tried with the greatest care to ensure myself the proper leisure for completing the *Meistersinger* by next winter. Unfortunately, everything has been very difficult for me because my continual indisposition and my sad frame of mind have kept company with my other trials, so as to make it more difficult for me to have any desire for work." He wrote again to Pusinelli in a long letter about his "poor wife" Minna, questioning whether he should return to her: "Under favorable conditions I finally *can* complete my *Meistersinger.* Very probably this work will quickly become popular, and it *can* bring in good returns for me. But one can't *count* on this, and my life from month to month must not depend on such possibilities; for if I have no 'good inspirations,' then I have nothing to write down, and with continual worries I no longer have very good inspirations now."

At Lucerne on May 10, 1866, he wrote that he had won for a little time the quiet for creating "a great and joyful work. Wish me this success and—perhaps I dare to say it—wish it to the world!" He had already completed Act I and was progressing well with Act II, which was finished in December.

In 1868 he wrote from Lucerne: "In Dresden I had in mind an attempt to procure some guarantee for the *Meistersinger* against abominable incompetence of the *Kapellmeisters* there, and with what a nice reception was I met there!" The principal *Kapellmeister* was Julius Rietz, who was hostile to Wagner, as he had been at Leipsic.

The prelude is scored for piccolo, two flutes, two oboes, two clarinets, two bassoons, four horns, three trumpets, three trombones, bass tuba, kettledrums, triangle, cymbals, harp, and the usual strings.

Wagner in his Autobiography tells how the idea of *Die Meistersinger* formed itself; how he began to elaborate it in the hope that it might free him from the thrall of the idea of *Lohengrin;* but he was impelled to go back to the latter opera. The melody for the fragment of Sachs' poem on the Reformation occurred to him while going through the galleries of the Palais Royal on his way to the Taverne Anglaise. "There I found Truinet already waiting for me and asked him to give me a scrap of paper and a pencil to jot down my melody, which I quietly hummed over to him at the time." "As from the balcony of my flat, in a sunset of great splendor, I gazed upon the magnificent spectacle of 'Golden' Mayence, with the majestic Rhine pouring along its outskirts in a glory of light, the prelude to my *Meistersinger* again suddenly made its presence closely and distinctly felt in my soul. Once before had I seen it rise before me out of a lake of sorrow, like some distant mirage. I proceeded to write down the prelude exactly as it appears today in the score, that is, containing the clear outlines of the leading themes of the whole drama."

Wagner conducted the two overtures. The hall was nearly empty; there was a pecuniary loss. This was a sore disappointment to Wagner, who had written to Weissheimer on October 12, 1862: "Good: *Tannhäuser* overture, then. That's all right for me. For what I now have in mind is to make an out-and-out sensation, so as to make money." He had proposed to add the prelude and *finale* of *Tristan* to the Prelude to *"Die Meistersinger"*; but his friends in Leipsic advised the substitution of the overture to *Tannhäuser*. There was not the faintest applause when Wagner came on the platform; but the prelude to *Die Meistersinger* was received with such favor that it was immediately played a second time.

One critic wrote of the *Meistersinger* prelude, "The overture, a long movement in moderate march tempo, with predominating brass, without any chief thoughts and without noticeable and recurring points of rest, went along and soon awakened a feeling of monotony." The critic of the *Mitteldeutsche Volkzeitung* wrote in terms of enthusiasm. The *Signal's* critic was bitter in opposition. He wrote at length and finally characterized the prelude as "chaos," a "tohu-wabohu and nothing more."

## A SIEGFRIED IDYL

COSIMA LISZT, daughter of Franz Liszt and the Countess d'Agoult, was born at Bellagio, Italy, on Christmas Day, 1837. She was married to Hans von Bülow at Berlin, August 18, 1857. They were divorced in the fall of 1869.

Richard Wagner married Minna Planer on November 24, 1836, at Königsberg. They separated in August, 1861. She died at Dresden, January 25, 1866.

Wagner and Cosima were married at Lucerne, August 25, 1870. Their son, Siegfried Wagner, was born at Triebschen, near Lucerne, on June 6, 1869.

In a letter to Frau Wille, June 25, 1870, Wagner wrote of Cosima: "She has defied every disapprobation and taken upon herself every condemnation. She has borne to me a wonderfully beautiful boy, whom I can boldly call 'Siegfried'; he is now growing, together with my work; he gives me a new long life, which at last has attained a meaning. Thus we get along without the world, from which we have wholly withdrawn."

The *Siegfried Idyl* was a birthday gift to Cosima. It was composed in November, 1870, at Triebschen. Hans Richter received the manuscript score on December 4, 1870. Wagner gave a fine copy of it to Cosima. Musicians of Zürich were engaged for the performance. The first rehearsal was on December 21, 1870, in the foyer of Zürich's old theater. The Wesendocks were present. Wagner conducted a rehearsal at the Hôtel du Lac, Lucerne, on December 24. Christmas fell on a Sunday. Early in the morning the musicians assembled at Wagner's villa in Triebschen. In order to surprise Cosima, the desks were put on the stairs and the tuning was in the kitchen. The orchestra took its place on the stairs, Wagner, who conducted, at the top; then the violins, violas, wood-wind instruments, horns, and at the bottom the violoncello and the double bass. Wagner could not see the violoncello and the double bass; but the performance, according to Richter, was faultless. The orchestra was thus composed: two first violins, two second violins, two violas (one played by Richter, who also played the few measures for a trumpet), one violoncello, one double bass, one flute, one oboe, two clarinets, one bassoon, two horns. Richter, in order not to excite Cosima's suspicions, practised for some days the trumpet part in the empty barracks. "These daily excursions and several trips to Zürich awakened the attention of Mme Wagner, who thought I was not so industrious as formerly." The performance began at 7.30 A. M. The *Idyl* was repeated several times in the course of the day, and in the afternoon Beethoven's Sextet was performed without the variations.

The *Idyl* was performed at Mannheim on December 20, 1871, in private and under Wagner's direction. There was a performance on March 10, 1877, in the Ducal Palace at Meiningen. Wagner conducted. The score and parts were published in February, 1878. The first performance after publication was at a Bilse concert in Berlin toward the end of February, 1878. The music drama *Siegfried* was then so little known that a Berlin critic said the *Idyl* was taken from the second act. And Mr. Henry Knight, a passionate Wagnerite, wrote verses in 1889 in which he showed a similar confusion in mental operation.

This composition first bore the title *Triebschener Idyll.* The score calls for flute, oboe, two clarinets, bassoon, trumpet, two horns, and strings.

Siegfried was born while Wagner was at work on his music

drama *Siegfried.* The themes in the *Idyl* were taken from this music drama, all save one: a folk-song, "Schlaf', mein Kind, schlaf'ein"; but the development of the themes was new.

## "THE RIDE OF THE VALKYRIES," FROM "DIE WALKÜRE"

AFTER an instrumental introduction to Act III of *The Valkyrie,* the curtain rises.

"On the summit of a rocky mountain. On the right a pine wood encloses the stage. On the left is the entrance to a cave; above this the rock rises to its highest point. At the back the view is entirely open; rocks of various heights form a parapet to the precipice. Occasionally clouds fly past the mountain peak as if driven by storm. Gerhilde, Ortlinde, Waltraute, and Schwertleite have ensconced themselves on the rocky peak above the cave; they are in full armor.

"Flashs of lightning break through the clouds, and from time to time a Valkyrie is seen on horseback with a slain warrior hanging from the saddle. We quote John F. Runciman's description of the Valkyries' Ride:[1]

"The drama here is of the most poignant kind; the scenic surroundings are of the sort Wagner so greatly loved—tempest amidst black pine woods with wild, flying clouds, the dying down of the storm, the saffron evening light melting into shadowy night, the calm, deep blue sky with the stars peeping out, then the bright flames shooting up; and the two elements, the dramatic and the pictorial, drew out of him some pages as splendid as any even he ever wrote. The opening, 'The Ride of the Valkyries,' is a piece of storm music without a parallel. There is no need here for Donner with his hammer; the All-Father himself is abroad in wrath and majesty, and his daughters laugh and rejoice in the riot. There is nothing uncanny in the music: we have that delight in the sheer force of the elements which we inherit from our earliest ancestors: the joy of nature fiercely at work which is echoed in our hearts from time immemorial. The shrilling of the wind, the hubbub, the calls of the Valkyries to one another, the galloping of the horses, form a

[1]John F. Runciman: *Richard Wagner, Composer of Operas,* 1913.

picture which for splendor, wild energy, and wilder beauty can never be matched.

"Technically, this Ride is a miracle built up of conventional figurations of the older music. There is the continuous shake, handed on from instrument to instrument, the slashing figure of the upper strings, the kind of *basso ostinato,* conventionally indicating the galloping of horses, and the chief melody, a mere bugle call, altered by a change of rhythm into a thing of superb strength. The only part of the music that ever so remotely suggests extravagance is the Valkyries' call; and it, after all, is only a jodel put to sublime uses. Out of these commonplace elements, elements that one might almost call prosaic, Wagner wrought his picture of storm, with its terror, power, joyous laughter of the storm's daughters—storm as it must have seemed to the first poets of our race. . . .

"It is worth looking at the plan of this Ride—which is, be it remembered, only the prelude to the gigantic drama which is to follow. After the *ritornello* the main theme is announced, with a long break between the first and second strains; and again a break before it is continued. Then it sounds out all its glory, terse, closely gripped section to section, until the Valkyries' call is heard; purely pictorial passages follow; the theme is played with, even as Mozart and Beethoven played with their themes, and at the last the whole force of the orchestra is employed, and Wagner's object is attained—he has given us a picture of storm such as was never done before, and he has done what was necessary for the subsequent drama—made us feel the tremendous might of the god of storms."

The arrangement for concert use calls for these instruments: two piccolos, two flutes, three oboes, English horn, three clarinets, bass clarinet, three bassoons, eight horns, three trumpets, four trombones, bass tuba, kettledrums, side drum, cymbals, triangle, and the usual strings.

## PRELUDE TO "PARSIFAL"

WAGNER, with his theatrical sense, was right: this music is not so impressive when it is performed, no matter how well, outside of the Bayreuth theater consecrated to the music dramas. We heard *Parsifal* the year it was produced at Bayreuth. No performance of the prelude has since awakened the same emotions. There was the silence of deep devotion; the presence of the worshipers, fanatics in the great majority; the expectation of marvelous scenes to come as the wailing first phrase rose from the unseen orchestra. Put this prelude in the conventional opera house, or in the concert hall, and it cannot be ranked with Wagner's greatest works.

The prelude to *Parsifal* was composed at Bayreuth in September, 1877. The first performance was a private one in the hall of the Villa Wahnfried at Bayreuth, on December 25, 1878, to celebrate the birthday of Cosima Wagner. The prelude was performed as a morning serenade by the Meiningen Court Orchestra, led by Wagner. The performance was repeated the evening of the same day, when guests were invited.

The score and orchestral parts were published in October, 1882. *Parsifal,* "a stage-consecration-festival play" in three acts, book and music by Richard Wagner, was first performed at Bayreuth for the patrons, July 26, 1882. The first public performance was on July 30, 1882. Hermann Levi conducted.

Wagner's version of the story of Percival, or, as he prefers, Parsifal, is familiar to all. There is no need in a description of the prelude to this music drama of telling the simple tale or pondering its symbolism. The ethical idea of the drama is that enlightenment coming through conscious pity brings salvation. The clearest and the sanest exposition of the prelude is that included by Maurice Kufferath in his elaborate essay, *Parsifal* (Paris: Fischbacher, 1890). We give portions of this exposition in a greatly condensed form:

Without preparation the prelude opens with a broad melodic phrase, which is sung later in the great religious scene of the first act, during the mystic feast, the Lord's Supper.

The phrase is sung, at first without accompaniment, in unison by violins, violoncello, English horn, clarinet, bassoon, *sehr langsam* (*lento assai*), A flat major, 4-4. This motive is repeated by trumpet, oboes, and half the first and second violins in unison against rising and falling *arpeggios* in the violas and remaining violins, repeated chords for flutes, clarinets, and English horn, and sustained harmonies in bassoons and horns. This theme is known as the motive of the "Last Supper." The second phrase of the motive is given out and repeated as before.

Without any other transition than a series of broken chords, the trombones and the trumpets give out the second theme, the "Grail" motive, because it serves throughout the music drama to characterize the worship of the holy relic. It is a very short theme, which afterwards will enter constantly, sometimes alone, sometimes in company with other themes, often modified in rhythm, but preserving always its characteristic harmonies. As William J. Henderson says: "The second theme of the prelude is that of the Grail itself, which is here presented to us in a different musical aspect from that of the *Lohengrin* score. There the Grail was celebrated as a potency by which the world was aided, while here it is brought before us as the visible embodiment of a faith, the memento of a crucified Saviour."[2] This theme is not original with Wagner. The ascending progression of sixths, which forms the conclusion of the theme, is found in the Saxon liturgy and is in use today in the "Court" Church at Dresden. Mendelssohn employed it in the *Reformation* symphony; therefore, zealous admirers of Mendelssohn have accused Wagner of plagiarism. The two masters, who knew Dresden well, probably were struck by the harmonic structure of this conclusion, and they used it, each in his own way. Anyone has a personal right to this simple formula. The true inventor of the "Amen" is unknown; the formula has been attributed to Silvani. Its harmonic nature would indicate that it belongs to the seventeenth century, but there are analogous progressions in Palestrina's Masses. The "Grail" motive is repeated twice.

Then, and again without transition, but with a change of tempo to 6–4, comes the third motive, that of "Belief." The brass first proclaims it.

The strings take up the "Grail" theme. The "Belief" motive reappears four times in succession, in different tonalities.

A roll of drums on A flat is accompanied by a tremolo of double basses, giving the contra F. The first motive, the "Lord's Supper," enters first (wood-wind, afterwards in the violoncellos). This time the motive is not completed. Wagner stops at the third measure and takes a new subject, which is repeated several times with increasing expression of sorrow. There is, then, a fourth theme derived from the "Lord's Supper" motive. The first two measures, which are found in simpler form and without the appoggiatura in the "Supper" theme, will serve hereafter to characterize more particularly the "Holy Lance" that

[2]William J. Henderson: ***Richard Wagner, His Life and His Works,*** **1901.**

pierced the side of Christ and also caused the wound of Amfortas, the lance that drew the sacred blood which was turned into the communion wine; the lance that fell into the hands of Klingsor, the Magician.

At the moment when this fourth theme, which suggests the sufferings of Christ and Amfortas, bursts forth from the whole orchestra, the Prelude has its climax. This prelude, like unto that of *Lohengrin,* is developed by successive degrees until it reaches a maximum of expression, and there is a *diminuendo* to *pianissimo.*

Thus the synthesis of the whole drama has been clearly exposed. That which remains is only a peroration, a logical, necessary conclusion, brought about by the ideas expressed by the different themes. It is by the sight of suffering that Parsifal learns pity and saves Amfortas. It is the motive of the "Lord's Supper" that signifies both devotion and sacrifice; that is to say Love, and Love is the conclusion. The last chords of the expiring lament lead back gently to the first two measures of the "Lord's Supper" motive, which, repeated from octave to octave on a pedal (E flat), end in a series of ascending chords, a prayer, or a supplication. Is there hope? The drama gives the answer to this question full of anguish.

The prelude is scored for three flutes, three oboes, English horn, three clarinets, bass clarinet, three bassoons, double bassoon, four horns, three trumpets, three trombones, bass tuba, kettledrums, and strings.

## "GOOD FRIDAY SPELL," FROM "PARSIFAL"

When Parsifal turns slowly towards the meadow, a hymn of tender thanksgiving arises from the orchestra. The melody is played by flute and oboe, which muted strings sustain. In the development of this theme occur several figures—"Kundry's Sigh," the "Holy Supper," the "Spear," the "Grail" harmonies, the "Complaint of the Flower Girls," which are all finally absorbed in the "Good Friday" melody. This pastoral is suddenly interrupted by the sound of distant bells, sounding mournfully from afar.

Gurnemanz and Kundry robe Parsifal. They set out for Montsalvat.

When Gurnemanz blesses Parsifal and salutes him king, horns, trumpets, and trombones play the "Parsifal" motive, which is developed imposingly and ends with the "Grail" theme, intoned by the whole orchestra *fortissimo.* A series of chords leads to the motives of "Baptism" and "Faith."

## CARL MARIA VON
# WEBER

(Born at Eutin, Oldenburg, December 18, 1786; died at London, June 5, 1826)

---

MR. WILLIAM APTHORP frequently spoke of the "Weberian flourish," of the chivalric spirit shown, not only in Weber's overtures to *Euryanthe* and *Oberon,* but in much of his music for the piano. Weber's operas are wholly unknown as stage works to the younger generation. *Oberon* is a dull opera, with some beautiful music. *Euryanthe,* too, is dull, dull beyond redemption, although at Dresden years ago we saw a most carefully prepared performance, for the cult of Weber in that city was then firmly established, and nowhere else was Der Freischütz so admirably performed. Yet Weber was a mighty man in his day, influencing composers of other countries than his own, praised to the skies by Berlioz and Wagner. The latter had good reason for his enthusiasm; the influence of *Euryanthe* is observed in his early operas. Weber was a romanticist of the E. T. A. Hoffmann order. The music for the scene of the Wolf's Glen in *Der Freischütz* is in no need of fireworks and ghostly apparitions for its terrifying effects. There is charming fairy music in *Oberon.* Then there is the mysterious *largo* in the *Euryanthe* overture. The grand arias, the set pieces for a soprano, with the final *allegro* section better suited to an orchestral instrument than the human voice, are now singularly out of fashion, but what could be better as music for a particular text than that for the opening scenes of *Der Freischütz?* The three overtures will long preserve the composer's name.

# CARL MARIA VON WEBER

## OVERTURE TO THE OPERA "OBERON"

*Oberon; or, the Elf-King's Oath,* a romantic opera in three acts, book by James Robinson Planché, who founded it on Villeneuve's story "Huon de Bordeaux" and Sotheby's English translation of Wieland's German poem, "Oberon," was first performed at Covent Garden, London, on April 12, 1826. Weber conducted. The first performance in New York was at the Park Theatre on October 9, 1828.

Weber was asked by Charles Kemble in 1824 to write an opera for the Theatre Royal, Covent Garden. Weber chose "Oberon" for the subject. Planché was selected to furnish the libretto. In a letter to him, Weber wrote that the fashion of it was foreign to his ideas: "The intermixing of so many principal actors who do not sing—the omission of the music in the most important moments—all these things deprive our *Oberon* of the title of an opera, and will make him [*sic*] unfit for all other theaters in Europe, which is a very bad thing for me, but—*passons là-dessous.*"

Weber, a sick and discouraged man, buckled himself to the task of learning English, that he might know the exact meaning of the text. He therefore took one hundred and fifty-three lessons of an Englishman named Carey and studied diligently, anxiously. Planché sent the libretto to Dresden an act at a time. Weber made his first sketch on January 23, 1825. The autograph score contains this note at the end of the overture: "Finished April 9, 1826, in the morning, at a quarter of twelve, and with it the whole opera. *Soli Deo Gloria! ! !* C. M. V. Weber." This entry was made at London. Weber received for the opera £500. He was so feeble that he could scarcely stand without support, but he rehearsed and directed the performance seated at the piano. He died of consumption about two months after the production.

Planché gives a lively account of the genesis and production of *Oberon.* He describes the London public as unmusical. "A dramatic situation in music was 'caviare to the general,' and inevitably received with cries of 'Cut it short!' from the gallery, and obstinate coughing or other significant signs of impatience from the pit. Nothing but the 'Huntsmen's Chorus' and the *diablerie* in *Der Freischütz* saved that fine work from immediate condemnation in England; and I remember perfectly well the exquisite melodies in it being compared by English musical critics to 'wind through a keyhole.' . . . None of our actors could sing, and but one singer could act, Madame Vestris, who made a charming Fatima. . . . My great object was to land Weber safe amidst an unmusical public, and I therefore wrote a melodrama with songs, instead of an opera such as would be required at the present day."

The first performance in Germany of *Oberon* was at Leipsic, December 23, 1826.

The overture begins with an introduction (*adagio sostenuto ed il tutto pianissimo possibile,* D major, 4-4). The horn of Oberon is answered by muted strings. The figure for flutes and clarinets is taken from the first scene of the opera (Oberon's palace; introduction and chorus of elfs). After a *pianissimo* little march, there is a short dreamy passage for strings, which ends in the violas. There is a full orchestral crashing chord, and the main body of the overture begins (*allegro con fuoco* in D major, 4-4). The brilliant opening measures are taken from the accompaniment figure of the quartet, "Over the Dark Blue Waters," sung by Rezia, Fatima, Huon, Scherasmin (Act II, Scene x). The horn of Oberon is heard again; it is answered by the skipping fairy figure. The second theme (A major, sung first by the clarinet, then by the first violins) is taken from the first measures of the second part of Huon's air (Act I, No. 5). And then a theme is taken from the peroration, *presto con fuoco,* of Rezia's air "Ocean! Thou mighty monster" (Act II, No. 13), and given as a conclusion to the violins. This theme ends the first part of the overture. The free fantasia begins with soft repeated chords in bassoons, horns, drums, basses. The first theme is worked out in short periods; a new theme is introduced and treated in *fugato* against a running contrapuntal counter theme in the strings. The second theme is treated, but not elaborately; and then the Rezia motive brings the spirited end.

## OVERTURE TO THE OPERA "DER FREISCHÜTZ"

WHAT WOULD conductors do without these three overtures of Weber? They are to them in time of perplexity what *Cavalleria Rusticana* and *Pagliacci* are to opera managers. And yet, in spite of countless performances, the overture to *Der Freischütz* is not stale. The part song for the horns still charms the ear, although it is now associated with "when the sun glorious" and other sacred words for service in the meeting house. The Samiel motive is still dramatically sinister and brings back memories of the red-cloaked fiend as we have seen him on the German stage. And the clarinet theme, typical of Max, is still worthy of the famous praise of Berlioz. When there is talk of this overture there is frequently a reference to an article about it written by Douglas Jerrold. Was this article ever republished in an edition of Jerrold's works? Has anyone now living ever read it?

*Der Freischütz,* a romantic opera in three acts, book by Friedrich Kind, music by Weber, was performed at Berlin, June 18, 1821. Weber wrote in his diary that the opera was received with "incredible enthusiasm; Overture and Folksong were encored; fourteen out of seventeen music pieces were stormily applauded. Everything went exceedingly well, and was sung *con amore.* I was called before the curtain and took Mad. [*sic*] Seidler and Mlle. [*sic*] Eunike with me as I could not get hold of the others. Verses and wreaths came flying. '*Soli Deo Gloria.*'" Some of these verses were malicious, and reflected on Spontini, much to Weber's distress.

Weber began work on the overture on February 22, 1820. On May 13 he noted in his diary: "Overture of *Die Jägersbraut* finished, and with it the whole opera. God be praised, and to Him alone be the glory" (*Die Jägersbraut* was the original title of the opera; it was kept until into the year 1820, when Weber changed it to *Der Freischütz* at the advice of Count Bruhl, Intendant of the Berlin Court theaters). Weber heard the music for the first time at a rehearsal of the Dresden Orchestra, June 10, 1820. This was the first music of the opera that he heard.

We have mentioned the success of this overture at Berlin, when it was played as the prelude to the opera and under Weber's direction; a success that dumfounded the followers of Spontini and settled the future of German opera in the capital. And so, wherever the overture was played, the effect was overwhelming—as in London, where the opera was first performed in English, July 22 (?), 1824, at the English opera house. W. T. Parke wrote: "The music of this opera is such a continued display of science, taste, and melody as to justify any praises bestowed on it. The overture embraces most of the subjects of the airs in the opera, ingeniously interwoven with each other, and is quite original. The grandeur of some passages and the finely contrasted simplicity of others produced an effect which was irresistible. It was vehemently encored."

Much has been written about the overture, from the rhapsody of Douglas Jerrold to Wagner's critical remarks concerning the true reading. The enthusiasm of Berlioz is well known: "The overture is crowned Queen; today no one dreams of disputing it. It is cited as the model of the kind. The theme of the slow movement and that of the *allegro* are sung everywhere. There is one theme that I must mention, because it is less noticed, and also because it moves me incomparably more than all the rest. It is that long, groaning melody, thrown by the clarinet over the tremolo of the orchestra, like unto a far-off lamentation scattered by the winds in the depths of the forest. It strikes home to the heart; and for me, at least, this virginal song, which seems to breathe skyward a timid reproach, while a somber harmony shudders and threatens, is one of the most novel, poetic, and beautiful contrasts that modern art has produced in music. In this instrumental inspiration one can already recognize easily a reflection of the character of Agathe, which is soon to develop in all its passionate purity. The theme is borrowed, however, from the part of Max. It is the cry of the young hunter at the moment when, from his rocky height, he sounds with his eyes the abysses of the infernal glen. Changed a little in outline, and orchestrated in this manner, the phrase is different both in aspect and accent." Compare with this the remarks of Berlioz in the section on the clarinet in his "Treatise on Instrumentation." The clarinet, he says, has the precious faculty of producing "distance, echo, an echo of echo, and a twilight sound. . . . What more admirable example could I quote of the application of some of these shadowings than the dreamy phrase of the clarinet, accompanied by a tremolo of stringed instruments in the midst of the *allegro* of the overture to *Freischütz?* Does it not depict the lonely maiden, the forester's fair betrothed, who, raising her eyes to heaven, mingles her tender lament with the noise of the dark woods agitated by the storm? O Weber! !"

The overture begins *adagio,* C major, 4-4. After eight measures of introduction there is a part song for four horns. This section of the overture is not connected in any way with subsequent stage action. After the quarter the Samiel motive appears, and there is the thought of Max and his temptation. The main body of the overture is *molto vivace,* C minor, 2–2. The sinister music rises to a climax, which is repeated during the casting of the seventh bullet in the Wolf's Glen. In the next episode, E flat major, themes associated with Max (clarinet) and Agathe (first violins and clarinet) appear. The climax of the first section reappears, now in major, and there is use of Agathe's theme. There is repetition of the demoniac music that introduces the *allegro,* and Samiel's motive dominates the modulation to the *coda,* C major, *fortissimo,* which is the apotheosis of Agathe.

## OVERTURE TO THE OPERA "EURYANTHE"

THE OVERTURE is not without a certain old-fashioned but veritable pomp; it has the spirit of ceremony which the admirers of Weber call "the chivalric spirit." It would be perhaps an idle task for an ultra-modern to insist that the only music in this overture that appeals to the men and women of the younger generation is that of the short episode which was originally intended to accompany a pantomimic scene on the stage, a scene of old-fashioned romantic melodrama, with tomb, kneeling heroine, gliding ghost, and an eavesdropping, intriguing woman. In these few mysterious measures Weber thought far beyond his period. The ultra-modern might say that the rest of the music is decorative and that the decorations are substantial till they are cumbrous; that the melodies are like unto a cameo brooch worn by a woman who remembers nights of coquetry and dances long out of fashion; that the few measures of counterpoint show Weber as a plodding amateur. Nevertheless, the conventionally jubilant swing and the impetuous pace still make their way in a concert hall.

*Euryanthe,* grand heroic-romantic opera in three acts, book founded by Helmina von Chezy on an old French tale of the thirteenth century, "Histoire de Gérard de Nevers et de la belle et vertueuse Euryant de Savoye, sa mie"—a tale used by Boccaccio (*Decameron,* second day, ninth novel) and Shakespeare (*Cymbeline*)—music by Weber, was produced at the Kärnthnerthor Court Opera Theater, Vienna, October 25, 1823. The composer conducted. Domineco Barbaja, manager of the Kärnthnerthor and the An der Wien theaters, had commissioned Weber to write for the former opera house an opera in the style of *Der Freischütz.* Weber had several librettos in mind before he chose that of *Euryanthe;* he was impressed by one concerning the Cid, by Friedrich Kind. The two quarreled. Then he thought of the story of Dido, Queen of Carthage, as told by Ludwig Rellstab, but this subject had tempted many composers before him. Helmina von Chezy, living in Dresden when Weber was there, had written the text of "Rosamunde" to which Schubert set music. The failure of this work apparently did not frighten Weber from accepting a libretto from her. She had translated a version of the old French tale mentioned above for a collection of medieval poems (*Sammlung romantischer Dichtungen des Mittelalters*), edited by Fr. Schlegel, which was published at Leipsic in 1804. She entitled her version, "Die Geschichte der Tugendsamen Euryanthe von Savoyen" (The Story of the Innocent Euryanthe of Savoy). The original version is in the *Roman de la Violette,* by Gilbert de Montreuil.

As soon as the text of the first act was ready (December 15, 1821), Weber began to compose the music. He wrote a large portion of the opera at Hosterwitz. The opera was completed without the overture on August 29, 1823. Weber began to compose the overture on September 1, 1823, and completed it at Vienna on October 19 of that year. He scored the overture at Vienna, October 16–19, 1823.

Weber wrote to his wife on the day after the first performance, "My reception, when I appeared in the orchestra, was the most enthusiastic and brilliant that one could imagine. There was no end to it. At last I gave the signal for the beginning. Stillness of death. The overture was applauded madly; there was a demand for a repetition; but I went ahead, so that the performance might not be too long drawn out."

Max Maria von Weber, in the life of his father, gives a somewhat different account. A grotesque incident occurred immediately before the performance. There was a tumult in the parterre of the opera house. There was laughing, screaming, cursing. A fat, carelessly dressed woman, with a crushed hat and a shawl hanging from her shoulders, was going from seat to seat, screaming out: "Make room for me! I am the poetess!" It was Mme von Chezy, who had forgotten to bring her ticket and was thus heroically attempting to find her seat. The laughter turned into applause when Weber appeared in the orchestra, and the applause continued until the signal for the beginning was given. "The performance of the overture," says Max von Weber, "was not worthy of the usually excellent orchestra; indeed, it was far inferior to that at the dress rehearsal. Perhaps the players were too anxious to do well, or, and this is more probable, perhaps the fault was in the lack of sufficient rehearsal. The ensemble was faulty—in some places the violins actually played false—and, although a repetition was demanded by some, the impression made by the poetic composition was not to be compared with that made later in Berlin, Dresden, and the Gewandhaus concert in Leipsic." Yet Max von Weber says later that Count Brühl wrote the composer, January 18, 1824, that the overture played for the first time in Berlin in a concert by F. L. Seidel hardly made any impression at all. To this Weber answered, January 23: "That the overture failed is naturally very unpleasant for me. It must have been wholly misplayed, which I am led to believe from the remarks about its difficulty. The Vienna orchestra, which is in no way as good as that of Berlin, performed it *prima vista* without any jar to my satisfaction, and, as it seemed, with effect."

The overture begins E flat, *allegro marcato, con molto fuoco,* 4-4, though the half note is the metronomic standard indicated by Weber. After eight measures of an impetuous and brilliant exordium the first theme is announced by wind instruments in full harmony, and it is derived from Adolar's phrase: *"Ich bau' auf Gott und meine Euryanth'"* (Act I, No. 4). The original tonality is preserved. This theme is developed brilliantly until, after a crashing chord, B flat, of full orchestra and vigorous drumbeats, a transitional phrase for violoncellos leads to the second theme, which is of a tender nature. Sung by the first violins over sustained harmony in the other strings, this theme is associated in the opera with the words, *"O Seligkeit, dich fass' ich kaum!"* from Adolar's air, *"Wehen mir Lüfte Ruh'"* (Act II, No. 12). The measures of the exordium return, there is a strong climax, and then after a long organ-point there is silence.

The succeeding short *largo,* charged with mystery, refers to Eglantine's vision of Emma's ghost and to the fatal ring. Eglantine has taken refuge in the castle of Nevers and won the affection of Euryanthe, who tells her the tragic story of Emma and her betrothed, Udo; for the ghost of Emma, sister of Adolar, had appeared to Euryanthe and told her that Udo had been her faithful lover. He fell in battle. As life was to her then worthless, she took poison from a ring, and was thereby separated from Udo; a wretched ghost, she was doomed to wander by night until the ring should be wet with the tears shed by an innocent maiden in her time of danger and extreme need (Act I, No. 6). Eglantine steals the ring from the sepulcher. She gives it to Lysiart, who shows it to the Court, swearing that he had received it from Euryanthe, false to Adolar. The music is also heard in part in Act III (No. 23), where Eglantine, about to marry Lysiart, sees in the madness of sudden remorse the ghost of Emma, and soon after reveals the treachery.

In *Euryanthe,* as in the old story of Gérard de Nevers, in the tale told by Boccaccio, and in *Cymbeline,* a wager is made over a woman's chastity. In each story the boasting lover or husband is easily persuaded to jealousy and revenge by the villain bragging of favors granted to him.

For these three overtures, Weber used the customary orchestration of woodwinds in twos, four horns, two trumpets, three trombones, kettledrums, and strings.—EDITOR.

## RALPH VAUGHAN
# WILLIAMS

(Born at Down Ampney on the Borders of Gloucestershire and Wiltshire, England, on October 12, 1872)

---

## A LONDON SYMPHONY

*I. Lento; Allegro risoluto*
*II. Lento*
*III. Scherzo (Nocturne): Allegro vivace*
*IV. Andante con moto; Maestoso alla marcia*
*Epilogue: Andante sostenuto*

It is doubtful whether without the title and descriptive programme a hearer, as the music was playing, would say, "Aha! London—I hear the Thames, the roar and bustle of the streets. Now we are in foggy, dismal Bloomsbury. Let's go to the Thames Embankment. And now we see the march of the unemployed." No. The austere, remote Delius wrote a symphonic poem *Paris,* which is anything but the Paris of *Louise,* and might be Rouen, Belfast, or Terre Haute.

A critic in London reproached Williams for introducing in this symphony a theme too much like the notes of "Have a banana!" from a song. "We'll All Go Down the Strand," a popular music-hall ditty in the London of 1897. Perhaps Williams did this deliberately for the sake of "local color."

The symphony contains pages of great worth. The first two movements are the richest in musical thought and in powerful expression. The idea of sleeping London is admirably brought out, and the contrast with London awake is symphonically, not merely theatrically, dramatic. The second movement is an excellent example of tonal painting. It seems to us that the succeeding movements lack varied and contrasting coloring. The "Hunger March" of the unemployed is disappointing. The subject called for a Hector Berlioz. The epilogue is of a higher flight of imagination. On the whole, the symphony is an important contribution to orchestral literature, one of the most important—and they have not been many—in a dozen years.

This symphony was composed in 1912–13. The first performance was at one of F. B. Ellis's concerts in Queen's Hall, London, on March 27, 1914. Geoffrey Toye was the conductor. On May 4, 1920, the revised version of the symphony was brought out at Queen's Hall, London, at a concert of the British Music Society. Albert Coates conducted. This performance was said to be the fourth. It was also said that the symphony had been "shortened a good deal, particularly at the closes of the movements, on the way."

The following description by Mr. Coates of the symphony was published in the bulletin of the society:

"The first movement opens at daybreak by the river. Old Father Thames flows calm and silent under the heavy gray dawn, deep and thoughtful, shrouded in mystery. London sleeps, and in the hushed stillness of early morning one hears Big Ben (the Westminster chimes) solemnly strike the half-hour.

"Suddenly the scene changes (*allegro*); one is on the Strand in the midst of the bustle and turmoil of morning traffic. This is London street life of the early hours—a steady stream of foot passengers hurrying, newspaper boys shouting, messengers whistling, and that most typical sight of London streets, the costermonger (Coster 'Arry), resplendent in pearl buttons, and shouting some coster song refrain at the top of a raucous voice, returning from Covent Garden Market, seated on his vegetable barrow drawn by the inevitable little donkey.

"Then for a few moments one turns off the Strand into one of the quiet little streets that lead down to the river and suddenly the noise ceases, shut off as though by magic. We are in the part of London known as the Adelphi. Formerly the haunt of fashionable bucks and dandies about town, now merely old-fashioned houses and shabby old streets, haunted principally by beggars and ragged street urchins.

"We return to the Strand and are once again caught up by the bustle and life of London—gay, careless, noisy, with every now and then a touch of something fiercer, something inexorable—as though one felt for a moment the iron hand of the great city—yet, nevertheless, full of that mixture of good-humor, animal spirits, and sentimentality that is so characteristic of London.

### "Second Movement

"In the second movement the composer paints us a picture of that region of London which lies between Holborn and the Euston Road, known as Bloomsbury. Dusk is falling. It is the damp and foggy twilight of a late November day. Those who know their London know this region of melancholy streets over which seems to brood an air of shabby gentility—a sad dignity of having seen better days. In the gathering gloom there is something ghostlike. A silence hangs over the neighborhood broken only by the policeman on his beat.

"There is tragedy, too, in Bloomsbury, for among the many streets between Holborn and Euston there are alleys of acute poverty and worse.

"In front of a 'pub' whose lights flare through the murky twilight stands an old musician playing the fiddle. His tune is played in the orchestra by the viola. In the distance the 'lavender cry' is heard: 'Sweet lavender; who'll buy sweet lavender?' Up and down the street the cry goes, now nearer, now farther away.

"The gloom deepens and the movement ends with the old musician still playing his pathetic little tune.

### "Third Movement

"In this movement one must imagine one's self sitting late on a Saturday night on one of the benches of the Temple Embankment (that part of the Thames Embankment lying between the Houses of Parliament and Waterloo Bridge). On our side of the river all is quiet, and in the silence one hears from a distance coming from the other side of the river all the noises of Saturday night in the slums.

(The 'other' side, the south side of the river Thames, is a vast network of very poor quarters and slums.) On a Saturday night these slums resemble a fair; the streets are lined with barrows, lit up by flaming torches, selling cheap fruit, vegetables, produce of all kinds; the streets and alleys are crowded with people. At street corners coster girls in large feather hats dance their beloved 'double-shuffle jig' to the accompaniment of a mouth organ. We seem to hear distant laughter; also every now and then what sounds like cries of suffering. Suddenly a concertina breaks out above the rest; then we hear a few bars on a hurdy-gurdy organ. All this softened by distance, melted into one vast hum, floats across the river to us as we sit meditating on the Temple Embankment.

"The music changes suddenly, and one feels the Thames flowing silent, mysterious, with a touch of tragedy. One of London's sudden fogs comes down, making Slumland and its noises seem remote. Again, for a few bars, we feel the Thames flowing through the night, and the picture fades into fog and silence.

## "Fourth Movement

"The last movement deals almost entirely with the crueler aspect of London, the London of the unemployed and unfortunate. After the opening bars we hear the 'Hunger March'—a ghostly march past of those whom the city grinds and crushes, the great army of those who are cold and hungry and unable to get work.

"We hear again the noise and bustle of the streets (reminiscences of the first movement), but these now also take on the crueler aspect. There are sharp discords in the music. This is London as seen by the man who is 'out and under.' The man 'out of a job' who watches the other man go whistling to his work, the man who is starving, watching the other man eat—and the cheerful, bustling picture of gay street life becomes distorted, a nightmare seen by the eyes of suffering.

"The music ends abruptly, and in the short silence that follows one again hears Big Ben chiming from Westminster Tower.

"There follows the epilogue, in which we seem to feel the great, deep soul of London—London as a whole, vast and unfathomable—and the symphony ends as it began, with the river, old Father Thames flowing calm and silent, as he has flowed through the ages, the keeper of many secrets, shrouded in mystery."

And yet the composer has been quoted as saying:

"The title might run *A Symphony by a Londoner*—that is to say, various sights and sounds of London may have influenced the composer, but it would not be helpful to describe these. The work must succeed or fail as music, and in no other way. Therefore, if the hearers recognize a few suggestions of such things as the Westminster chimes, or the lavender cry, these must be treated as accidents and not essentials of the music."

The symphony is dedicated "to the memory of George Butterworth," a young composer of great promise, Lieutenant of the Durham Light Infantry, who was killed on August 5, 1916, "after successfully taking an enemy trench at the head of a bombing party." It is scored for these instruments: three flutes (and piccolo), two oboes, English horn, two clarinets, bass clarinet, two bassoons, double bassoon, four horns, two trumpets, two *cornets-à-pistons,* three trombones, bass tuba, a set of three kettledrums, snare drum, bass drum, cymbals, triangle, jingles (the little cymbals, or plates, fixed in the wooden hoop of a tambourine), tam-tam, glockenspiel, two harps, and strings.

# INDEX

# INDEX

# INDEX

# PITCH of MUSICAL INSTRUMENTS

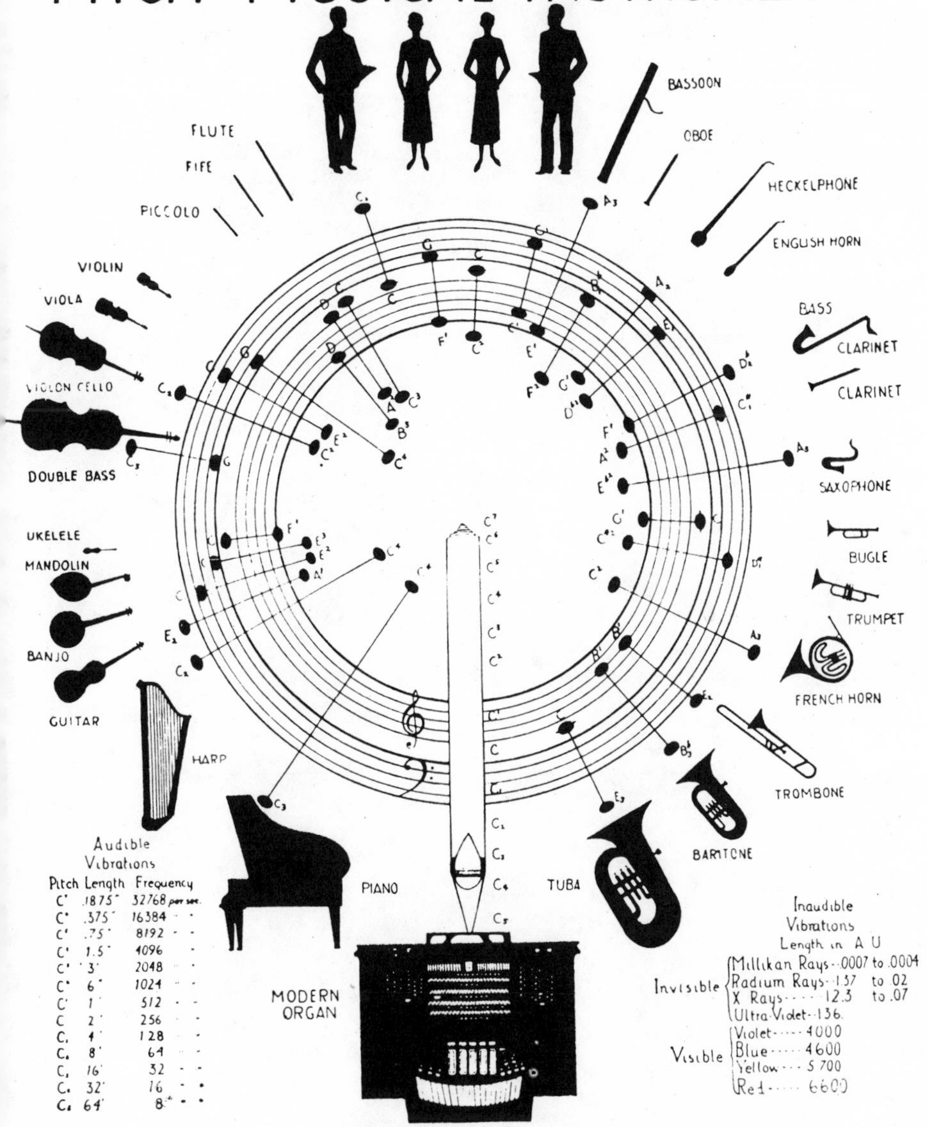

FLUTE
FIFE
PICCOLO
VIOLIN
VIOLA
VIOLON CELLO
DOUBLE BASS
UKELELE
MANDOLIN
BANJO
GUITAR
HARP
PIANO
MODERN ORGAN
TUBA
BARITONE
TROMBONE
FRENCH HORN
TRUMPET
BUGLE
SAXOPHONE
CLARINET
BASS CLARINET
ENGLISH HORN
HECKELPHONE
OBOE
BASSOON

Audible Vibrations

| Pitch | Length | Frequency |
|---|---|---|
| $C^7$ | .1875" | 32768 per sec. |
| $C^6$ | .375" | 16384 " " |
| $C^5$ | .75" | 8192 " " |
| $C^4$ | 1.5" | 4096 " " |
| $C^3$ | 3" | 2048 " " |
| $C^2$ | 6" | 1024 " " |
| $C^1$ | 1' | 512 " " |
| C | 2' | 256 " " |
| $C_1$ | 4' | 128 " " |
| $C_2$ | 8' | 64 " " |
| $C_3$ | 16' | 32 " " |
| $C_4$ | 32' | 16 " " |
| $C_5$ | 64' | 8 " " |

Inaudible Vibrations
Length in A U

| | | Length in A U |
|---|---|---|
| Invisible | Millikan Rays | .0007 to .0004 |
| | Radium Rays | 1.37 to .02 |
| | X Rays | 12.3 to .07 |
| | Ultra-Violet | 136. |
| Visible | Violet | 4000 |
| | Blue | 4600 |
| | Yellow | 5700 |
| | Red | 6600 |